FINAL
FIRE

FINAL FIRE

IS THE NEXT GREAT AWAKENING RIGHT AROUND THE CORNER?

THOMAS HORN, LARRY SPARGIMINO & DONNA HOWELL

DEFENDER

CRANE, MO

ISBN-10: 0998142603
ISBN-13: 978-0998142609

 Contents

1

A Vision of the Next Great Awakening

MANY YEARS AGO I (Tom Horn) died and woke up in heaven. Contemplating my surroundings, I wondered where I was, where I had come from, and why I had no memories of getting here—wherever *here* was.

At that moment, before it was shortly confirmed, I knew this was no dream; it was too vivid to be anything less than real. In fact, it felt *realer* than any previous *reality* I had known.

I became aware of these uncanny surroundings when abruptly I found myself standing somewhere before a spectacular pillar of light *(or was it a throne?)*. It was so bright, so intense and penetrating—glistening with vibrant streams of silver and blue and gold emanating with the most unexplainable yet awe-inspiring presence—that I could hardly keep my eyes open or my face toward the radiance.

And I was urgently exclaiming something, and didn't know why I was saying it: "Please, Lord, don't let me forget. Please don't let me forget! IT'S TOO WONDERFUL!"

How long had I been here and what was I talking about? Why was I so desperate to recall something I had obviously been told I would forget?

Suspended there like a marionette hanging on wires, I somehow knew that "memories" from moments before (but were there "moments"

1

or "time" in this place?) stood just beyond my ability to reckon them back into my conscience mind again.

But I *had* known something, something about the future. *I had seen it, and then I had been told I would not remember the details.* But why? What would be the purpose in that?

Something else had happened too. Somehow I knew that a scroll of some kind had unrolled before me…with scenes of a future, *my future,* playing out on what looked like a silvery parchment. It had been as clear and as believable as if I were watching a movie, with rich depictions of a destiny, or a possible future, where something extraordinary and miraculous was taking place—a cinematic conveyance of a personal fate, a "potential existence" that had been downloaded into my subconscious mind, or soul, and then…for some reason…had departed my intellect. Had a revelation of some type been sealed inside me? Something for a later time?

My thoughts raced, and I started to repeat, "Lord, please, don't let me forget," but I stopped short as, just then, a deep, still small voice countered, *"You will not remember…and it is time for you to go back now."*

And then I heard a thunderclap…and found myself falling backward, drifting swiftly, as if I had been dropped out of an airplane window or was let loose by some heavenly hands that had been holding me above, my arms and legs gliding up and down now against a cloudless sky.

As I fell, I gazed unblinkingly upward in amazement. The brilliance, which had just been in front of me, was moving rapidly away into the distance, and yet I wasn't afraid. A high-pitched whistling sound began rushing in around my ears, and I thought it must be the air carrying me aloft as I plummeted toward the earth. A moment later, I watched as the oddest thing happened: The roof of my house literally enveloped me as I passed effortlessly through it, and then it felt as if I had landed on my bedroom mattress with a THUD!

I sat straight up, took a desperate, shuddering, deep inhalation, and slowly let it out, realizing something extraordinary had occurred. Wherever I had been, whatever I had seen, I was back now to the so-called real world, and this material substance straightway felt far less authentic than the other place I had been.

It was the middle of the night and I sat there for a few seconds, possibly in shock, trying to determine what had happened.

I could feel my chest burning…and then I heard something.

Sobbing…right next to me…my young wife, Nita, with her head in her hands.

As my eyes adjusted to the darkness, I found her isolated stare. She looked as if she had been crying desperately, and had an unfamiliar expression conveying what I somehow already understood—we both had experienced something far more irregular than we ever could have prepared for.

"Nita," I said softly, "what's going on? Why are you crying?"

It took a while for her to collect herself, but once she did, she tearfully described how she had awakened to find me dead. No pulse, no breath, no heartbeat, cold to the touch, and not just for a few seconds either. I had remained in that condition for approximately fifteen minutes, she estimated, while she screamed for me to wake up, pounded on my chest, and attempted something like CPR.

We didn't have a phone in those days, and it was in the middle of the night. Nita had been unsure what to do and was about to try pulling me outside to the car to take me to the hospital when I abruptly jerked up, took in a deep breath, and looked at her.

For the reader, no matter how incredible the narrative above seems, it really did happen to me a long time ago. Later, and since then, I understood why God allowed my wife to wake up to find me in that condition. Without her eyewitness account that night, uncertainties about the supernaturalism of the experience would have undoubtedly crept into my mind over the years. Also, that I had been dead for a significant period of time, not breathing and therefore not taking in oxygen, and yet experiencing no brain damage (though I'm sure some would argue otherwise) also attested to the preternatural virtues of the event.

But why would God show me something and then not allow me to remember it? What would be the point in that—right? I can tell you that this was *the* question pressing me in the days immediately following the event, and in my youthful naiveté and impatience I first went about trying to find the answer to that mystery in the wrong way. I learned a valuable and biblical lesson as a result. In fact, that early mistake is why most have never heard this story until now.

What happened next was this: A couple days after my death and return from "over yonder," I told the pastor of our local church that I had an important question to ask him. In private, I recounted the events of earlier that week and probed what it could possibly mean. "Why would God show somebody something, then tell them they would not remember the vision?" I had inquired earnestly. His response was shocking for an honest and sincere young Christian man. Basically he offered that I had probably eaten too much spicy food, or maybe had accidently been poisoned and was therefore delusional or had a vivid dream.

No kidding.

Of course, I was not yet familiar with such admonitions as, "Give not that which is holy unto the dogs, neither cast ye your pearls before swine, lest they trample them under their feet" (Matthew 7:6). Not that I am saying my pastor back then was a dog, you understand, but that this was a lesson I would not soon forget about sharing sacred holy things with those who have not had similar supernatural experiences and therefore cannot appreciate or understand the otherworldly significance. In fact, besides my closest friends and family, from that day forward, I kept the event (and what I would soon understand about its measurable implications) a secret between me and them. Then, just a few years ago, well-known television personality Sid Roth asked me to repeat the story on his syndicated program, *It's Supernatural*. Because Sid, unlike some preachers, actually BELIEVES in the miraculous, I agreed that it was time to tell at least a part of that history. Albeit, as legendary radio broadcaster Paul Harvey used to ponder, what was the rest of the story?

After the disappointing experience following my pastor's less-than-enthusiastic response to my question regarding why God would give somebody a vision then not allow him or her to remember it, I struggled to make sense of what had obviously been an extraordinary incident in my and Nita's life. I prayed daily, seeking understanding, and it was during this same period (undoubtedly God had all this timing in control from the very beginning) when I happened to be reading through the Bible from cover to cover for the first time in my life. I had made it to the book of Job, and it was during these devotions that one day my eyes suddenly fell upon Job 33:15–17, and the Word of God dramatically came to life in what some charismatics might call a *rhema* moment, a time in which the Scripture went from being ink on paper to *the living Word of God!* The text that instantly conveyed the dynamic truth behind what had happened to me that fateful night read:

> In a dream, in a vision of the night, when deep sleep falleth upon men, in slumberings upon the bed; Then he openeth the ears of men, and sealeth their instruction [within them], That he may withdraw man from his purpose, and hide pride from man.

Though I was a very young and inexperienced believer, I clearly and instantly understood what this text was saying to me. Like the apostle Paul who could not tell whether he was "in the body…or out of the body" when he was "caught up to the third heaven" (2 Corinthians 12:2), God, on that momentous night, had taken me to a heavenly place and sealed "instructions" within me. These directions would be there when I needed them during life, as they were like a roadmap that the Holy Spirit would "quicken" when, at different times, I needed guidance or information. Nevertheless, I was not to remember these details ahead of time otherwise I might be drawn away into my "own purpose" and lifted up in "pride" according to this oldest book in the Bible—Job.

In other words, if as a young believer I had seen the ministries that God would later allow me and Nita to participate in—from pastoring large churches to owning a Christian publishing house and syndicated television ministry, to speaking at major conferences as a best-selling author, or any of the other opportunities he would give us permission to be associated with—I very likely would have made two huge mistakes: First, I would have immediately aimed at these later ministries and started working to try to make them happen all without the benefit of the struggles, trials, setbacks, side roads, and experiences that are necessary for "seasoning" and (hopefully) qualifying one to eventually operate in them (thus God "withdrew me from *my* purpose"); and second, I would have been tempted by pride to think of myself as more than I should have as a young man, if I had seen myself winding up in high-profile ministries, and so God in His benevolence also "hid pride" from me by keeping the revelations sealed until the appropriate times.

The Quickenings

In the Bible, it is clear that God does "seal" knowledge, wisdom, and revelations in the hearts of those who follow Him, and that these concealed truths can be "quickened" or made alive at the right moments as they are needed as depicted in such texts as Matthew chapter 10, where Jesus says to His disciples: "But when they deliver you up, take no thought how or what ye shall speak: *for it shall be given you in that same hour* what ye shall speak. For it is not ye that speak, but the Spirit of your Father which speaketh *in you*" (Matthew 10:19–20, emphasis added). That this reflects a deep partnership between our personal devotions and studies (2 Timothy 2:15; Psalms 119:11) and the indwelling Holy Spirit as part of the mystical union God has with all members of the true Church—the Body of Christ—can also be seen in Proverbs 3:6, which says, "In all thy ways acknowledge him [that's us doing our part], and he shall direct thy paths" [His part]. Again in the book of John (6:63) it refers to the Holy Spirit as the one "that quickens" (Greek *zōopoieō*—"to cause to live, to make alive at that moment") the Word of God as well as those "sealed instructions" that Job talked about.

I'm not sure how this experience plays out for others, but several times in my life and at times completely unexpected (always at night when I am asleep), I have been jolted from bed with an extraordinary glimpse that I believe is taken from that original storyboard God gave me years ago, and about which I begged Him not to "let me forget." One time, for example, I was shaken from sleep by a very powerful and detailed list of things that would happen in the former religious institution I had been an executive in. I jumped from bed, wrote down the vision as I had seen it—including names of people who would be involved and exactly what they would do and how it would greatly damage the ministry if the district leaders did not intervene (they didn't, and it did)—and then I sent that detailed letter to the state superintendent, plus gave a copy to my son, Joe Ardis, and to my wife, Nita. Within three years, everything played out exactly as I had seen it, down to the smallest details. In fact, it was so precise that it shook Joe up, causing him to come to me after the fact to express his utter amazement as to how it could have been possible for me to foresee such comprehensive events that accurately.

A more recent "quickening" revelation is one that the world kinda-sorta already knows about involving how I was able to very precisely predict the historic resignation of Pope Benedict in the book *Petrus Romanus: The Final Pope Is Here*, as well as on television and radio, a year in advance.

This began with a series of preternatural events too long to list in this book, but which ultimately brought me to investigate and write the best-seller, *Petrus Romanus*. During the research phase of that work, we uncovered the obscure manuscript of a Belgian Jesuit name Rene Thibaut, who predicted sixty years in advance that the papacy would change hands in 2012 based on his understanding of the nine-hundred-year-old prophecy by Saint Malachy that we were studying. We worked diligently to translate Thibaut's work into English and to verify his mathematical (and mystical) calculations using a software spreadsheet and language translator.

At first, we found Thibaut's speculations interesting partly because of the year 2012, which the world was abuzz about in the lead-up to that year. But as we made inroads behind the scenes with Catholic academics and historical artifacts, we began to believe something much bigger was afoot and that either the Malachy prophecy was genuine (that is, it was either divinely or demonically inspired) or that some of the Cardinal electors *believed* it was genuine and were therefore electing popes down through the years that could somehow be seen as fulfilling their lines in the prophecy, and therefore it had become a self-fulfilling oracle.

It was during this time that one night I was, once again, rattled from sleep and instantly convinced that we had been led by God to make this discovery and that in fact Pope Benedict would indeed step down in April 2012 using "health reasons" as a cover for abdication. I went on television and radio in 2011 (and out on a limb, quite frankly) as the book was being written and rushed through editing, typesetting, and print, so that it could be in stores before the anticipated resignation of the pope. We wrote specifically on page 470 of *Petrus Romanus* that Pope Benedict would "likely" step down in April 2012, but in media (which people can watch on YouTube in numerous interviews from 2011), we were more insistent that not only "could" it happen, but, we predicted, it would.

As the year 2012 came and went and Pope Benedict nor the Vatican made any announcement that he was stepping down, I thought perhaps, for the first time since I had woken up dead in heaven years earlier, the "sealed," Job-like, "instructions" mechanism had either not worked or I had been mistaken. Yet, as the months passed, I somehow remained convinced that we had seen the vision correctly! I would email research assistants and say "it's not over till it's over" while at the same time saying to myself, *What are you talking about? Benedict is still the pope!*

Then something happened that the world knows about now—February, 28, 2013, at 8:00 pm, the resignation of Pope Benedict was announced by the Vatican, who immediately gave the *New York Times* an interview in which they made the astonishing admission: Pope Benedict had SECRETLY AND OFFICIALLY resigned to select members of the Curia in April 2012, just as I (and Thibaut *and the quickening!*) had said he would. This was immediately confirmed by Giovanni Maria Vian, the editor of the official Vatican newspaper, *L'Osservatore Romano*, who wrote that the pope's decision "was taken many months ago," after his trip to Mexico and Cuba ended in March 2012, "and kept with a reserve that no one could violate"[1] (meaning it was to remain top secret and was to be known only to a handful of trusted Vatican cardinals until preparations for Benedict's housing and the public announcement was ready).

This revelation was astounding! Thibaut had mystically speculated the event sixty years in advance, and "the quickening" had confirmed for me this historic event with pinpoint accuracy all ahead of time. Media everywhere went crazy! My office phone did not stop ringing for weeks, with top media from around the world (including Rome) wanting to interview us to ask who "our insider at the Vatican was." CNN begged me to come on their program, which I declined. The History Channel featured our groundbreaking work in a special series, and so on. But why am I talking about this now? Is it so we can pat ourselves on the back and brag about how incredibly accurate our prediction was?

No. I'm raising this issue now because there has been another "quickening," and this time it involves the current Pope Francis (the last pope, Petrus Romanus, according to the Malachy list [OR IS HE!? More on that question later])—and the revelation I will shortly detail as being much bigger and more concerning than the last one was, yet it is with the same level of confidence I had when we foresaw that Pope Benedict would step down (an event that had not happened for hundreds of years and one that everybody was telling us would never happen…that is, until it did) that I will now convey what I (Tom Horn) predict is going to happen over the next few years.

ISIS, the Final Roman Emperor, and the Next Great Awakening

As for the role ISIS is and will play in the prediction that I (Tom Horn) am set to make, I need to briefly summarize how much of our modern world has been seized with fear over this mysterious group called ISIS (Islamic State of Iraq and Syria; sometimes "ISIL": Islamic State of Iraq and the Levant). Our Facebook newsfeeds have been inundated with blurred images of bloody beheadings. When we visit YouTube, unsolicited videos pop up off to the side with the latest reporting of death tolls by men in black clothing carrying threatening firearms with their faces covered. Whether we like it or not, when we Google-search something entirely unrelated, articles appear declaring that the seemingly unnecessary and irrational executions of nonhostile men in orange jumpsuits are still underway. Our confidence in national security has been rattled by the threat, the American collective consciousness lives in nail-biting suspense, and even our children have picked up on the fact that nameless and faceless "bad guys" are fulfilling repulsively dreadful feats of bloodshed that makes the boogeyman look like a comparative saint: at least we know he lives on only to torment our imagination.

Unbelievably, however, there lies a group of central questions at the forefront of our minds that even our country's leaders have not been able to effectively answer: What is their motivation? Where did they come from? Why are they killing? And what in the world is "the Islamic State"?

Reasonable questions, no doubt, and simple enough that one would assume they would render equally simple answers. Despite convoluted explanations, however, our government, as well as the American public, is largely mystified. Though many theories have surfaced, some of which are popularized as the most likely, getting in touch with ISIS and understanding the purpose behind their mission is puzzling to even Major General Michael K. Nagata, former US Army commander of the Special Operations Command Center, who said in an interview with *The New York Times*, "'We do not understand the movement, and until we do, we are not going to defeat it,' he said, according to the confidential minutes of a conference call he held with experts. 'We have not defeated the idea. We do not even understand the idea.'"[2] Former Defense Intelligence Agency Michael T. Flynn said of this comment, "The fact that someone as experienced in counterterrorism as Mike Nagata is asking these kinds of questions shows what a really tough problem this is."[3]

The Islamic religion is monotheistic and Abrahamic, and it holds its roots in the Quran (Arabic: "the recitation"), which Muslims (followers of the Islamic faith) believe to be the exact and literal words of Allāh (Arabic: "the God [of Abrahamic religions]"). There are many common elements between fundamental Islam and Christianity, such as beliefs in: only one God; the message and teachings of the prophets Noah, Abraham, Moses, David (and others), as well as Christ; Christ as a prophet (but not divine in Islam); Old and New Testaments are holy; wickedness of Satan; appearance of Antichrist; and heaven and hell…and so on. A peaceful start, one might think. However, just like there are different denominations within Christianity where fundamental beliefs and life-style practices fluctuate, there are varying sects of Islam (Sunni, Shia, Sufi, Kharijites, Ahmadiyya, etc.), under each of which are spawned numerous different schools of thought, and all with their own views on violence.

To which does ISIS belong? It is said they subscribe to Wahhabism, a branch of Sunni Islam. Wahhabism is described by neutral and unbiased sources as a "religious reform movement…[in which] followers believe that they have a religious obligation…for a restoration of pure monotheistic worship."[4] Even among many Muslims, however, such as those behind the As-Sunnah Foundation of America (ASFA) whose mission statement on the front of their page says "Unity, Knowledge, and Understanding for the Muslim Community,"[5] Wahhabism is "[t]he most extremist pseudo-Sunni movement today."[6] And it is the most extremist because this brand if Islam holds an apocalyptic vision involving a "worldwide caliphate"—a one-world, theocratic government, that envisions religious, military, and political power over all Muslims and the earth.[7]

In 2010, Abu Bakr al-Baghdadi became the leader of ISIS, and he has since strived for domination. Aggressively, he has led ISIS to control huge land masses in Iraq, Syria, Libya, Nigeria, and Afghanistan, among many other territories of Asia and Africa. In 2014, official ISIS spokesman Abu Muhammad al-'Adnani declared Baghdadi the "Caliph Ibrahim":

> 'Adnani demanded that all jihadi factions, not only those in Iraq and Syria, but everywhere, pledge allegiance to the Islamic State, for the "legality" of their organizations is now void. He stated: "Indeed, it is the State. Indeed, it is the khilāfah. It is time for you to end this abhorrent partisanship, dispersion, and division, for this condition is not from the religion of Allah at all. And if you forsake the State or wage war against it, you will not harm it. You will only harm yourselves."[8]

Many may read these words and believe they are—*at least*—the most emphatic definition of hubris fathomable, if not complete totalitarianism. Nevertheless, though the world caliphate is a self-proclaimed authority (which numerous Muslim groups find controversial), and though Baghdadi is the self-proclaimed caliph (of whom numerous Muslim groups deny support), ISIS continues to gain rapid support from fellow terrorists-in-training; American intelligence officials have estimated that one thousand foreign fighters *per month* travel to Iraq and Syria to join ISIS,[9] with Baghdadi now standing as dictatorial commander over every Muslim community in the world.

While their clandestine motives—political and religious—have baffled even US intelligence officials, their actions are loud and clear. They may be reclusive in keeping communication lines limited to themselves, allowing the rest of the world to draw whatever conclusions they will about the *whys*, but leaders of ISIS are social media savants, and at every turn they have blasted the Internet with execution videos, propaganda videos, rejections of peace, articles of demands, photos of their destruction of Christian artifacts and buildings, etc. Genocide, the likes of which this world has not seen since the domination of Nazi Germany, is one of ISIS' goals:

The Nazi destruction of stolen art was an act of gratuitous violence against Europe's cultural heritage, undertaken in service to a demented ideology… Similarly gratuitous destruction of ancient cultural centers and artifacts is now underway wherever the black flag of the Islamic State, ISIS, is raised in Iraq and Syria. And so is another genocide, this time of Christians.…

As the indefatigable human rights campaigner Nina Shea wrote…the wanton destruction of a sacred place is also a metaphor for "the genocide of Iraq's Christian people and their civilization."[10]

Nina Shea is not the only one who sees this horror for what it is. Even the European Parliament "passed a resolution declaring that the Islamic State terror group…'is committing genocide against Christians and Yazidis…(and) other religious and ethnic minorities.'"[11] Democratic presidential candidate Hillary Clinton said shortly before the 2016 election, "I am now sure we have enough evidence, what is happening is genocide deliberately aimed at destroying lives and wiping out the existence of Christians and other religious minorities."[12]

Is ISIS so far off in left field that their cries for dominance are driven by an apocalyptic landscape? Some rational minds would believe this to be an immediately sensationalistic notion, but if we look at how dramatic ISIS is in every other aspect, we begin to not only accept, but *expect*, their ideologies to be ceaselessly and recklessly grandeur…and we are not alone. ISIS driven by ancient eschatology and apocalypticism.

To begin, Islam's central figure, the prophet Muhammad, allegedly predicted the invasion and defeat of both Constantinople and Rome. The first of these two cities fell into the hands of the Muslims in the 1400s, bringing the prophecy to fruition. Rome has yet to be dominated. Sheikh Yousef Al-Qaradhawi, "one of the most influential clerics in Sunni Islam,"[13] explained this prophecy:

The Prophet Muhammad was asked: "What city will be conquered first, Constantinople or Romiyya?" He answered: "The city of Hirqil [i.e. the Byzantine emperor Heraclius] will be conquered first"—that is, Constantinople...Romiyya is the city called today "Rome," the capital of Italy. The city of Hirqil [that is, Constantinople] was conquered by the young 23-year-old Ottoman Muhammad bin Morad, known in history as Muhammad the Conqueror, in 1453. The other city, Romiyya, remains, and we hope and believe [that it too will be conquered].[14] (brackets and ellipses in original)

The idea that ISIS plans to wage war against Rome is more than clear through all of their speeches, posts, articles, and propaganda. To quote Baghdadi, himself, in a speech to fellow Muslims just two days after he was pronounced the caliph (translated by ISIS' subsidiary media company Al-Hayat; as quoted by the Middle East Media Research Institute):

So congratulations to you, O slaves of Allah, as Allah has allowed you to reach this noble month. Praise Allah and thank Him for having granted you long lives, thereby giving you a chance to correct your past deeds.... As for the religion of Allah, then it will be victorious. Allah has promised to bring victory to the religion....

So take up arms, take up arms, O soldiers of the Islamic State! And fight, fight!... So raise your ambitions, O soldiers of the Islamic State!...

Soon, by Allah's permission, a day will come when the Muslim will walk everywhere as a master, having honor, being revered, with his head raised high and his dignity preserved. Anyone who dares to offend him will be disciplined, and any hand that reaches out to harm him will be cut off.

So let the world know that we are living today in a new era. Whoever was heedless must now be alert. Whoever was sleeping must now awaken. Whoever was shocked and amazed must comprehend. The Muslims today have a loud, thundering statement, and possess heavy boots. They have a statement that will cause the world to hear and understand the meaning of terrorism, and boots that will trample the idol of nationalism, destroy the idol of democracy, and uncover its deviant nature....

So listen, O ummah [Arabic: "community"] of Islam. Listen and comprehend. Stand up and rise. For the time has come for you to free yourself from the shackles of weakness, and stand in the face of tyranny, against the treacherous rulers—the agents of the crusaders and the atheists, and the guards of the Jews....

O Muslims everywhere, glad tidings to you... Raise your head high, for today—by Allah's grace—you have a state and caliphate, which will return your dignity, might, rights, and leadership....

Therefore, rush, O Muslims, to your state. Yes, it is your state. Rush, because Syria is not for the Syrians, and Iraq is not for the Iraqis. The Earth is Allah's... The State is a state for all Muslims. The land is for the Muslims, all the Muslims....

Know that today you are the defenders of the religion and the guards of the land of Islam. You will face tribulation and epic battles....

So prepare your arms, and supply yourselves with piety. Persevere in reciting the Koran [Quran] with comprehension of its meanings and practice of its teachings.

This is my advice to you. If you hold to it, *you will conquer Rome and own the world.*[15]

Besides the aforementioned parallels between Nazi Germany and ISIS' genocidal agenda are the blatantly obvious parallels between Hitler's declaration-of-war speeches and this—Baghdadi's declaration of war against Rome and all enemies of Islam. His intonations are sometimes so Hitlerian that one could swap out the relative ethnic groups and enemy groups and post it online as a "lost speech by Hitler" and people would believe it. But I digress…

Under the leadership of Baghdadi, radical Muslim terrorist factions are, *in fact*, "raising up arms" for war. Islamic eschatology (from the Hadith) points to the town of Dabiq, Syria as a fester-pot of the *Muslim Malahim* (apocalypse; Armageddon). The "Romans" (or "Roman Christians," as some scholars put it) will "land" in Debiq, wage war against the Muslim soldiers, the Muslims will win, and the "Last Hour" heralds the arrival of Isa (Christ) and Dajjal (Antichrist). (Note also that ISIS' official magazine is also called *Debiq*.) From The Only Quran website, the prophecy reads:

Abu Huraira [Muhammad's recorder and companion] reported Allah's Messenger (may peace be upon him) assaying: The Last Hour would not come until the Romans would land…in Dabiq. An army consisting of the best (soldiers) of the people of the earth at that time will come from Medina (to counteract them).… They will then fight and a third (part) of the army would run away, whom Allah will never forgive. A third (part of the army), which would be constituted of excellent martyrs in Allah's eye, would be killed and the third who would never be put to trial would win.… And as they would be busy in distributing the spoils of war (amongst themselves) after hanging their swords by the olive trees, the Satan would cry: The Dajjal [Antichrist] has taken your place among your family. They would then come out, but it would be of no avail. And when they would come to Syria, he would come out while they would be still preparing themselves for battle drawing up the ranks. Certainly, the time of prayer shall come and then Jesus ["Isa"] (peace be upon him) son of Mary would descend and would lead them in prayer. When the enemy of Allah [Dajjal; Antichrist] would see him, it would (disappear) just as the salt dissolves itself in water and if he (Jesus) were not to confront them at all, even then it would dissolve completely, but Allah would kill them by his hand and he would show them their blood on his lance (the lance of Jesus Christ).[16]

For some time, ISIS has been goading worldwide military powers to bring vicious attacks against Debiq, believing that the Muslims will win, and subsequently take the battles therefore outward to Rome. These provocations have been seen in a number of recent terrorist activities, and now they have raised the incitement even higher, baiting up to sixty countries across the globe.

A couple of months ago at the time of this writing, a serious ISIS threat-video, *See You in Debiq*, was released, relating imagery of this upcoming war. Since the war has not yet happened, the media specialists in ISIS used some digitally altered stock footage as well as original footage filmed in Iraq, to make the film. At one point in the video, the ISIS flag is raised over sixty other nation flags, representing its domination over opposition. Another scene shows an armored battle tank driving toward the Roman Colosseum, with the voiceover saying, "This is your last crusade; the next time it is us who will take the battle on your own land."[17] From *Heavy News*:

> In the video, tanks can be seen driving towards the Colosseum crumbled in the sand. Footage then cuts to outside buildings of the Italian capital, before zeroing in on the Vatican....
>
> The film's dialogue makes claims that the "Dabiq Army" will race into Rome, destroy crucifixes, and enslave Christian women.[18]

This video trails another, which was released in December 2015. Two ISIS radicals sit on a peaceful beach, facing the camera. One speaks in (somewhat broken) English, regarding the November 2015 ISIS terrorist attacks in Paris, France, and goes on to list other targets, including the US:

It is a state [referring to the Islamic State]. When you violate its right, your hand is bound to get burned…. All you Crusaders, you claim to want to degrade and fight the Islamic State, while you fail to secure your nations and your capitols. How come shall you degrade us? You call your armies, like France called their armies in the streets of Paris, but rest assured, they will avail them nothing. We will come to them from where they do not expect…. The revenge has started, and the blood will flow. France was the beginning. Tomorrow will be Washington. It will be New York, and it will be Moscow. You Russians, don't you think that we forgot you! Your time is coming! It is coming! And it will be the worst…. You will not have safety in the bedroom of your houses…. Allah! This event healed our hearts.[19]

The article, "ISIS Release Chilling New 'End of the World' Video Showing Final Battle with Crusaders," from *Mirror News* has no problem linking all their past violence to their latest unsettling "See You in Debiq" bait, calling forth all powers of the world to challenge them on their own soil, and then taunts that nonbelievers will "burn on the hills of Debiq."[20]

How the Vatican Is—and Will— Play Right into Isis' Hands

Over the last few years and on more than one occasion, Pope Francis as well as top Vatican diplomats and spokespersons have argued in favor of a coordinated international force to stop so-called Islamic State (ISIS) atrocities against Christians and other minorities throughout the Middle East. In 2015, this included Italian Archbishop Silvano Tomasi, who called on the United Nations to "stop this kind of genocide…. Otherwise we'll be crying out in the future about why we didn't do something, why we allowed such a terrible tragedy to happen."[21] Pope Francis himself has tried to parse words between "stopping" ISIS and distancing himself from US-led bombing sorties, yet he, too, has used very specific language in recent days that has not gone unnoticed by these writers, hermeneutical efforts undoubtedly cultivated for theologians and knowledgeable persons to encourage them to see beneath his judiciously chosen phrases to his deeper, *sotto-voce* ("under-voice") communication, which clearly expresses his and Rome's intentions to sanction a coming war, using terms like "unjust aggressor," "genocide," and even the very idiom, "just war,"[22] which are directly connected not only to specific activities of ISIS but are particular vocabulary extracted from "Just War Theory" and "Just War Doctrine" (the latter is derived from Catholic Church 1992 Catechism, paragraph 2309, which lists strict conditions for "legitimate defense by military force").

Both "Just War" traditions mentioned above (thoroughly examined in the book *The Final Roman Emperor* [Defender Publishing, 2016] as it involves definitions by theologians, policy makers, and military leaders) repeatedly employ the very terms "unjust aggressor" and "genocide" for the purposes of ratifying those doctrines whenever "war is morally justifiable through a series of criteria, all of which must be met for a war to be considered *just*. The criteria are split into two groups: 'the right to go to war' (*jus ad bellum*) and 'right conduct in war' (*jus in bello*). The first concerns the morality of going to war and the second moral conduct within war," which postulates that war, "while terrible, is not always the worst option. There may be responsibilities so important, atrocities that can be prevented or outcomes so undesirable they justify war."[23] The fact that Pope Francis and other high-ranking churchmen have explicitly used precise "Just War" terms is telling and supports the PREDICTION made later in this chapter as well as clarifies why Archbishop Tomasi in his call to the UN for greater military action against ISIS admitted that his request for engagement was derived from "a doctrine that's been developed both in the United Nations and in the social teaching of the Catholic Church."[24] This is the dictum I believe certain power brokers at the Vatican (what Father

Malachi Martin called the Masonic "Superforce") and the Pontiff will knowingly use to eventually engage the self-proclaimed caliph of the ISIS regime, who wants nothing less than a final end-times holy war leading to the arrival of the Islamic Mahdi (Messiah). Once the proper balls are rolling, both ISIS and the Vatican will see themselves in the midst of unfolding prophecy. For their part, all the Vatican needs at this moment are the right trigger events. This is where the first part of my prediction comes in.

Prediction #1—Weapon of Mass Destruction

Sometime over the next forty-eight months, the Islamic State and/or their associates are going to use a weapon of mass destruction. It will be of such scope and impact as to raise the international outcry sufficient for Rome to play its first card, which, as we noted above, has been primed by subtle references to Just War theory in the lead-up to this predicted event. When this WMD (electromagnetic pulse, biological weapon, chemical weapon, dirty radiological bomb, or nuke that causes widespread damage) is used by ISIS, the Roman pontiff will call for the revitalization of the Christian rules for Just War. A coalition army similar to the 2003 invasion of Iraq will be formed to seriously engage the Islamic radicals. Geopolitics aside, the jihadis will see the Vatican's sanction of war as a new and final religious crusade—indeed, an actual fulfillment of their 1,300-year-old hadith, which allegedly quotes the sayings of the Prophet Mohammed concerning a last days caliphate that goes up against "the army of Rome" to initiate "Malahim"—the equivalent to Armageddon in Christian teachings, a battle that ISIS believes they will ultimately win. This war will, according to ISIS, provoke the coming of Mahdi, the Al-Masih ad-Dajjal (Antichrist), and Isa (Jesus), who spears the Antichrist figure and fights on behalf of the Muslim army.

It is this author's (Tom's) belief that Pope Francis likewise will view himself—and Rome—as amidst unfolding prophecy, which the pope has alluded to on several occasions, including connecting ISIS terrorism with the end of the world.[25] Francis has even recommended that people read *Lord of the World*—a related 1907 book by Monsignor Robert Hugh Benson that depicts the reign of Antichrist and the Vatican's relationship to the end of the world, which both Francis and emeritus Pope Benedict have called "prophetic." This is not surprising, as the reigning pope is an avowed prophecy believer and knows that he is "Petrus Romanus," the final pope (#112) from the famous "Prophecy of the Popes" attributed to Saint Malachy (that is, unless Francis was NOT canonically elected, which we will discuss later—an intriguing possibility that presents additional strange and prophetic alternatives to the narrative). The best-selling work titled *Petrus Romanus: The Final Pope Is Here* thoroughly and critically dissected this mystical prophecy and found widespread support for the document from Catholics and even evidence that, down through the years, cardinals elected popes who could somehow be viewed as fulfilling their line in this prophecy. As it involves Pope Francis, here is what the final line in the prophecy says:

> In the extreme persecution of the Holy Roman Church, there will sit Peter the Roman [Pope #112, Petrus Romanus], who will pasture his sheep in many tribulations, and when these things are finished, the city of seven hills will be destroyed, and the dreadful judge will judge his people. The End.

When elected Pope #112, Jesuit Jorge Mario Bergoglio (Pope Francis) immediately did several fascinating things to wrap himself in his "Peter the Roman" title.

First, he took as his namesake St. Francis of Assisi, an Italian (Roman) friar whose original name was Giovanni but that was later changed to Francesco di Pietro (Peter) di Bernardone—a man whose name can literally be translated "Peter the Roman" from the final line of the "Prophecy of the Popes."

Second, Pope Francis knows that Francis of Assisi was a prophet and that he predicted this final pope would "be raised to the Pontificate, who, by his cunning, will endeavor to draw many into error and death…for in those days Jesus Christ will send them not a true Pastor, but a destroyer." It is astonishing that Francis would pick as a namesake a man that foretold this of the final pope.

Third, Pope Francis named Pietro Parolin as the Vatican's new secretary of state—a man who could sit on the throne of Peter if Pope Francis retires like Benedict did, dies, or is killed, and whose name can also be viewed as "Peter the Roman." If Francis was not canonically elected, Pietro Parolin would actually become the real Pope #112 under that scenario.

And then there are those famous last words from the "Prophecy of the Popes" itself, which say: "When these things are finished, the city of seven hills will be destroyed, and the dreadful judge will judge his people." This idea, that the city of Rome will be destroyed during the reign of Pope #112 (and just ahead of the Second Coming of Jesus Christ as judge), is a vision repeated in numerous ancient prophecies from Greek, Jewish, Catholic, and Muslim cultures. This includes what ISIS draws from their hadith—that they will go to war against the army of Rome and destroy the Vatican's headquarters. ISIS has even produced a movie that depicts this apocalyptic event culminating in the destruction of Rome.[26] In tandem with the prediction, they have threatened to kill Pope Francis,[27] and the pontiff has responded by saying he is willing to be assassinated if that is God's will; he just hopes it doesn't hurt.[28] As this narrative continues unfolding toward the conflict I am predicting, it becomes increasingly clear that both Pope Francis and ISIS believe they are engaged in an end-times scenario, making some of what Francis has said and done since his "election" clearer within a larger oracular context.

For example, in addition to what the ISIS hadith and the "Prophecy of the Popes" say about the destruction of Rome, shortly after he accepted the pontificate, Pope Francis consecrated the world to "Our Lady of Fatima" during Mass in St. Peter's Square.[29] Francis knows the prophecies and controversies connected to Fatima, including the vision of the "Holy Father" (pope) walking among a destroyed city (the Vatican) when ISIS-like fighters run in and kill him. Francis believes in this prophecy (obviously why he dedicated the world to precisely this Marian apparition), and ISIS vows to make it happen. In *Petrus Romanus,* we noted:

> The third part of the Secret of Fatima, which was supposedly released in total by the Vatican June 26, 2000, seems to echo the visions of Pius X. A section of the material reads:
>
> *...before reaching there the Holy Father passed through a big city half in ruins and half trembling with halting step, afflicted with pain and sorrow, he prayed for the souls of the corpses he met on his way...on his knees at the foot of the big Cross he was killed by a group of soldiers who fired bullets and arrows at him, and in the same way there died one after another the other Bishops, Priests, men and women Religious, and various lay people of different ranks and positions.*[30]

It's interesting, given the prediction from Fatima, that Pope Francis has also reached out to Kabbalist rabbis, who in their Zohar (the most important work of Jewish Kabbalah, which was written in medieval Aramaic over seven hundred years ago) also foretell this destruction of Rome (Vaera section, volume 3, section 34) in connection with "Messiah's" secret arrival in the year 2013 (is this why top rabbis in Israel are saying Messiah's presentation to the world is imminent?) and, after this "Messiah" makes himself known to the international community, "the kings of the world will assemble in the great city of Rome, and the Holy One will shower on them fire and hail and meteoric stones until they are all destroyed."[31]

The deepness to which Pope Francis can be thought of as a mystic and believer in such prophecy involving the coming destruction of Rome may also be connected to his knowledge of the Cumaean Sibyl, whose prophecy about the return of the god Apollo (identified in the New Testament as the spirit that will inhabit Antichrist) is encoded on the Great Seal of the United States (for more information, see the last chapter of this book on the Sibyl's prophecies, the Great Seal, and the design and layout of the Vatican and Washington DC) as well as in Catholic art, from altars to illustrated books and even her appearance upon the ceiling of the Sistine Chapel, where four other Sibyls join her (Paul cast a demon out of one such prophetess in the New Testament) and the Old Testament prophets in places of sacred honor. Yet this Cumaean—who sits so prominently inside Catholicism's most celebrated chapel—gave forth other famous and forgotten prophecies, which we will examine later to show how she was quoted by early Church fathers and actually connected the end-times Islamic Mahdi with a "Last Roman Emperor" (who arguably developed into the "Holy Pope" legend)—eschatological figures whose time, and whose catastrophic war, may now have arrived.

Will Pope Francis be the one to play the role of the Last Roman Emperor? Or will it be another pontiff? Was there something strange about the conclave from which Pope Francis emerged to the pontificate? Something mentioned earlier in this chapter that suggests he was not actually "canonically elected?" Even some Catholics think "illegitimate" activity may have gone on behind closed doors during the last conclave[32] and that, for reasons we do not yet understand, Francis was put in as a temporary "placeholder" until the real Pope #112 (Petrus Romanus) could be installed. This too might echo the choice of St. Francis of Assisi as a namesake, as the ancient friar did predict that "a man, not canonically elected, will be raised to the pontificate." The mysterious reasons surrounding a "placeholder" pope—a false pope—is largely unknown to the public, but was foreseen by such mystics as Father Herman Bernard Kramer in his work, *The Book of Destiny*. During an unusual interpretation he made of the twelfth chapter of the book of Revelation concerning "the great wonder" mentioned in verse 1, Father Kramer wrote:

> The "sign" in heaven is that of a woman with child crying out in her travail and anguish of delivery. In that travail, she gives birth to some definite "person" who is to RULE the Church

with a rod of iron (verse 5). It then points to a conflict waged within the Church to elect one who was to "rule all nations" in the manner clearly stated. In accord with the text this is unmistakably a PAPAL ELECTION, for only Christ and his Vicar have the divine right to rule ALL NATIONS.... But at this time the great powers may take a menacing attitude to hinder the election of the logical and expected candidate by threats of a general apostasy, assassination or imprisonment of this candidate if elected.[33]

Although we disagree with Kramer's interpretation of the book of Revelation, his fear that "great powers may take a menacing attitude to hinder the election of the logical and expected candidate" echoes the sentiment of priests mentioned elsewhere in our book *Petrus Romanus*, who see a crisis for the Church coming, and the Final Roman Emperor (Antichrist) rising as a result. As we move through 2016, Pope Francis is publicly looking for a global political authority (such as the UN) to come alongside him to implement his religious and social agenda, President Obama has just set his eyes on becoming the UN Secretary General following the US presidential election,[34] and Israeli President Benjamin Netanyahu is very concerned about the ramifications of both. Will the pope or ex-president step forward to fulfill the Cumaean Sibyl's prophecy...or are there others waiting in the wings? Either way, I predict that an ISIS WMD and a call by Rome to sanction war will soon result in both Muslims and Romans engaging in their own apocalyptica.

Oh...and we should point out that nearly a decade ago, a major Islamic website set the date on which this war and its Mahdi would unfold: "Based on our numerical analysis of the Quran and Hadith," they concluded, "the official beginning of the End of Time and the coming of the Imam Mahdi will most likely be in...2016."[35] As this book heads to the typesetter, time is running out to see if their calculation was correct.

Prediction #2—On the Heels of War, a Great Awakening

In the same way that the last Great Awakening(s) grew out of the tragedies of war and disillusionment over civil authorities, today we are witnessing the most amazing similarities between cultural phenomenon (the threat of war, terror, an ISIS WMD, and the loss of faith in establishment politicians) that preceded many Awakenings of the past, including the "Age of Fire" that we write about later in this book that grew out of military conflict and the formation of the modern Jewish state of Israel.

I predict these similarities are not by chance, but providence, and that at least one final Great Awakening awaits the immediate future.

Unfortunately, I predict a terrorist use of a weapon of mass destruction and the military conflict following it will—like the Holocaust did— partly provide the impetus for both the Church and society's awakening. Nevertheless, the up side to the coming global spiritual stirring may be (in my opinion, *will* be) the greatest supernatural awakening in the history of mankind. Awakening could come without the need for such tragedy, and I pray that is the case. I also pray the history of awakenings and the parallels to current events outlined in the following chapters will stir your soul to believe as I do that we are on the cusp of a FINAL FIRE!

2

The Protestant Reformation

BETWEEN JUNE AND September of 2014, the Pew Research Center conducted a demographic study. According to their statistical findings, 70.6 percent of today's North American population identify themselves as Christian. As per the outline of this study, the Christian category covers Protestants (45.6 percent), Catholics (20.8 percent), Orthodox Christians (0.5 percent), Mormons (1.6 percent), Jehovah's Witnesses (0.8 percent), and a group of "other" Christian affiliations. These numbers, collectively, are down from 78.4 percent in 2007 within the Christian category, exposing a staggering, nearly 8 percent decrease of Christ-centered religion adherents during an interlude of only seven years. Not surprisingly, of those belonging to non-Christian groups, most are college age or younger, representing a much larger potential number of unbelievers in tomorrow's generation. Additionally, interreligious marital relationships are also increasing (one in four since 2010), which leads to a swell in the demand for answers regarding that age-old "unequally yoked" conundrum.[36]

For many within the Church, this is disheartening news. Not only does this statistic possibly show a lesser sum of our brother and sister saints inheriting the eternal kingdom of heaven alongside us, it points to a day when our own children and grandchildren are more at risk of being submerged in a confusing and unbelieving world, should the figures continue to dwindle.

But others are not so easily discouraged. *The Kingdom of God is not at all dependent upon a numbers game carried out by man's statistical reports.* And despite this dramatic recent dip amongst those classified as Christ-believers, the US "remains home to more Christians than any other country in the world."[37] With still over 70 percent of our nation's population claiming to believe in Christ, despite doctrinal or denominational barriers that cause variations to core beliefs and lifestyles, one is forced to acknowledge that a majority of our country's inhabitants have respect for Jesus Christ: the Man who came to die, and thus to conquer death.

Yet, these kind of reports, had they been conducted on a national level since the founding of our country, would show significant ups and downs throughout the years. This is certainly not the first time we have observed a decline in the number of believers. A quick submersion into the history of Christianity will reveal that, for centuries, the passion of the Church and number of new converts to the faith have considerably risen and fallen in parallel to major cultural events and/or social phenomena, leading to both widespread revival and the Great Awakenings.

"Great Awakenings"—a term the reader will see many times throughout this book—refers to periods of radical interest and enthusiasm from the secular world toward spirituality (specifically toward evangelical Christianity), accompanied by profound conviction of heart, sharp increases to conservatism and church attendance, and the development of new denominational movements. The term "Great Awakenings" differs from "revival" in that, although often occurring simultaneously, the revival of the Church affected those who already belonged to the faith, and were therefore "revived" by the season of growth, whereas the Great Awakenings affected the irreligious population, drawing multitudes into the faith for the first time.

Historians and theologians arrive at different conclusions as to how many Great Awakenings have been observed and documented through-out history. Whereas many agree that there have at least been three in the distant past (one occurring circa 1740, another circa 1800, and the third circa 1850), many, including these authors, propose that a fourth took place in the earth-loving era of the 1960s–1970s. Still others have added to this list, involving periods of growth within more specific denominations or religious movements.

But in order to understand how even the first of these Great Awakenings transpired, one need look further back to the early reformers of the Christian faith.

Bohemian Reformation

John Wycliffe

Scholastic philosopher, theologian, and Oxford University seminary professor John Wycliffe (1324[38]–1384) was born into a large family heralding from Wycliffe Village on the south bank of the River Tees in northern England. To the dismay of historians, several men in his locality were given the same name and attended the same schools, so the exact date he arrived at Oxford University (as well as many details regarding his childhood) is debated, but his identity comes out of obscurity as a prized student of Merton College in 1356 with an arts degree, a master (or "head of house") at Balliol College in 1361, the head of Canterbury Hall in 1365, and head of the clergy house in Ludgershall, Buckinghamshire, in 1368. It is said that by the year 1372, he had obtained a doctorate in theology from Oxford University, but he had held residence at Oxford for much of his life off and on since 1345.[39]

As several biographies on his life will attest, from his earliest days as a student, Wycliffe poured himself deeply into the pursuit of education, studying science, law (including the Roman and canon systems of jurisprudence), Latin, and most notably, scholastic philosophy and scholastic theology. Some of these fields of study were looked upon with fellow scholars' approval. Others, however, such as the municipal law of England, were considered a disdainful and suspicious waste of Wycliffe's time. He did not, however, allow his peers or his mentors to dissuade him from any subject of study that he saw fit to delve into, regardless of what threat it would hold to taint his reputation as a serious, budding Bible scholar. According to biographer Thomas Murray, "no prejudices or no authority could prevent Wycliffe from exercising his own judgment, or from devoting his attention to any department of science or literature which he thought might prove agreeable or useful…and thus early we find traces of that independence of thinking and steadfastness of purpose which so eminently marked his character, and [from which, after his passing] were productive of results [referring to his role in the Protestant Reformation] so beneficial to the world."[40] It wasn't only that he maintained to have a mind of his own in choosing what avenues of education he intended to follow, but also that he was able to defend his position articulately. So well versed was Wycliffe that, both personally and in a university debate setting, "he not only stood unrivalled among the most eminent Doctors of the university…but it is even admitted by one of the most illiberal of his enemies, that his powers of debate were almost more than human."[41]

It was during this time that Wycliffe took to a controversial practice: He studied from the Bible directly (in his case, a Latin translation), and *constantly*. At every mealtime, recreational activity, and strolls about the countryside, Wycliffe poured into the Book he found most sacred. Students and professors in noted universities across Europe had faced expulsion "for having made the Bible their text-book, and for having drawn their doctrines from that only infallible source."[42] In this era, such a brazen act as studying the Bible on one's own to such a degree would not have been allowed by fellow churchman, had Wycliffe not the ability to defend his actions eloquently and coherently, but study the Word he did, and with unparalleled fervor.

The Black Death spread across England during Wycliffe's studies in the summer of 1348. This devastating bacterial pandemic originated in Central Asia and made its way to Europe via merchant ships, causing several forms of plague outbreak, and overall has been estimated to claim the lives of between 100–200 million people in Europe by the year 1353. On February 10, 1355, during observance of St. Scholastica Day, one of the most notorious uprisings in the history of Oxford, England, broke out at the Swindlestock Tavern, when a couple students of the university fired complaints at the tavern owner about the quality of drinks he was serving. The argument came to blows, and immediately a retaliation from both sides led to the accumulation of hundreds of armed students and countrymen in a riot that lasted two full days. In the end, sixty-three scholars of the university were killed, as well as around thirty locals.[43]

After observing the destruction of the Black Death followed by the riot, Wycliffe was touched by the fragility of, and social wickedness within, humanity. It is said of Wycliffe at this time that "he seems to have looked on the state of society generally with painful foreboding, being equally affected by its manifest depravity, by its present sufferings, and by the prospect of the further retribution regarded as assuredly awaiting it."[44] Death and devastation left such an impression on him that from his perspective, divine judgment was upon the earth. When he penned his first manuscript in 1356, *The Last Age of the Church*, he wrote from an emotionally charged and defeated perception, making claims that the close of the fourteenth century would be the end of all mankind (a viewpoint that in later writings he corrected). However, within this manuscript came an outright attack upon what Wycliffe observed as corruption within the Roman Church priesthood. Whereas other writers following the Black Death attributed the pandemic to God's judgment upon sin in general, Wycliffe attributed it to divine condemnation of disgraceful clergy.

Wycliffe concluded that Scripture was the only reliable source for truth behind the mysteries of God. Man, as he came to believe, was capable of error, and therefore, Wycliffe encouraged people of God to dive into Scripture instead of resting on the advice and teachings of those in the Church. As a result of this unconventional religious lifestyle statement, Wycliffe eventually became somewhat of an early authority in challenging scriptural justification for the papacy, of which he found none.

Over time, involving his earlier writings, his conflicts with the Church often became political in nature, and his name was drawn into famous disputes when he was summoned by William Courtenay, bishop of London, in early 1377. The exact reasoning for this summoning is unknown because, at the entrance to the church, hostility broke out between Courtenay and those who had come to support Wycliffe, and the charges against Wycliffe were not efficiently documented. This event proved to cause an ugly rivalry between Wycliffe and well-known clergymen across the country, and heavy attacks came upon Wycliffe's written works from all sides. One of these attacks included a papal bull (a charter issued by the pope) sent by Pope Gregory XI to the Archbishop of Canterbury, King Edward III, the chancellor, Courtenay, and Oxford University detailing eighteen theses of Wycliffe's that were to be viewed as flawed, and of which presented a threat to church and state. However, much of this attention only proved over time to popularize his manuscripts, instead of silence them.

He fought against its institutional approach to appointing clergymen as well as to certain aspects of church property ownership. But in his later years, prior to his death in 1384, he devoted paramount attention to the reduction of papal power. Although a gross oversimplification of his writings, it is accurate to say that a main theme that resulted from Wycliffe's life work was that man should rely on God and His infallible Word, perpetuating, then, the notion that a relationship between God and man can be and should be a *personal* one, and not one with a priest as fascistic overseer.

He died after suffering a stroke in December of 1384, just after penning his magnum opus, *Trialogus*—a lengthy treatise on the subjects that he believed were theologically devoid of truth within the Catholic Church. Wycliffe was declared a heretic in 1415; his remains were declared unfit to rest in consecrated ground,[45] and thereafter his body was exhumed and burned.

To many of his time, Wycliffe was a dangerous man who set out to usurp the authority of the Church in trade for independent and liberal spirituality that could unearth generations of theologically uneducated religious leaders. To many of our time, after observing his influence in immortalizing the concept of the Bible as humanity's ultimate authority—one of the major founding principles in what became known as the Protestant Reformation—he is a legendary ecclesiastical pioneer.

Jan Hus

Jan (John) Hus (1369–1415), a Czech priest, was greatly moved by Wycliffe's writings. After earning his master of arts degree in Prague (Western Europe, in the Bohemian Kingdom; capitol city of modern-day Czech Republic) in 1396, he became an ordained priest in 1400. In 1402, he became rector (university chancellor) of the Charles University of Prague. By 1403, he was retained as the preacher of the prestigious Bethlehem Chapel.

Hus began passionately calling for reformation of the Church, carrying the convictions of Wycliffe ever close to his heart. He translated Wycliffe's *Trialogus* into Czech and recirculated it, despite that this particular volume had been banned by this time. In the few years following, Hus arrested every opportunity to promote Wycliffe's ideals from both his pulpit, as well as on the streets, to any and all who would hear, until this heresy was silenced and all writings of Wycliffe were confiscated by order of King Wenceslaus, the "King of Bohemia," after pressure from Pope Gregory XII in 1408.[46]

Just following this decree, the Charles University of Prague faced major division as a result of the "Western Schism" (or "Papal Schism," which began in 1378 and lasted until 1417), when two (and eventually three) leaders in the Catholic Church were concurrently claiming to be the one true pope. King Wenceslaus had a vision of becoming the Holy Roman Emperor, and he saw Pope Gregory XII as a threat to his agenda, so he denounced Gregory and proposed that the priesthood of the region (including the clergy of the university) take a neutral position during the schism. The university was largely formed from four regional governing sections: the Czechs (or "Bohemians"), the Polish, the Saxons, and the Bavarians. The Czechs, including Hus, agreed to the king's neutrality proposal, but the remaining university students and leadership did not, many of them choosing to side with Pope Gregory XII. After much deliberation and counsel from advisors, the king then declared that all affairs at the Charles University of Prague would be dealt with by vote. However, he furthered his personal agenda by assigning every Czechian voter with the power of three votes, leaving the remaining governing authorities with the power of only one vote. Consequently, up to twenty-thousand[47] students and leaders of the university left in anger in 1409 to attend native universities in the North. Upon their abandonment, Charles University of Prague was reduced to merely a Czech college, losing all of its international importance and regional influence, but with them the students and leaders took, *and effectively spread*, the unconventional Wycliffe "heresy" to various parts of Europe.

Although now a rector at a college with an all-but-destroyed reputation, Hus was personally launched into the height of his fame, as people were becoming more and more aware of Wycliffe's free-thinking principles through Hus' preaching between 1400 and 1408. As Hus' teachings gained momentous recognition, "free preaching" (any preaching outside designated areas such as cathedral, collegiate, and parish churches) was banned. A papal bull was published, issuing the confiscation of all Wycliffe materials, which were to be burned. Hus protested to no avail. He attempted to continue promotion of Wycliffe ideals under royal protection (he still had favor with royal governors as a result of adhering to neutrality during the schism), but by March of 1411, Hus was sentenced to excommunication from all churches in Prague by Alexander V (one of the church leaders attempting to lay claim to the "one true pope" title, today declared an "antipope" by the Roman Catholic Church).

Political unrest climbed, and John XXIII (Alexander V's successor, also later declared an "antipope") led a crusade against King Ladislaus of Naples, who stood in support of Gregory XII. John XXIII began to sell indulgences ("a way to reduce the amount of punishment one has to undergo for sins"[48]) as a way to raise funds for war against the king. People flocked to the churches, giving generous offerings in trade for the indulgences. Hus, as well as many others in the area, saw the selling of spiritual favor as a whole new corruption within the Church, and the excommunication sentence only ignited a fire within Hus to preach even louder. To all who would listen, Hus preached that the Church should pray for her enemies, bless their enemies, rely *only* on the Bible as an authority over men, and stand against the sale of indulgences for the sake of war, all the while continuing to read and quote from the then-condemned writings of Wycliffe.

His words gained extreme support, and a new level of resentment against Church hierarchy resulted when Hus took his convictions back to the pulpit of the Bethlehem Chapel, despite the controversy of his presence there. Roman authorities responded by reiterating Hus' excommunication status, placing an interdict upon the entire city of Prague: "No citizen could receive communion or be buried on church grounds as long as Hus continued his ministry."[49]

In order to protect the city, Hus went into hiding, but his voice continued to ring out from the pulpits of Prague through his supporters.

By 1413, Hus had penned a manuscript of his own: *De Ecclesia* ("The Church"). It has been said that this manuscript is only a rewriting of Wycliffe's book of the same name. However, Hus was driven by a passion to bestow truth on the residents of Prague at such an immoral period in its history, and merely sending them a copy of Wycliffe's prohibited teachings would not minister to anyone anew. It was *Hus'* name, *Hus'* voice that drew the attention of the spiritually hungry followers of Prague, so Hus feverishly composed *De Ecclesia*—a book that, although bearing sharp similarities to Wycliffe's book, also reflected Hus' convictions precisely—and sent it to the Bethlehem Chapel. Once there, it was read from the pulpit, blasting its listeners with intense claims that Christ, and Christ *alone*, is Head of the Church, and that carrying out opposition to an erroneous pope or priesthood was, in fact, "to obey Christ."[50]

Hus' and Wycliffe's words continued to broaden outward to Hungary, Poland, and Austria like a brushfire that could not be contained. So widespread was the enthusiastic acceptance of their doctrine and theology that King Wenceslaus' brother, King Sigismund of Hungary, sought to end the division within the Church, and invited Hus (with promises of safe conduct[51]) to appear at the Council of Constance in 1414 to represent his concepts of ecclesiastical reform. Hus agreed to represent himself before the officials, and in November of 1414, he was brought to John XXIII, who removed his excommunication status, but forbade him to say Mass, preach, or attend any ecclesiastical functions.[52] Hus continued to say Mass and preach to all present, violating his safe conduct agreement, and was therefore arrested and placed on trial, where he was asked to recant his beliefs. His response was: "I appeal to Jesus Christ, the only judge who is almighty and completely just. In his hands I plead my cause, not on the basis of false witnesses and erring councils, but on truth and justice."[53]

In June and July of 1415, during Hus' trial, excerpts, as well as propositions, from his *De Ecclesia* were read aloud. When he again publicly refused to retract his writings, he was declared a heretic and condemned to burn at the stake.[54] On July 6, he was taken to a cathedral dressed in his own priest robes and humiliated in front of the crowd as each piece of his church garments was ceremoniously removed as an act of degradation, and then he was brought to the stake. When given one final chance to deny his faith, he said, "Lord Jesus, it is for thee that I patiently endure this cruel death. I pray thee to have mercy on my enemies,"[55] and then the flames were lit.

His last words are said to have been, "Christ, Son of the Living God, have mercy on us!"[56]

When word reached Prague that Jan Hus had been executed, civil unrest exploded.

The Hussite Wars

Followers of Hus, referred to as "Hussites," directed their anger toward the organized Church over what they saw as a criminal murder, which led to the "Hussite Wars." Smaller factions of the Hussites split into groups with common goals. Just to name a few of these sub groups that would form in the years to come:

Utraquists: They introduced the "lay chalice," allowing the laity to participate in both bread and wine during communion. Prior to this movement, it was common practice for the Roman Catholic priests to be the only members to drink the wine at Eucharist.

Taborites: They declared that the relationship between servants and masters was unbiblical. The Taborites were considered one of the most radical departures from monastic dealings, stood unshakably by the theology that the Bible is the utmost authority, and defended the laws of God by all means necessary, including war.

Orebites (also Horebites): Similar to the Taborites, the Orebites would stop at nothing to liberate mankind from dependence upon papal order and dictatorial mandates from the hierarchy. When battles ensued, they fought alongside the other radical parties and were actively involved in burning down the Benedictine monastery in Mnichovo Hradiště (1420).

Just after Hus' execution, more independent churches began to adopt the new disciplines of Hus and Wycliffe during their services, encouraging the congregants to study the Word outside of religious establishment. Despite the Roman Catholic Church's attempt to fizzle Hus' teachings through silencing the "heretic," liberation from religious legalism was expanding. Some of the authorities who were present during the Council of Constance caught wind of this and sent strongly worded letters to both the civil and church leaders in Bohemia, demanding that a stop be brought immediately from practicing such heresy. In September of 1415, 452 Bohemian superiors placed their seals on a joint response to the council leaders in a written response claiming that the death of Hus had been "insulting to their country, that there were no heretics in Bohemia, that any assertion to the contrary was itself a heresy of the worst kind."[57]

Knowing that one man had already been put to death for this level of insubordination, the developing Hussite factions formed both offensive and defensive coalitions to protect and endorse, by the sword if necessary, religious freedom. On the defense, any preacher who required it was granted protection from these allies of new truth, who had proven ready to shield the movement from further prosecution under the label of heresy, as well as the ongoing threat of excommunication. On the offense, radical troupes of armed Hussite civilians invaded local monasteries and forcibly replaced any church leadership unwilling to adhere to the popular Hus and Wycliffe theology.

Classic Roman Catholic powers did not stand idly by, carrying out what at first was diplomatic intervention, such as the shutting down of the University of Prague, which quickly diminished the number of ordinations within the region. Without fresh, young priests to carry on the Hussite ideals, their mission would dwindle. In a response to this, the Auxiliary Bishop of Prague was captured and taken to a Hussite stronghold where he was forcibly coerced to ordain as many priests as was needed to replace traditional ministers. Other attempts at a more peaceful end were also met with failure.

When the Hussite factions only grew in number and fury, Pope Martin V—who had been the officiator over Hus' trial at Constance as well as the man who sentenced Hus to death—sent an appeal to King Wenceslaus to aid him in suppression of the movement, return the former ministers to their posts, reinstate their revenue, and drive the Wycliffites and Hussites to either renounce and discontinue their heretical practice, or die. The king initially refused, but when pressures from the pope continued, Wenceslaus caved, and much blood was shed upon Bohemian land between the Hussites and the royal armies.

The Hussites assembled upon nearby "holy hills"—Tabor, Horeb, and Olivet, thus named by the relating factions—and devised organized resistance, sending word to Wenceslaus that they were prepared to die for their beliefs. After allowing a few key Utraquist zealots to lead a procession to Prague, holding high the Blessed Sacrament, they stormed the town hall demanding the release of Hussite prisoners. When their demands were not met, a fight broke out and the Hussites "threw the judge, the burgomaster, and several members of the town council out of the window into the street, where they were killed by the fall."[58] King Wenceslaus swore retaliation, but due to the excitement of the event, he suffered a stroke and died on August 16, 1419.

The death of Wenceslaus led to significant outbreaks of war all across Prague and the outskirts of Bohemia—early on led by Wenceslaus' brother, King Sigismund, under influence of the papal legates (foreign representatives of the pope)—leaving a surge of destruction in its wake. Battles upon battles were fought, and the Hussites engaged in more proficient military style offensive tactics. Utraquism:

> ...abolished every traditional rite and liturgy. There were to be no more churches, altars, vestments, sacred vessels, chants, or ceremonies. The Lord's Prayer was the only liturgical prayer; the communion table was a common table with common bread and common appointments, the celebrant wore his everyday clothes and was untonsured. Children were baptized with the first water at hand and without any further ceremony they received Communion in both kinds immediately after Baptism. Extreme unction and auricular confession were abolished; mortal sins were to be confessed in public. Purgatory and the worship of saints were suppressed, likewise all feasts and fasts. [The Catholic Encyclopedia goes on to say:] Such a creed accounts for the fury of destruction which possessed the Hussites.[59]

As the Hussite wars continued, some of the Roman Catholic Church's original fears materialized as the zealots of the reforming faith continued to read into, and revise, certain aspects of Scripture that is central to the gospel. The longer this tension went on, the further the Hussites were swept away from Wycliffe's and Hus' convictions, and into what even today's Protestant Church would consider sacrilegious. So caught up in defending religious liberty practice were they that at times they completely strayed from the principles they had fought to introduce and defend in the first place, bringing violent invasions upon many bordering countries that had aided the crusades against them. Eventually, even the Hussites turned radically against each other in the struggle to establish each faction's doctrine (most notably between the Taborites and the Utraquists). The more blood that was shed, the more misguided their values became until, at last, the Council of Basle paved the way for peaceful negotiation. The main articles of amendment (known as the *Compactata* of Basle) produced by this council were:

- In Bohemia and Moravia, communion under both kinds [bread and wine] is to be given to all adults who desire it;
- All mortal sins, especially public ones, shall be publicly punished by the lawful authorities [as opposed to the Church];
- The Word of God may be freely preached by approved preachers but without infringing papal authority;
- Secular power shall not be exercised by the clergy bound by vows to the contrary; other clergy, and the Church itself may acquire and hold temporal goods but merely as administrators and such [in other words, they may administer over, but not claim to "own," secular possessions].[60]

The articles did not entirely appease all factions of the Hussites, but their support, troops, resources, and vigor had been spent. The details of every anti-Hussite crusade are lengthy enough that it would require more space than is lent for this historical review, but suffice it to say, this newfound voice thrust into existence by Wycliffe and Hus would not be silenced. Although there was a period of time during the Hussite Wars when the initial doctrines of Wycliffe and his martyred brother Hus had been misdirected in the enthusiasm and flurry of clashing swords, the world would never forget the freedoms from legalistic dogma—the Bohemian Reformation, as it has been called—that had inspired this time in history.

And even as early as this era, a pattern begins to form: The greater the attempt to silence a voice, the louder the voice is heard among the people. The harder the Church attempted to turn listeners away from Wycliffe and Hus, the more the listeners became the speakers, and the new message of a personal relationship with Christ as the Head and His Word as supreme authority spread with irrepressible heat.

Oddly, this does not apply in every case. For instance, when the Hussites became overly radical and began throwing their voices toward demands for reform that tore a rift between their mission and the gospel of Christ, and into inter-faction wars regarding doctrine, they were silenced or killed, and those who remained were pacified by the compromise brought forth at the Council of Basle, effectively silencing them through peace instead of the demand for blood. For the Hussites, when they were at their loudest, they were silenced. But modern-day theologians of the Protestant faith will likely propose that the Hussites were silenced only *after* they had successfully landmarked their ideology, suggesting that when *God* has something to say through His people, no power on earth can quiet Him, and it is only when His *people* confuse His mission with trivial disputes that He allows a hush.

In this case, the hush that God allowed would, also, be quite temporary.

Martin Luther

For about a century, the Bohemian Reformation experienced vast religious tolerance. As the Church became less of a governing power over the secular world, it gradually became viewed as another earthly kingdom competing with European monarchies for wealth and authority, trading its spiritual and religious integrity for ultimate control. The Bohemian Reformation is merely *one* example of the earliest enlightenments that spotted the globe. Conciliarism ("the theory that a general council of the Church is higher in authority than the Pope"[61]) led to a completely redefined creed for believers, beginning with movements like that of the Bohemian Reformation, and it was an idea that gained vital and overriding focus worldwide.

German professor of theology and friar, Martin Luther (1483–1546), was the eldest among several siblings born to Hans and Margarethe and baptized into the Roman Catholic faith during this time. (On modern roads, the drive between Prague and Luther's birthplace [the Mansfield Südharz District in Saxony-Anhalt, Germany] is less than four hours.) Like Wycliffe and Hus, Luther had his own reasons for believing that philosophy and reason only led men so close to God, and that Scripture was the most accessible of God's divine revelations to mankind. Luther, in his writings a century after those of Hus, would parrot many of the principles originally penned by Wycliffe and Hus.

Perhaps more than any other name in the history of the Protestant Reformation, Luther's is one that draws conflicting biographical accounts when referring to his nature. In some reiterations of his life, he is seen as a crazed and wild animal, painted as one driven by a struggle for self-serving personal power and popularity. In uncountable others, he is seen as a humble man, only lifting his voice when necessary, and whose unadulterated love of the true gospel was the single stimulus of his years on earth. Depending on the writer, Luther is either criticized or romanticized, with unbiased records lost in a sea of opinionated rants—whether for or against him. It's not inaccurate to say that because of his significance in religious history, his role as hero or villain may fall to the reader's personal faith and doctrinal convictions. (It is for this reason that the following review of Luther will only report details of his personal character when reliable sources are in agreement.)

Despite this dichotomy, no one can deny that the movements taking place during—and after—his life as a result of his stance against the Church redefined everything our modern world associates with evangelical Christianity.

In his youth, Luther attended local Latin grammar schools, primarily run by church leadership. Living in fear of a fellow classmate who loved to point the finger at his peers for moral flaws—and then revel in the physical chastisement from the faculty that resulted—Luther strove to keep his conduct above reproach.[62] In the area where he spent his earliest years, public displays of piety were the norm, and priests, nuns, and monks were around every corner, all with their own advice for how and when to approach the throne of God. The world that surrounded Luther was completely and entirely dedicated to Catholicism.

By age twenty-two, Luther had accepted a master's degree in the town of Erfurt, under the tutelage of Bartholomäus Arnoldi von Usingen and Jodocus Trutfetter. These men were mentors of Luther's, important advisors for his young mind, who had inspired him to become a free-thinking individual, never swayed by popular philosophy or human reasoning, no matter how persuasive the original author.[63] (This influence most likely marks the era that shaped Luther, one of the greatest names in Christian history.) As a result of a strong submersion into independent thinking, Luther quickly saw that the more he craved God and His love, the shallower human reasoning appeared as an instrument to bring about and solidify that relationship. God was above and beyond the understanding of men, and He left in the hands of men the only instrument capable of communicating His plan for humanity: His Word. Through learning to question every study and theory presented to him—particularly those of Aristotle's—Luther felt a personal conviction to question and test every theory and theological idea against the Book that he believed held the last word in every debate.

Wycliffe, Hus, and Luther had much in common in this respect…

In July of 1505, Luther was traveling back to the university after a visit home as a thunderstorm began brewing in the skies. As lightning struck the ground nearby, he cried out to St. Anna for help, promising to become a monk out of fear of what he believed to be divine intervention—the "terrors from heaven"[64]—upon the course of his life. Choosing to set aside his father's wishes that he make more of himself through a career in law, Luther dedicated himself to ministry, a choice that his father despised. (Noteworthy to this moment in Luther's life: At the ceremonial observance of this decision, Luther laid prostrate over the grave of one of the leaders at the Council of Constance who had assisted in the condemnation [and therefore execution] of Jan Hus. Luther would not understand the terrible irony of this act until later.)

Plunging himself into his new life as a friar,[65] Luther regularly spent six hours at a time in the confession booth,[66] ignored the pangs of hunger during fasting, prayed for long hours, and devoted himself to pilgrimage and spiritual journey. Day after day, he dutifully carried out the expected regiments of monastery life, surrendering himself and all his temporal urges and needs to those routines the priesthood deemed necessary to further personal growth in the Lord.

But when all of this did not deliver the enrichment he had anticipated, Luther began to feel an emptiness growing within; one that would not be filled by the disciplines of the life he had chosen. Now more than ever, he was feeling distanced from God. Alienated. A man devoured by a constant fear of damnation and purgatory, enslaved to rituals, and whose afterlife was drawn into question every waking moment of the day.

The means the Church had endorsed for shedding the guilt of sin might have been a comfort to the laity, but to Luther, they served as a constant reminder that God was far away, reachable only by customs and sacraments and ceremony. Such a feat as *earning* one's salvation through these methods all too soon became suspect to him, and as he furthered himself even deeper into his cloistral obligations to find answers to his growing list of questions, the concept of God as a loving entity to His children seemed to reveal a clash from the world he was immersed within. It appeared as if this holy place, this building, his rituals, his life of dedication to the Maker of Mankind, all of these were exposing a God of wrath and judgment rather than a God of tenderness and mercy. It was of this time in his life that Luther said, "I lost hold of Christ the Savior and comforter, and made of him a stock-master [by this, he meant "jailor"] and hangman over my poor soul."[67]

In the spring of 1507, Luther was ordained a priest. At his first Mass following ordination, Luther was presented with the privilege to partake of the sacred communion. As is common in classic Roman Catholicism, Luther believed that by eating of the bread and drinking of the wine, he would be absorbing not bread and wine, but the literal and physical body of Jesus Christ—an act that he did not take lightly. Feeling more than just estranged from God by this moment in time, how could he—this sinful, errant, unworthy friar—have the audacity to partake in the body of Christ, his Lord? How could he then follow this rite of passage into the same vocational footsteps that so many holy men before him had trod, mediating between the spiritually starving people and God, Himself, when he, Luther, had not yet felt the deep intimacy with the Lord that was essential for such a calling?

Nonetheless, despite his sentiment that he was undeserving, Luther ate of the bread and drank of the wine, making the righteous vow that the rest of his existence would be solemnly devoted to bringing the children of God ever closer to sacred enrichment.

As soon as Mass was over, Hans, Luther's father, confronted Luther about his choices, questioning whether the lightning and "terrors from heaven" had merely been a ploy from the enemy to derail Luther from the rewarding career in law that Hans had wished for his beloved boy. To add to his anger, Hans reminded Luther that he had completely forgotten about the fifth commandment, in which a child is commanded by God to honor his parents' wishes. However, these antics merely served to drive a wedge between father and son. Now, more than ever, Luther needed a fatherly figure to stand in for the earthly one who was slipping from his grasp. Vicar General Johannes von Staupitz, a superior within Luther's order, saw in Luther the need for such an individual, and it was a role he easily filled.

Luther and Staupitz became close, and soon Luther was being given important responsibilities. One of these involved heading to Rome to bring reconciliation between two Augustinian factions who were at odds. Rome was by far the city about which many young priestly imaginations had fantasized as the truest capital of holy behavior. The center of all purity and piousness. The metropolis of virtuous dealings. The sacred place where the saintliest of godly men worshipped.

For Luther, Rome was the opposite.

For the first time in his life, he observed a completely Catholic world guilty of heralding more blasphemy and loathsome conduct than holiness. In his writings, this trip to Rome would not produce awe and wondrous reflections of the holy city's architecture. Contrarily, everywhere he looked, he saw disorder and filth. Men were urinating on the streets and publicly soliciting prostitutes. Fellow priests showed a surprising lack of knowledge and wit, appearing as though they merely functioned in obligatory position, hurrying through Mass to have it over and done with, and even went as far as to rush Luther in his spiritual contemplations. Luther returned to his monastery shortly after, disenchanted.[68]

In October of 1512, by the request of Staupitz, Luther received a doctorate as a theologian. He held steadfast to his internal feelings of unworthiness, but he obeyed the request, and traveled to teach in Wittenberg (where he spent the rest of his career). Yet, it was not without complications of the heart. If he was to be seen as a teacher of the Lord, he had questions that needed answering, and quickly.

Fervently, Luther poured out his woes in confession, beseeching Staupitz to hear in great detail every miniscule transgression that he had committed. Luther seemingly didn't carry the burden of sexual sin as many of his peers did, but instead found error and blemish in even the mundane and regular proceedings of the day. Over time, every single act by Luther was self-analyzed to the point of obsession, and he felt he was incapable of living even a single moment without executing an atrocity. Staupitz, though ever patient and helpful to his son in Christ, rebuked Luther for confusing confession as a time to be consumed with "flummery and pseudo faults…these knotty phobias and specters,"[69] which were only a sin in the mind of Luther. But, as he later shared, Luther only "somewhat" feared eternal damnation; the sin he feared most was displeasing God…to the point that he "trembled."[70]

At every turn, Luther sought to either find the ultimate and supreme answer that would justify his self-punishment and bring satisfying and divine supplementation to his weariness, *or* a release from this unsustainably miserable existence of self-loathing via a breakthrough of enlightenment toward a new purpose for his life. Each day was met with a new record of abominable evils, under the weight of which he was suffocating. The longer he lived under the pressure, the longer he spent in contrite confession, prayer, and fasting, absolutely consumed every waking moment of the day to right his wrongs, that he may be seen as fit for fulfillment. But, as historians have thousands of times observed, it was from the depths of this turmoil that his epiphany was happened upon.

Slowly at first, with that familiar independence of thinking that had been instilled within him, Luther began questioning more than just the authority of human reasoning and philosophy as a basis for a relationship with God. He started to see fault within the Church's approach to God, no longer convinced that it was merely his own shame or sin that kept him from feeling closeness to Christ. The logic behind the ritualistic creed so often practiced around him had gradually exposed what he saw as contradictions. If one aimed to please God through constant confession and self-punishment, adhering always to the profound schedule of piety-through-religious-ceremony, how could they focus on anything outside of themselves and their own eternal destiny? And if they could not focus on anything outside of themselves, then what, besides selfishness, were they ultimately accomplishing? Wasn't the saturation of these rituals leading roundabout to a love of one's self instead of the love of merely pleasing the Lord? Were these holy men so consumed by the preservation of their own afterlife that they had completely missed the opportunity to *worship* the Lord for all He had done for His people?

And, wasn't that message and goal of Christ's all along? Wasn't that why He came? To convene with Him in love and not legalism?

Convinced that true closeness to God began with loving and praising the Lord, Luther traded in hours of penitence and sorrow over his own failings and redirected his focus to appreciation and admiration.

But, loving the Savior could only come after knowing the Savior. It was with this in mind that Luther poured into the Scripture with new-found aim, determined to find passages that revealed the loving nature of God rather than solely the God of reprimand. He had always believed that the Bible was the first authority over mankind, but it was now with fresh eyes that he was only just beginning to appreciate the depth of liberty Christ had come to offer. (The apostle Paul's letters to the Romans and Galatians were of particular interest.)

To say that Luther's epiphany led to quick liberation from his spiritual fatigue would be to ignore the subsequent years of excruciating internal unrest that he faced during the crest of his journey. In almost every answer he received, another confusion was revealed. His path had been retargeted, and the truth was certainly dawning, but the process was agonizingly slow and filled with moments of deep perplexity—so much so that at times even his faith in the existence of God was drawn into question. However, he was far closer now to the truth he had been seeking than before, as any reader of his lengthier biographical accounts will attest, and eventually he adopted a unique perspective that would help solidify his faith and make him strong. In Luther's view: God will sometimes allow one to feel lost and wandering in despair during one's journey to closeness with Him, because He knows it is only when one feels "robbed of all certainty" that a person will have "no place to go except to the God of mercy and grace,"[71] effectively constructing a more sturdy relationship in the end. For Luther's upcoming role in the Protestant Reformation, the foundation of the bond between he and God had to be made of the *sturdiest* metals.

Knowing, however, that the struggle to know and love the Lord had to come from within the heart, Luther proceeded to identify with a calling that associated much less with pilgrimages, rituals, relics, and the amount of monetary support flowing in during Mass, and more with an inward experience. By this point in history, because of the increase of international cohesion among nations (particularly England, France, and Spain) who contested the hierarchy—now viewing the Roman Catholic Church and its pope and leaders as a secular monarchy with more interest in power than in promoting holiness amongst the people—the Church's influence was weakening. This would make it much harder for Luther's voice to be terminated when he brought his disputes to Rome than it had been for Hus.

As it was, all across Europe, multitudes were sick or dying because of the plagues brought by the Black Death, and during this tumultuous period, *many* were falling on their knees before God, seeking personal closeness over favor with the priesthood. As a result, all over the land, recognizable corruption within the Church was being openly accused for what it was. So, by 1517, when Luther came against the powers that be—during the sales of indulgences by Johann Tetzel under the order of Pope Leo X to fund the rebuilding of St. Peter's Basilica—he was met with much societal support. Tetzel was seen by many in his endeavor as a scam artist. With the sale of each indulgence, the people were given a papal order that said they would not suffer in purgatory because of their charitable donations and good works. So long had Western society adopted the notion of penance and restitution that this extreme "quick-fix" method of releasing them from suffering in the afterlife was regarded with suspicion.

Luther was in great protest of such practice, believing that these indulgences would lead men to sin at will without fear of God's wrath as long as the offer to buy their spiritual assurance was on the table. The apostle Paul had written that the children of God were to "work out [their] own salvation with fear and trembling" (Philippians 2:12), a concept that was left void if salvation was for sale. But what outraged Luther most was the idea that the people were being fooled away from understanding salvation as the free gift God had given.

He wrote his grievances down in a letter to his archbishop, Albrecht (referred to commonly as "Albert of Mainz"). Within this letter was a document then called "The Disputation of Martin Luther on the Power and Efficacy of Indulgences" (now famously referenced as "The Ninety-Five Theses"), which addressed not only indulgences, but protestations of clerical abuses.

(Note: The story goes that Luther also nailed this document to the door of the All Saints Church [also "Castle Church," locally] in Wittenberg. For centuries, this deed has been celebrated by Lutheran biographers as an act of heroism and boldness and, according to university custom, it is still seen as fact.[72] It was also universally accepted as truth until the twentieth century. However, in 1961, Catholic Luther researcher Erwin Iserloh exposed that the first written account of this claim was penned by Wittenberg University professor Philipp Melanchthon, who did not appear at the university until the year 1518, and therefore could not have been a witness to this event. Today, the debate rages on as to whether Luther would have gone as far as to nail his criticisms to the door of a church without approval from his bishop to do so, but it's worthy of note that, this early on, Luther was still generally at peace with the Church and may not have yet seen reason for such unabashed provocation.)

Article 86 of Luther's theses posed the following bold question: "Why does not the pope, whose wealth is today greater than the wealth of the richest Crassus, build this one basilica of St. Peter with his own money rather than with the money of poor believers?"[73]

At first, Luther was ignored, written off as a lowly, meddling monk with no executive power or influence within the papacy. Because of how underestimated he was at the time, no ramifications were threatened against him as a result of his bearing his disregarded opinion to Albrecht and the colleagues within his own circle, so when the "Disputation" fell into the hands of the people, the "poor believers"—*and successively to the printing press*—circulation was wide…and immediate. Simultaneous to circulation of the document was translation from its original Latin to other native languages, and soon, access to Luther's arguments was everywhere.

If the pope *did* have the authority to condense or completely alleviate purgatorial misery, why, then, would he not place this blessing on all his people freely as the caring father-in-Christ he claimed to be, including those who could not afford the indulgences? These questions and comparable others began as a murmuring amongst believers in Germany, but within a period of a couple months, it grew to an angry roar across all of Europe.

Luther had no way of knowing at the time that he had just birthed the catalyst of the Protestant Reformation.

It was begun…

By the hordes, students of the Scripture traveled far and wide to hear Luther speak. Some of these included key names who would become important reformers within their locality as a result of personal meetings with Luther (such as Dominican Martin Bucer of Strasbourg and Johannes Brenz of Württemberg[74]). Luther's central ideology was music to their ears: justification—God's declaration that a sinner is righteous— was *sole fide*, "by faith *alone*," not by works. Salvation, Luther preached, was only attainable by faith in Christ as Messiah, and it was *free*.

The following December, Albrecht forwarded Luther's theses to Pope Leo X, who would spend the next three years responding with a series of theological messengers sent to challenge Luther's claims. In August of 1518, Luther was summoned to appear for examination in Augsburg, a trek he agreed to make, arriving at the appointed time in October of the same year. There, Cardinal Cajetan (Jacobo di Vio de Gaeta) heatedly questioned Luther in front of the Imperial Diet (the general assembly of the Imperial Estates of the Holy Roman Empire). The hearing became and intense, fiery exchange of shouts over Luther's ninety-five theses, and in the end, Luther was ordered to recant his positions on indulgences, justification by faith, and the pope's authority over the Church—an order he blatantly disregarded.

According to almost all accounts of Luther's life, he was that night informed by his supporters that Cardinal Cajetan had been given a papal brief issuing the arrest of Luther (who would then be sent directly to Rome), but before the arrest could take place, Luther fled back to Wittenberg and found refuge under Frederick III, elector of Saxony. However, to bring clarity and fairness to a famous moment in his life story, note that according to the *Catholic Encyclopedia*, this papal brief was "no doubt written in Germany, and is an evident forgery." It goes on to say, "Like all forged papal documents, it still shows a surprising vitality, and is found in every biography of Luther." So, whether Luther either fled in fear of arrest or simply traveled home after his shouting match with Cardinal Cajetan, he arrived back in Wittenberg a year after having penned his celebrated theses.

With tension rising between Luther and Rome—and with a growing voice from the laity in support of Luther's convictions—a champion theologian of the papacy by the name of Johann Maier von Eck emerged as the next challenger of Lutheran heresy. Cardinal Cajetan had put forth great effort to silencing Luther, so Eck staged a disputation at Leipzig between himself and Luther's colleague Andreas Karlstadt, who had previously defended Luther's theses. But, interestingly, Eck invited Luther to appear in person to defend his unorthodox doctrine, an invitation Luther accepted. Prior to the scheduled debate, Luther, his associates from Wittenberg, and many others who had begun to strike back at the hierarchal religious structure of Rome openly expressed their concerns in letters that widely circulated throughout prestigious leadership circles from the smallest church councils to the pope. From seemingly everywhere at once, there was an eruption of discussion involving many new ideologies, such as whether the pope should be seen as a fallible human capable of error via human reasoning, or as the chosen one of God who convenes directly with the Divine and, therefore, is of higher authority than an individual's scriptural interpretations. By the time the debate at Leipzig took place in July of 1519, everyone was listening.

According to many records covering the disputation, Luther was not wholly against the papacy, but saw it as a human institution with *equal* rights of authority as any other institution within the body of Christ. The Greek (or Eastern) Church, for instance, had not yielded itself to functioning under the weight of the papacy, and yet it showed itself capable of shaping, in Luther's opinion, more learned theologians than Rome.[75] Matthew 16:18, he said, was not to be taken as God's ultimate ordination that the exclusive rights of interpreting Scripture belong to the pope or the priesthood. And when Luther spoke, he did so with intensity.

Such impertinence resulted in his being labeled as the new Jan Hus.

When the event came to a weary and inconclusive end, Luther returned once again to Wittenberg. Locally, he was seen as the victor of the oratory tournament, while Eck remained champion in papal channels. However, while Luther had not officially and publicly been declared underdog in every arena following Leipzig, the comparison of his zeal to that of Hus imbibed from him any remaining soft spoken restraint.

It was a turning point.

If the Church was to be so quick to identify another Hus—the implications of which whispered pending excommunication and perhaps even execution—then Luther would give them a performance worthy of their shock. From the mouth and writings of the now emboldened reformist came daring, outright attacks against the powers of Rome. According to the *Catholic Encyclopedia*:

> He addresses the masses; his language is that of the populace; his theological attitude is abandoned; his sweeping eloquence fairly carries the emotional nature of his hearers.... In one impassioned outburst, he cuts from all his Catholic moorings—the merest trace left seeming to intensify his fury. Church and State, religion and politics, ecclesiastical reform and social advancement, are handled with a flaming, peerless oratory. He speaks with reckless audacity; he acts with breathless daring. War and revolution do not make him quail.... The "gospel," he now sees, "cannot be introduced without tumult, scandal, and rebellion."...

Luther the reformer had become Luther the revolutionary; the religious agitation had become a political rebellion. Luther's theological attitude at this time, as far as a formulated cohesion can be deduced, was as follows:

- The Bible is the only source of faith; it contains the plenary inspiration of God; its reading is invested with a quasi-sacramental character.
- Human nature has been totally corrupted by original sin, and man, accordingly, is deprived of free will. Whatever he does, be it good or bad, is not his own work, but God's.
- Faith *alone* can work justification, and man is saved by confidently believing that God will pardon him. This faith not only includes a full pardon of sin, but also an unconditional release from its penalties.
- The hierarchy and priesthood are not Divinely instituted or necessary, and ceremonial or exterior worship is not essential or useful. Ecclesiastical vestments, pilgrimages, mortifications, monastic vows, prayers for the dead, intercession of saints, avail the soul nothing.
- All sacraments, with the exception of baptism, Holy Eucharist, and penance, are rejected, but their absence may be supplied by faith.
- The priesthood is universal; every Christian may assume it. A body of specially trained and ordained men to dispense the mysteries of God is needless and a usurpation.
- There is no visible Church or one specially established by God whereby men may work out their salvation.[76]

Luther had gained not only followers amongst the laity, but also supporters and guardians of his doctrine within important political groups, including, but not limited to: Ulrich von Hutten, the leader of the Imperial Knights of the Holy Roman Empire; Franz von Sickingen, a German knight of noble birth (and later imperial chamberlain and councilor under Holy Roman Emperor Charles I of Spain); Silvester von Schaumberg, an Imperial Knight and bailiff of Münnerstadt, Velden-stein and Parkstein;[77] Frederick III ("Frederick the Wise"), elector of Saxony from the House of Wettin; and Georg Burkhardt (pseudonym "Georg Spalatin"), Frederick III's well known personal assistant, who served as an agent between Frederick III and Luther.[78]

Around the time that Luther personally sent his manifesto *On the Freedom of a Christian Man* to Pope Leo X,[79] Eck—Luther's opponent at the debate of Leipzig—appeared in Rome carrying many of Luther's works for examination. The pope in turn responded on June 15, 1520, with the renowned *Exsurge Domine* ("Arise O Lord") papal bull, cen-suring forty-one propositions from Luther's ninety-five theses and later works, demanding that Luther's works be burned within sight of the clerics and people, and threatening Luther with excommunication if he did not agree to publicly recant within sixty days of publication.

Eck was commissioned to publish the bull across Germany along-side Cardinal Girolamo Aleandro. Arriving in Meissen, Merseburg, and Brandenburg in late September, Eck and Aleandro were met with instantaneous and ardent resistance by Lutheran supporters, who responded to the bull by throwing it into the rivers or publicly defac-ing it. Defense of Lutheran dogma was so concentrated that Eck's and Aleandro's lives were placed in danger several times in the midst of ensuing mayhem. The commanded burnings of Lutheran works were only partially successful, as many students either openly refused to adhere to the pope's order or staged mock burnings where anti-Lutheran literature was instead put to the flames and Luther's works were hidden away.

On December 10, amongst a proud assembly of Wittenberg Uni-versity students chanting *Te Deum laudamus* ("Thee, O God, we praise You") and *Requiem aeternam* ("Eternal rest grant to them"), Luther set fire to the papal bull by the city gate in Wittenberg. Once Luther's bra-zen response to the demand of recanting reached Rome, Pope Leo X formally excommunicated him on January 3, 1521, in the bull *Decet Romanum Pontificem* ("It Pleases the Roman Pontiff").

The bull of excommunication seemingly only served to set afire a raging passion within the hearts of those who sought liberty from the hierarchy. This included Luther, who then flew to his desk feverishly night and day composing new treatises and proposals appealing to local nobility to join with him in further opposition of papal malpractice. It was around this time that he composed *Address to the Christian Nobility of the German Nation* and *The Babylonian Captivity of the Church*, attacking the sale of indulgences, condemning the power and control of the pope, proclaiming equality of all believers based on faith, and asserting that baptism and communion are the only two sacraments the people of God should have to recognize.

Luther's popularity amongst both the laity and now the clergymen of his area was strong enough that the excommunication bull stirred but little fear and even less cooperation from the people, so the enforcement of it was given to secular authority, and Emperor Charles V (previously Charles I of Spain) sent a summons for Luther to appear at the Diet of Worms (thus named by its location in Worms, Germany) for thorough examination and trial. Jan Hus' famous execution had occurred after the promise of safe conduct had been voided over superficial cause. Knowing this, Frederick III went out of his way to acquire a safe passage agreement ensuring that Luther would be safe on his journey to the Diet of Worms—as well as his journey back home. Despite this, Luther's associates feared fatal repercussion for his appearance at the assembly, and urged him not to go lest he risk martyrdom. But risk it he did, and on April 17, 1521, he appeared as ordered before the presiding Emperor Charles V. On his travels to Worms, Luther was seen by civilians as an "unconquerable hero," and to the dismay of the papal administrators, when he entered the final city for the hearing, "people trumpeted and cheered."[80]

The first day of the hearing, Luther was asked if the writings presented were his, and if he wholly and strictly stood behind them. In the midst of the attention, he was at first quiet and timid, and the day ended when he asked to return to his quarters and reflect upon the contents of his writings. His request was granted, and he was given until the following evening to recant. (Note that Luther's request to delay his response has historically drawn much speculation, and to this day, it is not known why he did not immediately refuse to recant. However, many believe he felt the need to spend time in prayer and preparation over his retort.) When he appeared the second day, he stood steadfast and sure of himself in his refusal to recant, saying, "I neither can nor will recant anything, for it is neither safe nor right to act against one's conscience… God help me, Amen."[81]

Having already bound himself to allow Luther safe passage, Emperor Charles V made the order that Luther was to return home immediately and without harm. However, in late May, an edict was signed demanding a ban against Luther. This time, the orders came not from papal authority, but from that of secular, civil command. A call was issued for his immediate arrest, and an award was promised to anyone aiding in his capture; his writings were to be destroyed; he was to be viewed as a criminal heretic; and no one in Germany was permitted to offer him accommodation, whether that be food, drink, or housing. Not surprisingly, friendly allies intervened on Luther's behalf. In a dramatized abduction staged by Frederick III, armed horsemen descended upon Luther during his stroll at the edge of a forest, grabbed him, blindfolded him, took him by force upon horseback, and galloped away. From there, they escorted him to the safe haven of Wartburg Castle. This mock-capture proved to deliver the desired reaction, as rumors of this abduction quickly spread about Germany. Lutheran supporters mourned, believing the worst, but also, papal authorities could not immediately conclude that Luther had been assisted by collaborators.

Taking on a disguise, Luther grew a beard and allowed a full head of hair to replace his tonsure. Going by the alias of "Junker Georg" (Knight George), he remained in Wartburg Castle in confinement to only two rooms.

There is much discussion regarding the writings composed by Luther during his stay at the castle. Lonelier than he had ever been, and taken from a world of constant access to the pulpit and thrust into hiding, he fell into a pit of depression deeper than any he had faced prior. Some of his musings at this time have led biographers to suggest he was within an inch of losing his sanity. His words held newfound darkness, and the secret letters written from the castle to his associates in Wittenberg spoke of wily attacks upon Luther by the devil. Desperately alone, Luther found solace only in the quill and the Word. He began translating the New Testament into German vernacular, but this endeavor is not without criticism today. Attempting to speak in words the commoners would understand, he didn't shy away from using informal and unsophisticated expressions that were frequently heard in the lower social circles. As a result, his New Testament translation has been declared errant and uninspired. But to the recipients of the work—the members of lower society much excluded by the holy church crowds— this document spoke on their level, and the demand for it was momentous. According to the *Catholic Encyclopedia,* "In less than three months the first copy of the translated New Testament was ready for the press.... [I]t was issued at Wittenberg in September. Its spread was so rapid that a second edition was called for as early as December."[82]

This bold, unashamed translation—despite controversy connected with Luther's choice vocabulary—would be one of the most dominant historical benchmarks associated with Martin Luther's name. But it was not merely this endeavor that diverted Luther's mind from isolation. While holed up in his gloomy castle sanctuary, Luther continued putting his thoughts on parchment, and the following titles make up only a short list of those formed at that time: *On the Abrogation of the Private Mass, On Confession, Whether the Pope Has the Power to Require It,* and *The Judgement of Martin Luther on Monastic Vows.*

As these and other works of Luther made their way into the hands of the priesthood, one by one, priests and nuns left the organized Church, dropped all but the two sacraments from their observance, and adhered to the notion that any "good works" carried out for the sole purpose of gaining favor with God and diminishing their own suffering in the afterlife was selfish and void of heart. This resulted in a huge declination of traditional religious practice in trade for what believers saw as a restoration of fellowship between God and humankind.

Yet, perhaps the boldest of all Luther's assertions popularized at this time was that priests, monks, and nuns were free to break vows of celibacy and enter into a new vow of marriage. This institution, Luther said, was blessed by God, Himself, and was given as a gift for men and women—including leaders within the Church—to enjoy. The proof of this, as Luther saw it, was not only in Scripture, but within the functions and design of the human body, itself. To resist the natural and sensual passions of the body would not alleviate the urges and render them nonexistent. Contrarily, ignoring the body's needs served only to exacerbate them, causing in the end a much greater distraction between God and His servants than marriage. Within this frustration, the enemy gains far stronger a hold on the ministers, and it was with this thread of thought in mind that Luther suggested a vow of celibacy was the devil's tool, and further encouraged ministers to marry, remain as teachers of the Word, and free themselves from the binds of passion.

By the scores, men and women of the faith traded in tradition for reform. Although the reformation had long since already begun the restructuring of religious practice, it was this amendment that brought about revolutionary change. With it, however, was another wave of radicalism, comparable to that of the Hussite Wars.

Luther's defender, Andreas Karlstadt, who had appeared at the disputation in Leipzig, caused significant disturbance to the locals of Wittenberg. Although he attempted to cling most precisely to Luther's teachings, his shedding of the old ways was aggressive and fanatical, which even Lutheran devotees found bristling. The laity was guilty of sin, he said, if they did not personally handle the cup and bread before observing communion. On Christmas Day, he publicly appeared to conduct Mass without his clerical garments. Disregarding monastic vows, he married a young girl—an act that, although slowly gaining support, was still in its infancy of toleration and approval.[83] He published 152 theses against indulgences, demanded that images and statues be removed from churches, protested the ritual of prayers to the deceased, and insisted that Mass be pronounced in its dialect native to the laity. His reasoning for such deliberations was: "We must begin sometime…or nothing will be done. He who puts his hand to the plough should not look back."[84]

But Karlstadt was not alone in his harsh contempt for authoritarian church regulations. Others of the Augustinian order joined in ignoring longstanding procedure and guidelines, determined to free themselves from their perceived lifelong oppressions:

> On 9 October, 1521, thirty-nine out of the forty Augustinian Friars formally declared their refusal to say private Mass any longer; Zwilling, one of the most rabid of them, denounced the Mass as a devilish institution; Justus Jonas stigmatized Masses for the dead as sacrilegious pestilences of the soul; Communion under two kinds was publicly administered. Thirteen friars (12 Nov.) doffed their habits, and with tumultuous demonstrations fled from the monastery, with fifteen more in their immediate wake; those remaining loyal were subjected to ill-treatment and insult by an infuriated rabble led by Zwilling; mobs prevented the saying of Mass; on 4 Dec., forty students, amid derisive cheers, entered the Franciscan monastery and demolished the altars; the windows of the house of the resident canons were smashed, and it was threatened with pillage. It was clear that these excesses, uncontrolled by the civil power, unrestrained by the religious leaders, were symptomatic of social and religious revolution.[85]

As tension grew, angry, armed mobs on the streets defaced church buildings and smashed sacred statues, and these exploits were only met with retaliation.

Anxiety grew to a boiling point at the appearance of the Zwickau Prophets—Nicholas Storch, Thomas Dreschel, and Markus Stübner— hailing from Zwickau, Saxony. Having already been cast out of Zwickau for their theological diatribes, they eagerly swept the streets with claims that true authority is not from the pope *or* from Scripture, but from personal revelations by the Holy Spirit. Infant baptism, they said, was immoral, affronting many mothers and fathers who had believed their children would be forever saved by their own virtuous interventions. The most riling of all their esoteric declarations was related to an imminent apocalypse that they allegedly foresaw—and with it, the return of Christ. Although a portion of what they said reflected Lutheran ideology, much of it did not, and when word of the propaganda being preached in Wittenberg reached Luther, he left immediately for his hometown, arriving March 6, 1522.

At once, he took to the pulpit, firing passionate pleas for the people to return to core Christian values such as love and charity instead of airing out their weariness through hatred and violence. Eight successive sermons fell from his mouth imploring for a truce from quarrel.

These eight sermons had great effect on the listeners, who thereafter settled their zeal for a time. (Later, Luther recalled these sermons in a manuscript he called his best work: *The Eight Wittenberg Sermons*.) However, by removing the threat of false prophets and banishing the men from Zwickau, Luther was now not only in opposition to the established Church, but also to radical reformers who endangered progress toward religious liberty through violence and bloodshed.

As a result of this, Luther's name would be dragged into extreme acts of revolt all across Central Europe, in the Great Peasants' War of 1524–1525.

Turbulence had been seething between the peasants and upper classes for the last century, and Luther's writings, when taken out of context, could be twisted into statements that suggested his support of hostility toward the socially elite. In Franconia, Swabia, and Thuringia, attacks were led by laborers and farmhands against the aristocracy.

Within a short time, these revolts became a full-fledged war. Although the war was, at its core, between social classes in a feud over lifestyle extremes—the lust for money and the dire reality of poverty—it was often with Luther's name at the center that assaults were carried out in the interest of divine justice. What was truly a war on the upper crust became interwoven with a radical religious groups, frequently led by Protestant clergy.

Despite the short duration of the conflict, the body count was sub-stantial enough that the Great Peasants' War "threatened the national life of Germany,"[86] and by no means was this war the beginning or end to what had been over a hundred years of societal feuding. It was, in truth, a devastating time. "More than 1000 monasteries and castles were levelled to the ground, hundreds of villages were laid in ashes, the harvests of the nation were destroyed, and 100,000 killed.... [O]ne commander alone boasted that 'he hanged 40 evangelical preachers and executed 11,000 revolutionists and heretics.'"[87] And as far as the true nature of Luther's response to, and involvement in, the rivalry, it is difficult to find an unbiased account. According to the *Catholic Encyclopedia*, which has generally painted Luther to have been somewhat of a radical (which is understandable and somewhat expected, considering the source), "This smouldering fire [the war] Luther fanned to a fierce flame by his turbulent and incendiary writings, which were read with avidity by all, and by none more voraciously than the peasant."[88] However, historians, theologians, and Protestant Reformation researchers have weighed in on his role much differently. Like Wycliffe, who has been described as one whose "powers of debate were almost more than human,"[89] there was something about Luther during this time of civil hostility that people have had a hard time putting into words. From one account to another, he is canvased as a man with a piercing gaze, and who one minute was found blessing his listeners with love and grace incomparable to any other speaker, filling their hearts with hope abounding—and the next minute berating them for their lack of faith and willingness to shed blood for temporal gain, convicting them with a strangely powerful influence that could only come from supernatural authority. Catholic biographers have sometimes pointed to this as proof of Luther's wildly unpredictable character, and a means of implying that his role was nothing more during this era than a heretical ticking time bomb who fed the bloodthirsty farmers with the fire they needed to ignite further fallout. Yet, many others see him as one who sympathized with peasants against members of society who lavished in luxury while the poor starved, but who always came back to one central principle: the authorities of the land must be obeyed,[90] and violence is to be avoided at all costs.

The debate of Luther as instigator of the war rages on with enthusiastically different perspectives, depending on the reporter. But one need only look as far as the treatises and manuscripts that Luther wrote during this time of strain to see that by default, the defense of the gospel under spiritual authorities tended to clash with the promotion to obey secular or religious authorities (which were often seen as the same thing once the Roman Catholic Church had established itself as more of a monarchy than an institution endorsing holy behavior), and, therefore, his stance was controversial by nature. Luther couldn't have detached himself from either extreme if he had wanted to, standing as the voice of the peasants in one pamphlet and the voice of the princes in the next. From his serene *Eight Wittenberg Sermons* and his *Exhortation to Peace* to his hounding *Against the Murderous and Robbing Rabble of Peasants* (amongst others), Luther stood strongly for one side or the other on a case-by-case basis, reiterating his passionate positions relative to specific instances. (At one point, Luther deserted the peasantry, seeing that despite their unfortunate role in society, it was their revolts that caused the war, and that much like a rabid dog that could not be trained for any purposes other than to strike out and kill for purposes unjustifiable, their battles must be put down, even if that endeavor resulted in the loss of life for those who, under the placard of the gospel, would shed blood. Following this, when royalty responded even more vehemently against the low class than was necessary to regain peace, Luther used his writing skills to reprimand them as well.[91]) However, just as select Scriptures of the Bible, when taken out of context, have historically been used to feed the personal agendas of radicals, so, too, would Luther's writings be recited indiscriminately when one group wanted the words of a weighty influence on their side.

The longer the war raged on, and the more lives were lost, the more the leaders, royalty, high class, and peasants alike dropped Luther's name into their agendas, and the more Luther has gone down in history as the man with mass blood on his hands. This period would be the most controversial of Luther's involvement in the Protestant Reformation to date (and years later, Luther would take upon himself the guilt for all the destruction[92]). In the end, key frontrunners on the side of the peasants were executed, and the rebel citizens were left with little resources or voices of havoc to throw any coals into the burner, and the war ended in May of 1525.

Then, the following month, Luther did something that finally solidified his lifelong goals of religious amendment—and religious free-dom—for God's people.

He got married.

Since the beginning, clerical personnel had engaged in sexual exploits, sometimes without much effort in the interest of discretion. But until now, such behavior had been seen as a corruption of the clergy. In Luther's opinion, many of these individuals were merely taking vows to win favor to God through good works, and then defiling those vows by soliciting the services of concubines and mistresses. As followers of Luther continued to watch his every move, listen to his every word, and shadow the lifestyle he had advocated, ministers were now, more regularly than before, violating their vows of celibacy and taking wives, some of them even continuing in their endeavors to preach and spread the gospel. Luther was certainly not the first cleric to marry, but it was *his* marriage that drove the people toward aspirations of eliminating rules of celibacy altogether in trade for an agreeable and matrimonial com-promise. If the human body was, as Luther said, created for enjoying marital intimacy—and if ignoring the body was, as Luther had pointed out, of greater carnal threat to the leaders of the Church—then why should these vows exist at all? Cannot a man and woman still minister to the lost and maintain holiness simultaneously? That was the question of the century. And when Luther bellowed his loudest answer to the priesthood in the form of his own marital vows on June 13, 1525, to Katharina von Bora (a nun he had helped escape from her convent two years prior), the seal of approval on clerical marriage was set in stone.

This is not to say that Luther's choice did not cause a stir. Many saw his decision as reckless and immature, especially for a man in his position, who had joined in his happy nuptials as the world around him was toiling in the aftermath of slaughter. But after all the tension, war, and efforts of religious reformation, Luther longed to live out the rest of his life quietly.

In the years following both tragedy for all of Germany and personal contentment with his new bride, Luther made it his duty to organize the new Church. Summarizing the new faith in his catechisms, Luther sought to bring the cross evermore at the center, reestablish Christ as the only Head, and reinstate Scripture as mankind's ultimate authority. Positioning himself at a church in Upper Saxony that had completely broken ties with Rome, he pursued slow transformation, so as not to replace one system of control with another. As Church leadership from neighboring regions grew more familiar with the theological foundations Luther was implementing, they began seeking his advice, and he obliged.

In 1526, he wrote a German Mass in order to incorporate the laity's understanding during service, and as expected by this point, it included the giving of bread and wine directly to all participants, and made many other traditional rituals optional so each church could, in turn, celebrate as they saw fit with their congregants. Baptismals and weddings were likewise simplified.

In his writings of 1529, *Large Catechism* and *Small Catechism*—the former as a manual for leadership and the latter as a manual for the laity—he included an innovative questions-and-answers section so the Christians would personally understand the words they spoke when prompted in service, as opposed to merely voicing memorized aphorisms. (Today, the *Small Catechism* is still widely used in religious teaching, and has a reputation for being one of the most comprehensible tools for educating recent converts, as well as an excellent resource for parents to help instruct their children.) These handbooks deeply explained the Apostle's Creed, and broke down in clear terminology the traits and qualities of each member of the Godhead: God the Father, God the Son, and God the Holy Spirit. The Father is the Creator of all, whose hand sets in motion all that exists and all that transpires. The Son is the Redeemer, the Rescuer of all whose souls would otherwise be condemned for all eternity, a price He paid with His blood. The Holy Spirit is the Supreme Sanctifier, without which no man could be made holy. In every article of these works, Luther stressed the importance of the Trinity as individuals to whom closeness could be achieved, as opposed to the faraway, ruling personalities they had been established as in the past.

Now free from his captivity at the Wartburg Castle, Luther revised his Bible translation, pouring methodically over every word, and added in the Old Testament. The complete work was published in 1534. He would spend the rest of his life polishing every verse. Luther's translation, though not accepted by all at the time (or even today), quickly spread across Germany, then Europe, and eventually the world, and was the inspiration for William Tyndale's English Bible (the first Bible printed in English) published around the same era. Tyndale's translation stands as a forerunner for the King James Bible, which was more responsibly translated by forty-seven scholars of the Church of England from the original Hebrew, Aramaic, and Greek.

In his later years, Luther did not shy away from confrontation when new ideologies or doctrines were brought into the Church. Certainly, he is known for far more than what is stated here. His name is closely associated to disputes concerning what happens to the soul after death, the precise meaning of Christ's words at the Last Supper (and therefore the exact observance of the Eucharist), and his position against the Turks. He is frequently brought into provocative debate for his treatises *On the Jews and Their Lies* and *On the Holy Name and the Lineage of Christ* (in which he showed no mercy in his anti-Semitic attacks), and for the following final sermon in his birth town Eisleben, when he further blasted Jews with animosity.

Luther's slate is not perfectly clean, and as much as he is celebrated, he is also despised. Yet, for the purposes of understanding the portions of his life that contributed to the Protestant Reformation, we will now bring a close to our reflection of this famous historic figure whose actions splintered the Roman Catholic Church into new sects of Christianity across the globe.

On February 18, 1546, following a long bout of mounting health problems and a painful evening wrought with chest pains, Luther passed away. Other than uttering the word "yes" when asked by his companions if he was ready to die, his last words were a quote from Psalm 31:5: "Into your hands, I command my spirit. You have saved me, Father, O faithful God."

John Calvin and Huldrych Zwingli

Germany was by far the hot spot wherein the fires of the Protestant Reformation began to burn. However, the stories of Wycliffe, Hus, and Luther are not the only relevant accounts that contributed to the fracture of the Roman Catholic Church.

John Calvin

Originally trained in law, French theologian John Calvin split from the Roman Catholic Church after he experienced a personal faith epiphany in 1533, believing that he had been called by God to bring reformation. In November of the same year, Calvin's close friend Nicolas Cop dedicated his inaugural address at the Collège de France (then "Collège Royal") to the need for reform. The address was condemned as heretical, and Calvin was associated with the outrage that ensued, so he fled to Basel, Switzerland.

In 1536, he wrote *Institutes of the Christian Religion*, his ground-breaking revelation of Protestant systematic theology, offering validation of popular Reformation topics such as the sacraments and justification by faith. It was an instant bestseller.

When Calvin set off for Strasbourg (Eastern France) the following summer, he stopped for what was supposed to be a one-night stay in Geneva ("Genève," the second-largest city in Switzerland). There, he met Guillaume ("William") Farel, a somewhat distraught and frazzled reformer who had heard of this bright author, and convinced the reluctant Calvin to stay and assist him in bringing the new faith to his city. Initially, his residency in Geneva was peaceful, and the city council supported his *Articles on the Organization of the Church and its Worship at Geneva*, which detailed revisions of religious practice citywide. Later, when the proposed modifications proved difficult to keep, anxiety grew between the council and Calvin, a heat that intensified when whispers of an alliance with France brought doubts as to the allegiance of Farel and Calvin, who were both French. But the most notable quarrel involving Calvin's days in Geneva occurred when the allied city of Bern, Switzerland, propositioned a standardization of ceremonies, including an implementation of unleavened bread during communion. Calvin and Farel refused, and in protest of an order issued by the city council, communion was not observed on Easter. Because of this, both men were asked to leave the city; they tried to appeal to Bern, but to no avail. Calvin's reputation by this time was already beginning to take on that free-thinking and independent agitator quality so closely tied to leading reformers.

By September of 1538, Calvin had been invited to direct the Saint-Nicolas Church in Strasbourg by reformist Martin Bucer (who had previously traveled to hear Luther speak in Wittenberg). Once there, he was given a position in the Sainte-Madeleine Church and the Temple Neuf also, and spent his time preaching and lecturing for hours every day to congregations numbering in the hundreds. What little time he had left in his day was spent in devotion, as well as in the rewriting of his *Institutes of the Christian Religion* (which was exceedingly lengthened). Another book materialized in 1540, the *Commentary on the Romans*, Calvin's first of many historically important commentaries. In it was a translation of Scriptures from the original Greek into Latin, integrating Calvin's expository preaching and notes on scriptural interpretation.

Matrimony was a choice that still held some controversy for head ministers, but it was also a lifestyle statement that rang as a loud and clear example to the people that it was time to abandon the old ways. After some urging by his associates to consider marriage, Calvin married Idelette de Bure in August, 1540.

Following this, he received word that times had changed for Geneva. Church attendance was down since he had left, and the theological and political issues that had driven him from the city earlier on were no longer a concern when the allied city of Bern proved interested in petty land disputes. Cardinal Jacopo Sadoleto of the San Callisto Church in Rome (previously secretary to Pope Leo X) was aware of the goings-on in Geneva, and wrote to the city council with a peaceful plea that their churches return to the traditional Catholic faith. Rejecting the notion of losing Protestant progress, city officials asked Calvin to respond directly to Sadoleto. Calvin consented to help uphold the movement within Geneva, and endorsed their modern practice in a letter to the humble cardinal.

When Geneva saw the lengths at which Calvin would take to defend the gospel, even for a city that had previously exiled him, they believed he was the leader they had been praying for. Calvin loathed the idea of returning amidst a sea of people who had so recently caused strife, but he felt it was the Lord's calling upon his life to do so, and in September of 1541, Calvin was stationed back in Geneva. Again, his stay was to be temporary (as an advisor for six months), but once more, Calvin was met with inarguable reason to oversee the growth of a healthier adherence to the mission of Christ, and the pulpit of St. Pierre Cathedral became his next domicile.

Immediately, Calvin brought proposals to the city, and they adopted his ideas into a list of mandates known as the "Ecclesiastical Ordinances." In addition to this, Calvin, along with two musically inspired refugees of Geneva, composed updated hymns of praise and implemented them into the services. Later that year (1542), he published *Catechism of the Church of Geneva*, the first edition of which is said to have been based on Luther's *Large Catechism*. During his term at Geneva, Calvin's sermons were frequent (usually five sermons per week), consistent, and expertly arranged. (In the year 1549, a scribe was brought in to record Calvin's sermons, and they have since been analyzed by modern scholars.)

But despite his faithfulness to the call, trouble and heartbreak were no strangers.

That July, Idelette bore Calvin a namesake. A premature birth resulted in his loss quickly thereafter, and in 1545, Idelette became sick and weak. While caring for his wife and attempting to keep up with all the demands of his ministry, Calvin fell into confrontation with some of the aristocratic members of Genevan society. In a similar manner as appears in church quarrelling today, troublemakers with hefty political influence rose against Calvin, finding any and all trivial reasons to insult him and make his tenure a nightmare. Although these mischief-makers were apprehended for their public insults and scheming, their hold on Geneva was larger than the reprimand, and by 1547, Geneva's civil magistrates had joined the others in their detestation of Calvin. When a placard written in ominous hostility against Calvin and the Church leaders was found on the pulpit where Calvin preached, an investigation was launched by the city council. Atheist and libertine Jacques Gruet, today known for his blasphemous mockery of Christ and Scripture, was implicated. His home was searched, and incriminating evidence found. Amidst this evidence were secret notes he had written in opposition to the state and other threatening blasts referencing Calvin. In July, he was beheaded for his crimes.

This event supplied the influential upper class with fodder for retaliation. The flames of hatred for Calvin only intensified, and just when it felt like the turbulence couldn't become any more chaotic, on March 29, 1549, Calvin's ailing wife passed away. He never remarried, and grieved her loss desperately.

In early 1552, Ami Perrin, the same public figure who had bargained to gain Calvin's presence in Geneva, was elected as a principal magistrate. Calvin met with the council in an appeal for his resignation, but it was denied. He would stay in Geneva in misery.

Throughout this drama, Miguel Serveto (frequently "Michael Servetus")—a Protestant theologian and Spanish physician who believed he had found fault in the doctrine of the Trinity and who had been intensely debating these issues with Calvin through letters since 1546—had caused quite a stir in Basel, Switzerland. Having written works against the Trinitarian doctrine (which, it is said, Luther had passionately opposed in several of his writings), he gained enemies in both the Protestant and Catholic spheres, and was therefore expelled. The Inquisition of Spain put out an order for Serveto's arrest, so the fugitive fled to Vienne (a couple hours' drive from Geneva on modern roads) in 1553. Because of the threat Serveto's theology posed upon the gospel, Calvin intervened for his capture. Through various letters sent to local officials and the inquisitor-general of France, Serveto was found and arrested.

Brought in for questioning, the letters between Serveto and Calvin were presented as evidence of heresy, and Serveto strictly denied having anything to do with them. Shortly after, he escaped from his imprisonment and was sentenced *in absentia* (absent from court) to execution by the stake.

Inexplicably, Serveto made a stop in Geneva during his trek to Italy to hear Calvin, his theological adversary, preach in person. He was recognized and arrested immediately after the service. The trial of Serveto in Geneva dragged on for months. Although Calvin had no civil authority, it is clear through his correspondence at this time that he was the mastermind behind Serveto's persecution. On October 27, 1553, Serveto was burned alive atop a pile of his own books at the edge of the city.

Serveto's execution brought several critics against Calvin, including the celebrated reformer Sebastian Castellio, who had previously been in good standing with Calvin as the rector of the Collège de Genève. However, countless other names of importance responded with emphatic support of Calvin's victory as the defender of Christianity who would stop at nothing—including participating in another man's execution—to preserve the integrity of the Reformation. The group of high-society headaches who had pestered Calvin for the last decade, or "Libertines," as Calvin had taken to calling them, began to lose their powerful grip. As Geneva's population had slowly come under the sway of French refugees who declared allegiance to Calvin, the voting populace against the Libertines grew, and during the city elections in 1555, the Libertines' power in office faded.

In retaliation, the Libertines rioted in the streets and endeavored to burn down a house that was allegedly occupied by the French. The chaos and disorder continued until a magistrate appeared and convinced one of the Libertine leaders behind the bedlam to proceed to the town hall. Some of the key agitators fled the city, but the others were soon found and, through Calvin's endorsement, executed.

With the ongoing clash of the Libertines now finally put to rest, Calvin's leadership became central, and unchallenged. Having already risen to international fame as a result of his *Institutes of the Christian Religion* (amidst his other writings), and now given uncontested authority in one of the most vital cities associated with religious reform, Calvin was able to relax after years of strain.

From 1553 to 1558, Mary I—daughter of King Henry VIII, fourth crowned monarch of the Tudor dynasty, and queen of England and Ireland—executed nearly three hundred Protestants. Her reign as the slayer of religious men was such that, to this day, she is most frequently referred to by her infamous label "Bloody Mary." Those who either escaped her clutches or chose exile over execution sought shelter with other respected Protestants, and Calvin was among them. Geneva welcomed these refugees and placed them under the city's protection. Soon, a church for the Marion exiles was established (led by John Knox, later the founder of the Protestant denomination in Scotland), and these congregants fell under Calvin's wing. And later, upon the refugees' return to England, Ireland, and Scotland, Calvin's convictions were spread throughout the three countries, a significant contribution to Calvin's role in the Reformation. France, however, in Calvin's purview, had yet to be reached with such success. From 1555 to 1562, Calvin's church pooled resources and sent more than a hundred Protestant missionaries to France. Even in the face of persecution from King Henry II, reform spread across France by the fires Calvin had lit.

In 1558, illness descended upon Calvin, but so absorbed was he in leaving his mark on the world that he ignored his body's warnings and slaved away on yet another edition of *Institutes of the Christian Religion*, expanding it once again. Despite a temporary recovery, a passionate sermon delivery led to an outburst of coughing spasms, which ruptured a blood vessel in his lung. His health took an extreme dive, and on May 27, 1564, Calvin passed away.

His legacy rivals that of Luther's. Over time, Calvinism—a highly disputed doctrine most often associated with predestination—became a prominent principle of faith among Protestants, and it is widely practiced today.

Huldrych Zwingli

Just after Luther wrote his ninety-five theses, a Swiss personality by the name of Huldrych Zwingli, who penned an equivalent "67 Conclusions," brought reform to Switzerland.

Many argue that Zwingli's ideas and passions were merely pseudo-Lutheran in nature, and saw Zwingli as Luther's copycat. Historians are unable to prove this theory, stating that Zwingli had been writing of his disputes with the Roman Catholic Church years before he could have gotten his hands on Lutheran literature. Admittedly, numerous works by Zwingli hold uncanny similarities to that of Luther's, serving to strike against the corruptions within the ecclesiastical hierarchy in comparably informal diction. He held that Scripture was the highest authority over the Church, rejected many sacraments, diligently defended the poor, and protested against teachings of justification through good works. Like Luther, Zwingli promoted clerical marriage.

When cantons (member states) within the Swiss Confederation showed resistance to the Reformation, Zwingli gathered his resources and associates, forming alliances between the reformed cantons, causing distinct division nationwide. Zwingli was subsequently banned by the Church, and the distribution of his writings was to be brought to a halt, but this did not silence the movement he had begun. When a fellow reformed preacher was captured and executed, Zwingli declared war on the Catholic cantons. After raising an army of only nine thousand men against the Catholic states' thirty thousand, the opposing sides met at Kappel. At the last moment, Zwingli's relative Hans Aebli appealed to everyone with a truce, and the war was avoided.

German Prince Philip of Hesse visualized an alliance between Luther and Zwingli for the purposes of uniting a political coalition of Protestant strength. In 1529, a famous meeting took place at his castle to discuss this potential, but when Luther and Zwingli broke into an argument regarding key elements of communion (Luther subscribed to belief in consubstantiation; Zwingli believed the "body" and "blood" were merely representative), the meeting resulted in complete failure. (This famous event has become known as the "Marburg Colloquy.")

Tension grew between the Catholic cantons and Zurich (the largest city of Switzerland, where Zwingli was pastor), and on October 9, 1531, Zwingli was among the casualties who fell by the sword. His legacy was carried on by his successor, and, like other crucial reformers, he has left a vital impact on Protestant movements throughout Switzerland and the neighboring countries. He has been referred to as the "Third Man of the Reformation" (Martin Luther being the first, John Calvin being the second).

Conclusion

A comprehensive and exhaustive list of all the early reformers and their corresponding roles in the movement could easily fill thousands of pages of religious world history textbooks. Because this has already been done by others, and because the central focus of this book regards the authors' predictions of an upcoming Great Awakening, we will not use the space herein to thoroughly reflect upon every accomplishment during the Protestant Reformation. The narration for this period however, could include the following names. Note that we are listing these names because of their association with the movement and their role as an eventual perpetuator of Reformation—*not* as beloved, holy men who had solid, honest, upstanding lives, as *some* of their legacies have been extremely spotted by controversy:

- Jerome of Prague (often "Hieronymous"), key follower of mentor Jan Hus. Played a significant role in the precursory reformers as a praised public speaker and educator. Burned at the stake on May 30, 1416, at the Council of Constance, just after the execution of Hus, becoming the first martyr behind the cause of the Hussite Wars.
- Gustav Vasa, king of Sweden. Gained national freedom from the papacy in 1523. Reformation occurred in Sweden circa 1536.
- Henry VIII, king of England; head of the English Church (or "Anglican Church"). Administratively and personally terminated ties with the Church of Rome between 1529 and 1537. Succeeded by young Edward VI upon death, under whose leadership England embraced the Reformation on a greater level (despite

a brief return to Catholicism under the reign of Queen Mary I ["Bloody Mary"] between 1553 and 1558). Other primary countries affected by this administration were Ireland and Scotland.

- Francisco de Enzinas, Spanish scholar and author. Translated and published the Greek New Testament in Spanish between 1543 and 1556 and was subsequently arrested and imprisoned. This translation paved the way for countless Spanish cities to secretly distribute the gospel into the hands of commoners during the Spanish Inquisition.

- John Knox, theologian and Scottish clergyman who became personal chaplain to Edward VI, later exiled by Queen Mary I. Mentored by John Calvin in Geneva. Partnered with Scotland nobility in bringing the Reformation to Scotland circa 1560.

3 ♨

The First Great Awakening

ALTHOUGH THE TERM "Great Awakenings," as stated earlier in this book, is more often a reference to the enthusiasm of irreligious people turning to the faith for the first time, a significant feature of this first movement is a massive revival of believers, as that is primarily how the first Great Awakening began. In the same way that it is hard to grasp the Protestant Reformation without first learning about the forerunning Bohemian Reformation, regarding the first Great Awakening, we must first turn our attention to early eighteenth-century America (New England).

Jonathan Edwards

Philosopher, revivalist preacher, and Protestant theologian Jonathan Edwards was the only son born into a Puritan family of thirteen including parents Timothy Edwards and Esther Stoddard on October 5, 1703, in East Windsor (modern South Windsor), Connecticut. The glorious blessing of his birth was announced at the same time terrible news came from Deerfield, Massachusetts, just fifteen miles from Edwards' birthplace.

Eunice Williams (Jonathan Edwards' older sister) and two of her young boys (a six year old and an infant less than two months old), were brutally murdered at the hands of the Indians during an event that has become known as the "Deerfield Massacre." Queen Anne's War (1702–1713)—the second in a string of European dynastic wars—was a raging battle on North American soil between France and England for control of the continent. Independent Native American tribes, referred to most often in wartime documents of this era simply as "the Indians," allied themselves with both French and English forces on a case-by-case basis, the Deerfield Massacre being one instance when the Indians supported the French with bloody and ruthless fury. Deerfield was an English frontier settlement, and thus was centered in the crosshairs of French Commander Jean-Baptiste Hertel de Rouville, who led his men and the Mohawk allies in an attack against the village. In the end, almost half of the village was burned to the ground, lifeless bodies decorated the landscape, and most remaining settlers were forced to flee. Over a hundred were taken captive, some of whom were killed, including family members that the newborn Edwards would never meet.

Although North America did become a great nation reflecting a worthy charge of allegiance between its government and its people—one that eventually diminished the power of foreign militaries attempting to stake land claims—such a vision wasn't reached until the victory of the American Revolutionary War (1775–1783). It is easy for some today to assume that Edwards was born an American and automatically associate that with impressions of a life lived in "one nation, under God, indivisible, with liberty and justice for all," but in 1703, no such free country welcomed Edwards. Houses' yards were not lined with white picket fences, but with fortifications from attack. Scenery was not regarded for peaceful sunsets and serene fog resting amidst the trees, but for the rising smoke of distant feuds. Church services were attended not by relaxed congregants donning their Sunday best and carrying fresh baked bread for a potluck, but by a people whose hearts were filled with sorrow over the loss of loved ones or fear for their own survival.

It was within this uncertain world that Edwards was born, and his character was critically defined by the exposure to the fragility of human life.

From his earliest memories, Edwards was drawn into prayer meetings amongst his family circle numerous times each day, wherein he was updated on the tales of bloodshed and the dire needs within his community. However, as noted by biographer George M. Marsden of *Jonathan Edwards: A Life*, Edwards would soon become aware that "the real war was among spiritual powers, a nation God had favored with true religion versus peoples in Satan's grip, [whom Marsden refers to as the] Catholics and pagans."[93]

John Williams, Edwards' uncle and minister of Deerfield, was a famous captive of the Massacre who later authored *The Redeemed Captive: Returning to Zion*, a memoir of the attack on the village, the inhumane slaughter of his wife and sons, and his days in custody of the Mohawks. One need not read desperately between the lines to see Williams' outright disdain for the Roman Catholic Church and the papacy. To some, his musings against Roman corruption parallel those of Wycliffe, Hus, and Luther.

This memoir would be one of the first books Edwards would read.[94]

Edwards' father Timothy was a devout revivalist preacher whose success was more in the spoken word than written, and whose oratory emphasis never waned from the threats of eternal hellfire and lives surrendered to godly dedication. By the age of nine, Edwards was stirred by a sermon Timothy preached a while after his return from war. (It is about this time that the word "awakening"—thus coined by Timothy[95] denoting "an awakening sense of a person's sad estate with reference to [their own] eternity"[96]—begins to work its way into common historic phraseology.) Not only did Edwards passionately engage in personal prayer often throughout the day, he took to the swamp with his friends, building a makeshift prayer stall, where he led prayer meetings and religious teachings, the model of holiness to his peers that he truly was. This fervent and enthusiastic "awakening" of young Edwards lasted only months, after which he returned to typical boyish activities, such as the role-play of battle between himself and the Indians from a covert hide-out he and his comrades frequented in the woods.[97] Despite that this sudden craving for God was merely a fizzled high (which is understandable considering his adolescence at the time), Edwards and historians regard it as *the first of his awakenings*.

Edwards was not the only one touched by his father's words, however. As Timothy continued to preach animatedly about the damnation of nonbelievers, reportedly "hundreds"[98] of people in East Windsor were moved to newfound consideration of their eternal fates.

In 1716, at twelve years of age, Edwards began attending college in Wethersfield (later "Yale"). (It was not entirely uncommon at that time for male students to enroll for college as soon as they were capable of proving an adequate educational background.) In his senior year, he was stricken with a ghastly case of pleuritis (the inflammation of the lining around the lungs), and, believing he would not survive, once again ardently yielded himself to God and pious conduct—this time out of fear. When he was met with recovery, however, he relaxed his anxieties and went about his studies, not directly against his rearing of upright behavior, but not in perfect adherence to it either.

Angst over the journey toward holiness had always been present in Edwards' life. A still, small voice in his spirit always had a hold upon him as he matured, keeping him from complete abandonment of all morality, but something about the spiritual journey of which his father taught (largely favored by the Calvinistic ideology of predestination, leading Edwards to believe that nothing he strived to do ultimately mattered anyway) was tedious, "melancholy," and "unpleasant."[99] And, like Luther, Edwards would come to experience deeply troubling and confusing seasons in his relationship with God as a result of stringent self-discipline. God was far away. A Being who lived above and outside of Edwards' own realm. One who held the ultimate last word on who was and was not on His invitation list for the pearly gates in the afterlife. Accessible only by means of strict religious obedience, and by being lucky enough to be chosen as one of His elite.

But not a God of love and affection. How could He be, when His ears were only opened to the privileged who fit into the "unconditional election"[100]? From Edwards' personal narrative, written years after this tumultuous time: "From my childhood up, my mind had been full of objections against the doctrine of God's sovereignty, in choosing whom he would to eternal life, and rejecting whom he pleased; leaving them eternally to perish, and be everlastingly tormented in hell. It used to appear like a horrible doctrine to me."[101]

From feeling tempted to toss religion and piousness out the window altogether, to recognizing that very temptation as the rebelliousness that his beliefs most strongly opposed, to realizing that his own eternity depended upon his ability to work out this perplexity, Edwards lived in a state of constant, unrelenting bewilderment. It didn't help that his relationship with fellow schoolmates was almost always strained. To state that he was lonely, antisocial, and didn't connect with the rowdy boys he studied with would be an understatement, and those inexperienced and zealous students of Scripture who loudly proclaimed to have all the answers to the enigmas of spiritual integrity only served to irritate him. Perhaps some of this social mismatch could be attributed to his being the only son in a household of many sisters, but apart from that, he was viewed as serious and stern, landing himself the role of killjoy among his colleagues, and leaving him with nearly no one in whom he could find solace or peace.

As he neared the end of his college days, his battle between the foolishness in human reasoning of God's total sovereignty on one extreme—and the foolishness of blindly following an entity he did not know how to identify on the other—came to a sudden halt. God *was* sovereign and supreme in His authority over the fate of men, but that didn't necessarily make Him the tyrant who sat atop His throne in heaven, casually rolling the dice for His children's eternal destinies, whom Edwards had come to fear and resent. Even Edwards, *himself*, cannot explain exactly how he arrived at this conclusion. His writings about this realization reflect his own surprise both at the time and in later reflections. Biographers have also had a tough time assigning a cause for this change. However, if one were to dig deep enough into Edwards' later ruminations, it proves to be around this time in his life that God's *character* began to expose itself to him. Edwards began to recognize the nature and personality of the Man above, and not just the Judge.

This, Christian biographers agree, appeared to be "the work of the Holy Spirit."[102] And this, *the intercession and intervention of the Holy Spirit*, many Christians will also agree, is a miracle that by default completely defies human reasoning. Without human reasoning, the person it affects may, in turn, never be able to "reason" (or explain) the "hows" or "whys" that contributed to the change, such as in the case of Edwards.

Then, one day, in his fresh contemplations of this God, this Character, Edwards found himself all of a sudden so hungry to know that a single verse stood out among the others. It was 1 Timothy 1:17: "Now to the King eternal, immortal, invisible, the only God, be honor and glory for ever and ever. Amen." He was no stranger to this verse, but unexpectedly, he found himself to be a stranger to its meaning until now. As Edwards explains:

> As I read the words, there came into my soul, and was as it were diffused through it, a sense of the glory of the Divine Being; a new sense, quite different from any thing I ever experienced before. Never any words of scripture seemed to me as these words did. I thought with myself, how excellent a Being that was, and how happy I should be, if I might enjoy that God, and be rapt up to him in heaven, and be as it were swallowed up in him for ever! I kept saying, and as it were singing over these words of scripture to myself; and went to pray to God that I might enjoy him, and prayed in a manner quite different from what I used to do; with a new sort of affection....

From about that time, I began to have a new kind of apprehensions and ideas of Christ, and the work of redemption, and the glorious way of salvation by him. An inward, sweet sense of these things, at times, came into my heart; and my soul was led away in pleasant views and contemplations of them. And my mind was greatly engaged to spend my time in reading and meditating on Christ, on the beauty and excellency of his person, and the lovely way of salvation by free grace in him. I found no books so delightful to me, as those that treated of these subjects.... This I know not how to express otherwise, than by a calm, sweet abstraction of soul from all the concerns of this world; and sometimes a kind of vision, or fixed ideas and imaginations, of being alone in the mountains, or some solitary wilderness, far from all mankind, sweetly conversing with Christ, and wrapt and swallowed up in God. The sense I had of divine things, would often of a sudden kindle up, as it were, a sweet burning in my heart; an ardor of soul, that I know not how to express.[103]

This incredible revelation of God's personality, and the intimate exchange between Himself and Edwards, led to what became the decisive fusing between sovereignty and mercy:

Not long after I first began to experience these things...I walked abroad alone, in a solitary place in my father's pasture, for contemplation. And as I was walking there, and looking up on the sky and clouds, there came into my mind so sweet a sense of the glorious *majesty* and *grace* of God...I seemed to see them **both in a sweet conjunction; majesty and meekness joined together;** it was a sweet, and gentle, and holy majesty; and also a majestic meekness; an awful sweetness; a high, and great, and holy gentleness.[104]

Edwards was on fire, the flames of which would only become further manifest. Nothing was the same after this. Everything in his surroundings reflected a new, serene loveliness. Although he, like any human, would still struggle in his own understanding of sin, not completely given into the untroubled and lighthearted images of all things wonderful and beautiful (at times his struggle was immense, especially in the meshing of his theology with his knowledge of physics), his spiritual walk with God from that day on would never be the same.

He was "awakened"…

It was around this time that he began a diary. Unlike most private journals, however, his was not one that spoke of day-to-day occurrences and casual affairs, but it was a curious record of his own behavioral resolutions, and of how closely he kept them. Whether he failed or passed the tests he had written for himself to follow, he documented it each time, creating a paper trail of celebrations alongside weaknesses. Yet, these writings allowed him to track his own progress and review what highs and lows he was most vulnerable to, thus strengthening his willpower toward godliness over time. (It goes without saying that a man like Edwards, who went on to lead some of the most acclaimed early revivals in Protestant Christian history, would need to grow in great strength for the days ahead.)

In the summer of 1722, and for eight months following, Edwards was a "supply" pastor (one who preaches from the pulpit for a decided allotment of time, usually when a church is between pastors) for a small Presbyterian church in New York City. These were, outside of college walls, his first sermons before a congregation, and it was in these experiences that he sharpened his homiletics. On September 20, 1723, he delivered his master of arts oration in Latin at Yale. In November, at the age of twenty, he was appointed the pastor of Bolton Congregational Church in Bolton, Connecticut. Several notable sermons materialized at this time, among which were "The Pleasantness of Religion" (wherein one's embracing the harmless pleasures of the world such as food and drink was stressed), and "Nothing upon Earth Can Represent the Glories of Heaven" (wherein he animatedly envisioned the "pure gold" and "clear glass" of heaven as promised in Revelation 21:18). However, he struggled with the conviction that he should be preaching more on revival and holy living than on enjoying the promises and freedoms in Scripture, and therefore, in May of 1724, he left Bolton and returned to Yale in New Haven as a tutor and to take some time to reflect upon what he was called to do.

Edwards had known of a young girl named Sarah Pierpont since his initial move to New Haven in 1719. Over the years, he had observed her sweet and gentle nature, and on occasion he wrote of his adoration of her, noting the similarities they held in their love for nature and quiet moments of reflection in God's presence. By spring of 1725, his affection had grown into a mature love, and a few months later, the two were engaged to be married. Although the engagement would last two full years, when Sarah would reach the age of seventeen, Edwards was taken with a new bout of joy, understanding even deeper the significance of the relationship between God as the Groom and His people, the bride (a topic that he would frequent in his later sermons).

In late 1726—after an invitation by his grandfather, Solomon Stoddard (1643–1729), the renowned hellfire-and-brimstone preacher of the Northampton Congregationalist Church in Northampton, Massachusetts Bay Colony (and who was known for his extension of the gospel truths to the Indians)—Edwards traveled to work as Stoddard's personal pastoral assistant. Stoddard was now in his eighties, and saw the need to mentor a successor, so in February of the following year, Edwards was ordained and began preaching alongside Stoddard. Five months later, he married Sarah Pierpont. Sarah proved in every way to be an integral support to Edwards' developing theology and his relationship with God. Together, they held the same convictions of heart and mind, and naturally appeared to seek the Lord in the same ways. Edwards had, since his revelation years prior, been subject to occasional internal battles of despair. It is not clear whether it was his marriage that brought him out of this, but it was at the time of his wedding when his spirits were raised higher than ever before, and shortly afterward, his bizarre diary entries documenting his achievements and failures were nearly forgotten altogether.

Back in 1712, Stoddard had regaled his congregation with a famous sermon—"The Efficacy of the Fear of Hell, to Restrain Men from Sin"—heralding the most vivid imagery of hell the imaginations of Northampton had ever been exposed to. Historical debate lands this sermon in controversy. Some see it as the harbinger sermon that launched uncountable imitations in the following years, driving listeners to their knees in sincere repentance like so few sermons were capable of doing. Others, mostly those of modern times, view it as a fear-mongering, sensationalistic rant encouraging congregants toward little more than an emotional experience driven by terror, and argue that the changes brought about on an individual level by a sermon such as this delivers, at best, a temporary commitment to God. Despite this contrast, to the parishioners of 1712, it was inspired, and resulted in an extraordinary "outpouring of the Spirit of God."[105] (Stoddard and his colleagues believed that warning believers of the reality and horror of eternal hellfire was an act of compassion.)

It was this sermon and similar others that later, in 1726, bombarded Edwards' conscience with the duty to reach the lost with unadulterated gusto. One of his own first sermons called "The Warnings of Future Punishment Don't Seem Real to the Wicked" paralleled the earlier sermon of Stoddard's. Already, Edwards' career as a legendary revivalist was beginning to form. When an earthquake on October 29, 1727, thrust swarms of terrified locals into the church, the stage was set for Stoddard and apprentice preacher Edwards to further educate the congregation on what awaited them if drastic faithfulness did not become their standard of living. For nine days following the earthquake, the land continued to shudder.[106]

About a year and a half later, on February 11, 1729, Solomon Stoddard passed away, leaving the church—and therefore the spiritual condition of the city—in Edwards' hands. (Noteworthy to the character and disciplines of Edwards: By this time, he had adopted the practice of rising as early as four o'clock in the morning, when he would retreat to his study for prayer, devotions, and writing for *thirteen hours a day*.

To Edwards this was, in itself, an act of worship.[107]) Stoddard's death was seen by those in the area as the loss of a great leader...the loss of a "Joshua."[108] Nobody doubted Edwards' capability to hammer out a well-versed lecture, but nobody *yet* saw in him the preacher of the Great Awakening that Stoddard's death would propel.

For the most part, Edwards and Stoddard shared the same doctrinal views. However, one area in which they differed was the personal nature of Edwards' ability to see God as more than just a Judge. (Or, if Stoddard *did* hold a softer tone regarding the love and mercy of God, and not just on His judgments, those moments are few and far between the harsher tones found in Stoddard's sermons and publications. One can only guess how Stoddard regarded God away from his pulpit, as those moments are not what he was remembered for.) Several biographical reflections suggest that Edwards followed immaculately in the footsteps of his grandfather's articulations, at times even memorializing his words, but his approach was lesser toward *repentance through terror* than it was *repentance through reverence*. His countenance was one of sincerity and tenderness.[109] Nevertheless, in spite of a different skill set than his predecessor, Edwards was never mute when given the opportunity to arouse his listeners to the dangers, and realities, of hell. Edwards' sermons had undertones of demonstrable and enthralling logic, as well as great clarity and comprehension, and although they didn't get to the point as quickly as Stoddard's, some suggest they held more longevity in the hearts of the listeners, who would find difficulty disputing them as a result of Edwards' persuasiveness.

Subjects of his sermons included, but were not limited to: the Northampton Judases who would easily betray loyalty to Christ for temporal frivolity; the degeneracy within the youth, including premarital pregnancies, and the parents' role in advancing it; the declination of the earthly consequences for sin, including newly established social and cultural tolerance toward shamelessly wicked behaviors; God's allowance of mankind's despair as a tool for growth, strengthening, and ultimately for redemption; and predictably, the enemy's vices and their inexplicable hold upon, and cooperation with, the wicked nature of mankind. All of these subjects and many others laid a platform upon which Edwards could remind the churchgoers of his city that everlasting torment and agony awaited the men and women who refused to turn from their depravity. And as the documented respect from Northampton parishioners attests, kindhearted Edwards' pleas were well received, and even the youth eventually discontinued their reckless behaviors as a result of his impact.

After delivering a public lecture in Boston called "God Glorified in the Work of Redemption…" wherein Edwards challenged Arminian doctrine (primarily associated with the idea that one is awarded salvation through his or her own faith, as opposed to the Calvinistic reliance upon God's sovereignty alone), Edwards became a celebrated and esteemed personality, quickly intersecting with international and clerical persons of importance (including Thomas Prince, Benjamin Colman, and William Cooper, all of whom held influential connections within the Protestant Church). In no time at all, from this one lecture, Edwards' thorough knowledge of Scripture and refreshing approach to its delivery catapulted him into a position of theological authority among church elders. As his popularity climbed, however, Edwards' attention was first and foremost upon the thirsty souls of Northampton, who now, after the event in Boston, were all the more eager to attend his services with open minds.

In late 1733, Edwards felt the winds of change blowing. For some time he had noticed small local behavioral changes here and there, leading him to believe he was merely on the cusp of a revival.

It was then that he came up with a most ingenious plan…

Holding a meeting in the privacy of his home among some of Northampton's central public figures, he asked them to take his convictions and meet in smaller groups around their own respective neighborhoods to implore the cooperation of the households to adhere to a truer moral code of living under Edwards' outline. In so doing, Edwards' "preaching," by extension, would occur through town elders even while he was not present; therefore, it would spread through society with more fervency than one man alone could achieve. Smaller groups held outside of church is common practice today, but in Edwards' time and locality, families who attended church had done their holy duty for the week, and the rest of their time was occupied with secular focus, some of which involved habits that did not compliment Scripture. But through these more acutely focused and personalized meetings (or, rather, mini-services), men, women, and children might be reached by Edwards' words through respected and cherished leaders in their own social circles. The distant pastor they only saw once weekly or biweekly might, with God's direction and blessing, touch their hearts frequently throughout the week via the willing servants of Northampton.

It was a novel idea…

And it worked.

Immediately.

Beginning in the smallest nearby settlement of Pascommuck, people young and old were feeling an unusual conviction of heart. It was infectious. Tavern crowds were diminishing. Marital beds were mending. Teens were turning in early, and premarital abstinence was returning as a priority. Public conversations were changing from those of gossip and negativity to discussions of God's grace.

And as the resurgence of decency was lifting to a defining peak, community tragedy escalated it.

In April of 1734, a beloved young man of Northampton developed a fatal case of pleuritis, and died two days later.

Everyone in the area was affected by his death, especially the youth, and Edwards' church was packed with mourners at the following service. His sermon was, as usual, gentle and sincere, but his message hit hard in light of the boy's recent passing. From his pulpit, Edwards loaded his listeners with the critical truth of Psalms 90:5–6: "Yet you sweep people away in the sleep of death—they are like the new grass of the morning: In the morning it springs up new, but by evening it is dry and withered." This man, this *boy*, so loved by his comrades and elders, at the prime of his life—hearty, strong, handsome, and admired like the "new grass of the morning"—had no more seen it coming than had anyone else. Death comes unexpectedly. There is never a guarantee of tomorrow. Each day of life presents choices, and those choices cannot be squandered upon the endeavors of temporal gain. Edwards did not use this death as an excuse to rail upon the public about the dangers of hellfire. (According to some biographers, this is exactly what Solomon Stoddard would have done.) Instead, Edwards focused upon painting a celebratory picture of the beauty of the life that had just been lost, and promised the congregation that this beauty could not begin to compare with that of heaven. But the elephant in the room had to be addressed: This life was but a vapor in the light of eternity. How, then, would one wish to be remembered, if his or her time on earth was cut short? Were the congregants *prepared* for eternity?

At the close of his sermon, the crowds were in tears. They had not only *heard* his message, they had *felt* it. Young people gave their hearts to the Lord.[110]

And before the mourning of this death had passed, another fell ill and died. Because there was little question of this youthful wife's recent commitment to, and excitement about, the Lord, the sermon preached just after her passing was one that spoke of afterlife security.

About this time, Edwards preached, and then published, a defining sermon, *A Divine and Supernatural Light…* from which we derive this excerpt:

That there is such a thing, as A SPIRITUAL and DIVINE LIGHT, immediately imparted to the Soul by GOD, of a different Nature from any that is obtain'd by natural Means…

[T]hat some Sinners have a greater Conviction of their Guilt and Misery than others, is because some have more *Light*, or more of an Apprehension of Truth, than others. And this *Light* and Conviction may be from the Spirit of GOD; *the SPIRIT convinces* Men *of Sin*.[111]

The idea that God would, in fact, impart knowledge directly to the people through this "light" (brought through a connection with the Holy Spirit after true conversion) quickly became the central principle of the revival. (Again in history we see that when the rituals and rules are trumped by the notion of a personal communication line between God and His children, hearts are stirred toward that communion.) In a short period of time, followers of Edwards would refer to themselves as the "New Lights," those who had embraced the new earnest and paramount seeking of God—in comparison to the "Old Lights," the spiritually dead or stunted (or, non-revivalists). (Later, the ministers who heralded from this season of revival would be called "New Light Ministers.")

As time went on, the small groups grew into larger ones, and they agreed to meet in even more specific gatherings (the youth among the youth; the adults among the adults; and so on, much like today's youth groups, men's groups, women's groups, etc.). The sales of prayer books were rising and hymns of praise were implemented into the smaller meetings.

Each day provided access to revitalization for the spiritually starving, and finally, the lifelong dream of Edwards came to fruition: Northampton was experiencing genuine revival. *Permanent* change was taking place. The most unlikely of foul-mouthed and ostentatious citizens were coming to know the Lord, subsequently taking the gospel to the scandalous company they had previously kept, and each time this occurred, instead of raising skepticism among the conservatives, it fanned the flames of "awakening" in even the darkest areas of town. As the revival grew, sickness and disease miraculously evaporated, word spread to the Connecticut River Valley, to New Haven, to the coastlines, then to the outer colonies, and soon, all of New England was aware of these events. Independently from Northampton, churches all over the region were adopting similar worship, service, and small group studies under the standards that Edwards had generated, which led to the awakenings of many other church bodies, piling passion upon passion until the intensity of the development could hardly be explained. (Although, for those biographers who identify as Protestant Christians, the explanation for this is easily one of clear, dvine intervention, with obedient Edwards merely as the mouthpiece.)

Despite a few delays (involving claims from rivals that the revival was merely the spreading of sensationalism, as well as a tragic suicide by Edwards' uncle who feared he would never be worthy enough to achieve the security of salvation), the movement continued to expand across neighboring territories and eventually reached Scotland and England. Amidst this fire, Stoddard's original pleas for the extension of the gospel to the Indians became a priority, and through church leaders, Indian tribes of various heritage met at the Conclave of Deerfield (at the site of the Deerfield Massacre) for a four-day treaty negotiation. In the end, Yale tutor John Sargeant was ordained as a minister of the Mahicans along the Housatonic River, and shortly after his success, resources poured in from supporting churches to further the mission, adding much of the Indian population to the wave of spiritual activity. (Though, for most of the Indian population at this point, it was not a "revival," but an "awakening" *into* an initial enthusiasm for religion/relationship with God.)

Although the first Great Awakening had now officially begun through the works of Edwards—and the rest of the world was beginning to tune into the frequencies of transformation—it was only in its infancy, still as of yet principally affecting the area around Connecticut and Massachusetts. The whispers of change were present, but the majestic wind gust that would spur the Great Awakening into its heights was yet to come. By this time, Edwards' reputation had preceded him to various parts of England, Scotland, and the States, and his writings had reached two other revivalists, whose names were eventually added to the preachers of the Great Awakenings list: George Whitefield and John Wesley (of the "Wesley brothers").

Our narrative of Jonathan Edwards carries on through that of Whitefield.

George Whitefield

Famous English Anglican priest George Whitefield (also "Whitfield"; 1714–1770) was the fifth son born to Thomas Whitefield and Elizabeth Edwards of Gloucester, England. The Bell Inn on Southgate Street, which Whitefield's family owned, had suffered a decline in business. As a result, Whitefield was admitted to Pembroke College at Oxford as a servitor (a student who paid for tuition through tutoring and "serving" the other students, and in Whitefield's case, this often involved ministerial duties).

In 1729 (nine years before Edwards' writings would fall into the hands of John Wesley), the Wesley brothers, John and Charles, had formed an organization at Oxford called the "Holy Club"—thus named "by their fellow collegians in mockery of their emphasis on devotions."[112] The mission of the club was to meet for prayer and Bible study, participate in organized fasts, and carry out good deeds for the needy, including contributions of food to the poor, visits to prisoners, and educational assistance to young children (primarily orphans). Membership throughout the years included John Gambold (later "a Moravian bishop"); John Clayton (later "a distinguished Anglican churchman"); James Hervey (later "a noted religious writer"); Benjamin Ignham (later "a Yorkshire evangelist"); Thomas Brougham (later "secretary of the SPCK [Society of Promoting Christian Knowledge]"[113]); and of course, George Whitefield, whose life was—through his experiences in the Holy Club and as an associate of the Wesley brothers—thereafter righteously affected. (Many, including Charles W. Keysor, who authored *Our Methodist Heritage*, are of the opinion that today's Methodist Church holds its origins in this "Holy Club.") When the Wesley brothers left Oxford for Georgia, Whitefield became the club's leader.

Whitefield, through both an illness as well as the intense religious literature he was exposed to at Oxford, felt most passionate about the gospel and, early on, dedicated his life to the ministry. Additionally, one *crucially important detail* surfaces around this time: Whitefield got his hands on a copy of *A Faithful Narrative of the Surprising Work of God in the Conversion of Many Hundred Souls in Northampton*—Edwards' narrative following Northampton's first wave of awakening. The work was a celebration of a clear and real revival, and Whitefield was not alone in being moved by its contents. He was, however, unique in how he would respond to it…

As a child, one of Whitefield's greatest loves was the theater (which at the time was seen as a worldly enterprise). He proved adept in his acting abilities, and when his attention turned full-throttle toward Scripture, the experience of his listeners was more than a stagnant, cold sermon. Much to the contrary, many preaching sessions were only a hairline away from a staged reenactment of Bible stories, his gestures and expressions wildly demanding attention of spectators (the likes of which must have been even more fascinating and energetic as a result of his being born cross-eyed, a feature that has been brought up in much discussion throughout the years). As a result of this, when he became an ordained deacon by Bishop Benson of Gloucester in 1736, preaching his first sermon in the St. Mary-le-Crypt, he riled the congregation with animated modernizations, bringing the Scripture to life in ways that some found offensive. However, "Bishop Benson remarked, that he only hoped the madness [the emphatic delivery] might continue."[114]

Evidently the bishop was not the only one who felt Whitefield's unorthodox method of teaching was a refreshing break from the lethargy that so frequently haunted the pulpits of England's finest churches. From Gloucester, he was invited to preach at the parish churches of Islington, Bishopsgate, and Westminster, among many others. According to biographer John Charles Ryle, "From the very beginning he attained a degree of popularity such as no preacher, probably, before or since, has ever reached. To say that the churches were crowded when he preached, would be saying little. They were literally crammed to suffocation. An eye-witness said, 'You might have walked on the people's heads.'"[115]

In 1738, Whitefield traveled to meet up with the Wesley brothers in Savannah, Georgia, in order to help them establish and manage an orphanage. (Orphanage work would become a central focus of his life's work as a result of this endeavor, though at times, he admitted, it was a burdensome task.) When money for the orphanage was scarce, he returned to England to raise funds, but his reception home was not ideal. Concern over his openly preaching the doctrine of regeneration had upset church leaders while he was away, and consequently, he was no longer invited to stand at the pulpits he had once found familiar.

However, being shunned from the doorways of the churches contributed nothing against Whitefield's determination to teach, or *entertain*, an audience wherever he could find it. In fact, it fortified his resolve, launching an ironic backfire. If he was not allowed to preach *within* the confines of a building, he would preach *outside* the confines of a building…but his preaching would not be confined.

And thus, George Whitefield became, as he is so famously associated, the "outdoor preacher" (often "open-air preacher"). It was, as history will tell, a practice he would continue for the rest of his life. The following biographical account is astounding:

From that day, he regularly took up the practice of open-air preaching. Wherever there were large open fields around London; wherever there were large bands of idle, church-despising, Sabbath-breaking people gathered together—there went Whitefield and lifted up his voice. The gospel so proclaimed was listened to, and greedily received by hundreds who had never dreamed of visiting a place of worship. In Moorfields, in Hackney Fields, in Mary-le-bone Fields, in May Fair, in Smithfield, on Kennington Common, on Blackheath, Sunday after Sunday, Whitefield preached to admiring masses. *Ten thousand, fifteen thousand, twenty thousand, thirty thousand, were computed sometimes to have heard him at once.* The cause of pure religion, beyond doubt, was advanced. Souls were plucked from the hand of Satan, as brands from the burning.…

There was hardly a considerable town in England, Scotland, and Wales, that he did not visit. When churches were opened to him, he gladly preached in churches. When chapels only were offered, he cheerfully preached in chapels. When church and chapel alike were closed [or, as stated prior, refusing him], he was ready and willing to preach in the open air. For thirty-four years he labored in this way, always proclaiming the same glorious gospel, and always, as far as a man's eye can judge, with immense effect. In one single Whitsuntide week, after he had been preaching in Moorfields, he received *one thousand letters* from people under spiritual concern, and admitted to the Lord's table *three hundred and fifty persons*. In the thirty-four years of his ministry, it is reckoned that *he preached publicly eighteen thousand times*.[116]

Mankind, Whitefield said to the crowds, was fallen; his heart was corrupted from birth as a product of the original sin, and it was only through the redemption of Jesus Christ that humans stood any chance of inheriting that blessed kingdom above. Justification, Whitefield heralded to his eager listeners, was by faith in Christ, *alone*. God's children, Whitefield spoke, were in a constant need of regeneration through the power of the Holy Spirit; a complete surrendering of heart and mind to the Almighty. And a life of holiness, Whitefield declared, *must* be apparent in order for one to label himself a "Christian." These were the four staples of Whitefield's evangelistic theology.[117]

Although London was usually home to Whitefield, his travels were extensive, taking him to Scotland fourteen times, Ireland twice, over the Atlantic and back seven times, and to every corner of England and Wales. Anywhere and everywhere he could, and often up to thirteen times per week, he engaged the masses with unparalleled appeal, so much so that his initial fame was principally a result of the self-promoting, in-person appearances (as opposed to others mentioned in this book, whose renown came about largely through the quill). As the account quoted previously attests, his gospel reveals were "received by hundreds [and later tens of thousands] who had never dreamed of visiting a place of worship," but by those in the established Church, the story is far different: "Once he was nearly stoned to death by a Popish mob in Dublin." Travel, alone, put him at constant risk: "Once he was nearly murdered in bed by an angry lieutenant of the navy at Plymouth. Once he narrowly escaped being stabbed by the sword of a rakish young gentleman in Moorfields."[118] Nevertheless, nothing stood in his way of plowing ahead and past all obstacles, so that the world might continue to be reached with the good news of Christ.

Throughout his ministry, Whitefield was given many opportunities to serve in prestigious positions (including that of the president of the first Methodist conference, which he took, and later relinquished), but he always fell back on his love for the theatrical sermons of the open air. Evangelizing the lost was the backbone of Whitefield's ministry and the passion he would return to all the days of his life. He cared not whether he was popular or liked among men, but carried a sense of disinterest in matters of reputation, simply choosing most often to ignore any attacks against him. It was to the *hungry* he spoke, to the *lost* he directed his attention, to *Christ* that he dedicated his work…and to the naysayers he offered a shrug of indifference. Though his lack of concern for the Church's opinion of him caused many ripples, and he was certainly not without association to turmoil, the Messiah was far more important. Whitefield's words were delivered to all social statuses without bias: rich, poor, educated, ignorant, man, woman, child, and youth. His sermons were loved by many within the aristocratic or noble circles, including "Marquis of Lothian, the Earl of Leven, the Earl of Buchan, Lord Rae, Lord Dartmouth, Lord James A. Gordon…[and] Lady Huntingdon,"[119] among many others. Getting through a single sermon of his without tears was nearly unheard of, as he not only read and spoke Scripture, but he *cried* it. When offered money, he immediately refused, unless the donor understood that the money would merely be forwarded on to a charity, ministry, or orphanage. At the time, as well as today, several churches and orphanages were named after him.

In late 1739, Whitefield made a trip across the ocean to Philadelphia, Pennsylvania, where he met one of the most remarkable personalities of his career: Benjamin Franklin. Franklin was, at this time, nowhere near the legendary status he would eventually reach as president of Pennsylvania or as a forefather to our later-forming United States of America, but he was already a force to be reckoned with. Since 1729, one decade prior to Whitefield's arrival, Franklin had been the chief publisher of *The Pennsylvania Gazette* (one of the most successful and widely read newspapers throughout the colonies), which offered him a forum to voice his thoughts to an enormous audience. Among his commentaries on the arts and sciences were his reflections on local reforms and matters of the Church. The intellect and articulations within Franklin's writings were such that his societal influence by 1739 was authoritative and prevailing.

When Franklin initially heard about this open-air-preaching George Whitefield character, known for his ability to gather crowds by the tens of thousands during lively sermon illustrations in England, Franklin's first impulse was to dismiss the stories as sensational rumor. However, when Whitefield appeared in person to oversee a revival meeting from the steps of the Philadelphia courthouse, Franklin saw the masses for himself. Whitefield's charisma had not only served to collect the rumored thousands, including the skeptical Franklin, but his powers of speech and ability to deliver a lesson were so impressive in the flesh that Franklin thought the stories he had heard could never do Whitefield justice. Although Franklin did not agree with his theology (Franklin was a Deist), he found Whitefield's teaching so magnetically captivating— and his doctrines so supportive of upstanding conduct (and therefore of paramount importance to the world)—that immediately following the revival meeting he abandoned all other articles from his mind and devoted his paper entirely to Whitefield's cause. In *forty-five* following issues, *The Pennsylvania Gazette* covered Whitefield's whereabouts, dealings, and news of his effect on the globe, as well as the publications of Whitefield's sermons and journal writings.

Previous to this moment in history, Whitefield had been a celebrity of his own unintended making. But now, with the press reporting his every move, word spread about this cross-eyed revivalist like a brushfire, and this time, the source was a celebrated statesman who had formerly been only cynical. (A lifelong friendship was established during this era between Whitefield and Franklin; they kept in close contact throughout the years with mutual respect for the others' beliefs, and anytime Whitefield stopped in Pennsylvania during his travels, he stayed at Franklin's residence.)

While Whitefield's impact was resulting in revival throughout England, peppering Scotland and Ireland with smaller movements, and influencing the colonies through Franklin's publications, Jonathan Edwards was leading a triumphant awakening in his area. Each man was familiar with the other's reputation, publications, doctrines, and ministry. Joint efforts toward a brave new world—a brand new era of Christly fire and passionate believers brought on by the grace of God through His mouthpieces—was the next natural step.

"The Whole World in a Flame"

In February of 1740, Edwards wrote to Whitefield and asked that, while on his following trip to the colonies, he make a stop in Northampton. Whitefield's response to Edwards via a mutual Bostonian acquaintance was: "[S]urely our Lord intends to *put the whole world in a flame.*"[120]

Whitefield arrived in Boston, Massachusetts, the following September. One of his first crowds was so large that the floor of the balcony began to collapse underfoot. Panic ensued, five were killed, and many were injured. Whitefield moved the crowds outdoors, an environment that he had long since grown accustomed to, and continued to preach the gospel in the cold rain in front of thousands.[121] From Boston, Whitefield traveled to Northampton and stayed in Edwards' personal home. The two men bonded immediately, and Whitefield fell in love with the entire Edwards clan, even going as far as to visit with Edwards' wife and children about Scripture.[122] While there, Whitefield preached several times in the area, and although the numbers gathered were not as large as they had been in England or Pennsylvania, the congregation included the masses that had been reached five years prior by Edwards, as well as thousands of others.

Many in Northampton had maintained their spiritual fervor between the initial awakening and Whitefield's visit, but it was at Whitefield's entrance that the biggest boom of enthusiasm spread to date, reinvigorating those who had grown lax in their dedication, as well as drawing in souls who had until then ignored Edwards' first wave of revival.

Long after Whitefield had left the region, the zeal of the people raged onward. Men, women, and children of every age had found the promises of Scripture so imprinted in their imaginations through Whitefield's melodramatic delivery that the Word had been brought to life for them. *Years* of educated preaching from Edwards—and the ministers who followed in Edwards' footsteps—had instilled the *knowledge* of Scripture within the people, but now it was a living, tangible thing, something evidenced by unmatched imagery through Whitefield.

And so it was. We now see the *three waves* that unfolded over the lands like a blanket of all-consuming fire that encapsulates the first Great Awakening:

The first wave: Edwards' widely distributed works touched parts of the world, inspiring radical adherence to Christ and igniting a passion within Whitefield to preach in a way no minister had prior.

The second wave: Whitefield's incredible and refreshing magnetism brought a second wind to the readers of Edwards' literature, and that inspiration came around about to bless Edwards' homeland. That which Edwards had begun was strengthened by Whitefield.

The third wave: Just like before, once the precedence had been set—once the bar had been raised to reflect both the charisma of Whitefield's speaking method and the gentle, steady balance that was Edwards' approach at the pulpit—both ministers' techniques were fused together and adopted by surrounding churches and implemented across both colonial and international borders, and eventually, *the world*, which was, as prophesied by Whitefield, "in a flame."

(The timeline most commonly associated with the first Great Awakening is from 1730 to 1755.)

Conclusion

Jonathan Edwards went on to preach one of the most famously referenced sermons in Christendom: *Sinners in the Hands of an Angry God*. The sermon speaks of hell as a real place, and the motive behind the message was to cause listeners to "wake up" to the reality that awaited them if they did not repent and devote themselves to Christ. Depending on how the sermon is delivered, it can easily be twisted into a hellfire-and-brimstone classic and compared to Stoddard-style presentation. However, Edwards was well-known for his quiet and emotional speaking, so it behooves one to remember that even the most vivid imagery from Edwards would have been far gentler than that of his predecessor, or those of various modern, vociferous ministers. The effect of the lesson was powerful, and it has been said that during the preaching of *Sinners in the Hands*, Edwards was interrupted by congregants who cried out in despair, pleading with him to tell them how they may be saved. When the sermon was published, the reception was incredible, and it stands today as one of the pinnacle sermons of all Great Awakening theology, as well as a common homily studied in religious and academic settings.

In the 1750s, Edwards had become an advocate of smallpox inoculations. The smallpox vaccine was not perfected until the close of the century, and Edwards' health had been dwindling. Still, believing that he had to set an example, he agreed to the experimental injection, and died from feverish complications on March 22, 1758. His last words were of love for his wife, who was absent at his time of death.

After George Whitefield's visit to the Boston and Northampton area, he continued to travel abroad, consistent in his preaching efforts for the rest of his life. His trips around the world were so impressive that he set records of the farthest distances traveled by a white man in his time. Not surprisingly, he also set records for the numbers who gathered to hear him speak. Beginning with Benjamin Franklin's support (and eventually extending to other sources), a total of seventy-eight of his eighteen thousand formal sermons have been published. Between his ventures, he continued to assist orphanages, primarily those that were established by through the Wesley brothers in Savannah, Georgia, circa 1738.

In September of 1770, while dealing with asthmatic difficulties, Whitefield arrived to a crowd of listeners in Newburyport, Massachusetts. On the way there, feeling his strength failing, he looked upwards and prayed, "Lord Jesus, I am weary in thy work, but not of thy work. If I have not yet finished my course, let me go and speak for thee once more in the fields, seal thy truth, and come home and die."[123] He preached for two hours to those who had assembled, but his usual luster and drama was gone, and he was barely able to stand upright. The following morning, on September 30, just before sunrise, he passed away. His last words were, "I am dying."[124] John Wesley delivered the funeral sermon at his memorial service.

John Wesley outlived Edwards and Whitefield, as well as his younger brother Charles. Like Whitefield, John Wesley played a key role in fanning the flames of revival through outdoor preaching. Like Edwards, he assisted in establishing small-group discipleship programs wherever he traveled. Through his personal ministry, as well as other evangelists he inspired, Methodists became central to many social matters, seeing to the needs of the poor and parentless and comforting prisoners, among a long list of other good deeds. He is credited as the founder of Methodism.

Charles Wesley remained an English leader of the evangelical Methodist movement alongside his brother. However, to this day, he is mostly remembered as the illustrious writer of more than six thousand hymns, many of which allude to a personal indwelling of the Holy Spirit.

The Wesley brothers together are credited with having played critical roles in the later development of Pentecostalism.

4

The Second Great Awakening

UNLIKE THE PROTESTANT Reformation and the first Great Awakening, which stemmed from the efforts of specific men before it spread to the masses, the second Great Awakening is episodic in nature, involves several subsidiary movements, enmeshes denominations, spans intermittent periods over a century, documents the ministries of many, and came about partly as a result of the formation of America as its own independent country. One key element of this awakening was the rigorous clash between—and later harmony within—denominational borders. Much like the fourth Great Awakening or "Jesus Freak" revival mentioned later in this book, the roots of the second Great Awakening took on a life of their own, and it has been referenced as a phenomenon by numerous historians. (Note that some have popularly suggested this awakening was merely an emotional phenomenon, and that God was not the initiator, but as some might expect, there are details of the story that render such a conclusion rudimentary. More on this later.)

Rather than focus on the lives and passions of individuals (except for a certain level of focus on James McGready, through whose meetings the awakening was propelled), we will instead center our attention upon the various waves of awakening, the relevant dates, and their causes.

A Country Sleeps (1755–1787)

The impressions left upon the churched world by John Edwards, George Whitefield, the Wesley brothers, and other associates of their time were lasting:

- **Edwards:** The discipleship group-style small gatherings that Edwards fostered grew in popularity, even across denominations. By the late 1700s, modest study groups not only increased, but a great number of them formed into their own independent churches. This inaugurated some split between classical or traditional scriptural interpretation of leading denominations at the time of Edwards, and allowed for developing churches (and a number of unordained lay ministers) to hold subjective prerogative in claiming their affiliate denomination. The three most prominent denominations in the US by the close of the century were Methodist, Presbyterian, and Baptist. Additionally, the indigenous awakening/revival of the Indians and minority ethnic groups—those that had started with Samuel Stoddard and were fueled through Edwards' associates at the peak of the Northampton awakening—was substantially furthered by two dedicated missionaries circa 1745: William Robinson and Samuel Davies.
- **Whitefield:** The "outdoor" and "open-air" preaching methods that Whitefield had started were also adopted throughout the states, beginning what can be seen as the first "revival meetings" (or "camp meetings," though that term was not familiar until 1802, two years after the Revival of 1800 in Logan County, Kentucky). The massive "tent crusades" during the Age of Fire would not occur until centuries later, when the organizational structure supporting them was stronger and well-funded, but they can trace their origins to these earlier revival meetings, and even farther back to Whitefield. By the time the winds of the second Great Awaken-

ing would blow, these meetings would be a commonplace across racial, denominational, and social borders.

- **Wesleys:** Methodists were appearing all over the states, responding to many social issues, bringing food and shelter to the poor, unifying relief groups, and truly ministering to the needy as they believed Christ, Himself, would have done. Their ministries were also to reach the lost with the gospel, but were never limited merely to preaching, as their efforts were carried into the secular world wherever required, which is precisely what John and Charles Wesley had influenced as far back as the good deeds of the "Holy Club." By the late 1700s, the Methodists were rising up as a growing body of believers, viewable as a collective saint to the disadvantaged.

However, despite these developments, the States at large were experiencing significant shifts that caused hiccups in the flow of services and the focus upon God. The previously dominating Anglican (England) Church—*along with its well established groundwork and institutionalized foundation*—largely fizzled after the American Revolution, which on many social and political levels also saw the dwindling of British aristocracy and monarchy throughout the country. When the weight of British managing was lifted, the English Church was rejected in favor of American religious independence. Somewhat overnight, disdain for British Church practice erupted, and anything that even smelled of the English hierarchal Church was tossed out by the newly liberated American patriots. Freedom of choice was a novelty, driving believers to attend whatever congregation fit their personal convictions—and far be it from them to worship the way the English told them to, so Anglican religious authorities mostly packed up and evacuated (though the Methodists remained under Anglican sway for a while). Yet, although Baptists, Methodists, and Presbyterians by this point had formed the three central denominations, the sudden shift away from English-inspired services caused a sharp upward curve of attendance within these three denominations that *quickly outgrew their own limited structure.*

Larger cities were able to respond to the surge to some degree, simply instating deacons and respected congregants to rise up as ministers in nearby buildings, and the Presbyterians were the most prepared to respond with a religious educational infrastructure in largely populated areas. For the rural folks who had transferred to these denominations, an entire generation of spiritually hungry people tripped all over themselves in the lack of leadership. Uneducated farmhands began to lead countryside services, speaking at the pulpit from memory (many of whom could not even read), filling the pastoral void because it was necessary, not because it was a passion, and questionable theology replaced learned theology. Baptisms and communions were almost completely dropped from many countryside churches, as the people saw the sacraments as an ordained minister's duty only, and the ordained ministers were all serving in the cities. And when squabbles about the services ensued, there was no board of directors or official clergymen to respond, so what had started as a celebration of religious freedom was developing into a carnival of inexperienced amateurs, albeit they were motivated by sincerity.

As this temporary disaster escalated, leaders within the three key denominations reacted by sending in the pros to nurture the churches to health. Sometimes, as with the Methodists under John Wesley's outline, this endeavor delivered great success; other times, as with the Presbyterians, some Baptist sects, and many other minority groups, the intervening big-city ministers arrived on the scene calling shots like dictators, ruffling feathers, and leaving lists of instructions the puzzled congregations didn't know how to follow. Historians frequently adopt an air of sarcasm when explaining these interventions by the city ministers who traveled to the smaller establishments, and the explanation has been given in similar words as these: The "learned" ministers saw themselves as better than the "country-bumpkin preachers," who therefore needed to be put in their place. It wasn't the fault of the "superior city man" that they spoke over the heads of the underlings. If the Church was going to thrive, the ranchers either needed to throw their pitchforks aside and keep up, or get out of the way and let the chosen ones do their job.

Methodists, Baptists, and Presbyterians respected each other in the pursuit of two goals: Jesus Christ and patriotism (or alleviation of English clerical control). However, in almost every other area, they quarreled. As could be expected after a fresh, national, religious restart, so many churches were just getting their doctrinal bearings nailed down that their tenets of faith and standards of worship were fiercely adhered to in the zealous discussions of freshly forming church bodies. Through the abandonment of one perceived tyrant (the Anglican domain) came another (disputes between authoritarian personalities within their respective denominations). Richard McNemar, author of the 1808 documentation *The Kentucky Revival*, describes it like this:

> The writings of these churches instead of uniting the people in righteousness and peace, had kindled up endless controversies and angry disputes…. According to the scriptures, [the early] Christians were united all of one heart and one soul; they laid aside all anger, wrath, clamor, envy and evil speaking; were kindly affectioned one towards another, and loved one another with pure heart fervently. But daily observation proved, that those who now assumed the same name ["Christians"], were full of envy and strife, railing and backbiting, hateful and hating one another; and in every sense different from those holy men of God, who were formerly called by the name of Christ….
>
> [T]he ministers of Christ [circa 1785–1795]…appeared to be proud, aspiring, contentious men, striving who should be the greatest, overlooking common people as an inferior rank of beings, deeply immersed in the cares of the world, eager after salaries, or posts of profit in civil government.[125]

So, for a time—in the interim between the forthcoming second Great Awakening and the previous influences of Whitefield, Edwards,

and the Wesleys—Christ-centered religion was swallowed up in squabbling, interdenominational wars. Biographers and journalists of the day
reflected this, and many lingering comments suggest that even leaders
of the three denominations scrambled to iron out their own theology
while doggedly berating anyone who didn't follow their vague-at-best
convictions. From the well-known diary of Baptist David Barrow who
wrote of his experiences in the South during this era of transformation: "Of all the denominations I can remember to have seen in that
country, the Deists, Nothingarians and Anythingnarians are the most
numerous."[126] Harvard student and tutor from Richmond, Virginia,
William Ellery Channing, said, "Christianity is here breathing its last.
I cannot find a friend with whom I can even converse on religious
subjects."[127]

Although there were certainly little spark revivals that sprouted here
and there across the states during the excitement following the American
Revolution, the disorganized mess *within and between* denominations
caused a period of religious stagnation and chaos.

Often, denominational leaders who traveled to help build or correct
a church would form panels whose responsibility it was to crack down
on or eradicate the sinful members in the congregation. Many were
asked to leave their own churches by unlearned and unproven committees or councils, and these numbers were left wandering, unwelcome,
and shunned. It was the blind leading the blind in an unprecedented
and preposterous "church cleansing." And the supposed "sinners" without a nurturing congregation surprisingly did not retaliate *against* God,
but instead helplessly and aimlessly drifted about in their hunger *for*
God, anticipating with baited breath the day when all these earthly trivi-
alities would stop hindering His movements.

It took years before everyone would finally begin to band together in
the interest of winning souls for Christ, but by approximately 1787—
when the three denominations finally settled upon their own structural
foundations, directing personalities, and theological frameworks—the
stage was set for that to happen.

A Country Stirs (1787–1790)

The revival that hit Virginia in 1787–1789 was local. Compared to others spoken about in this book, one might even say it was "small." It didn't necessarily spread throughout the States and shower international borders with news-waves of any great and powerful church leaders. It did not pull all of the heathens out of their cabins in the woods and propel them to their knees at the altar. However, with the English powers out of the way, the flag of freedom raised, and finally the implementation of order within the ranks of the three main denominations, factions within the Church began to work together.

Skirmishes among the outskirt Indian tribes were no longer a British problem to solve, but an American one, and compassionate hearts bled for them with newfound determination since their advocates were nowhere to be seen. Children were being raised without hearing the gospel of Christ, and they were not receiving it from their untaught parents or farmer/pastors at church, and that had to be corrected. The Great Commission, itself, was crumbling under pitiable direction, and that, certainly, was not what the good Lord would have wanted for an uninhibited and glorious country like America. If this country was going to be founded on strength, love, freedom, and *God*, the people had to start acting within that interest.

Evangelical ministers suddenly sprang forth from the farmlands and sought theological education and credentials, so many at once that Virginia was rife with revivalist preaching. Students chattered excitedly about Scripture. Young children who had frolicked in the fields without much prior word of this "Christ" personality were catching the buzz and asking questions. Mothers were extending their kitchen talents to bless their communities with potluck contributions. Fathers were seeking the advice from the now-available mentors…

And amidst the new generation of schooled "country bumpkin preachers"—whose passion and drive had led them to even higher understanding of the Word than their pious predecessors—empathy and consideration for the people abounded.

Yes, the sermons spoke of hellfire and damnation, but in words the general population of the South could understand.

Yes, the Scripture was read and theology was taught, but without the self-inflating rhetoric and oratory competition that had plagued those parts in past years of interdenominational conflict.

Yes, each person was called forth in the duty of the Great Commission, but no pitchforks need be cast aside for Christ and His works to be remembered.

Although Lincoln's Gettysburg Address was still almost a hundred years in the future, the concept of a government—*and religion*—"of the people, by the people, [and] for the people" was gaining rapid ground. With workhands at the pulpit, no man would be left behind. Right?

Well…*almost*.

One major issue remained: Those who had been exiled from church as a result of immorality remained spiritually destitute, and it was from *them* that the deepest hunger for renewal was planted, soon rendering a greater harvest than the most proficient of earthly agricultural surroundings. According to the records within John Boles' *The Great Revival: Beginnings of the Bible Belt*:

> The self-examination and rigorous moral policing [within the three denominations]…maintained a pure remnant…. [C]hurch minute books [of that time] contain little else than the record of those excluded from fellowship. Alcoholism, profanity, mistreatment of slaves, and sexual immorality were common malfeasances. Some churches, in their rigid observance, almost decimated their own membership. Thus was produced a large body of churchless people who desired reconciliation and renewal of religious fellowship.[128]

From these and other isolated groups, a ravenous craving for a touch from God materialized, but the States, so recently established, were still a good ten years away from religiously diplomatic maturity, so willing to ostracize imperfection that the 1787–1789 Virginia revival sputtered out after the virtuous moral crackdown from clergymen to the laity. Although the revival only lasted a couple of years before the voices again quieted, the river of enthusiasm that had been uncorked could not be placed back in the bottle. The waters may have calmed, but the flow didn't stop.

Something was stirring.

For a decade, the South returned to an irreligious society, but ministers prayed harder than ever. South Carolina Baptist leader Richard Furman encouraged all that through trial comes strength, and through faithfulness comes victory.[129] North Carolina Methodist leader Jeremiah Norman spoke that with the Lord's help, anything is possible.[130] Georgia Baptist leader Sanders Walker appealed to an increase of individual prayer time and worship within the private family home.[131] Methodist preacher George A. Reed repeatedly reminded his listeners that God answers prayer.[132] The denominations gathered their strongest men in conferences and meetings and poured their hearts out to the Lord requesting that the previous Virginia hype would not be all the Divine had in store for them. Extensive fasting was instructed and urged to any who were willing to experience a lasting revival. From all corners of the South and across denominations, ministers were exchanging letters, gathering assemblies, merging initiatives, revising sermons, and calling for drastic repentance.

The sheer magnitude of discussion related to widespread restoration making its way beyond state borders, beginning with leaders and trickling into congregations, was enough to convince the entire land that it had embraced a sinful, spiritual plague, and only through diligent seeking would God provide the antidote. Although America was indeed facing huge changes politically and economically—with uncertainty contributing to a sense of urgency especially after the American Revolutionary War and during the land disputes between the natives and the Americans over the Northwest Territory (1785–1795)—there was no longer a supreme, central, *national* crisis that drove the Church to feel the *need* for God equivalent to those of other awakenings or revivals featured within this book (such as the Vietnam radicalism in the "Jesus Freak Movement" and the silencing of Protestants during the Reformation). America hadn't achieved complete peace, and minor wars were still rifling about with the French (the Quasi-War had not occurred yet, and when it erupted, it was fought almost entirely on oceanic territories), but this was the first era of American sovereignty and self-determination. In a time when the principal enemy of the people was the lack of religion, in and of itself—not war, not famine, not affliction, not bloody persecution of believers, not excommunication, not hierarchy… just irreligiousness—a pardon was pursued for the national offense, and people were penitent.

The spiritual malnutrition was a crisis of its own.

The upcoming awakening and revival occurred primarily because *awakening and revival was sought…*

When the South was effectively oiled up and seasoned for fire, a young farmworker entered the scene with a glowing match in his hand.

James McGready

James McGready was born in Pennsylvania and worked the fields alongside his siblings. Very little is known about him (including his mysterious birthdate), but that he had been a devout prayer warrior since childhood, and that he made an astounding impression on his uncle who consequently petitioned young James' parents to allow him to pursue a theological education under the uncle's supervision. After consent was given for McGready to go, he set forth in his studies under the tutelage of revivalist preacher Rev. Dr. John McMillan, who later opened a school of theology. (This small school opened by McMillan later became the Washington & Jefferson College just miles outside of Pittsburgh.)

At around the age of thirty, McGready was licensed as a preacher by the Presbytery of Redstone, Western Pennsylvania. With his studies behind him, now equipped to begin his own ministry, he had intended to travel back home to his parents who were then living in North Carolina, but he made a stop in Virginia in 1788, at the peak of the aforementioned interdenominational revival. His stay there wasn't lengthy, but the effect the revival had on him was profound, and it was with earnestness that he made his way to North Carolina to see how the believers in his parents' home town were faring.

Immediately, he found reason to be surprised when the immorality revealed itself in the crude behaviors of the backwoods residents. As he observed the overindulgence in whiskey during a funeral, he subsequently refused to say grace for the food and drink that had been brought to a wake, throwing his name into local controversy. Once attention throughout the region had been directed at him, McGready didn't hesitate to utilize this attention to sound the alarm on the importance of upright conduct. Soon after being stationed as the pastor of two churches in his area, he brought the gavel down on unsuspecting listeners, and the conviction he ignited was prevalent. With the South in a tizzy for revival, this new minister's brand of conviction was instantly popular.

McGready married, opened a school in his own home, and made guest appearances at local academies and churches. The more he spoke, the more he was asked to speak. Nobody tired of his lengthy prayers, and he frequently moved his audience to tears as his boisterous and condemning voice—and body language—found even the holiest among them guilty of atrocity. He was less focused on theological, denominational, or doctrinal combat than some of his peers, who still clung to beliefs that only one truth (their personal truth) existed, which placed him in a position to minister just about anywhere he went. Salvation through Christ was his message, and just as often as he spoke of the fires of hell, he spoke of the joy of heaven, but the distinction between the two was so animated that each hearer was consistently ping-ponged between jubilant elation and deep fear. It was not that McGready's concepts were new, but that they were freshly and passionately delivered in a way that no man or woman could ignore. Listeners were encouraged to put their doctrinal differences aside and focus on the cross. Like George Whitefield, McGready's pulpit executions were quite theatrical. According to Reverend Barton W. Stone (a key figure in the later Kentucky Revival):

> [M]y room-mate…politely asked me to walk with him a short distance in the neighborhood, to hear a certain preacher. I consented, and walked with him. A crowd of people had assembled—the preacher came—it was James McGready, whom I had never seen before. He rose and looked around on the assembly. His person was not prepossessing, nor his appearance interesting, except his remarkable gravity, and small piercing eyes. His coarse tremulous voice excited in me the idea of something unearthly. His gestures were *sui generis* [unique; in a class by itself], the perfect reverse of elegance. Every thing appeared by him forgotten, but the salvation of souls. Such earnestness—such zeal—such powerful persuasion, enforced by the joys of heaven and miseries of hell, I had never witnessed before. My mind was chained by him, and followed him closely in his rounds of heaven, earth and hell, with feelings indescribable. His concluding remarks were addressed to the sinner to flee the wrath to come without delay. Never before had I comparatively felt the force of truth. Such was my excitement, that had I been standing, I should have probably sunk to the floor under the impression.[133]

McGready focused his railings upon materialism, especially that which corrupted members of the higher social classes. Like John Calvin, whose personal safety and ministerial security was threatened by the "Libertines" (see "John Calvin" in the "Protestant Reformation" chapter), when McGready's teachings were taken personally by the upper class, a retaliation was organized. Sometime in the middle of the week, the pews were thrown about, his altar was burned to the floor, and he received a letter written in blood threatening the end of his life if he did not flee the country.

Despite his arrival to the disarray, and among the shocked laity, McGready gently approached the pulpit and quoted from Matthew 23:37 (also Luke 13:34): "O Jerusalem, Jerusalem, thou that killest the prophets, and stonest them which are sent unto thee, how often would I have gathered thy children together, even as a hen gathereth her chickens under her wings, and ye would not!"

His point had been made, and the whispers followed. Such a daring response in the face of menace was unexpected, and his boldness intensified the revival-hungry residents of small-town, North Carolina.

Whether McGready left to Kentucky after this as a result of fear or simply because Kentucky was becoming a booming populace is unknown. From 1790 to 1800, the population of Kentucky had tripled, and unlike the peaceful Virginia, its churches were still in the lingering heat of interdenominational squabble. Believers were exhausted and drained, and many had been kicked out of the fold completely, left to thirst for living waters on their own. Young people were bored to tears with services that had become so wrapped up in the definition of their respective denominational theology that they only appealed to the elderly. Sacraments were all but forgotten, and those still carried out were done so obligatorily.

McGready arrived in Logan County, Kentucky, in 1796, taking over three congregations within his first year. Fervently, he fasted and prayed for the outpouring of the Holy Spirit, and gathered all who were willing to pray and fast alongside him. It started slowly at first, seeds of flame just sprouting from the hearts of the most faithful, and then gradually germinating across the river lands.

In May of 1797, excitement erupted when a particularly inspired sermon from McGready resulted in almost ten conversions and led many others to repentance.

Then it settled again.

But Kentuckians continued to pray.

In July 1798, another sermon by McGready stirred the listeners of the Muddy River and Red River congregations, and the whole river region soared into a fervent religious mindset within a month. From one gathering to another, testimonies were shared, lives were being changed, and murmurings of revival were on the rise. When Presbyterian James Balch arrived and declared that the entire movement was rooted in pure human emotion, the churches were thrown into uncertainty.

Then it settled again.

But Kentuckians continued to pray.

In July of 1799, when yet another inspiring sermon was delivered, followed by a passionate communion reflection, the congregants refused to leave the church until they could be assured of their salvation. The service was brought back into the church, where McGready and his associate ministers feverishly prayed for the hungry people. As a result, the crowds began to feel a communication line opening between themselves and God, and they repented of their sins, experienced loving reassurance, and sensed a resurgence of the Holy Spirit within them, urging them to embrace the resuscitation of their own languished souls. At a succeeding service, people were so affected by the power and presence of God that they fell to the floor and wept bitterly for hours in their conviction.

Rumors were abounding throughout the state by now, and converts were emerging from every service. Each one took his or her testimony to friends, family, and acquaintances, so much so that before the scoffers could react, they were confronted by other acquaintances with tales of what God had done for *them*. Other ministers materialized, some of whom worked alongside McGready, or whose personal ministries mirrored his—such as Presbyterians William McGee, William Hodge, and John Rankin, and Methodist John McGee (William McGee's brother)— and a devout camaraderie could be seen from church to church, again across denominations, again despite social spheres, and now across state lines (into Tennessee, primarily) like an invisible joining of friendly hands toward the cause of revival fire.

A Country "Awakens" (Summer of 1800)

In June of 1800, up to five hundred heartfelt congregants of Muddy River, Gasper River, and Red River gathered together in the Red River Meeting House for a four-day communion observance led my McGready, with the McGee brothers, Hodge, and Rankin in leadership attendance. Friday, Saturday, and Sunday were a great success, bringing many together in obedient "remembrance of Me [Christ]," but something brilliant and unusual happened on Monday…

A young woman had been searching diligently for long time to feel that sweet sensation of reassurance. She had been present at revival meetings and church services, living as close to the Christian law as she humanly could, but despite this, there was still a void of confidence in her spirit. If her earthly days expired, she did not know what direction she would go, and she was not alone in this concern.

In the middle of a lengthy sermon by Reverend Hodge, she suddenly sprang up from her seat, joyously bellowing and singing, alerting all those around her that the unrelenting question of her eternity had been wonderfully and solidly answered. All eyes were upon her, and all ears were alert to her delight. This went on for a time, and when she had said all she had to say, she returned to her pew. When all was again quiet, Hodge finished his sermon, but there was a certain peculiar aura amidst the gathering afterward that didn't immediately subside. At the conclusion of the service, some stood to leave, but many sat motionless, as if in unconscious submission to an unseen presence still standing at the pulpit, poised to deliver the most important portion of the teaching.

William McGee stood up from his chair, and then slumped to the floor in an unexpected fit of tears. Others had begun to cry across the building.

Brother John McGee stood on the platform and addressed the crowd. There was another Preacher amongst them, he said, and this was the greatest Preacher of all, One whom the people needed to surrender themselves to fully.[134]

A drone fell over the congregants. Sobs openly emanated. To an outsider, it might have appeared as if a national leader had just been assassinated in front of them through the wailing sadness and despair that flooded the hall. McGready, Rankin, and Hodge observed the room carefully. It was within their interest to be sure that any outpouring *had to be* from God, and was not purely human emotion. After speaking with each other momentarily, they decided that rather than immediately intervene and hinder some mass conviction God might be conducting, they would survey the scene prudently…

The loudest voice of all of them was from the woman who had been touched first. John McGee heard her cry, and set out to check on her, but he was pulled aside by one concerned fellow who cautioned him against promoting further emotional disruption. The response he had to this warning was one he shared later in a *Methodist Magazine* interview, and it has since been quoted hundreds of times as the turning point of the meeting: "I turned to go back and was near falling; the power of God was strong upon me. I turned again and, losing sight of the fear of man [read: "disregarding the warning of mere man"], I went through the house shouting and exhorting with all possible ecstasy and energy, and the floor was soon covered with the slain [referring to the "slaying of the Holy Spirit"]."[135]

Once the other ministers saw this behavior from John McGee, as well as the spontaneous pre-Pentecostal manifestation across the meeting house, they became confident that it was the Lord at work, and the deluge of tears continued. Exclamations of anguish and depravity boomed, and appeals for heavenly mercy bucketed from the helpless. As for how long this meeting went on, how many may have found joy as the one woman had, and for what other events transpired that day, almost all documents of this account merely move on to what happened next…

McGready and the other ministers, convinced this was the work of God, laid plans for another sacramental service, to be held at the Gaspar River Church the following month. McGready took pains to circulate the news, but a media campaign was hardly necessary. Speaking of the hundreds who flocked to Gaspar River, one minister [Rankin] said, "The news of the strange operations which had transpired at the previous meeting had run throughout the country in every direction, carrying a high degree of excitement to the minds of almost every character."[136]

All surrounding congregations, regardless of denomination, were in commotion over the news that an entire hall was filled with hundreds of people who had fallen and cried in their conviction. Perhaps the information would have been received differently if the meeting had produced a majority of jubilant converts, but this was something poles apart from the concept of celebratory life-changing. It wasn't crowds of jumping revelers, but convicted, weeping multitudes.

Sadness.

Despair.

Guilt.

The three-day sacramental service scheduled for the following month (July 1800) drew in scores of people, the numbers of which could not be housed by the local church families. By the time the meeting took place, this was a known issue, and many had traveled hundreds of miles from far and wide with the intention setoff setting up a tent and camping on the outskirts of the gathering. (McGready also saw the potential of this idea and promoted camping as a regularity for these several-day-long gatherings, and although the term "camp meeting" would not be a commonplace until 1802, this became the first of many official American camp meetings.)

Ministers from churches in the territory attended to pray and assist. Some believers came with insatiable spiritual hunger, others came simply to see what all the talk had been about, but the sentiment that infused all believers together was *anticipation*.

Just as before, the first couple of days were successful in their reverent focus, but it was a few days later when a stirring began to dramatically affect the attendance. On Saturday evening, when the sermon had finished and all the campers had returned to their tents, two women began to speak openly about the things God had done for them to others nearby. Conversation from others ensued, and a whispering spread through the camp encouraging all present believers that the long-promised revival had already begun, that they were located at the front and center of it, and that God was about to bring incredible deliverance to the desolate at this very meeting. (Whether or not anyone slept that night is unknown, and any lay-ventured and impromptu services occurring outside among the tents is also a mystery, but many interpretations of this evening suggest that well after the five main ministers had retired for the night, the campers *at least* talked, prayed, and cried well beyond nightfall. Ministers who had come to camp were among them.)

As stated before, revival had been occurring purely because revival had been sought... And *now*, revival was about to explode, purely because revival was *expected*.

(It is not surprising that this awakening has been referred to as a phenomenon. But again, those historians who personally believe in the intervention of divine order hold to the probable theory that "phenomenon" should be read "work of the Holy Spirit." Note that some historians have chalked this awakening up to an emotional marvel. The idea that the people wanted revival and would stop at nothing to get it could, from a secular sphere, support that the movement spawned from human means: a bunch of excitable groups gathering around late-night campfires and getting hyped over theories of supernatural relief from their despair. *However*, this argument immediately falls flat when one considers both common sense and the denominational governance of this era and regional vicinity. First, Pentecostalism was *not* a leading denomination at the time; in fact, Pentecostalism did not emerge until the early twentieth century. And yet, the events of these services clearly indicate that Pentecostal outpourings of the Holy Spirit were occurring in a primarily Presbyterian/Baptist/Methodist setting. This happened *despite* the fact that the leaders of the three denominations were particularly and historically wary of emotionalism in the church. It's not surprising that McGready, Rankin, and Hodge stood by carefully observing when these episodes began to take place at the first of these two meetings. Additionally, regarding our note on common sense, although there certainly was joy among some of the people, many who had attended these first two meetings were documented to have cried out in anguish and despondency over their own salvation insecurity [perhaps as a side effect of Calvinistic predestination theology, which had been a prevalent study in the world of Christendom up to this point]. The crowds were sad, lonely, terrified, and begging for mercy. They were not jumping around shouting "hallelujah" in an attempt to usher in supernatural demonstrations. Therefore, it is safe to assume that much of the conversational exchange that night in July would have been regarding this salvation insecurity and the personal gloom that resulted from it. It isn't a worthy exegetical reading of the historic records and texts on the Kentucky Revival [actually, it's quite preposterous] to assume that groups gathered around a campfire brooding about their agony, and that it was through the saturation of negativity that a happy revival later occurred. It is in these authors' opinions that there would have had to have been an Answerer meeting them where they sat to bring about anything beyond bouts of vast, communal depression. It *is* conceivable that excitable groups could join together in anxiety, as misery loves company. But it is inconceivable based on eons of human psychology that this pessimism would spawn anything but immense revival failure and a lot of souls returning home discouraged.)

The following morning, the sermon was once again disrupted by groans and shows of hopelessness. Yet, that evening, the final scheduled sermon by William McGee struck a chord. His focus was on Matthew 14:24–33:

But the ship was now in the midst of the sea, tossed with waves: for the wind was contrary. And in the fourth watch of the night Jesus went unto them, walking on the sea. And when the disciples saw him walking on the sea, they were troubled, saying, "It is a spirit"; and they cried out for fear. But straightway Jesus spake unto them, saying, "Be of good cheer; it is I; be not afraid." And Peter answered him and said, "Lord, if it be thou, bid me come unto thee on the water." And he said, "Come." And when Peter was come down out of the ship, he walked on the water, to go to Jesus. But when he saw the wind boisterous, he was afraid; and beginning to sink, he cried, saying, "Lord, save me." And immediately Jesus stretched forth his hand, and caught him, and said unto him, "O thou of little faith, wherefore didst thou doubt?" And when they were come into the ship, the wind ceased. Then they that were in the ship came and worshipped him, saying, "Of a truth thou art the Son of God."

The apostle Peter, McGee said, had doubted his Lord's saving power, and he had begun to sink under the surface of the sea. Christ extended His hand, and pulled Peter out from his peril.

The thing that *condemned* Peter was his own "little faith." The thing that *rescued* him was the God who reached beyond Peter's inadequacies and met him where he was.

The people of Kentucky were crying out constantly, petitioning God over and over again to save them from peril. They, too, had "little faith." Their Rescuer was standing there, reaching out to them despite their own inadequacies, waiting to meet them where they were, and it would only be through the taking of the Savior's hand that they would come up from the sea and walk with God.

How could such a people who claimed to have so much faith in the supremacy of God also be the people who doubted His capability to salvage those He loved?

According to the journal accounts of McGready, nobody returned to their tents that night. Physical hunger was nonexistent in comparison to spiritual hunger. Thirst was not for temporal refreshments, but only for the hand of God, hovering within reach just above the surface of their own tumultuous seas. Sleep wasn't even a thought in the minds of those who strove for a rest that could not be delivered through warm milk and a mattress. Though the hours of night crept upon them, they continued in worship, devoted themselves to repentance, and finally, *finally* experienced joy and blessed assurance. The power of God moved throughout the throngs. Believers fell to the floor, once again slain in the outpouring of the Holy Spirit.

Again, it is not clear how long they remained in such a state of acute reverence. Nearly all of the reflections indicate that the night simply went on and on, with the xx quite possibly extending throughout the entirety of the following day. So many lives were changed that, when the camp meeting reached its end, testimonies poured forth from the participants like a statewide siren blaring to the other regions of the country, alerting all Americans to the authorities and powers of God being revealed near these humble and unassuming rivers of Logan County.

Soon, all of Kentucky had adopted the practice of several-day or weekend services, and people traveled in wagons over great distances ready to pitch tents and stay as long as it took for the Lord to do a mighty work, and their expectations were repeatedly met:

[T]he falling, crying out, praying, exhorting, singing, shouting, etc. [during one of these meetings in May, 1801] exhibited such new and striking evidences of a supernatural power, that few, if any could escape without being affected. Such as tried to run from it, were frequently struck [by the Holy Spirit] on the way, or impelled by some alarming signal to return: and so power-ful was the evidence on all sides, that no place was found for the obstinate sinner to shelter himself, but under the protection of prejudiced and bigoted professors. No circumstance at this meeting, appeared more striking, than the great numbers that fell [slain] on the third night: and to prevent their being trodden under foot by the multitude, they were collected together and laid out in order, on two squares of the meeting-house; which, like so many dead corpses, covered a considerable part of the floor. There were persons at this meeting, from Caneridge, Concord, Eagle-Creek, and other neighboring congregations, who partook of the spirit of the work, which was a particular means of its spreading.[137]

Unprecedented numbers of distinguished ministers (including the famous Barton Stone, Thomas Campbell, and Alexander Campbell, from which we derive the term "Stone-Campbell Movement," the colossal continuation of McGready's revival) rose from rich plantations and modest farmlands alike to take their position behind makeshift pulpits in the trees. With meeting houses and church facilities long since outgrown, the masses worshiped and celebrated outdoors under the sun by day, and via the light of torches by night. (It is such a tragedy that the "open-air" preacher George Whitefield could not be present for such events.) Every meeting was bigger than the last. Each stimulation was more effective than the former. Thousands upon thousands were flocking with provisions in tow to the campsites, arriving with bleak hope and departing with exultation. Denominational walls were crumbling. Church membership soared. The fuse had been set alight, beginning in Kentucky, and rapidly the self-perpetuating sparks flew and traveled across Tennessee, Virginia, and North Carolina toward an explosion of Southern revival like a detonated bomb…

And it would not be long until every other state within the US was irreversibly affected by its blast.

America was *awakened.*

Conclusion

In the days and months following this crest, children played an enormously important role in the recently popularized camp meetings. Their participation in church services and sacraments prior had been greatly limited, and their voices had been silenced in pursuit of reverence.

However, at the camp meetings where the family-tent revival was thriving, Christ's words, "forbid [the children] not to come unto me, for such is the kingdom of heaven," took on new meaning. Not only were the children allowed to celebrate their own conversions and unite with their parents in joy, it is said that their conviction was unusually mature, and that they understood with wisdom beyond their years precisely what spiritual manifestations they were sharing in. Through the mouths of babes, many came to believe in a simplified concept of salvation, and mental barriers built by the overanalytical adult skeptics collapsed under the weight of their own children's uncompromising transformations. In one account from Richard McNemar (in which he was an eyewitness), we read of two little girls early on in this development of children's involvement, their advanced exhortations, and the positive outcome it ultimately had:

> At a sacrament, near Flemingsburgh...the power of God was very visible among the people through the whole of the occasion; under which there was much weeping, trembling and convulsion of soul: But what was the most solemn and striking, was the case of *two little girls*, who in the time of meeting, cried out in great distress. They both continued for some time praying and crying for mercy, till one of them received a comfortable hope; and then turning to the other, cried out "O! you little sinner, come to Christ! take hold of his promise! trust in him! he is able to save to the uttermost! O! I have found peace in my soul! O! the precious Savior! Come just as you are! He will take away the stony heart and give you a heart of flesh! You can't make yourself any better, Just give up your heart to Christ, now! You are not a greater sinner than me! You need not wait another moment!" Thus she continued exhorting, until her little companion received a ray from heaven, that produced a sudden and sensible change: then rising with her in her arms, she cried out in a most affecting manner, "O here is another star of light!" These children were perhaps *nine or ten years old...*

And here a new scene was opened, while some trembled like one in a fit of the fever, wept and cried out, lamenting their distance from God, and exposedness to his wrath; others were employed in praying with [the children], encouraging them to believe on the Son of God, to venture upon his promise, give up their wicked rebellious heart, just as it was; for God to take it away, and give them a heart of flesh; singing hymns, and giving thanks to God, for the display of his power, without any regard to former rules of [childless] order. At this, some were offended and withdrew from the assembly, determined to oppose it, as a work of the wicked one. But all their objections only tended to open the way for the true nature and spirit of the work to shine out; and encourage the subjects of it, to set out with warmer zeal to promote it…. At this meeting, one man was struck down and lay for about an hour [another Pentecostal/Holy Spirit-infused occurrence, prior to the Age-of-Fire Pentecostalism that would arise later]…. This put the matter beyond dispute, that the work was supernatural; and the outcry which it raised against sin, confirmed a number in the belief that it was from above.[138]

Certainly at first, the role of children as the callers-to-Christ for their parents, grandparents, older siblings, ministers, and elderly within their community was a surprise that, as McNemar stated above, caused some to leave the meetings. In due course, however, the effect it had on the masses was a considerable *increase* in the fold, far more than it ever was a disruption:

From these small beginnings, it gradually spread. The news of these strange operations [involving young people] flew abroad, and attracted many to come and see; who were convinced, not only from seeing and hearing, but feeling; and carried home the testimony, that it was the living work of God. This stirred up others, and brought out still greater multitudes. And these strange exercises still increasing, and having no respect to any stated hours of worship, it was found expedient to encamp on the ground and continue the meeting day and night. To these encampments the people flocked in hundreds and thousands, on foot, on horseback, and in wagons and other carriages.[139]

Before long, the testimony of the babes was not only expected and tolerated, it was endorsed. Not only did the little ones exhort, they *preached!* McNemar shares one example when a young boy's wise preaching resulted in an outpouring of the Holy Spirit amidst present adults:

> The general meeting at Indian creek, Harrison county... continued about five days and nights.... But there was very little appearance of that power which strikes conviction to the heart of the sinner, until the third day about two o'clock in the afternoon. A boy from appearance *about twelve years old*, retired from the stand-in time of preaching under a very extraordinary impression, and having mounted a log at some distance, and raising his voice in a very affecting manner, he attracted the main body of the people in a few minutes. With tears streaming from his eyes, he cried aloud to the wicked, warning them of their danger, denouncing their certain doom if they persisted in their sins, expressing his love to their souls, and desire that they would turn to the Lord and be saved. He was held up by two men, and *spoke for about an hour*, with that convincing eloquence that could be inspired only from above. When his strength seemed quite exhausted and language failed to describe the feelings of his soul, he raised his hand and dropping his handkerchief, wet from sweat from his little face, cried out, "Thus, O sinner! Shall you drop into hell, unless you forsake your sins and turn to the Lord." At that moment some *fell like those who are shot in battle*, and the work spread in a manner which human language cannot describe.[140]

Such young children would grow into the next generation of adults, remembering the power they witnessed as a personal experience, and not just as something mystical they saw their parents living through. The revival would not end when the grown-ups became idle in their spiritual appetite. It's no wonder then that the second Great Awakening was episodic and lasted longer than others. Unlike some awakenings and revivals that ascended into almost overnight enthusiasm and then slowly descended into another period of stagnation, the second Great Awakening produced movements that would continue to radiate for over half a century. Among these were:

- Adventism. The "Millerites," followers of William Miller, believed the Second Coming of Jesus Christ was imminent.
- The Holiness Movement. Roots of this movement trace back to the Wesley brothers' Methodist "good deeds" theology established as early as the "Holy Club." However, the second Great Awakening refueled this movement (and it is still alive and thriving today, comprised of millions of followers).
- The Restoration/Stone-Campbell Movement. Led by Barton Stone, Thomas Campbell, and Alexander Campbell. Believers wished to restore church practice and concepts of Christianity back to its purer form, without an extravagant hierarchy.

In addition to Barton Stone, Thomas Campbell, and Alexander Campbell of the Restoration/Stone-Campbell Movement is a lengthy list of other religious leaders rising out of obscurity during or immediately following the second Great Awakening. Among these were:

- Francis Asbury (1745–1816), author, founder of American Methodism, and pioneering circuit-rider (clergymen assigned to travel by horseback to minister and organize new congregations).
- Benjamin Randall (1749–1808), central figure behind the expansion of Free Will Baptists.

- Harry Hosier ("Black Harry," 1750–1806), an illiterate Methodist minister, never formally ordained. The first African-American man to preach to a white congregation, an endeavor that he carried out powerfully.
- Richard Allen (1760–1831), author, teacher, minister, and African-American founder of the African Methodist Episcopal Church (AME; the first independently black denomination on US soil).
- Lyman Beecher (1775–1863), key Presbyterian leader in the second Great Awakening and cofounder of the American Temperance Society. Father of thirteen children, most of whom also rose up to be great leaders, including, but not limited to, Harriet Beecher Stowe, Henry Ward Beecher, Charles Beecher, Edward Beecher, Isabella Beecher Hooker, Catharine Beecher, and Thomas Beecher.
- Lorenzo Dow (1777–1834), eccentric preacher and author. Rumored to have preached to more people during the second Great Awakening era than any other man. Written works were almost all best-sellers; one title was said to have been the second best-selling book in the States for a time, just under the Holy Bible.
- Asahel Nettleton (1783–1844), Connecticut pastor and theologian. Leader during the second Great Awakening. Said to have led tens of thousands to Christ.
- Jarena Lee (1783–1855), African-American female author and preacher. Composed the first ever published autobiography by an African-American woman in the United States (*The Life and Religious Experience of Jarena Lee*). The first woman given the rights to preach publicly by Richard Allen, founder of the African Methodist Episcopal Church, after the release of her memoir in 1819.
- Peter Cartwright (1785–1872), Methodist revivalist, missionary, opponent of slavery, and twice-elected legislator in Illinois. Significant leader toward the beginning of the second Great Awakening. Is reported to have gone on to personally baptize twelve thousand new converts into the faith.

- Nathaniel William Taylor (1786–1858), Protestant theologian and leader behind the New Haven Theology (or "Taylorism"), which attempted to mesh revivalism with traditional Calvinism.
- Charles Grandison Finney (1792–1875), Congregationalist and Presbyterian minister, author, social reformer, revivalist, and opponent of slavery. Advocated mixed-gender and interracial revival meetings. Often credited as the "father of modern revivalism." Posthumously added to the list of "Preachers of the Great Awakenings."
- Antoinette Louisa Brown Blackwell (1825–1921), women's rights activist, author, public speaker, and the first woman to be ordained as a mainstream Protestant minister in the US.
- Ellen Gould White (1827–1915), author and Christian pioneer. Formed the Seventh-Day Adventist Church.

5

The Third Great Awakening

BEFORE WE BEGIN our overview on the accounts of this period, one significant debate needs to be addressed, as it appears to come up frequently in hot discussion, continuously addressing the following questions: When did the third Great Awakening begin? What caused it? Who were the central figures behind it? How was it different than the second? And was it even a qualified "awakening" at all? Such staunchly opposing opinions thrive behind this analysis that these questions are not easy to answer.

Perchance even the readers of this book have heard someone suggest with plausibility that "there never was a third Great Awakening." These same skeptics will agree that there was definitely *something* going on in the states at this time, but the never-ending potato/*po-tah-to* dispute of the immortal "third Great Awakening" terminology leaves scores of lay researchers questioning—or wholly discounting—the importance of this period. So, let's briefly take a look at the hot-button deliberation...

In many ways, the third Great Awakening is as impossible to tie to one or two specific individuals' efforts or passions as its predecessor, and it is often considered to be a continuation, not an awakening in itself. In the decades following the second Great Awakening:

- Protestant churches increased across the land, attendance was up, and seminary training was taken seriously, with the construction of colleges and universities of theology observing a climb. Add to this the fact that several of the key figures from the bullet list in the previous chapter had carried on proficient ministries across state lines, and not just in the South. Because many of these establishments and ministries grew well into the third awakening (some of which are even in their highest points of fruition at the time of this writing), this is a "continuation."

- Camp meetings peppered frontier lands from the day they were initiated through McGready and his associates and forward (in some denominations, such as Methodist and Pentecostal, they are still quite a prominent practice), so this feature, too, is a "continuation."

- Missionary endeavors amplified, and many denominations quickly expanded their outreach programs to minister internationally. Based on clear and present evidence of missionary work in the years following the Revival of 1800 (and through to today), this is a "continuation."

- Although interdenominational wars have always, and probably will always, exist in Christendom, today's comparatively peaceful amity between Christian denominations holds origin in the revival and awakening of McGready's day, when the Baptists, Methodists, and Presbyterians cast aside their squabbling to focus on the character and mission of Christ. Obviously, this is a "continuation."

These and other developments carried well into the third Great Awakening with equal or escalating momentum, so by that rationality, it makes sense to assume that from several angles the second awakening never officially ended when the archives say it did. But perhaps the "end" is not asserted by the experts based on programs, attendance records, practices, or establishments. Could it be based on a national fizzling of religious passion?

Stagnation of the enthusiasm in the second awakening set in anywhere from 1820 through 1850, depending on the specific sect of Christianity in focus (which explains the varying reports), and a lot of the Presbyterian/Methodist, McGready-style camp meetings had observed the culmination of vast Holy Spirit manifestations (such as mass slayings in the Spirit) by that time. (Also note that through the ministries and extemporaneous preaching of Charles Finney [mentioned in the closing bullets of the previous chapter], intermittent and powerful revivals continued to spring up throughout the states during this time.) However, most scholars who study Christian revival unrelated to specific groups or sects attribute the mid-to-late 1850s as the official, national end of the second Great Awakening interdenominationally. Strangely, the start of the *third* Great Awakening is recorded as beginning in the late 1850s (the exact group of years that marks the end of the *second*), making the notion of a "continuation" a literal one accountable by historic timeline. This renders one lengthy and episodic awakening beginning around 1790 and drawing to a close circa 1920, incorporating the second and third together.

Most ardently debated is the following: Numerous scholars and historians have claimed that the second Great Awakening *did* end circa 1850, and that the third Great Awakening never occurred at all, based on their own list of "awakening" qualifiers, which the third Great Awakening does not meet. When one considers their argument open-mindedly, one will likely find it sound, as their definitions are logical. (These same scholars tend to discount the fourth Great Awakening as well.) Yet, a vast majority of others persist in recognizing religious history from 1850 to approximately 1920 to be the official years of the third Great Awakening, based on an *equally* valid and logical list of qualifiers.

We will not take the time here to dig deeply through all the lines of reasoning that support or undermine the status and legitimacy of the third Great Awakening, nor will we build a complicated list of comparisons between the second and third to qualify the third as its own historical period deserving of its own title. *But*, to bring simple clarity to why at least most in the mainstream see these two epochs as different:

1. **Momentum:** Zealousness and supernatural manifestations *did* stagnate in many areas across the US prior to 1850, even though the attendance, education, and programs were maintained through robust infrastructure, albeit with less excitement. This was a result of several factors: disillusionment of spirituality after the extremism of the date-setting Millerites errantly proclaimed 1844 as the year Christ would return; emotionalism eventually replacing sincere Holy Spirit-manifested outpourings (which was a major concern for the three leading denominations covered in the second Great Awakening study); agitation of slavery quarrels; acute focus on political issues, and so on. So, judging *only* by the momentum of enthusiasm, the second Great Awakening had, in fact, diminished, along with the declination of new converts, paving the way for believers to call for another revival/awakening.

2. **Cause:** The 1840s and 1850s mark a time of extreme escalating political tension. Anti-slavery and pro-slavery parties had been in heated conflict for decades. American states were drawing hard lines in the sand that identified with "free state" or "slave state" labeling. Approaching the 1850s, this civil rights/constitutional rights clash reached one of its first cataclysms, piloting the "Bleeding Kansas" warfare (alternatively, "Border War of Kansas") beginning in 1854, and blood was spilled not only on US soil between our citizens, but even at times between political representatives and senators upon the floors of the US legislature. (This and other events—including the Pottawatomie Massacre and the Marais des Cygnes Massacre—directly triggered the American Civil War after the formation of the Confederacy [the seven Southern states declaring secession following the 1860 presidential election, of which Abraham Lincoln triumphed as the first Republican president].) As such, while the religious ardor of the second Great Awakening was fading away, with many focusing on incoming political turmoil, by

1850, the country was falling on its knees again, pleading for divine assistance. As stated in the previous chapter, the second Great Awakening happened primarily because the Church sought revival. The third Great Awakening occurred as a blunt consequence of obvious national turmoil. Thus, the *cause* behind the two awakenings can be seen from two completely different angles of origin.

3. **Traits:** And *when* America fell on its knees again circa 1850, it launched a new generation of religions (including Christian Science and the Unity Church), denominations (including the Salvation Army), movements (including the Social Gospel Movement and the Bible Students Movement, the latter of which later splintered into today's Jehovah's Witnesses), and activism (the prohibition, pornography, and prostitution protests; women's rights to vote; and a certain marriage of church and state), therefore birthing traits of a variable religious influence on social issues in the third Great Awakening than the second had.

The third Great Awakening may be disputed where terminology and scholarly qualifications lists are concerned, but nobody can deny that the latter half of the nineteenth century was privy to a brand of revival that would leave a lasting stamp on Christianity from that day on.

The last remaining question left unanswered then, as posed at the beginning of this overview, regards the central figures of this awakening. Although the list could go on and on, especially considering some of the international revivals who inspired America to follow suit, the most notable names appearing in literature are the following: Dr. Walter Palmer and wife Phoebe, camp meeting evangelists in Ontario and Quebec, Canada, who arrived by Wesleyan minister Samuel Rice's invitation in New York in late 1857, leading six hundred nonbelievers to the Lord and later thousands of others in the States (some say this endeavor propelled the official beginning of the third Great Awakening); Jeremiah

Lanphier of Fulton Street, one of the great prayer-meeting organizers of the 1850s (this prayer-meeting period was a phenomenon, drawing in multitudes for national prayer, which shortly turned into crusades, and some believe this was the true cause behind the third Great Awakening); Dr. Henry Ward Beecher (listed in the bullets of last chapter's conclusion), a prominent devotions and prayer-meeting leader; William Joseph Seymour, African-American initial leader of the famous 1906 Azusa Street Revival (the event that tremendously affected the formation of today's Assemblies of God Pentecostal denomination, holding almost sixty million members in 2006); and of course, the aforementioned Congregationalist/Presbyterian Charles Finney of the second Great Awakening, whose revival work in 1825–1835 on the East Coast was supremely influential long after he had drawn back from his ministry efforts (he maintained a position of religious authority until his death in 1875).

A few other names that plead mentioning are Richard T. Ely, Josiah Strong, Washington Gladden, Lyman Abbot, Charles Monroe Sheldon, and Walter Rauschenbusch, all of whom were either leaders or pioneers of the Social Gospel Movement—an activist Protestant movement that applied scriptural ethics to social issues such as poverty, alcohol abuse, child labor, labor unions, economic and racial equality, and survival preparedness during times of political schism—the followers of which believed that through human effort, the world could be cleansed of social evils and marshal in the Second Coming of Christ. (Note that many of their actions were worthy, and some were controversial; much of their theology was biblically sound according to modern scholars, and much of it was not. However, the Social Gospel Christians' motives were largely pure, and through their persistent ventures, influence was provided for beneficial labor reforms under Franklin D. Roosevelt's "New Deal" organized labor legislation in the 1930s.)

By far, however, the name that comes up more than any others as it relates to his role in the third Great Awakening—and for good reason—is preacher, author, publisher, and evangelist Dwight Lyman Moody (frequently "D. L. Moody"), toward whose ministry this overview will now turn.

A Regular Tom Sawyer Is Called

Dwight Lyman Moody was the sixth child born to Edwin J. and Betsy Moody in Northfield, Massachusetts, on February 5, 1837. Although it's likely he was never aware of it, Moody was related to Franklin D. Roosevelt, Grover Cleveland, Harriet Beecher Stowe, Oliver Wendell Holmes, and the same Jonathan Edwards who led the revival of Northampton, Massachusetts, the previous century, which unleashed the first Great Awakening.[141] His parents were well known to have been happily married, and the respect they had for each other built a firm foundation for a happy home, even though they were absurdly poor.

Edwin owed a great deal of money in many directions. At the time of his marriage, he didn't have two nickels to rub together, so Edwin and Betsy from the beginning had to beg and borrow just to secure the land that biographers refer to as "the poor farm." By the birth of Dwight Moody, their sixth mouth to feed, they were haunted by debt, and by the time he entered school, he had a younger sibling, and Betsy was pregnant with twins.

As a result of the most heartbreaking tragedy ever occurring in D. L. Moody's young life, however, Edwin would not be present to welcome his twin babies into the world. No one is certain at the time what caused Edwin's sudden death , but a modern evaluation of his symptoms reveals that it appears to have been a massive heart attack after a long day of hard labor in the field. Little Dwight was four years old.

Betsy, now a single mother of seven with two on the way, grieved for her beloved, unable to mourn in peace as creditors harassed her for payments. Before long, the creditors had confiscated everything the Moody family owned, even down to the wood for their fireplace.[142] Then the twins were born, and the total number of children who huddled in their beds for warmth was nine. Betsy was still in her postpartum bleeding when the landowner came to collect payment—a payment Betsy expressed to the landowner under the covers of the birthing bed in her own bedroom that she did not have. Well-meaning but nosy neighbors suggested that Betsy rehome some of her children elsewhere. Not only was she cold and desperate, and living in depravity, but a single woman couldn't raise that many children on her own and still expect them to turn out well.

Criminals, they said.

That was what Betsy's children would become.

Ironic…

Betsy disregarded her neighbors' advice and devoted herself all the more to giving her children everything they could possibly need, including the parenting and love that would make them grow into great men and women of God. Their lives were not easy: their cupboards were bare, their house was cold, their bellies grumbled, and their father was gone, leaving an ever-vacant hole in their daily lives that could not be filled.

But *love*… love was abundant.

When Reverend Oliver Everett, pastor of the First Congregational Church in Northfield, heard the state the Moody house was in, he began bringing food and money. During his visits, he connected well with the children, especially the boys, and he left a lasting impression on Dwight Moody, who would later journal about the kind man's ministry and the hope he inspired within them all. In 1842, the entire Moody clan was baptized by Everett "in the name of the Father, Son, and Holy Ghost."

The accounts of Moody's earliest years are likely to make a reader laugh out loud. So taken with him were all his elders; so charismatic were his dealings; so beguilingly humorous were his harmless shenanigans; and so confident was his determination and wit, that his character lifts off the pages of his biographies with so much charm one might think him too fascinating to be real. He was a regular Huckleberry Finn, living a new chapter each daybreak. A clever Tom Sawyer, painting the fence on Saturday out in the sun.

He loved to pull pranks, like the time he hung a bogus sign on the schoolhouse door advertising a temperance lecture. There was, of course, no lecture. Nonetheless, the schoolhouse was heated and lit for the date and time stated on Moody's phony ad, a hefty gathering arrived in anticipation of the teaching, and as one might expect, no lecturer arrived. (Nobody knew at the time that Moody had been behind the stunt.)

He was also constantly negotiating with an ingenuity even businessmen could not ignore, like the time he convinced the stagecoach driver to transport him to his grandma's house. The fare for children was ten cents. Moody had five. After a short conference with the driver, Moody was stationed on the luggage rack, as if he were a suitcase, five-year-old baggage, having earned a half-priced ride. On the return trip home, he was penniless, so he once again talked his way into a significantly discounted journey, this time with a bouquet of flowers and a useless handful of wild parsley as his fare.

In the face of extreme mounting poverty, Moody made a constant impression on those around him. He was well-liked, openly accepted, and supported. From his youngest years, he always had a hands-on job., At his first of many posts, he earned one penny per week in exchange for milking cows. School was a lower priority, because reading, writing, and arithmetic didn't fill one's belly (and for the majority of his life, Dwight would struggle with abysmal spelling, deferring much of his communications to a stenographer).

At the age of seventeen, Dwight left home and went to Boston to work with his uncle Samuel at a shoe store. The young man's allure was such that he quickly became a successful shoe salesman. Between flattering his clientele with wit and cracking jokes that put them in the spending mood, he was soon sending home bundles of new shoes and cash for his mother and siblings when he wasn't playing tricks on the cobbler.

And it was there, during his days of peddling footwear, that Moody began to trip into the snares of enemy traps, casting aside his focus on boyish games in exchange for a more mature kind of thrill. There were so many things he hadn't experienced, a void where excitement should have been, and now that he was no longer living under his mother's roof, the big city was his oyster, the hidden pearl his quest. *Something* in this life had to be more fulfilling than sizing the feet of strangers and pitching the latest heels, and as soon as nobody was looking, he was determined to find it, regardless of what that meant for his spiritual well-being.

But...it was there, during his days peddling footwear, that Moody would meet Edward Kimball, a man who intervened the day the young jokester became the laughingstock.

Uncle Samuel had made Moody promise that if he had been given a sales position at the store, he would have to attend a church of Samuel's choosing. The Mount Vernon Congregational Church was the place of worship Samuel stipulated, and Moody agreed, if for no other purpose or sense of duty than to keep his job. Kimball was a Sunday school teacher there. One Sunday morning, fellow Harvard students had been present with Moody when Kimball directed his listeners to open their Bibles to the book of John. Moody had no clue where in the Bible that book was, and he instead opened to Genesis, paging from right to left in search of the targeted text. Sniggering erupted from the students, and snide remarks were whispered loud enough for Moody to hear that the others regarded him as an ignorant country dolt. Back home, Moody was accepted, and this abrupt disapproval from his urban peers was mortifying.

Immediately, Kimball took his own Bible, which was already opened to the New Testament book of John, and placed it in Moody's hands, trading out the one still lingering in Old Testament Genesis. The gentle fix had its intended effect, not only bringing an end to the pettiness, but kindling a friendship between Kimball and Moody that would last. Kimball saw in Moody the unharnessed free spirit on the cusp of downfall, unlikely to steer toward God's path without mentorship. Somewhere below the jovial surface, Kimball would later write, Moody was a dark and troubled youth: "I can truly say, and in saying it I magnify the infinite grace of God as bestowed upon him, that I have seen few persons whose minds were spiritually darker than was his [Moody's] when he came into my Sunday School class."[143]

Sometime after that first meeting, feeling led by the Lord and over-whelmed with the urgency to hear Moody commit his soul to Christ, Kimball walked to the shoe store, entered, asked for Moody, and then boldly made his way behind the employee counter where Moody stood organizing the merchandise. Placing his hands on Moody's shoulders, Kimball poured his heart out, telling Moody of this Savior who loved him so much that He *died* for him, so that Moody might spend eternity in His presence. Moody had heard of Christ before, as Betsy and Everett had seen to that, but Kimball, with tears falling down his cheeks, made this Christ fresh.

Personal.

The hidden pearl of the oyster.

Perhaps *this*—no…perhaps *He*—was the answer to the void.

To this day, there still remains a memorial plaque fixed to the build-ing just outside where Moody was wrapping shoes in tissue papers the day Kimball dropped by. It says, "D. L. MOODY: Christian evangelist, friend of man, founder of the Northfield schools, was converted to God in a shoe store on this site: April 21, 1855."

First, it had been Reverend Everett ministering to Moody and his family's earthly needs. Then it had been Kimball ministering to Moody's eternal needs. The example set for Moody was a strong one. The desire to know God more was pulsating. The prior darkness within Moody that Kimball would years later record had recently begun to manifest itself in youthful delinquency, and Moody's harmless prank-ing had even grown into vandalism of neighboring farmlands. The young girls outside his apartment who swore like sailors and made their risqué intentions known with the batting of handsome eyelashes were becoming intoxicating of late. Temptation in Boston soared in ways it hadn't back home, and the parental accountability the fledgling Moody had in the city was almost nonexistent. He had been, just prior to Kimball's visit, at the very door of moral corruption. He was at the threshold of giving himself over to the wiles of worldly lure. But, as Moody would later say in tribute to the sudden and divine swerve of new direction upon his life, "a gracious hand leads us in ways we know not, and blesses us."[144]

From the moment the free gift of salvation had been imparted upon him, Moody saw the world and everything in it differently: The birds no longer sang for the springtime, but for a reminder of Christ's sacrifice. The sun was shining brighter, lending its rays to illuminate Moody's surroundings, so that the landscape, itself, could join in his delight. The branches of the trees swayed in rapture and greeting, not just for the breeze.

And "all nature was at peace."[145]

For two years, Moody worked hard in his uncle's shoe store under the spiritual counsel of Kimball and his associates of the Mount Vernon Congregational Church. From somewhere deep within, a yearning to bestow the same assistance on others that Kimball and Everett had given him began to cultivate. Everyone he met was in need of something, and in the name of Christ, Moody sought to help meet that need. By the time he arrived in the slums of Chicago in September of 1856 (a move his uncle Samuel advised against), God had prepped Moody for a ministry.

Almost in an instant, Moody was stationed in another shoe store owned by relatives, raking in record sales and increasing profit margins, and soon he was taking on more professional responsibility. He became a member of the Plymouth Congregational Church amidst a support group of adoring comrades, one of which described Moody as one of the most joyous men he'd ever met.[146] Just like in his childhood, Moody was loved by almost everyone he crossed paths with, despite his lackluster education. This made it much easier for him to fill the pews of his new church when he filed out to the streets and into the saloons, relaying his notable shine of Christ as he entered the scene, turning heads and gaining attention. Kimball had taken the gospel into a shoe store to speak to a young man who would have never gone to church had he not been forced to in order to secure a job. Now, Moody would take the gospel to the surrounding corners and into businesses where others would be just as unlikely to attend a service.

It was within a church that the Word would be maintained among believers, but it was within taverns, boarding houses, and shoe stores where the Word would reach the lost and hopeless. Moody, of all people, had confidence in this logic.

It didn't matter for a moment that Moody was new flesh in a murky and industrialized city like Chicago. Whenever he observed someone struggling, wherever an alienated soul was wandering, an outstretched hand was thrust into view, one that traced upwards to the smiling, cheeky face of a new best friend. If one held a different opinion than Moody— on any subject, religion or otherwise—it was with a sincere nod and a handshake that the matter was settled, allowance paved for both sides to agree to disagree, all the while holding steadfast to a harmonious and refreshing bond. The impression Moody made was enduring. As the previously quoted memorial plaque stated, Moody was truly a "friend of man," meaning *any* man, from any background, with any conviction, and of any personality. With a wink, a chuckle, and a pat on the back, no one was left behind, and soon the church had to rent additional pews to seat those who had responded to Moody's jolly and fun-loving invite.

In addition to his merry witnessing, Moody made fast money, investing in real estate, selling at a high profit, sending money to his mother and siblings in Northfield, and soon he discovered that the same good-ol'-Southern-boy banter with which he had led others to church could lead people straight off the trains and into his store. His upright business dealings from both Boston and Chicago are well documented, and this led to a long-lasting trust between himself and new and returning customers. The pursuit of ministry and an honest living were then married in Moody's life, and when he became a successful traveling salesman, he simultaneously became a successful traveling disciple. Although the Plymouth Congregational Church remained his home church for a time, he found himself welcomed with open arms at Baptist, Methodist, and Presbyterian churches as well (one of which was where he met the future Mrs. Moody, Emma Revell).

Settling into a boarding home under the supervision of Mrs. Herbert Phillips—known by her residents as "Mother Phillips," an endearing accolade to her maternal nature—Moody could not contain the internal joy for volunteer work and ministry. Mother Phillips pointed him in the direction of the Wells Street Mission Sunday School, as it was located on the north side of the city, which was home to some of the poorest folk in all of Chicago. Moody made haste to the mission school and pitched himself as volunteer. There were too many teachers there already, and only sixteen students in total, the superintendent said. However, if Moody managed to collect a congregation of his own, he would be welcome to minister. According to biographer Kevin Belmonte of *D. L. Moody—A Life: Innovator, Evangelist, World Changer*:

> That was all Moody needed to hear.
>
> The next Sunday, [Moody] appeared with eighteen ragged and dirty children, gathered off the streets. Turning them over to some of the other teachers, he sought out more children, until the school was full to overflowing. He had no thought of teaching the children himself but saw it as his place to "drum up" recruits for the school. When he saw these poor children, he remembered the poverty of his youth. He'd known what it was for hope to be a stranger. A flame of compassion flared within him. This was work he could give himself to.[147]

When the school was filled with the head count Moody had solicited, his sights fell on a section of town appropriately called "Little Hell." Crime, filth, seediness, and immorality had earned the slum its devilish moniker. Depravity soaked the sidewalks like a blanket of sin, steaming up from the sewer grates and wafting like a stench above rafters, alerting any casual passersby of the innate need to clench their fists around their wallets and bound like a frightened stag to the nearest town border and onto safer territory. And yet, regardless of the reputation of the slum—in fact, *because* of the reputation of the slum—Moody honed in, a cheerful beam upon his features so wide one might think he had wedged a clothes hanger in his mouth. With a Bible in one hand, the other hand remained perpetually open for a friendly shake.

Fearlessly, Moody recruited a couple friends from church and self-appointedly took over a deserted freight car on a dirty street that was known to see several muggings per day (not to mention the terrors that occurred after nightfall), where he launched a rapid, uproarious, and exhilarating meeting. Moody knew he was not going to get anywhere if he didn't speak the language of the locals, so the quiet serenity of the pulpit was tossed to the wayside. Harsh reprimand and the fear of hell was likewise disregarded.

No, these sinners didn't need to be reminded of their hopelessness via the condemning shouts of a pious do-gooder. Nor did they need a gentle voice to bury itself under the rowdy din and spitting retorts of scoffing spectators. Those forms of teaching had their time and place, and it wasn't here or now. Those forms of teaching had their leaders, and Moody wasn't one of them.

Loud and exciting was what would get their attention, so loud and exciting is what Moody would give them; and, as was his typical approach by this time, it would be *joyous*, for "joy" was altogether a novelty to the likes of these weary and despairing youths.

The name Jesus Christ resounded with a mighty echo off the narrow walls of the alleyways. Juvenile gangsters stopped midstride and glanced at the crazy twenty-one year old. Young boys who on any other evening appeared seconds away from producing a rusty pocket knife approached the freight car with intrigue. Crooked dealings and nasty whisperings halted through the distraction, and before long, a gathering of the scariest-looking bunch had surrounded Moody from all sides.

There is no telling whether it was because of Moody's genuine smile, his fresh approach, the deeply rooted spiritual hunger of his listeners, or merely because Christ was responding when His Name had been called (which is likely), but within minutes there was jumping, singing, whooping, and hollering, and all the sons of chaos were banding together in a merry round of the hymn, "Stand Up for Jesus." God was using just the right minister at just the right time and in just the right place, and before Moody left that night, he was the "big brother" of the gangs of Chicago…and the boys lined up for more.

Needless to say, the meeting was only the first of many. If the street gangs arrived to Moody's freight car charged and full of life, unable to stand still in their youthfulness, unable to pay attention to a lesson from the Good Book, drawn in only by the hype of something buoyant, that was perfectly fine with Moody. It was a step in the right direction to simply be their buddy in the name of Christ. God willing, a lasting conviction would reveal itself in due course, and when anyone among them proved ready to hear of Christ, Moody was Johnny-on-the-spot. But in the meantime, these boys had been chewing the cud of debauchery for the entirety of their lives, and Moody was simply taking in their eagerness for their own pearl in the oyster. He brought them food they couldn't obtain through any avenue other than theft; he brought wood for their fireplaces so their mothers and siblings would be warm; he challenged them to races around the block; and when it was time to convene at the freight car, he jumped and shouted right along with them, in an almost fraternity-brother, high-five-style intimation. There were those who threw insults his way and jeeringly attempted to provoke him to anger, but Moody found a charming means of joining in the needling and affable goading that brought all parties to laughter, as *equals*, as *peers*…as *friends*.

He was one of *them*…and yet…he was different.

Moody had almost *literally* been one of them, but thanks to Kimball and his passionate pleas, Moody, who was now only barely older than the boys on the street, had taken a different path. He was determined to see them make the same decision. And if any among them refused to truly accept Christ as their personal Savior, it was enough for him to have been the companion who brought a smile to their face and a salve to their weariness. Unlike so many ministers who have gone before Moody or followed him, it was never a numbers game. He cared so profoundly for those he reached out to that he was never driven by arguing theology or carving another notch on his belt when the sinner's prayer was spoken. The central force that carried Moody into the dangerous slums of Chicago was first and foremost *love*. He led by example, his influence was inarguably alluring, and those touched by his outreach eventually did begin asking substantive questions about this Christ fellow, who was evidently responsible for instilling the "it" factor within big brother Moody. (Of the most changed was Jimmy Sexton, who later became a hero of the Civil War and the commander-in-chief of the Grand Army of the Republic. The crowds that flocked to Moody were primarily made up of young children and teens, and there are paintings and drawings in existence today of Moody laughing, hugging, and celebrating like an older sibling to hundreds. Some photographs still circulate showing Moody standing behind a group of young kids he had endearingly rewarded the title "Moody's bodyguards.")

A church was growing, right then and there, on those urine-stained boulevards of "Little Hell." By November of 1860, the crowd of children and young teens had grown to fifteen hundred,[148] requiring the abandonment of the freight car. A shanty of an old saloon became the new meeting house for Moody's ministries, and it was still a tight fit. It was a sight to see, and when the newly elected US President Abraham Lincoln was invited to observe the mission work in person, he agreed. Even though Lincoln had stipulated that he could not be put on the spot to give a speech, on his way out of Moody's saloon-church, he stopped, turned, and addressed all those present. He told of his own life, his own meager means during childhood, and inspired the children to believe that even when hailing from the slums of Chicago, one still had the potential to be anything they wanted to be when they grow up...

Who knows? They may even become the president of the United States, Lincoln said...

War

The children, teens, and leadership of Moody's mission school had been inspired through the personal visit of President Lincoln, and within the following months, a levity bathed the whole city of Chicago in a merriment that could only be credited to Christ, to whom praises were raised. But, sadly, as Moody would later write, this lightheartedness would crash to a sudden and thunderous halt: "Little did we know that our nation was soon to be baptized in blood, and that we would soon hear the tramp of a million men, that hundreds and thousands of our young men, the flower of our nation, would soon be lying in a soldier's grave."[149]

Less than half a year from Lincoln's visit to Moody's school, the American Civil War was in full swing. Many of Moody's associates, and scores of his young teen "brothers," were enlisted to fight. Moody could not stomach the thought of taking another man's life—even that of an enemy of war—so he went about supporting his country in a nonviolent way.

Erecting a temporary chapel in Camp Douglas, an army training ground at the southern outskirts of Chicago, Moody held church services for both the soldiers stopping through for rest, as well as for those still in training. He wasn't usually the speaker, but the organizer who attended to all the needs of those responding to invitations for Christ. (More than fifteen hundred services would be held in this makeshift church during the war, and according to Moody's associate Edgar Hawley, there was at least one meeting that held twelve thousand men.[150]) Moody placed all his efforts in ministering to those coming and going from duty at the battle lines, and even assisted in the formation of the United States Christian Commission (USCC)—a religious and recreational relief organization branch of the Young Men's Christian Association (YMCA).

Both independently and in the line of official duty, Moody tirelessly visited the barracks, bringing supportive religious print materials to the soldiers. The entire nation was submerged overnight in violence, injury, and death, and Moody's prayers—and smiles—landed upon the armed forces like a juicy steak tossed to a starving canine. When General Ulysses Grant (later the eighteenth president of the United States) led his troops to capture ten thousand Confederate soldiers at Fort Donelson in February of 1862 and the prisoners were transported to Camp Douglas, Moody's usefulness and determination escalated.

The prisoner holding was difficult to obtain entrance to, but Moody had established himself by this point as a trustworthy friend to the ranks, and when he was cleared, he set to observing chapel services alongside pal Edgar Hawley. Hawley wasn't a minister, but he was a believer, and once the two men were surrounded by massive crowds of spiritually confused POWs, they conducted a brilliant service. Hawley preached and Moody supported the responders. These soldiers were scared, lonely, emotionally devastated by their capture, far away from their wives and children, and fraught with regret and trepidation, and it was through the power of only one Source that their souls could be reached, strengthened, and saved for all eternity. The Civil War was *man's* business. The spiritual war was fought between supernatural entities, and Moody knew the Victor. The Son of God was at the ready, a smile on His face, and a hand stretched out, ready to be a Best Friend. The pearl in the oyster. The filling of the void.

Hundreds of prisoners came forward to give their hearts to the Lord, and it was the first of many other meetings heralding similar response.

But, it was around this time that the lists of casualties were being announced. Moody's proximity to the war until this point was in ministry to those who were training to serve or had served in a limited capacity, *not* to people who were preparing to die. Once the death tolls were read, the reality of war dawned on him suddenly and heavily.

Moody had always ministered because he cared about the *person*— not the numbers, the warm fuzzies, the notch on his belt, or the recognition. When the young boys on the streets hadn't accepted Christ, Moody had considered himself blessed just to have been a companion, knowing that he had set a good example as a brotherly mentor, and that

he had time for them to come around. He had never really been the
teacher as much as the man who had led the children to the teachers.
Sure, he had spoken to scores of youth on the casual streets of Chicago,
and certainly, that had been its own form of instruction. But they were
kids! They accepted Moody's simple gospel of Christ. A thorough understanding of Scripture wasn't necessary in his ministry before.

A sadness and a sense of urgency gripped his innermost preacher.
Now was not the time for high fives and street races and slum-speak.
These soldiers were coming into the barracks and heading back out to
the frontlines, some of whom would never be seen again. These weren't
just men with rank numbers and badges, they were *individuals*. They
had hearts and souls. Each one was crucially important, each one was
loved by God…and each one was leaving soon, without any guarantee
of tomorrow.

At Camp Douglas, Moody could hear the sounds of young soldiers
on the training ground of war, and wondered which of their voices
would someday once again bellow over the turkey at their Thanksgiving dinner tables, and which would soon be quieted, only living on as
a violent echo in the throes of wartime memorial. But though many
around him were in training to fight against men, Moody was training
to fight for men's souls. Ready or not, war had come, young people were
dying, and he now had a decision to make: Get out of his comfort zone
and preach like he never dreamed he'd preach, or watch men go to battle
who had never been reached with the gospel.

The choice was an obvious one.

But how—*how on earth*—would Moody find time to study or educate himself to the levels of biblical understanding that was required of
a preacher when he had become the celebrated chaplain of thousands of
soldiers? Up to eight hundred men per day depended upon him to bring
their daily rations, and he had to travel by horseback into the country
several times a week to gather supplies.[151] Not to mention his fundraising duties. Through his efforts alone, *millions* of dollars had been chan-
neled all over the place in various ministries and organizations, including

school houses, orphanages, the YMCA, mission works, and construction of churches.[152]

Moody was no theologian.

He didn't have all the answers.

What could *he* do?

The famously referenced dying-soldier scene in Moody's life occurred in January of 1863, during the Battle of Murfreesboro in Tennessee. A soldier lay on his deathbed, with Moody at his side. The soldier was convinced that God would never accept him, because he had spent his entire life in sin. Moody tried to bring solace to the younger man, but to no avail. Then, Moody turned to the third chapter of John, verses 14 and 15, and read: "And as Moses lifted up the serpent in the wilderness, even so must the Son of man be lifted up: That whosoever believeth in him should not perish, but have eternal life." The soldier stopped him, and asked if that had *actually* been read from the Scriptures. Yes, Moody assured him, it had been. When Moody was asked to read the Scripture again, he obliged. When he was asked to read it a third time, he agreed again, patient and willing to give the man any comfort he sought in his final hours. However, at the end of the third reading, the man's eyes were shut, and his lips were moving silently, as if in a prayer. Moody leaned in close and heard that the man was repeating the verse, weak as he was, at a barely audible whisper. The soldier spoke once more to Moody, telling him he had heard what he needed to hear. Moody took to his sleeping quarters for a short few hours, and when he awoke, he returned to find the soldier's bed empty. The attendant informed Moody that the soldier had died peacefully, the words "whosoever believeth in him should not perish, but have eternal life" on his lips.

As it turned out, Moody was not far away from having already achieved the level of biblical understanding required to reach the lost. Christ was all that mattered. Christ was *always* all that mattered, and for as long as he was called, Christ would be his sermon. (As an interesting note: In these war surroundings, Moody drew strength from the published sermons of George Whitefield.)

By the war's end in 1865, Moody had served at the battlefront on nine different occasions. He had assisted the attendants in bringing medical relief to the wounded; prayed for the sick, infected, and dying; and saw many a soldier pass away. In those final hours, just before a man's journey into the afterlife, he had observed a hope unfolding across the battered features of their faces, and these were memories that he would never forget. For the rest of his life, he would tell others about the great men who had died, the cause for which they died—and the Man who had died for them thousands of years prior, in whose presence they now resided.

In addition to spending his time making personal bedside visits, Moody preached a simple gospel message like a man on fire for Christ from any wartime pulpit he could find and, as the surviving soldiers' journal accounts attest, he led multitudes to Christ. His words were no more complicated than they had been during his one-on-one meeting with the dying soldier, but the confidence the other soldiers accrued from such endeavors not only brought them internal peace, but it followed them onto the battleground, and into the ears of fellow combatants. Such was the spread of Moody's Civil War ministry, and to this day, only God could possibly know how many were converted during those years.

Several important relationships were fostered during the latter part of the war (or in the years immediately following the war), including such names as D. W. Whittle (later a celebrated coworker of Moody's) and General Oliver Otis Howard (who later founded the African-American Howard University). Of contacts made overseas, Moody had left an impression on Lord Shaftesbury (an important social reformer) and Fountain J. Hartley (secretary of the London Sabbath School Union; Hartley had invited Moody to speak at an anniversary meeting at the school, and Moody's speech left such an impression on the gathering that he quickly became somewhat of a celebrity in England, which paved the way for his later London gospel campaign). He closely befriended legendary Baptist leader Charles Haddon Spurgeon and intermingled with the renowned George Müller's orphanage ministries, and through his relationship with Henry ("Harry") Moorhouse, Moody's skills as an evangelist were further sharpened. (His basis of the foundational love message was directly triggered by hearing young Moorhouse's passionate orations on John 3:16.)

Connections for Moody had been formed, and between those and Moody's infectiously upbeat personality (along with his lifelong pattern of esteemed negotiating and fundraising skills), his ministry had more of a future than ever.

Worldwide Awakening

Following the war, and during the American Reconstruction Era (the age of the process of restoring national unity and the final workings of civil rights laws for the now-freed slaves), Moody had bitten off more than he could chew. He had continued his work with the YMCA, worked regularly on up to twelve committees at any one given time, and founded the Illinois Street Church, where he taught on a regular basis. The first Farwell Hall of the YMCA was built and dedicated through Moody's fundraising efforts, but it caught fire and burned to the ground in 1867 (four months after its dedication). Sadly, it would not be the last casualty of conflagration. Immediately, Moody saw to raising the funds for a second Farwell Hall, which was constructed quickly and efficiently.

In October 1871, the Great Chicago Fire began in the O'Leary family barn just behind 137 DeKoven Street. For two full days, the blaze spread out of control, killing an estimated three hundred civilians and rendering more than one hundred thousand Chicago residents homeless. Moody was present in the second Farwell Hall when the fire alarm blared throughout the city. Moody and his associates poured out into the streets, observed the fire a half mile off, and without even bidding each other a formal farewell, they fled to their homes. Moody alerted his wife (whom he had married in 1862). Together, they dressed their children (one boy and one girl), grabbed a few of their most precious valuables (including their family Bible and a sentimental [but now famous] painting of Moody), and ran from the scene, taking refuge with friends. By midnight of that very night, Moody's home was naught but ashes and rubble. The *second* Farwell Hall met the same glowering fate as its predecessor. The Illinois Street Church was only a memory, now lying in smoky ruination. Nearly every material possession and building that meant anything to Moody and his ministry was devastated by the roaring inferno.

Now Moody was back to relief work. At every turn, people were helpless. The loss of lives and land this time around had nothing to do with national pride, war, serving a country, or fighting for what one believed in. It was tragic and futile. A seemingly senseless loss. For four months, Moody despaired. He tried to keep the Lord in focus as he ministered to those who had lost their homes and had nowhere to settle, but trial had so long been his closest companion since the war had broken out a decade before that he found himself not caring about anything anymore. Deeper down, however, in the most faithful crevices of this preacher's heart, hope continued to manifest in the prayers of rejuvenation. The hardship of life was eternity's temporal game, giving up was the coward's play, and Moody knew he had to beat it. Despite his dive into the depths of apathy and depression, his lips never completely retired from asking for God's patience and grace. It was for the outpouring of the Holy Spirit that he most often prayed during his season of spiritual unproductivity.

And just when it felt he had hit rock bottom, God spoke back.

Like so many other turning points in this book and within other testimonials, Moody's "Upper-Room Pentecost" experience is difficult—if not altogether impossible—to explain. It isn't that nobody has ever documented the event, as many have. It is the simplicity of what transpired *in contrast to* the unfathomably profound effect it had upon Moody that confuses researchers.

Moody was stationed for a time in New York to oversee fundraising for Chicago reparations, including a new church. One day, as he was minding his own business walking down Wall Street, he was taken in an instant by the overwhelming notion that God had something to relay to him. A friend of Moody's lived nearby, so he made haste to his home. After a quick greeting, Moody awkwardly told the man that he needed to be alone, and then diffidently asked him if he had a room he could enclose himself in. Moody's friend led him to a room upstairs (a literal upper room), and Moody closed the door. Then, falling to his knees, he felt God encircling him with a greater force and presence than he'd ever felt. In Moody's own words: "Ah, what a day!—I cannot describe it. I seldom refer to it, it is almost too sacred an experience to name—Paul had an experience of which he never spoke for fourteen years—I can only say God revealed Himself to me, and I had such an experience of His love that I had to ask Him to stay His hand."[153]

Moody later described this sensation to D. W. Whittle, who documented it thus:

> God blessed him [Moody] with the *conscious* incoming to his Soul of a presence and power of His Spirit such as he had never known before. His heart was broken by it. He spent much time in just weeping before God so overpowering was the sense of His goodness and love.... [Moody] lost interest in everything except the preaching of Christ and working for souls. He determined to go to England that he might be free from all entanglements in the rebuilding of his church and the [Farwell] Hall.[154]

Moody took to the pulpit zealously. His sermons were based on the same words and Scriptures as they had always been, but through forces unseen, his deliveries landed differently on his hearers, and "hundreds were converted" when he spoke.[155]

During one of his sermons following this incident at the church of an associate, he felt surprisingly drained. He had not been given the chance in his day to prepare for his lesson as well as others, and therefore he felt that his teaching was uninspiring. Nonetheless, the listeners had been remarkably attentive, and when he invited the people to stand and receive Christ at the end of the sermon, hundreds across the building stood. Moody thought perhaps they didn't understand what he had said. They were not being dismissed to leave…they were being invited to stay for prayer. He repeated the invitation, and further explained that anyone looking to accept Christ should follow him into the inquiry room. Almost the entire congregation filed into the room behind him, additional seating had to be set up, and the situation was so unbelievable that Moody repeated his charge a *third time*. Anyone wanting to become a Christian—by making Christ their Savior—was to stand. For a third time, everyone present stood. Nearly beside himself with wonder, and completely unprepared to respond to so many inquirers at once, Moody panicked and told the responders to go home and come back the next day to speak with the church's regular leadership, who were equally as skilled in assisting new believers during the conversion process. It wasn't that Moody hadn't cared about them. This was a response he had only envisioned in his dreams! But feeling inexperienced to handle the situation, he deferred the crowds to other ministers, much in the same way he had led the children to other teachers back in Chicago years prior. The next day, it came to his attention that the people had been serious when he received a dispatch requesting his immediate return. Moody was cooperative to the appeal, returned to the church, and led ten full days of follow-up meetings, in which hundreds of people were converted. (In the future, Moody would be prepared for such large numbers.)

That one hour in the upper room would be the hour to which all future moments in his life were compared. It was a simple, unpretentious setting. It was an uncontrived, unscheduled incident. The details of what happened that day would not flatter the human imagination with ceilings splitting apart, lights pouring from the sky, audible voices shaking the walls, or visions of grandeur. But, as Moody is a witness, the Holy Spirit is a gentleman, and sometimes He chooses to reveal Himself as a gentleman when love—*just* love…without smoke, mirrors, bells, or whistles—is what is needed to carry God's intentions to the weary. That one experience launched an intensity within his heart that would be the foundation for raising up one of the greatest evangelists our country has ever known.

As D. W. Whittle explained above, Moody's ties to Chicago's reparations held him in a position to maintain relief work, and because of his recent upper-room encounter, preaching the love of Christ was a passion that required the immediate dissolution of his role in that city. Additionally, he had left an impression on his international companions, who had promised him ample opportunity to speak in territories all across Europe, with paid travel expenses. So Moody finished masterminding the North Side Tabernacle (which took the place of the recently burned Illinois Street Church), alerted his associates of the desperate evangelism call on his life, found replacements for his numerous ministerial posts, and left for Britain in June of 1873.

Although slowly at first, news spread of this colorful American minister with an ability to strike directly into the hearts of his listeners. From the hundreds of converts within five weeks of gospel meetings in York, London, Moody traveled to Sunderland to capacity crowds with equal response, and the building was quickly outgrown, requiring the meetings to be moved to one of the heftiest North England halls. Neither Moody nor Ira D. Sankey—the gospel singer traveling with him—were ordained ministers, and they were therefore met with some resistance from the religious powers that be. However, newspapers—including secular papers—picked up the trail of Moody's success and furthered the rumors of those whose lives were being radically changed through his preaching, and naysayers were buried under mounding shouts of instant European revival.

Invitations for meetings to be held in Scotland were answered enthusiastically by Moody and Sankey, and the duo saw more of the same ardent reaction there, despite those who criticized Sankey's singing style. Even the largest of buildings could not hold the masses of people who attended Moody's preaching, and overflow services had to be conducted. More newspapers circulated updates, and for his last meeting in

Glasgow, Scotland, fifty thousand people showed up.[156] The assembly was so overwhelming that Moody didn't even bother attempting to file the crowds into the palace that had been secured for the meeting, instead opting to stand and shout from a horse-and-carriage box outside in the open air, George Whitefield-style. By September of 1874, Moody and Sankey had taken their revival-meeting ministry to all of Ireland as well, and although open-air preaching had never been Moody's preferred setting as it had been for Whitefield, there simply weren't buildings large enough to accommodate the masses, and Moody by default became somewhat of an outdoor preacher there. Aside from both Christian and secular newspaper outlets, Moody's meetings were promoted by major church leaders, including Charles Spurgeon and Free Church of Scotland superior Andrew Alexander Bonar.

Thousands, then tens of thousands, then hundreds of thousands of people were coming to accept Christ through the gospel as spoken by the humble war chaplain and relief worker. (And those who were already saved at the time they attended one of Moody's meetings were greatly strengthened.) Even the Royal Opera House of London, seating five thousand, proved only capable of housing one-fourth of the numbers that were typical of some of Moody's smaller congregations. Before long, newsstands had little else to report about besides the miraculous outpourings of the Spirit wherever Moody went, and Moody-endorsed publications were in nearly every home.

Of particular fascination is the fact that he *never did* mature into a great spokesman. Moody's speaking attire was mundane, his vocal intonations unpolished, his strings of words too simple to come from a minister. He pounded no pulpits. He frightened no one with the stirring of fear. His speeches were no more than a regular expository of Scripture. His presence was childlike and unassuming and unvaryingly *regular*. Although he often cried or at least choked up when he spoke of Christ's abounding love for sinners, very little else can be said about his style that would have drawn such numbers other than, perhaps, the will of God, Himself. Lord Shaftesbury once said:

Here come two simple, unlettered men [Moody and Sankey] from the other side of the Atlantic. They have had no theological training, and [have] never read the Fathers [referring to the Church Fathers]; they refuse to belong to any denomination; they are totally without skill in delivery, and have no pretensions to the highest order of rhetoric. They are calm, without an approach to the fanatical, or even the enthusiastic. They seek neither to terrify nor to puff up; eschew controversy, and natter no passions. So it is, nevertheless, thousands of all degrees in station and mental culture bow before them. Are we not right in believing—time will show—that *God has chosen the foolish things of the world to confound the wise?*[157] (emphasis in original)

Yet, with the same inexplicable charisma that had bounded from him since his youth; with that same down-to-earth negotiation logic that had stemmed from his days of selling shoes; with those same unsophisticated and unassuming hanger-mouth smiles that had inspired the street gangs of "Little Hell," Chicago; this unordained, nondenominational, misspelling and nearly illiterate, mid-thirties Tom Sawyer was leading every territory from one European border to another to its knees. Walls between church factions were peeling, Bibles were being dusted off and opened, theologians were hovering over the quill, study groups were popping up everywhere, and discipleship of young believers returned as an international priority.

And when British publishers sent astonishingly high royalty checks for the recently published Moody and Sankey hymnbooks (an amount equivalent to three-quarters of a million dollars by today's currency), Moody and Sankey forwarded every last cent of the money to the London gospel campaign committee to further the ministry they had started. The London committee refused to take such a sum, and the funds were therefore forwarded to the Chicago Avenue Church (a church that Moody had founded back home, but which had never completed a sufficient structure). By the close of the century, the Moody and Sankey hymnbooks would approach today's equivalent of almost twenty-eight million dollars in profit. Again, not one cent of the profit was ever received by the duo. Instead, the money continued to propel schools, churches, and the YMCA.[158]

In late 1875, Moody and Sankey returned to the States. Their message remained the same—the *love* of God versus the *wrath* of God (which was the popular theme of the day)—despite their arriving as two world-famous celebrities who could have gloated in their distinction, had that been their intention. Moody had already been a known figure in the US prior to his British campaign, but when he returned to the land that had been so saturated with news from credible sources internationally, masses unlike those he had ever seen before were standing around every pulpit he graced in every major city in the country.

The first stop was Brooklyn, New York, in huge ice skating rinks and massive tabernacles, which weren't nearly large enough, and thousands of people were turned away when even the standing areas were packed beyond levels of discomfort. Nearby churches opened their doors for the additional overflow services, and, not surprisingly, thousands gave their lives to the Lord.

Next was Philadelphia. Accommodations had been secured for twelve thousand people in an outdoor tabernacle, and when the meetings were immediately packed and thousands were turned away, more overflow meetings were scheduled. This was an exhausting demand not only for Moody and Sankey, but for nearly all Christian churches from varying denominations in the surrounding area, from which leading ministers dropped everything to assist. At one of these meetings, US President Ulysses Grant was present with government leaders, and seated nearby were other notable names such as future US President James A. Garfield, former Speaker of the House James G. Blaine, and members of Congress. Media reporters were present as well, and the torrential flood of complimentary reviews from the nation's most eminent chiefs on this strangely simple yet powerful bumpkin preacher soared into the following day's headlines.

Because Moody and Sankey refused even the smallest payment for their engagements, and no offerings were ever gathered for their benefit, some of the most prominent Christian and secular facilities in America personally funded the expenses for the meetings to take place in their own buildings (primarily the Hippodrome [later Madison Square Garden], which held two separate halls each capable of seating seven thousand). Because Moody spoke in front of thousands as if he were sitting in an intimate one-on-one setting over tea with a fellow—bringing his listeners into what felt like a personal and conversational engagement instead of a church service—the crowds were mixed with men, women, and children of every race and social class, having come to hear the friend of Christ and having left with a filling of the void. Because his words were not only a powerful calling for new converts but also a strengthener of existing believers, some hungry crowds attended his meetings over and over again, necessitating Moody's unprecedented act of asking some repeat attenders to leave the meetings and give their seats to the throngs outside—ensuring once again, with that old Moody flair, that no man would be left behind. Because Moody did not set out to praise men (even great national leaders), he had nothing to lose when he sweetly diverted flattery from those who did not believe in God and then gently reminded them with great social risk that they needed to be saved.

Moody was a man, and yet he was a child.

Moody had almost no education, and yet he spent a lifetime teaching the greatest lessons that could be conveyed.

Moody was a minister, and yet he was an unordained and unprofessional country bloke.

Moody's words were lackluster and common, and yet they are remembered as some of the most powerful ever uttered.

Moody began as a Tom Sawyer selling shoes in his uncle's shop, and yet he ended having led uncountable multitudes to Christ.

Moody was underwhelming and regular, and yet God used him for extraordinary things.

On and on he preached from San Diego to San Francisco to Vancouver to Boston to New York City, and on and on the people gathered by the thousands and tens of thousands. His legacy is unchallenged. His footprint on the world is celebrated. And through his obedience and commitment, the nation—no, the *world*—was revived…

Awakened.

And now we come around to one of the questions posed at the beginning of the chapter: Was the third Great Awakening even an awakening at all?

It is a question that naturally branches another: How could it *not* be considered so?

Conclusion

Moody went on to assist in fundraising efforts for numerous good-deed charities, relief funds, church building funds, missionary works, and cross-cultural Christian mission organizations. Before his death, he had founded two schools in Northfield, Massachusetts, as well as the Chicago Bible Institute (later Moody Bible Institute).

After Charles Spurgeon invented the "Wordless Book" evangelism tool in 1866—a book or banner with no words, each page its own color (black: sin; red: the blood of Christ; white: washed white as snow)—Moody incorporated one final color: gold (or yellow), representing heaven. The Wordless Book has been used in churches ever since Moody's modification for both children and illiterate adults as something they can "read," always reminding them of the most simple gospel truths. Additionally, it serves as an excellent device for missionaries speaking to foreign countries where language barriers require visual imagery. It remains immensely popular today, and many editions now include other colors to incorporate other aspects of the gospel.

Moody preached his last sermon in November 1899 in Kansas City,

Missouri. The following month, on December 22, he passed away in the presence of friends and family. His cause of death is unknown, but congestive heart failure has been deemed by modern speculation as the most probable trigger. In the later years of his life, he had lost two grandchildren, whom he loved dearly. Just before his death—after telling his family that his ascension to Christ's side was not something he feared, but rather, was his "coronation"[159]—his features lit up and he lucidly spoke that he had seen the faces of his deceased grandchildren. He then voiced grateful parting words to his wife and fell asleep. The nitroglycerin that had been hypodermically administered to him revived him a while later, however. He propped himself up on his elbow, gazed around curiously, and informed his family that he had already been to the gates of heaven, and that he found it very strange to be back. Shortly thereafter, he went back to sleep and did not awaken.

Posthumously, the Chicago Avenue Church was renamed the Moody Church.

The vast revivals that had begun through Moody's efforts (and the efforts of others mentioned prior) in the late 1800s thrust easily into the first two decades of the following century. In 1900, when the national revival threatened to wane after Moody's death, prayer meetings were called by leaders of the Moody Bible Institute, and the 1904 Revival was the emphatic response. By the Pentecostal Azusa Street Revival in 1906, America observed another surge, and it wasn't until circa 1920 that the states settled into stagnation. The Roaring Twenties was one of many economically celebratory periods, and when heads were turning to the raised hemlines of flapper skirts and young performers were appearing on liberal theater stages all across the world, the priority of religion suffered great decline, due in part to the interest in the entertainment industry. But, as history will tell, and as the next chapter will reveal, the entertainment industry would soon bow to the Shepherd during the Age of Fire, surrendering its capricious hold over the American people in trade for a whole new conduit for the gospel.

(Many of the others through whose ministries the third Great Awakening propelled were listed at the onset of this chapter, as they related to the questions of the awakening's origins and legitimacy discussed early on. Therefore, we will not list them here as the other surrounding chapters have done.)

6

The Age of Fire

THE "AGE OF FIRE"—or "Healing Revival" or "Evangelical Revival" as it is often called—occurred chiefly in the United States following World War II. The events of WWII began with international conflicts involving Italy's invasion of Ethiopia in 1935, the Spanish Civil War in 1936, and the Japanese invasion of Manchuria in 1931 and China in 1937. After Hitler's political seizure in 1933 and establishment of the Nazi Party, tension brewed across the globe, eventually leading to Hitler's German invasion of Poland in 1939, the event that launched France and Britain against Germany only days behind. Tumultuous times trailed this invasion, and by the time the Second World War was over, humanity would be desperate to reunite with God in a fresh, electrifying way.

The following is in no way an exhaustive account of everything that transpired in WWII, and many historical landmarks of that era will be omitted intentionally for the sake of space. Our focus is upon how the world arrived at a state of religious awakening following the shock of the Holocaust, and what effect those events had upon the Jewish nation, and by extension, upon evangelical Christianity. Let's visit a brief overview of these incidents, specifically that of Hitler, in order to understand the nature of the world at that time.

Hitler's Beginning

Causes behind WWII, as well as starting dates and ending dates, have all been highly debated, since WWII is generally viewed as merely a boiling point of the turmoil that began in WWI. Economic downfall and governmental chaos affected many countries in the aftermath of WWI, and dictators rose to form controlling fascist regimes (including Francisco Franco of Spain and Benito Mussolini of Italy). Germany was forced by the Treaty of Versailles to accept all responsibility for damages to the Allies and pay reparations after WWI, bringing the health of the economy, administration, and national pride to an all-time low. As a result of this, Germans were looking for any new leader who would promise restoration for their country and the dignity of its people, and they found that promise in their new Führer, Adolf Hitler, who rallied support through his voiced detestations and resentment of the treaty. Hitler's Nazi Party views of the inferior *Untermenschen* ("lower humans," or "subhumans") did more than just revitalize the nation's pride as the better people, more deserving of dignity. It led to radical arrogance.

While the Hitler regime nurtured the ideology that the *Übermensch* (literally "overman" and "superman," meaning the "higher humans")— the biologically superior "master race" of Aryan decent—were justified in ruling and/or enslaving the *Untermenschen*, quickly and daringly, Hitler saw to rearming Germany, and after ironic speeches about peace, he allied with Italy in his takeover of Austria in 1938. When the League of Nations (an intergovernmental organization established in 1920 during the Paris Peace Conference with a goal of disarmament, which led to the end of WWI) failed to stop Hitler, his barefaced battle cries were emboldened, and he led his troops to Prague in 1939, breaking his Munich Conference vow that Czechoslovakia would be allowed to maintain its territorial integrity.

Contrary to rising dictatorial agendas at that time, many countries within Europe were weary of conflict. When Germany and Italy (among others) began showing signs of antagonism, forming alliances and building up military strength, Britain and France initially attempted to appease Hitler by complying with his demands. Although this had been carried out as an effort to avoid further bloodshed by rendering unto Hitler all that he desired (a "give him what he wants so he'll leave us in peace" endeavor), it boomeranged, allowing Hitler even more time to bolster his armies. Additionally, it fed Hitler's ego as the man to whom surrounding countries bow, and he only grew more fearless in his lust for domination. Consequently, France and Britain changed tactics from appeasement to deterrence after Hitler's exploits in Czechoslovakia, but this stance, also, would not last.

Modern discussions most often attribute the pinnacle blastoff of the international reaction of WWII to 1939, when Hitler's aggressive foreign policy resulted in the invasion of Poland. France and the United Kingdom retaliated, abandoning their deterrence approach, and within a matter of days, they were joined by Australia, New Zealand, South Africa, and Canada in a declaration of war against Germany. Yet, it would not be until 1945 that the defeat of Nazi Germany would be signaled after the capture of the Reichstag building in Berlin. The six horrific years between 1939 and 1945 involved bloodshed incomparable to anything human history has ever observed prior…or since.

And millions of the most senseless, pointless, and cruel murders occurred as a result of Hitler's striving for the "perfect race."

The Holocaust

Also referred to as the *Shoah* (Hebrew: "catastrophe"), the Holocaust (Greek: *holókaustos*: "wholly burned," referring to animal-sacrifice offerings to God) was a systematic elimination through genocide (1941–1945) by Hitler of primarily the Jewish people throughout both Nazi Germany as well as other regions highly inhabited by German population. If only the Jewish headcount were to be considered, casualties of Hitler throughout the duration of the Holocaust would be around six million (about two-thirds of the Jewish population within that locality). If the numbers of other ethnic groups (Romanians, Poles, Slavs, etc.) Hitler found justification for eliminating were added to this, it would calculate to approximately eleven million irrational murders in total. Within these millions, many were women and children.

The word "Holocaust" was not used as a reference for this string of mass murders until circa 1960. Hitler and his Nazi Party instead called it the "Final Solution to the Jewish Question." This "Jewish Question" relates to one initially posed by the Jews, and can be summarized as: "How might the Jews achieve civil, societal, and legal independence as a nation—instead of always inhabiting foreign lands as a scattered people (diaspora)—and what steps were necessary to bring this freedom fantasy into fruition?" The "Jewish Question" also refers to one posed by non-Jewish populations who found this group—claiming to be "God's chosen people"—a nuisance and inconvenience, and can often be rendered: "What are we going to do about these bothersome Jews?"

The term came into use as early as the middle of the eighteenth century in Great Britain, and from its origin, although many theories and propositioned answers to the ongoing question arose from notable well-meaning Jewish defenders, this ideology of liberation and autonomy was not given priority focus by any one influential power long enough to find an answer.

For Hitler, the "Final Solution" to the "Jewish Question" was to systematically exterminate them from the planet.

The Motive

In addition to the eradication of "unwanted" racial genes, Hitler sought to weed out anyone with physical or mental disabilities (including homosexuality, which was regarded as a psychiatric disorder at the time). And often, even those who did not fit into these categories were likewise purged in the interest of Hitler's political advantage. But there is no doubt that the Jews were Hitler's key victims in his pursuit of creating the master race.

Many contend that Hitler's central motivation was that of pure control, a narcissistic urge to prove himself all-powerful in a time of war via the massacre of the masses: If he was to lead a nation to greatness, he had to be taken seriously, and the Jewish people were merely the peaceful and defenseless pawns who represented the least threat of organized counterattack. Others shake their heads in bewilderment, claiming that Hitler was no more than a homicidal maniac who achieved great personal (and sickening) satisfaction from inflicting unimaginable pain on helpless men, women, elderly people, and children. Due to the absurdity of the Holocaust, these motives tend to hold their ground as the only explanation necessary in most modern discussions. However, still others contend that the Holocaust was a product of fanatical belief in an anti-Semitic conspiracy theory: "The basic motivation...was purely ideological, rooted in an illusionary world of Nazi imagination, where an international Jewish conspiracy to control the world was opposed to a parallel Aryan quest."[160]

The Method

The death camps (or "extermination camps") established were the first of their kind, *ever*, in world history. Unlike the concentration camps, which were primarily built initially to retain and torture political rivals and union organizers—although by 1941 they were packed to the brim with Jews also—the sole purpose of the six death camps in Poland was for mass execution usually by gas chambers.

Outside the gas chambers, signs saying "baths" were hung, and the Jews were stripped naked and told they were merely going to be cleaned. As an additional deception to avoid panicking the crowds, the Jews were known to have been handed towels and soap before they entered the "showers." From there, the doors to the "showers" were screwed shut, vents in the walls were slid open, and solid Zyclon-B (hydrogen cyanide-based pesticide) pellets were dropped into the structure. Immediately, screams could be heard outside the locked chambers, and, depending on the victims' proximity to the pellets, sufferers could last up to twenty minutes before dying. Afterwards, the remains would be scoured (by other Jewish prisoners) for gold teeth fillings; women's heads would be shaved and the hair preserved for future use (felt, thread, upholstery, boot liners, socks, bomb-ignition mechanisms, mattress stuffing, etc.). The Nazis were told to keep the gas chambers a matter of secrecy, but as Auschwitz camp commandant Rudolf Höss relayed in the Nuremberg testimony, "The foul and nauseating stench from the continuous burning of bodies permeated the entire area and all of the people living in the surrounding communities knew that exterminations were going on at Auschwitz [one of the most prominent Holocaust death camps]."[161] (Note, however, that although Höss claims that "all of the people living in the surrounding communities knew" what was going on, other reports suggest that in many areas [apart from Höss' Auschwitz, which was known for the highest death tolls] the people were either unaware, or at the very least they did not understand the depth of the persecution. This is evident even on film, when bystanders are seen having extremely emotional reactions to the later camp liberations. More on this later.)

Another essential method of execution was "extermination through labor," the death of prisoners via severe heavy labor and simultaneous starvation. Prior to Hitler, no buildings or camps had ever been constructed purely for slaughter. Before their extermination, the unfortunate captives of both the death camps and the concentration camps were subjected to extreme medical experiments, including dangerous drug testing, and often these were performed upon the physically or mentally handicapped (including "dwarfs and hunchbacks"[162]). The details of these experiments are so disturbing that they cannot be listed in this book, but many have said (and these authors agree) that the excruciating testing was a fate far worse than death. Sometimes the tests were merely a means to see how much abuse the human body could tolerate, as "Nazi scientists were curious about the limits of human endurance."[163] The remains of those who died—whether by gas chamber, extermination through labor, or horrible medical experimentation—were subject to equally disturbing fates that, again, are too revolting to include here.

The ghettos (1939–1945) were established to contain Jews who were supposedly destined for the less tragic outcome of deportation. Under German law, each ghetto was to be managed by a Jewish council called a *Judenrat*. Each council was to oversee the distribution of food and labor (among other daily tasks). As a test of loyalty, the council leaders were coerced to file a report with the Nazis listing ghetto inhabitants who were to be collected and subsequently killed. If council leaders refused to compile this list, they, themselves, were put to death. Several famous Holocaust suicides took place as a result of council leaders' refusal to comply with these lists, deciding that they would end their own lives before being responsible for the death of their fellows. Others cooperated, condemning to death the weakest amidst them, admitting that their motive was ultimately to save as many as they could and remain in a position to protect who was left of their people at every opportunity. Over time, starvation and disease plagued the ghettos, causing hundreds of thousands of casualties. Uprisings resulted from Jewish resistance, but every attempt eventually fell under the weight of Nazi military power; those who remained on the Jewish side were executed. (One famous incident was the Warsaw Ghetto uprising in Poland in 1943, when Jewish resistance opposed the Nazis in a bloody battle after orders had been given by commander SS-Brigadeführer Jürgen Stroop to transport the Jews to the Treblinka death camp. From April 19 to May 16, 1943, by Stroop's order, one block after another in the ghetto was burned to the ground, and thirteen thousand Jews died, many of whom were burned alive or died from suffocation.) In the end, simple relocation of the Jews within the ghettos never occurred, and they were instead transferred to death camps.

Because Jews were at the epicenter of such violent focus, their presence—among what might have otherwise been neutral communities outside the superiority of Nazi Germany—caused trouble, however innocently so. Consequently, anti-Semitic paranoia broke out across Jewish populated territory, and as a matter of self-preservation, pogroms (riots) were rallied against the Jews, even by fellow persecuted peoples such as the Romanians (as was the case in the Ia i pogrom), adding another layer of death. Homes were pillaged, individuals were robbed and humiliated, and tens of thousands were shot, burned alive, or beaten to death. Repeatedly, those who attempted to defend the Jews were also killed.

By the time Germany invaded the Soviet Union in 1941, Nazi Germany had already been indoctrinated with anti-Semitism through the publications of pamphlets, flyers, and books, as well as through radio broadcasts and lectures. The Holocaust "death squads" (*Einsatzgruppen*: German "task forces") were therefore dispatched to Lithuania, Ukraine, Estonia, and Belarus (just to name a few) to oversee mass public killings of defenseless Jewish civilians. Men were forced to dig their own family members' graves prior to their execution, and survivor accounts (primarily by one man who was assumed dead as a result of his own fainting) portray the terrifying last moments of Jewish children screaming as their parents were murdered in front of them (as well as other heart-wrenching details). By the hands of the death squads alone, an estimated 2.2 million victims, almost all of whom were Jewish, were slaughtered.[164]

Under Hitler's leadership, every branch of the German administration participated in the mass executions of the Holocaust:

Every arm of the country's sophisticated bureaucracy was involved in the killing process. Parish churches and the Interior Ministry supplied birth records showing who was Jewish; the Post Office delivered the deportation and denaturalization orders; the Finance Ministry confiscated Jewish property; German firms fired Jewish workers and disenfranchised Jewish stockholders; the universities refused to admit Jews, denied degrees to those already studying, and fired Jewish academics; government transport offices arranged the trains for deportation to the camps; German pharmaceutical companies tested drugs on camp prisoners; companies bid for the contracts to build the crematoria; detailed lists of victims were drawn up using the Dehomag (IBM Germany) company's punch card machines, producing meticulous records of the killings.[165]

The Mask

Hitler didn't mind if the public knew of his detestation for the *Untermenschen*, as in many of his speeches he made that much quite clear. However, the exact lengths to which he persecuted the so-called subhumans was ordered to remain a clandestine operation.

The legendary Nazi propaganda film, *Theresienstadt: Ein Dokumentarfilm aus dem jüdischen Siedlungsgebiet: Der Führer schenkt den Juden eine Stadt* ("Terezin: A Documentary Film from the Jewish Settlement Area: The Führer Gives the Jews a City") of 1944, is merely one example among thousands of largely successful attempts to fool the world into believing that the Jews, although captives, were living healthy, productive lives under their benevolent protectors. From the subtitle alone, *The Führer Gives the Jews a City*, we can see that the purpose behind the scheme was to paint Hitler as a kindhearted and generous guardian over even the worst of his enemies. (The complete list of Nazi propaganda films included many titles that solidified anti-Sematic indoctrination across Europe as well as a profound number of justifications for euthanasia and sterilization. Whereas some of these were subliminal or gentle in their delivery, most were blatant.)

Just before this film was shot, when the Red Cross expressed an interest in visiting the camp in Terezin, great lengths were taken prior to their arrival to clean up the grounds, trim all the hedges, and scrub all the buildings from top to bottom in order to convince the Red Cross that the living conditions of the camp's inhabitants were industrious and thriving. As a smokescreen for the overpopulated camp, all the sickly, frail, and starving Jews were transported to Auschwitz and gassed, leaving only the few remaining Jews who were healthy enough to greet their concerned visitors. The torn rags and striped prison garments that the Jews had been living in for months on end were replaced with clean, fresh, well-tailored clothing, and the living quarters were adjusted to appear as if each "resident" (not "prisoner") was given ample room and all the required basic amenities.

This ploy was such a success that the shooting of *Theresienstadt* was ordered by the "Reich Ministry of Public Enlightenment and Propaganda" (a government agency formed in 1933 with a mission to endorse Nazi ideology) just after the Red Cross' departure.

Although most of the film was destroyed after the war, a good twenty minutes of the recording was later found in a vault in Czechoslovakia. Sequences and fragments were restored and pieced together, some of which can now be viewed online at the United States Holocaust Memorial Museum website.[166] An excerpt of the film's description reads:

> Documentary footage depicts the life of Jews in the ghetto of Theresienstadt [Terezin] in Czechoslovakia as harmonious and joyful. They wear yellow stars on their civilian clothing but are euphemistically called residents ["Bewohner"] instead of inmates. They look well-dressed and well-fed and keep smiling. No SS guards or other armed Germans are shown.
>
> Shots include: men and women work contentedly on farm, in factories, making pottery and sculpture, seamstresses and tailors, cobblers, etc. Yellow stars visible on their clothing, but people smile, implying satisfaction. Recreational activities include spectator sports event in an enclosed, porticoed courtyard; concert (various views of attentive, mannered, well-dressed crowds); library; flourishing community garden; children at play; women and men socializing. Final view is family dinner scene.[167]

These authors have viewed this film and can attest that it is unrealistically utopian in nature. The young children sitting on their beds and repeatedly hugging their dolls is clearly staged. The expressions of "focus" on the faces of the men in the forges are underlined with evident fear and misery. Moments when women are laughing and showing each other their prized needlework are unnaturally artificial. Several spots, if the viewer is looking for them, reveal side glances by the nervous Jews who are pretending not to notice the camera pointed at them. Nothing about this film was candid, and yet, to the spectators of the 1940s who had been exposed to only a short history of this fake kind of happiness as portrayed in movies, the Jews were quite at home in "the city the Führer gave them," and the lie was bought, hook, line, and sinker.

It took eleven days to compile the footage for this great hoax. Jewish actor and director Kurt Garron had been promised the right to live in trade for his arranging and shooting the film. Immediately following the close of the project, however, Garron and almost all the cast members—real actors, actresses, musicians, potters, athletes, scholars, doctors, grandmothers, grandfathers, mothers, fathers, husbands, wives, and children—were taken to Auschwitz and gassed upon arrival. Few Jews survived to confirm the inaccuracy and deceptiveness of *Theresienstadt*.

As mentioned, *Theresienstadt* was only *one piece* of the ongoing efforts by Hitler to mask the true terror of the Holocaust.

Because of the limited spread of information at the time, the only reports of war that many homes had access to internationally were radio updates or print media (mostly newspapers). The recently invented television was a luxurious commodity, and with the US suffering from the Great Depression, it wasn't until the 1950s that television became a staple item in American homes, a realistic medium for relaying world news, and a vital part in influencing public opinion. As a result, the radio and print channels until then were highly controlled by the biased powers that be. The public only needed to know what the political authorities of each earthly region deemed necessary.

In America at the time, *details of Jewish extermination were not released.*

The general public was mindful of the fact that war and turmoil festered on foreign territory, and the occasional Jewish refugee was able to pass through the red tape of the complicated American-entry visa process, bringing their heartbreak to the States, but because of the non-existent information highway just discussed, their testimony was limited to those they could reach in person (the Jews could not log online and start blogging about their experience), and surely, these stories were sensational. As far as the gas chambers, death camps, death squads, and rapid obliteration of one specifically peaceful race, the OWI (United States Office of War Information [1942–1945]) had concluded that this information would make Americans believe the war was singularly a Jewish crisis, [168] so our population lived on unaware of the millions who had perished at the hands of Hitler's men. From the Holocaust Encyclopedia at the United States Holocaust Memorial Museum, we read:

In August 1942, the State Department received a report sent by Gerhart Riegner, the Geneva-based representative of the World Jewish Congress (WJC). The report revealed that the Germans were implementing a policy to physically annihilate the Jews of Europe. *Department officials declined to pass on the report to its intended recipient*, American Jewish leader Stephen Wise, who was President of the World Jewish Congress.

Despite the State Department's delay in publicizing the mass murder, that same month Wise received the report via British channels. He sought permission from the State Department to make its contents public. Undersecretary of State Sumner Welles asked Wise *not to publicize the information* until the State Department confirmed it. Wise agreed and after three months the State Department notified him that its sources had confirmation. On November 24, 1942, Wise held a press conference to announce that Nazi Germany was implementing a policy to annihilate the

European Jews. A few weeks later, on December 17, the United States, Great Britain, and ten other Allied governments issued a declaration denouncing Nazi Germany's intention to murder the Jews of Europe. The declaration warned Nazi Germany that it would be held responsible for these crimes.

During the era of the Holocaust, the American press did not always publicize reports of Nazi atrocities in full or with prominent placement. For example, the New York Times, the nation's leading newspaper, generally deemphasized the murder of the Jews in its news coverage.

As the magnitude of anti-Jewish violence increased in 1939–1941, many American newspapers ran descriptions of German shooting operations, first in Poland and later after the invasion of the Soviet Union. *The ethnic identity of the victims was not always made clear.* Some reports described German mass murder operations with the word "extermination." As early as July 2, 1942, the *New York Times* reported on the operations of the killing center in Chelmno, based on sources from the Polish underground. *The article, however, appeared on page six of the newspaper.* Although the *New York Times* covered the December 1942 statement of the Allies condemning the mass murder of European Jews on its front page, it placed coverage of the more specific information released by Wise on page ten, *significantly minimizing its importance.*[169]

Despite the information being muted, the rumors of mass death continued to materialize, and eventually, the news was taken more seriously. By late 1942, word was reaching not only the US, but several other countries that had been largely oblivious to Hitler's depths of malevolence:

• In October of 1942, British radio spread the word to the Netherlands.

- The following December, the United Nations published the "Joint Declaration by Members of the United Nations" describing, and strictly condemning, Hitler's extermination plot.
- Resistance soldier Jan Karski brought reports throughout 1942 to leading politicians within his own Polish government, as well as key leaders in Britain and the US, regarding the devastation of the Warsaw Ghetto and the overall harsh treatment of the Jews in Poland.
- In 1943, Karski informed the celebrated London journalist Arthur Koestler, bringing the information to England.
- That same year, as Karski's momentum was growing, he made a *second* voyage to the US, meeting personally with Supreme Court jurist Felix Frankfurter, Tennessee Secretary of State Cordell Hull, "Father of Central Intelligence" and wartime head of the Office of Strategic Services William J. Donovan, the aforementioned president of the World Jewish Congress Stephen Wise, and US President Franklin D. Roosevelt (this was a turning point for the illumination of the extermination in the West); his attempt to convince numerous others (such as artists in Hollywood and many noteworthy bishops) was fruitless, as his stories were found to be too unbelievable.
- In August 1943, the Office of Strategic Services in London comprised a lengthy report covering gas chambers, sterilization, and Jewish death tolls at Auschwitz based on the information gathered from escapee Witold Pilecki.
- Later that year, news of the gas chambers was published in Dutch resistance underground papers; again, many assumed the stories were merely propaganda, and the circulation ended abruptly.
- In April of 1944, Jewish prisoners Rudolf Vrba and Alfred Wetzler escaped from Auschwitz, writing thirty-two pages of information on the Jewish persecution (known as the Vrba-Wetzler report), and brought it to Slovakian officials; one month later, in May, Arnost Rosin and Czesław Mordowicz escaped from Auschwitz, adding

more details to the report by Vrba and Wetzler (and informing the officials that since Vrba's and Wetzler's escape, one hundred thousand Hungarian Jews had been killed), creating what is now known as the "Auschwitz Protocols" document.

- That summer, *The New York Times* published material from the Vrba-Wetzler report, resulting in an outcry from world leaders to put an immediate stop on the deportation of Jews from Hungary to Auschwitz; an approximate two hundred thousand Hungarian Jews were therefore saved from deportation to the death camps.

Approximately halfway through 1944, all Jewish populations within, or close to, Nazi Germany had been obliterated. It was about this time that the US, as well as parts of the world elsewhere, were becoming less oblivious and more riled to the mistreatment of the Jews, but by then, nearly six million of them had been murdered. As Germany was losing its control of the war, major military efforts were taken to obscure all proof that the death camps, concentration camps, and ghettos had been the places of persecution that the survivors described: gas chambers were torn down, enormous graves holding hundreds and thousands of deceased were excavated and the bodies burned, and crematoria were destroyed. It would not be until after the war's end that the world would know the *whole* truth and the full lengths of Nazi debauchery would be unearthed.

Deliverance

In the closing weeks of the war, lingering Jewish groups were herded by gunmen and driven like cattle from the camps, through the snow, into open freight cars, and then to camps that had not yet been dismantled. If one were to fall during the trek or hesitate for even a moment, he or she was shot, and many did not survive the freezing journey due to low temperatures. These "death marches" consumed the lives of about two hundred and fifty thousand Jews, and it was one of Hitler's final oppressions before his suicide on April 30, 1945.

From July of 1944 through May of 1945, armed troops from Soviet, British, and American militaries advanced upon the last nine major operating concentration and death camps, including Auschwitz. The German guards were captured and lined up for inspection, and the prisoners were given food and water.

The testimonials that materialized after these liberations are terrifying. Soldiers arriving at the camps were blasted by the stench of rotting corpses; thousands upon thousands of bodies were strung out across the grounds and in grave pits; and because many prisoners were lying down waiting to die of starvation, it was nearly impossible to differentiate between the emaciated, unmoving bodies of the living and those who had already died. Within the living was an internal death that witnesses have had a hard time putting into words: a vacancy in their eyes, mechanical wandering, a lack of enthusiasm in responding to their rescuers who attempted to feed their malnourished bodies as they subsequently vomited. Too sick to eat, too weak to drink, and too damaged to believe in hope. Many of the "living" weren't really "alive" anymore, in the view of the testifiers.

Parts of these liberations were filmed, and the footage shows German guards ironically set to the task of digging the mass graves for the burial of all the bodies…a task they carried out with their arrogant heads held high and proud as they mercilessly hurled the skeletally starved remains onto carts for transport, and later into the deep burial pits. Bystanders who had gathered to watch as the liberations commenced are seen in videos weeping, shouting, shaking their fists, and some quietly praying, while others appear to be in complete, dumbfounded disbelief that such malice had been taking place so near where they lived.

As a contrast, between scenes of tragic heartbreak, tears, and anger come scenes of joyous celebration by the Jews who were healthy enough to clap and cheer.

Political commotion and global uproar followed world leaders into an extensive and chaotic aftermath. As the Nuremberg trials and Germany's reparations negotiations were underway, whole nations were in pandemonium over the outrage of the Nazi regime. So much had been hidden and so many cries for help had been ignored, but, finally, the vile wickedness of Hitler's rule was being unveiled. It was a contrariety like nothing else in human history: At the same time the fury rang from the lips of the people now enlightened, praises of gratitude to God and defensive governments rang from the lips of millions of others in thanks that the nightmare was over.

Zion

The word "Zion" (Hebrew: "Jerusalem," from the hill upon which the City of David was built) was a comfort to the Jews long before the Holocaust. Ever since the Jews had been driven from their land by the Romans in the Siege of Jerusalem in AD 70, they had lived dispersed. From that day forward, they had made an effort to return to Jerusalem, but it was not until more recently that their efforts consolidated into an effective energy.

In the 1800s, Jewish voices rang out more proficiently for a return to their mother country. They dreamed of a day when they would travel back to their ancestral Canaan, Palestine, and the Holy Land, revitalize Hebrew as the common language of their people, authenticate national self-governance and independence, and establish ownership of Israel as their homeland, as promised by God to Abraham of the Old Testament: "In the same day the Lord made a covenant with Abram, saying, Unto thy seed have I given this land, from the river of Egypt unto the great river, the river Euphrates" (Genesis 15:18).

In 1896, leading Zionist, author, and political activist Theodor Herzl, an Austro-Hungarian Jew who passed away almost forty years before the death camps were at their highest level of operation, wrote a distinguished book that received much attention: *Der Judenstaat: Versuch einer modernen Lösung der Judenfrage* ("The Jewish State: An Attempt at a Modern Solution of the Jewish Question"). The argument was this: For centuries, Jews have lived in persecution. They have been made to exist under the imposed restrictions of foreign governments; they have been confronted with hostility; they have been robbed of their rights to a peaceful camaraderie amongst neighbors of their own faith and made to live in minority ghettos as a result of economic and social burdens; the wealthiest among them are despised for any temporal luxury they have obtained, either through hard work or inheritance; the destitute among them are left miserable and hungry; those within the middle class must work much harder to gain the same level of confidence and trust in their professions than is freely given to their non-Jewish peers; and their dire circumstances do not appear to be getting better on their own.

Herzl saw a day when the final political liberation of the Jews would benefit the whole world and set a precedent—one of freedom and rights to autonomy—for all races, faiths, and nations. On the final page of his book, Herzl writes:

> Therefore I believe that a wondrous generation of Jews will spring into existence. The Maccabeans will rise again.
>
> Let me repeat once more my opening words: The Jews wish to have a State, and they shall have one.
>
> We shall live at last as free men on our own soil, and die peacefully in our own home.
>
> *The world will be freed by our liberty, enriched by our wealth, magnified by our greatness.*
>
> *And whatever we attempt there to accomplish for our own welfare will react with beneficent force for the good of humanity.*[170]

Herzl's vision inspired many, and he is credited as the founder of the Zionist Organization (later "World Zionist Organization"). The First World Zionist Congress was one among many of Herzl's initiatives, establishing legislative powers for the organization in the concert hall of the Basel Municipal Casino in Basel, Switzerland, 1897. The declarations made at this assembly became known as "the Basel Program" and can be summarized as the following:

> Zionism aims at establishing for the Jewish people a publicly and legally assured home in Palestine. For the attainment of this purpose, the Congress considers the following means serviceable:
>
> 1. The promotion of the settlement of Jewish agriculturists, artisans, and tradesmen in Palestine.
> 2. The federation of all Jews into local or general groups, according to the laws of the various countries.
> 3. The strengthening of the Jewish feeling and consciousness.
> 4. Preparatory steps for the attainment of those governmental grants which are necessary to the achievement of the Zionist purpose.[171]

Over time, an increasing number of Jewish populations adopted these ideals, but the support from non-Jewish powers was sluggish, and in many areas, nonexistent. During the Holocaust, Zionism was a symbol of hope that those who were persecuted latched onto with tenacity, but when the Jews were liberated from the camps, their wishes were magnified to a whole new level, and a piercing and unparalleled harmony resonated among nations across the planet to bring this dream to fruition. By this time, it was no longer a solely Jewish endeavor. The world had heard stomach-turning details about the persecution of this people, and whereas the Jews had previously occupied various countries around the world as a minority, they now had friends in high places as a result of the Holocaust.

Some hold to the notion that because of the activities of Zionist leaders in the late nineteenth century, the establishment of Israel as a nation would likely have occurred on its own despite Hitler's regime. But the most typical reflection from historians suggests that the Holocaust's role in the creation of Israel was imperative. Tomer Kleinman of the University of California Santa Barbara gets straight to the point on this outlook:

> The establishment of the State of Israel would have been possible without the Holocaust due to the Zionist movement, however the reparations from the Holocaust given by West Germany gave Israel the resources necessary to survive.... [T] he Holocaust played an important role in the founding and long term visibility of the State of Israel in three respects: The Holocaust motivated large numbers of immigrants to move to the new country, providing the necessary population; secondly, the Holocaust enabled Israel to pressure Germany into supplying the economic base necessary to build infrastructure and support those immigrants; and finally, the Holocaust swayed world opinion so that the United Nations approved the State of Israel in 1948.[172]

With the Jewish populations ready to uproot the lives that had already been destroyed by Hitler throughout central and eastern Europe and resettle to Israel, the monetary support in place to fund the establishment of the nation, and worldwide political power more graciously focused upon their priorities, it was the perfect time and place for Zionism to reach its pinnacle thrust.

On September 29, 1923, the British Mandate for Palestine (frequently the "Palestine Mandate") came into effect by the authority of the League of Nations, decreeing Britain the legal ruler of Palestine. The mandate was set to expire at midnight on May 14, 1948. As the Jews were freed from the Nazi camps years later throughout 1945, Zionist leaders consolidated and united remaining Jewish groups, leading militant raids against Britain to relinquish control of Palestine. Britain consequently turned the situation over to the now-existing United Nations to handle. In response, the United Nations manifested "Resolution 181(11)," in the interest of separating Palestine into a Jewish and Arab

State (the Arabs were also vying for control over their homeland through their nationalism movement), and providing a means of official withdrawal of the British Mandate for Palestine.

Resolution 181(11) was an attempt to please both the Arabs and the Jews, appealing for a peaceful cohabitation of both states, the security of religious rights, and the protection of both minorities. Most Jewish groups went along with this plan willingly, but the Arabs rejected the partition plan, unwilling to share the territory. A series of skirmishes between the Arabs and the Jews emerged, leading to the 1948 Arab-Israeli Civil War. During these battles, the Jews were, again, the peaceful party (at least in the beginning), usually only resulting to bloodshed upon the Arabs in self-defense. As the heat raged onward, approximately two hundred thousand Arabs and Jews were killed in battles that peppered lands populated by the Jews, which eventually continued upon Palestinian soil, and a blockade was set up around Jerusalem, isolating an estimated one hundred thousand Jews in Jerusalem alone (other Jewish settlements apart from the coastline suffered from this as well).

The morale dropped for Palestinian Arabs and Jews alike; eventually panic settled in the middle-class Arab-Palestine society, and tens of thousands of Arabs fled (the exact number of Arabs who evacuated has been listed from sixty thousand to one hundred thousand, depending on the report) in the first wave of refugees. Military support was promised to the Arab Liberation Army, but the support was never delivered as a result of intervention by the Haganah (a Jewish paramilitary organization). As the Arabs' support dwindled—both by foreign governments as well as armament supplies, which were only obtainable now through black market channels and independent contractors—the first "Iron Lady" Golda Meir (later the fourth prime minister of Israel; the term "Iron Lady" was afterward applied more famously to British Prime Minister Margaret Thatcher) appealed to North America for financial assistance.

By January of 1948, via the efforts of Meir, over twenty-five million dollars had been raised from American sympathizers of the Zionist movement (a number that continued to grow to 129 million by March of 1949). Shortly thereafter, the Haganah became a legitimate army on the offensive in the interest of reopening supply lines to Jerusalem and the surrounding settlements, adding infantry brigades and drafting thousands upon thousands of Jewish men and women to support their cause.

On the morning of April 8, 1948, Palestinian Arab nationalist leader Abd al-Qadir al-Husayni fell in the battle of Al-Qastel (a village just outside Jerusalem). His death resulted in a significant interruption of organized Arab military in the Jerusalem area. More battles and sieges thundered upon the Jews, but the Arabic forces were losing their grip. After the Deir Yassin massacre (executed by radical Zionist groups, not the Haganah), the local press reported a great fear spreading through the Arab Liberation Army, and more of them fled. By this time, the Jews had obtained support from the US, as well as many other nations across the world, and the "Palestinian Arab military power was crushed."[173]

In the midst of this civil war, however, revisions had been made to Resolution 181(11). On May 12 (a little over a month after key Arab military leader al-Husayni was defeated), the *Minhelet HaAm* (Hebrew "People's Administration") assembled to vote on the last remaining issue: to declare independence or agree to a truce. The former was the prevailing vote, one that was endorsed by the then-current chairman of the World Zionist Organization.

Moetzet HaAm (Hebrew: "People's Council") met two days later to hash out the final debates regarding borders, religion, the name of the state, and freedom of language, and finalize the Declaration of Independence document for Israel. The name of the state was voted six to three in favor of "Israel." The borders were not agreed upon, due to the ongoing clash of Arabic culture, and therefore, borders were not specified in the Declaration. Regarding the official faith and religion of the Jewish nation, the words "and placing our trust in the Rock of Israel" became the official lingo of the end of the document, allowing each individual the freedom to perceive said "Rock" as "*God* of Israel" or as the land of Israel, itself, as an independent state. The Hebrew language was agreed upon as the central language of the state, but because of the scattering of Jews throughout foreign lands, provisions were granted allowing freedom of language for the incoming Jewish settlers to be able to still feel at home.

The Declaration ceremony took place on May 14, 1948, at the Tel Aviv Museum (today Independence Hall) only hours after Britain's rule over Palestinian territory expired. In fear that British authorities (or the whispered threat of another Arabic invasion) would prevent it, the ceremony was to be attended by only those two hundred and fifty who had received a hand-delivered invitation by messenger, and all in attendance had been instructed to keep the event a secret. At 4 o'clock in the afternoon, Executive Head of the World Zionist Organization David Ben-Gurion brought down his gavel and a silence fell upon the gathering in the hall. He then began to lead the people spontaneously in the singing of "The Hope" (Hebrew: *Hatikva*, which later became Israel's national anthem) in front of a portrait of Theodor Herzl. The Israeli Declaration of Independence document was then read aloud, followed by the *Shehecheyanu* blessing (a Jewish prayer of blessing used on special occasions) by Rabbi Yehuda Leib Fishman.

After the blessing, the signatories made the document official. Literally overnight, the Palestinian lands transferred from British rule to the hands of the Jews. Israel was now a state, backed by international support (including the US), and the now-established Jewish nation had a homeland. A Zion. The restoration of the Promised Land by God to Abraham.

According to Rabbi Yechiel Eckstein of the Jewish Virtual Library:

> After the Holocaust, we Jews gazed dumbfounded at what had occurred. Was it possible to go on believing in a God of love after losing 6 million individuals, one third of the Jewish people, almost 2 million of whom were children? Was it possible to go on believing in God's covenant with Israel and their election?...
>
> Like Ezekiel before us, we Jews stood amidst the ashes of

[death camps] Auschwitz, Buchenwald, and Treblinka and [when] we looked down in the valley of Sheol we asked, "Can these dry dead bones again live [Ezekiel 37]?" Can we Jews possibly recover from this devastation? And behold, a miracle— God breathed life into those dry bones and they came together, sinew to sinew, bone to bone. They took on flesh and spirit. They arose and were reborn in Jerusalem. "For the Lord has comforted His people, He has redeemed Zion [Isaiah 52:9]."

What does Israel mean to the contemporary Jew? It means that God has not abandoned His people. It means that He is true to His Word! Israel's existence gives us our very will and determination to continue living...as Jews.[174]

The Jews were home.

The Age of Fire

Many adhere to the idea that there is only one earthly place that God has declared "holy," based on the words of the prophet Isaiah (24:23): "Then the moon shall be confounded, and the sun ashamed, when the Lord of hosts shall reign in mount Zion, and in Jerusalem, and before his ancients gloriously." Several other verses equally point to this (Deuteronomy 11:12; 33:13; Ezekiel 20:6). Likewise, the Jews, and Israel, are considered "God's chosen people" by many verse translations (Exodus 19:5; Deuteronomy 14:2; Deuteronomy 26:17–19; 2 Samuel 7:23–24; 1 Kings 8:53; 1 Kings 10:9; 1 Chronicles 17:20–21; Psalm 135:4; Isaiah 41:8; Isaiah 43:1–3; Isaiah 44:21; Jeremiah 31:1–4; Jeremiah 46:27–28; Ezekiel 36:24–28; Ezekiel 37:21–25; Joel 3:1–2; Amos 3:1–2; and Romans 11:1–2). Again from the prophet Isaiah (51:16), we read, "And I have put my words in thy mouth, and I have covered thee in the shadow of mine hand, that I may plant the heavens, and lay the foundations of the earth, and say unto Zion, Thou art my people."

The relevance of understanding Israel as the Holy Land and the Jews as God's chosen people as it relates to the Age of Fire lies in the Parable of the Budding Fig Tree (not to be confused with the Parable of the Barren Fig Tree). This parable appears in three New Testament Gospels locations (Matthew 24:32–35; Mark 13:28–31; Luke 21:29–33): "Now learn a parable of the fig tree; When his branch is yet tender, and putteth forth leaves, ye know that summer is nigh: So likewise ye, when ye shall see all these things, know that it is near, even at the doors. Verily I say unto you, This generation shall not pass, till all these things be fulfilled. Heaven and earth shall pass away, but my words shall not pass away."

The word "it" in Matthew 24:33 has been rendered also "He" or "the Kingdom of God." This passage, along with those that refer to the Holy Land and God's chosen people together, make up the base Scriptures of what has become known as the "Fig Tree Prophecy."

The Fig Tree Prophecy

On the Mount of Olives, the disciples asked Jesus Christ about the end of the world (or "end of the age")—"And as he sat upon the mount of Olives, the disciples came unto him privately, saying, Tell us, when shall these things be? and what shall be the sign of thy coming, and of the end of the world?" (Matthew 24:3). After speaking for a moment about His Second Coming and the threat of the Antichrist, Christ tells His listeners that the first sign of the end of the age would be when the fig tree "putteth forth leaves" (or "buds"). Because the fig tree is the last of the trees to flourish in the springtime, when it puts forth its leaves, it is an indication that "summer is nigh" (or "imminent").

Note that in Hosea 9:10a, Israel is referred to as a fig tree: "I found Israel like grapes in the wilderness; I saw *your fathers as the firstripe in the fig tree* at her first time" (emphasis added). Joel 1:6–7a makes the same comparison: "For *a nation* is come up upon my land, strong, and without number, whose teeth are the teeth of a lion, and he hath the cheek teeth of a great lion. He hath laid my vine waste, and barked *my fig tree*" (emphasis added). In addition to these references, nations have historically been typified by symbols and/or emblems (America: eagle; Russia: bear; Canada: beaver and maple leaf; Britain: lion; and so on), and for Israel, the emblem is a fig tree.

Jesus also spoke the following:

> "I tell you, Nay: but, except ye repent, ye shall all likewise perish." He spake also this parable; "A certain man had a fig tree planted in his vineyard; and he came and sought fruit thereon, and found none. Then said he unto the dresser of his vineyard, Behold, these three years I come seeking fruit on this fig tree, and find none: cut it down; why cumbereth it the ground? And he answering said unto him, Lord, let it alone this year also, till I shall dig about it, and dung it: And if it bear fruit, well: and if not, then after that thou shalt cut it down." (Luke 13:5–9)

In Isaiah 5:7a, the "vineyard" is the property of God, and the "house of Israel" ("For the vineyard of the Lord of hosts *is* the house of Israel"; italics original). At the time Christ spoke the parable above in Luke 13:5–9, He was three years into his public ministry. God's people (the vineyard) needed to "repent" or they would "likewise perish." Also note that Christ explicitly refers to the vineyard owner as "Lord" ("Lord, let it alone this year also"). So, in the parable, the "certain man" who owned the vineyard (God; "Lord") approached the "dresser" (Christ), and told him that for "three years" (Christ's public ministry up to that point), the vineyard owner had tried to find fruit from this fig tree (Israel). Because the tree would not produce fruit, the vineyard owner ordered the dresser to cut it down. (Translation: God told Jesus to cut Israel down.) But the dresser requests that the vineyard owner give the fig tree one more season of growth, during which the dresser will "dig about it" (make the ground around it healthy) and "dung it" (fertilize it). (Translation: Jesus requested more time to bring the nation of Israel to repentance.) If further efforts to see the fig tree produce fruit did not deliver, then the vineyard owner would cut it down.

Then, in AD 70, Israel was cut down by the Romans in the Siege of Jerusalem…

In Ezekiel, it is prophesied:

But ye, O mountains of Israel, ye shall shoot forth your branches [bud], and yield your fruit to my people of Israel; for they are at hand to come. For, behold, I am for you, and I will turn unto you, and ye shall be tilled and sown [made healthy again]: And I will multiply men upon you, all the house of Israel, even all of it: and the cities shall be inhabited, and the wastes shall be builded: And I will multiply upon you man and beast; and they shall increase and bring fruit: and I will settle you after your old estates, and will do better unto you than at your beginnings: and ye shall know that I am the Lord. Yea, I will cause men to walk upon you, even my people Israel; and they shall possess thee, and thou shalt be their inheritance, and thou shalt no more henceforth bereave them of men. (Ezekiel 36:8–12)

And in Amos, we are told of a replanting:

And I will bring again the captivity of my people of Israel, and they shall build the waste cities, and inhabit them; and they shall plant vineyards, and drink the wine thereof; they shall also make gardens, and eat the fruit of them. And *I will plant them upon their land, and they shall no more be pulled up out of their land which I have given them,* saith the Lord thy God. (Amos 9:14–15; emphasis added)

Then, in 1948, Israel was replanted…

We now arrive at an important conclusion: If Christ said the "end of days" was "even at the doors" when the fig tree "putteth forth leaves," and that "this generation shall not pass, till all these things be fulfilled," then the establishment of Israel as a nation marks the last generation before the end of days.

This is the core of the Fig Tree Prophecy.

The amount of time in a single generation is greatly varied from source to source. Some believe it to be forty years, some seventy, some eighty, some a hundred, and still others refer to when the last person within that generation passes away. When Christ told the disciples that "this generation shall not pass," He was telling them that Israel would be cut down before the end of their current generation. A generation in the Bible is typically forty years. If Christ was born in AD 1, as it is traditionally thought, then He would have prophesied the cutting down of the fig tree sometime during His public ministry in AD 30–33. Israel was destroyed in AD 70, about forty years later. Scholars in 1948 then presumed that the last generation would end by 1988: 1948 + 40 = 1988. The '80s birthed a *great* number of date-setter ministers who claimed the world would end, or Christ would return, by the year 1988. And, obviously, they were wrong…

(Note: According to Psalm 90:10, "The days of our years are three-score years and ten, and if by reason of strength they be fourscore years" meaning *seventy or eighty* years, which brings us to the following equations: 1948 + 70 = 2018 and 1948 + 80 = 2028, two or twelve years from the time of this writing. Yet again, the account of Genesis 15:13–16 assigns one hundred years to a generation, when God warns Abraham of the coming slavery of his people: "Know of a surety that thy seed shall be a stranger in a land that is not theirs, and shall serve them; and they shall afflict them *four hundred years*…But *in the fourth generation* they shall come hither again" [emphasis added]. This, of course, leads modern date-setters to assume the last days will arrive on or before 2048. Aside from all this math, in 2 Peter 3:8, we are instructed: "Be not ignorant of this one thing, that one day is with the Lord as a thousand years, and a thousand years as one day," which is why these authors do not subscribe to any particular dating methods. To strengthen this stance: "But of that day and hour knoweth no man, no, not the angels of heaven, but my Father only" [Matthew 24:36].)

When Christendom was shaken by the notion that the world would end, or Christ would return, within forty years of the Israeli Declaration of Independence, preachers rose to alert the world of these "last days" with unadulterated fervor. Thus began the "Age of Fire."

The Prosperity of the '50s

The 1950s was a glorious economical time for the United States. Americans made more money than ever before, purchasing houses, cars, and businesses. Funds left over were given to churches, resulting in the unprecedented raising of new buildings for worship and the remodeling of church grounds in disrepair. In the euphoric conclusion of WWII, love was in the air, and birth rates spiked (more than seventy-eight million Americans were born between 1946 and 1964), ushering in the era known as the "Baby Boom."

While Dwight D. Eisenhower was being sworn into office as the thirty-fourth American president, Jonas Salk was perfecting his polio vaccine, Ian Fleming was releasing his first of many James Bond adventure novels, and Patti Page was inquiring how much was that doggie in the window. Homes were being built luxuriously with extra living quarters called "family rooms"; artistic expression was teeming with promise as the entertainment industries soared into brand-new television sets across the country, shepherding in the "Golden Age of Television"; science and technology reached new heights; agriculture, industry, and manufacturing thrived; the US military drew in tens (and later hundreds) of billions of dollars of financial backing; labor unions climaxed; and the newly formed Council of Economic Advisors raised employment.

Community support and strong families were at the heart of American praying homes, not singularly as a result of worldwide support pouring in for Jews, but strongly affected by it. Fresh on everyone's mind was the concept of banding together as a people to steer the human race farther away from Satan's grip and ever closer to God. Although it wasn't quite the era of blamelessness that the movies, television shows, and radio broadcasts of the time projected, compared to the bloody paw-marks of war that had so recently riled the American psyche, we were a regular poodle-skirt wearing, soda-sipping, doo-wop bopping culture, and when compared to today, we were *innocent*. We may never know exactly who it was that put the *bomp* in the *bompah bompah bomp*, but as to whether our nation was ready to embrace an age of modest virtue on the trails of war, at least socially, that much is clear. Daughters still blushed when holding hands with a boy for the first time, mothers per-fected the skills of being housewives, sons worked hard to achieve higher grades, and fathers were more than happy to bring home the bacon. Churches were brimming with incomparable numbers, and those num-bers would only grow over the course of the decade. According to Gal-lup, an American research-based polls company:

> The most religious era of the past 74 years…was from the mid-to-late 1950s into the early 1960s, when, at some points, almost half of American adults said they had attended religious services in the past seven days. During this era, marked by the high fertility rates and family formation that was the foundation of the baby boomer generation, the percentage who reported that religion was important also reached high points, and almost all Americans identified with a religion.[175]

The gospel had always been available to anyone with ears to hear or eyes to read, and the Great Commission had always played a significant role in America's religious societies since the founding of the country, but when televangelism began to take root in 1951 through minister Fulton Sheen after approximately twenty years of forerunning radio broadcasts, preaching finally landed in the comforts of people's homes *visually*. No longer did men and women nonchalantly tune in to a Bible lesson and then wander through the dining room with coffee in one hand and a paper in the other, only hearing every fourth word of the program as they casually talked over the top of it about their daily schedules. No longer was a human's auditory system the only recipient of the sermon outside the church. One of the human body's most important sensory processors was now involved when the TV flickered on and the man in the suit was dramatically pummeling his pulpit. Now we could not only *hear* the gospel, we could *see* it…as could those who would otherwise never attend a church in person.

It was a whole new way of reaching people for Christ, and it was met with instant and powerful success.

One of the biggest legacies left behind in this new concept of witnessing, which started the great Healing Revival, was by that of televangelist pioneer Oral Roberts. This man's name has been spotted throughout history as a leader of the "Prosperity Gospel," and although he did believe that God wishes His children to be prosperous (based on his concept of 3 John 2), proposing that this was all he brought to the world through his ministry is an uncouth oversimplification. According to Ted Olsen of *Christianity Today*, "The 'faith-healer' (who hated the term) may have done much to mainstream Pentecostalism, but he was no architect of the Prosperity Gospel."[176] It would be wise for one to note, also, that the inclusion of Roberts' story in this book is only marginally to do with him. He is the central character, certainly. However, as he so openly admitted thousands of times in public, and as the masses of people likewise attest, this is a story about the conviction of the *people* and God's intervention through their lives as a result of where individuals stand in their faith, rather than an exposé of one man's charismatic career.

Keep in mind as you read the following pages that we are not relaying his biography because he was a spotless or sinless man who brought only the holiest and most theologically sound doctrine to the world through television, but because his life and works greatly affected one of the most profound Christian revivals of modern history, and inspired a chief swell in Pentecostalism.

The Healing Revival of Oral Roberts

In January of 1917, Oral Roberts was born into a family of five kids (two boys, three girls) to Reverend Ellis Melvin and Claudia Priscilla. Because their main source of income was through the donations offered at Roberts' father's revival meetings, their lives were wracked with poverty. One story is told of how Claudia called her boys to the porch and informed them that they would have nothing to eat that night. They made a visit to a neighbor's house and prayed in gratefulness about how good the Lord has always been to their family (but nothing is said in the story that the prayer had anything to do with the lack of food in their house), and when they arrived back home, the door was wedged shut with a huge box of groceries. Their faith was strong as a unit, and when "Mama" prayed, she did so while "shouting happy."[177]

As a boy, Roberts had a terrible stutter, frequently overwhelming him to the point of complete silence. (It's interesting to note that he has since gone down in history as one of the most important speakers in televangelism.) The bullying from schoolmates escalated to the point that when he was sixteen, Roberts ran away from home. He had told his mother and father he was leaving, and they certainly understood his motive, so they let him go, knowing he had to learn a lesson on his own. While he stayed away in another town for almost a year, he often awoke in the middle of the night with a desperate fever, and blood would expel from his lips when he coughed.

At the age of seventeen, Roberts collapsed during a basketball tournament in the town he had run away to. As he was wheezing and spitting up blood, his coach intervened, helped him to the car, and drove him home (where he lay bedridden for a 163 days after a second collapse weeks later). While too sick to eat, he rapidly dwindled to little more than a pile of bones on a sheet. Eventually, after several examinations, the doctor broke the sad news to Roberts' father: Roberts had tuberculosis in both lungs. Roberts' brother came to see him, throwing himself on the bed and pleading with God to transfer the disease upon him, instead. Roberts pushed him away, and then told his family he refused to ingest medicines that could not guarantee his survival, but would only serve to lengthen his suffering. (His mother's father and sister had both died from tuberculosis, so he had been exposed to whispers of how miserable and deadly the disease was.)

Within one fatal announcement from a doctor, every lifelong aspiration of Roberts died—including the goal of becoming a lawyer and governor of his state—leaving him in a fit of screaming hysterics and tears. Local ministers didn't help. In his autobiography, he relates that one pastor came to pray for him while he was sick, but instead of praying for answers, faith, miracles, or healing, the pastor merely prayed that Roberts would somehow be patient through his anguish.[178] The prognosis was bleak, and patience was equally futile as a medicine for tuberculosis. Roberts goes on to say, "Had I remained patient with tuberculosis, I would either have been in a sanatorium or in my grave today. Patience does not heal tuberculosis."[179]

Religious people told Roberts that *God* had placed this disease upon him, and then tried to convince him that he needed to get right with God—the same God they were claiming had afflicted him. Bitterness set in, and he only became more confused at the notion that there was nothing he could do but accept that God comes to save *and* to afflict. The very thought that people must accept this as reality and serve Him anyway would not settle in Roberts' spirit. But his breakthrough came just after this, through the gentle words of his mother.

Sitting on the edge of the bed, Roberts' mother explained that it was not *God* who had placed this torment upon him, but the devil. When Roberts asked why the devil would have wanted to destroy him so, she answered that it was because her son had been called by the Lord, and it is when one has a great calling on their lives that they are stricken by the enemy who wishes to keep them from fulfilling their purpose for Christ. (Years prior, she had told Roberts that while he was still in the womb, the Lord spoke to her and told her that the baby she was carrying belonged to God, that He had already chosen this boy for His work.) She went on to claim something extremely bold: *If Roberts would accept Jesus Christ into his heart and dedicate his life as a service to God, he would raise up out of his bed and be healed.*

A few days later, when Roberts' sister came with a similar plea saying she believed God wished to heal him, hope soared within him, and he found himself believing it also.

Letters were written from Roberts' father to surrounding prayer warriors in the community. Word reached the "Lindsay saints," friends of Robert's mother and father from the Full Gospel Church in Lindsay, Oklahoma, and they traveled to Roberts home to pray in person, arriving around midnight. Instead of praying with the same forlorn and pitiful expressions that Roberts had seen until that point, they prayed with hope, joy, and in expectation of a miracle.

Roberts was not healed that night...but something else happened. He saw a new form of prayer he had never seen, and his soul was stimulated.

From boyhood, Roberts had been primed for a life in ministry through the prophetic words of his revivalist father, who had said, "Oral, someday you will be a preacher. God will give you the largest meetings of your day. They will be so large others will go before you and prepare the way."[180] Because of his stutter, nobody believed little Roberts would amount to anything, claiming instead that his brother had the gift of words. (Often they unkindly said this right in front of the boy.) How wrong they were...

One night, Reverend Ellis Melvin Roberts dropped everything, including his preaching duties, to get on his knees by his son's bedside, refusing to get back up until young Roberts had surrendered his life to God. From his autobiography, we see the turning point: "I found myself listening to Papa's prayer. Pretty soon I began to feel something going all through me. I looked up and saw his face, and when I did, I guess I must have had a vision, for there just as clear as anything I saw the face of Jesus in Papa's face.... I began to cry. I couldn't help it. My heart was broken into a thousand pieces, and pretty soon I was asking God to save my soul."[181] Roberts prayed then and there, that if God would merely keep him alive, he would give everything to Him from that day forward. Roberts had nothing to give Christ. His stutter would keep him from effectively preaching. His social skills were dreadfully immature. His body was weak, and at any moment, he would start coughing and sputtering blood from his mouth. How, *how on earth*, could anybody like himself be of use to the Man who had come to die on the cross so many years ago? What could he possibly have to offer?

Immediately following Roberts' internal promise to the Lord, something supernatural happened in that room in front of his father, mother, and nurse. Starting at his feet and creeping up his body like a gentle river came the presence of God. When it reached his head, his face began to glow with light. As anyone in his position would do, he quickly got his father's attention and pointed out the strange and curious glow. Then, the fullness of the Lord's mighty presence descended, and Roberts found a thread of strength, sprang up in his bed, stood instantly to his feet, and shouted that his soul had been saved. The tuberculosis still tormented his body, but his *soul* was healed.

Shortly after, a man who had seen healings in a nearby tent revival came for Roberts. Roberts' mother and father did not need to be convinced that this was the Lord's will. On the way to the tent, Roberts listened to the man speaking of all the healings he had seen, and Roberts believed every word of it, *convinced* that God was about to heal him from disease. So strong and solid was his belief that before they arrived, he had already begun wondering what he was going to do with his life in his new body. His thoughts were interrupted by a plainly audible voice calling him from his mattress on the back seat of the man's car. The voice, which Roberts recognized as God's, told him that he *was* going to be healed…*and that he would use that healing power to bless his entire generation of hurting people.* When the voice quieted, Roberts no longer wondered what he was going to do in his new body. The calling was clear. (Those words Roberts heard would repeat themselves in his thoughts over and over for the next twelve years.)

That night, Brother George Moncey, preacher of that revival, gave a sermon, and people gave their hearts to the Lord for the first time. When he passed Roberts on his mattress, he told him God had sent him to this meeting to be healed. Roberts was too weak to walk, so his parents had to carry him to the front of the tent. When Moncey laid his hands on Roberts, he demanded that the tuberculosis come out of the young boy's body in the name of Jesus Christ. His prayer was not a plea, but a *command*. He spoke with authority, and his prayer was only about ten seconds long.[182] Roberts' body began tingling, and a force raided his lungs. The glow rematerialized, and within seconds, Roberts was once again on his feet, racing all over the tent shouting about his healing.

As Roberts tells this story in his own words in the autobiography, he doesn't spend prolonged sections of text drawing out the miracle. He doesn't go to lengths to describe all his feelings, all the peoples' reactions (except to point out that those who knew him immediately began rejoicing and praying), or all the thoughts that no doubt must have been racing in his mind. He gets straight to the point of the healing, as if the book was written by a man who believes so much in the power of God and the reality of healing miracles that no further explanation besides the act itself is necessary.

But another healing happened that night that Roberts did not expect. When Brother Moncey saw that the healing had driven about a thousand people to their feet, and many to their knees, he took hold of Roberts, led him to the microphone, and instructed him to tell the crowds what God had done. Roberts, who scarcely could string two words together in front of people he had known his whole life long before falling into a fits of stammerings, opened his mouth and started to testify. Without a single prevention, his words flowed forth from him as if he had been a public speaker for years. While he spoke, he filled his lungs with air so the people could see that there was no longer a stabbing pain in his chest in doing so. He ran across the platform of the tent so the believers could observe the strength that had so suddenly come into the legs that had been scarcely used for five straight months. The confidence that came over him and the words that flowed so freely now were the testimony given by a young man whose doctor was about to be floored by the following fluoroscopy showing that his lungs were now miraculously in perfect condition.

At his first sermon, two months later, two people gave their hearts to Christ. A collection plate was passed around to support Roberts and a fellow schoolmate who had also come to preach. It was the first offering of his ministry, and by the time it was divided between them, Roberts had acquired eighty-three cents.[183]

Twelve years of local preaching later, Roberts' Bible was casually opened to 3 John 2: "Beloved, I wish above all things that thou mayest prosper and be in health, even as thy soul prospereth." The verse had a paramount effect on him, and he had an epiphany of faith: God did not make people sick. Satan did. According to John 10:10: "The thief cometh not, but for to steal, and to kill, and to destroy: I am come that they might have life, and that they might have it more abundantly." It was the thief, the enemy, who came to hurt. *Christ* had come to give life, restoration, and wellness. In this moment of clarity, all of Roberts' questions were finally answered. In his fresh determination, he sought Scripture like never before, as if he had not poured through the gospels and Acts hundreds of times previously. He began sleepwalking and awakening to find himself crying in various places around his home, and at least on one occasion, his wife had to bring him back to bed. Something was stirring, but he hadn't quite gripped it yet. But when he added fasting to his regimen, clarity dawned yet again. After losing thirty-two pounds over the course of three months, he increased his personal devotional time to four hours per day, in addition to his ministerial duties and homiletic preparations.

About that time, another friend prophesied that Roberts would not be in his little town much longer. There were massive crowds awaiting him, his friend said, and God was preparing him to do great things. The interesting part of this story is that Roberts' friend was not a believer when he prophesied. He had snuck into Roberts' church a few times to hear him preach, and that was all it took for him to be convinced of spiritual things outside his own realm of belief. (This man was saved through one of Roberts' meetings seven months later.)

Then another woman who knew Roberts because of his ties with the local university prophesied that he would be the man who brought new faith among men, that she believed in miracles through faith, and that she would be watching in interest to see what God would do through him.

But until now, Roberts—who had been given the most important prophecy from the mouth of God, Himself, on that mattress in the car so long ago—had felt stifled. What follows is the commencement of what became his intense healing ministry: Falling to his face in his church office, Roberts told God that he had been long seeking for this power God had promised, this power to lead afflicted men and women to healing through faith, and as he lay right there on the floor, he told God he was refusing to get up until God spoke to him. He has never been able to explain how long he spent on the floor of his office because he chose not to look at the clock, nor can he explain the militant voice that came to him after what felt like an eternity seeking. Eventually, however, he heard loud and clear a command that he was to stand up. (Unlike the voice that spoke to him before, Roberts does not tell whether this one was audible.) Then the voice told him to get in his car. Once there, he was instructed to drive down the road one block and then turn to the right. When the instructions stopped, just down the road from his parsonage, he stopped the car and listened. Distinctly, he heard a new directive. From that very hour, he was to heal the sick and cast out demons by the power of the Lord.

The first healing meeting took place within days of that moment. Twelve hundred people attended. Ten minutes into his sermon, that familiar tingling came back and he began to prophecy that before Christ's return, power from the heavens would flow onto men and women, healing the sick, casting out devils, and liberating mankind to the ends of the earth. Halfway through his sermon, Roberts abandoned his sermon notes, and literally jumped off the platform toward his listeners. They followed suit, as if it had been planned, leaping from their chairs and surrounding him. One by one, he laid hands on the sick, and many were healed.

Resigning his post at the local church, Roberts moved to Tulsa, Oklahoma. His preaching took on a decidedly Pentecostal flare. But despite the reputation Pentecostal preachers at that time assisted in developing, it has been reported that "while many of colleagues in healing evangelism were flamboyant in their preaching, Roberts was subdued in his delivery."[184] In an early healing meeting, a man across the street attempted to shoot him, but the bullet missed Roberts' head by inches and tore through the tent. Newspapers across the country exploded in coverage over the mystery shooter who tried to take Roberts' life, but Roberts cared very little. He believed that the shooter was of little importance and continued to preach as if it never happened. However, after Roberts' reaction caught wind in the press, letters came in from all over the nation inviting Roberts' to come and speak about his own healing testimony and pray for the masses. The incoming mail became more than Roberts and his wife could handle alone, and they proceeded to hire assistants to type responses to the letters. They added onto their garage and brought in more help, but before long, their modest home had outgrown the space needed for what was turning into a full-fledged office building, so they moved to a larger house…which quickly became too small as well. It was during this time that Roberts wrote the first of his many books: *Healing Waters*. Between that title and the next one, Roberts saw that his words were reaching many, so he formed *Healing Waters Magazine*, a monthly paper that served to minister as well as advertise his upcoming meetings.

Stories of this "healer" were spreading, both from Roberts' publications as well as the personal testimonies from those who had been healed from blindness, deafness, crippled limbs, and disease, and from those who had been delivered from demons. Upon Roberts' arrival at the locations he had agreed to go, the crowds were larger than the churches or buildings had seating for, and many stood in the aisles and at the back. As a solution for this unsustainable situation, Roberts began piecing together an enormous tent as he could afford it. As he had done every time up until this moment in his ministry, he paid for everything with his own money, borrowing from friends as well as obtaining bank loans. (Later, his ministry would draw in much wealth, but for *years,* every lead he followed was done in faith, even when he couldn't rub two nickels together.) When the throngs continued to increase, "colored folk" were not permitted to enter the tent, so Roberts held additional meetings only for them, so that *all* God's people could be included.

His popularity climbed to the point that he felt the need to remind the congregations that it was not *he* who healed, but God. He was merely the messenger.

By 1950, Roberts was on the road full time, carting that mammoth tent from city to city. When the tent could no longer hold the numbers, it was replaced by another, which seated seven thousand. At the next city, when twenty-two thousand arrived, Roberts knew his latest tent investment was below par, but it was just about the largest mobile building that could be purchased at the time, so people squished together, stood outside, wedged between seats, and crumpled their bodies in tight corners until the end of the meeting.

One miracle witnessed during those early tent revivals had nothing to do with healing. On one evening, lightning ripped across the heavens, winds began to blow, and the electricity shut off. The tent, itself, weighing tens of thousands of pounds, was pulled up from the ground and tossed into the sky. Roberts settled the people quickly and told them not to panic, and the tent gently floated to the ground like a gentle bubble. When the support beams landed, it was between chairs and crowds, instead of upon the men, women, and children who were seated there. Only seconds later, as the storm raged on, the support beams fell. Metal chairs were beaten and twisted, and people had to crawl out from under the canvas of the tent, but amazingly, nobody panicked, and the direction of the beams' descent was between the throngs instead of atop them, as if each piece of the tent had been guided by invisible hands safely to the ground. In the end, not one person among the thousands was seriously hurt. (Only one man suffered a broken bone, but at a follow-up visit to the hospital, he was healed.) When the firemen arrived to scout the tent, they affirmed that nobody was stuck underneath. The news picked up the story, just on the tails of the Hartford circus fire that killed almost two hundred people and seriously injured seven hundred in a similar tent in 1944 (involving the death of the famous Jane Doe, "Little Miss 1565"). The event made national headlines, and even secular papers were calling it a miracle.[185] Following this, the United States Tent and Awning Company based in Chicago agreed to make a bigger, better tent—in fact, they built two: one that seated ten thousand, and another that seated twelve thousand five hundred when the first of the two was outgrown—and Roberts reports that both of them withstood even greater storms than the other, but they weren't fazed by the weather. The largest of Roberts' tents was still far too small for the gatherings that appeared (estimated by local police to be around twenty-five thousand), but they made do.

Other miraculous incidents unrelated to healing occurred during Roberts' many crusades. At times, an exact number of unsaved were placed into his thoughts, and he would announce from the platform that this was their night to respond. When the numbers were later counted, they added up exactly to the numbers that had popped into his mind. On one occasion, Roberts felt led to share that two men and one woman from the congregation were planning their own suicides, but that God wanted to reach them. Without hesitation, three people—two men and one woman—came forward in front of the thousands, admitted their plans of suicide, and then gave their hearts to the Lord.

Throughout Roberts' ministry, he directed more than three hundred crusades on six continents, and it is said that he laid his hands on well over two million people. In 1954, his crusades were televised, and in 1963, he commissioned the Oral Roberts University in Tulsa, Oklahoma. In 1981, he opened the City of Faith Medical and Research

Center, combining medicine and prayer together for the sick. The medical center was only in operation for six years, but it had a major effect on the medical staff, who carried their training to other healing centers across the states.

And it is at this point in the account of Roberts' life that the elephant in the room must be attended to: As the years rolled by, rivals attacked his reputation, and he became known in cynical media rants as the "faith healer." He resented this label, and always referred back to the fact that it was *God* healing the people as a result of their own personal faith, and that he was simply the messenger. Respected ministers across the globe have since defended his sermons as "abundant life teachings," instead of agreeing with the labels "prosperity gospel" or "faith healer." Grant Walker, author of *Heaven Below* had this to say: "Roberts was the most important religious figure in the second half of the 20th Century.... [H]e brought Pentecostalism out of the backwoods and made it respectable. One cannot imagine the modern day Pentecostalism without him. He transformed its image, but also its practice."[186] And as mentioned at the onset of this biographical overview, Ted Olsen of *Christianity Today* said, "The 'faith-healer' (who hated the term) may have done much to mainstream Pentecostalism, but he was no architect of the Prosperity Gospel."[187] Many televangelists followed in Roberts' footsteps, and among that number, many took his teaching to a completely elevated level, declaring that this "abundance" the Lord wants people to have can only come through giving more at every offering and supporting thriving ministries, and then the mailing address and phone number of these televised sermons would be posted on the TV screen. Countless of these ministers were later investigated for money scandals and sex offenses, forever tarnishing Roberts' name by association. Certainly Roberts had played a key role in the development of the Prosperity Gospel (and some of the things he said on air during his fundraisers have drawn controversy), but those who knew him personally say that it was unintentional, and that the Prosperity Gospel took place via the ministries of others who sought to mirror Roberts' ministry model and carry out their own exploitations of believers' pockets. Famous evangelist Billy Graham even said, "Oral Roberts was *a man of God* and a great friend in ministry. I loved him as a brother."[188]

Despite his defenders, though, Roberts was not always the spotless lamb guided by the Shepherd. Like anyone, he made mistakes, and some of them were devastating to his name. There is much evidence that as his fame catapulted, his words became bolder, and in his later years, he made provocative statements on the air. It didn't help that Roberts unabashedly wore nice clothes and jewelry, drove nice cars, and owned large homes—all luxuries that he continued to claim had been given to him from a loving God who wished him to "live abundantly." When one of Roberts' sons came out as gay, then received a court order to receive drug counseling, then committed suicide by shooting himself in 1982, the media had a heyday, and even some of the most conservative news centers sarcastically dragged Roberts' parenting skills (and by extension, his authority as a minister) through the mud.

Scores of biographical accounts today reflect upon Roberts as an individual who started his career in ministry with fervent sincerity, but whose direction took a queer turn as the result of national attention. And they may be right in this seemingly unbiased declaration. Perhaps he *did* turn wayward at one point, embracing celebrity status and riches as his hope for the lost dwindled underneath the constant demand for a posh public appearance. Perhaps he *was* the man who began as David in a field of sheep and retired like a king amongst the giving servants of his will. These are accusations that will follow his name into the future as long as the Lord tarries. (And it is for this reason that we focused this synopsis of his ministry on his earlier years.)

However, nobody can deny that in the beginning, he was radically saved, radically healed, and radical about bringing the gospel of Christ to millions of people. And although these authors would not claim that Roberts' life was in perpetual alignment with God's will, one fact cannot be denied...

It was never about Oral Roberts!

Through Roberts' crusades, millions were touched forever by the hand of God. Millions were healed of their afflictions. And at least hundreds of thousands gave their hearts to the Lord during a period of fiery revival. It was about *the people*. At times, people's focus gets skewed from the message and they look instead to the messenger. But to those crowds who met God at the tents, Roberts was a tool, not the Savior. Through individual belief and faith, lives were touched. Did it happen because *Roberts* was amazing? No. It happened because *God is*. It only goes to show that when man is not perfect, God has a way of using anything, anyone, working in those "mysterious ways" so often referred to, in order to meet mankind at the fallen position in which they stand.

Whether he ended his career the way he began it or not, his mark upon the world of revival is such that his legacy cannot be ignored.

The Evangelism Revival of Billy Graham

While tent meetings were becoming the norm, greatly inspired by Oral Roberts, another rising name in Christendom, whose reputation has remained historically above reproach, was evangelist Billy Graham.

Born in November of 1918 on a humble dairy farm, Grahams younger years were carefree and lighthearted, despite the heavy load of chores. Everywhere he went, he surprised people with his extreme abundance of energy, and he only settled down long enough to immerse himself into the rapturous tales of Robin Hood and Tom Swift. He would hang upside down like a monkey from the branches of trees on his farm, hollering and practicing his "Tarzan yell."[189] Sometimes he was ornery; while disembarking from the school bus, he would slip his hand under the bus and twist the shutoff spigot connected to the gas tank. The bus would travel a short distance away and then the engine would sputter and stop. The bus driver of course found this to be infuriating, but to Graham, it was hilarious, and it "made him a hero to the other kids."[190]

Unlike many families in their area who had not yet taken to owning a radio, the Grahams quickly became riveted by the inpouring of audible news updates. Little Billy loved it, and passed the time away enraptured by the spokesmen on the other end of the relay. (He did, however, find himself frightened at the voice of a strange German speaker by the name of Adolf Hitler.)

Between cow-milking sessions and working the plow, Graham's family once in a while took a shopping trip together or went to the movies. On one special occasion, Graham's father took him to hear a sermon by a great preacher. His name was Billy Sunday, and although Graham would remember being fascinated by the huge crowds of people who had come to hear this man's teaching, he wouldn't grasp the celebrity status of the preacher until years later.

Overall, Graham was an obedient child. Prayer and Bible study were part of a daily regimen of his household, and his parents were attentive and caring. Their disciplines were consistent, and sometimes tough, but Graham knew he was loved, and when given the opportunity to disrespect his parents in any way, he almost always chose instead to show them love in return for theirs.

In 1934, when he was sixteen, Graham was one among thousands attending a revival meeting led by Baptist evangelist Mordecai Ham. Although he could not later recall all of what was said, he remembered being "spellbound" by Ham that night, and when he returned home, he retreated to his bedroom in thought, staring out the window at length.[191] Continuing to go to these meetings day after day, a deep conviction gripped his heart. Graham had been to church every time the doors were open since birth, but something now tore at his conscience with intensity. No matter how many times he justified himself in his head, no matter who in his community reassured him that he was an upstanding young man, a tugging at his heartstrings to make his life right with God would not disappear. He realized after much reflection that although he had always parroted moral behavior and attended church regularly, he had not yet personally given his heart to Christ as an individual decision. Growing up in a Christian and God-fearing home did not save a person's soul. At the next meeting, he responded to the invitation to accept Christ as his personal Savior. Nothing miraculous happened, and externally, he felt no different, but Graham believed his heart was sincere that night, and the event brought him peace.

In the following years, Graham sought any opportunity he could find to tell those he came into contact with about Christ.

After graduating from high school in 1936, he attended Bob Jones College in Cleveland, Tennessee, but at his parents' urging, he transferred to the Florida Bible Institute the next semester in 1937. The educational programs there encouraged the students to go and preach in their local arenas—whether or not they planned to go into the ministry. Graham did so, and before long, he was telling the residents of neighboring trailer parks about Christ. The following Easter, he was put on the spot by an associate when his name was suggested as a person to preach in the local Baptist church. He studied all night long and practiced his words allowed, but when it was time to take the pulpit, he rushed through four sermons in eight minutes, and then returned to his seat.[192]

Believing that he had a calling on his life—though he didn't know what that was—Graham continued to practice his preaching in solitude when he wasn't sharing the gospel with the residents of trailer parks. Eventually, he took his passions to the streets in Tampa, Florida, a short distance from his college. His theology was evangelical from the beginning (and later, his boisterous vocal intonations and rhythmic sermon delivery would set the pattern that many Pentecostal preachers would follow). One day in 1938, he prostrated himself and wept, telling the Lord that he was willing to surrender his life in service to Him. Despite his nervousness and lack of experience, he knew in his heart that he had been called to preach, and to that end he applied himself from that day forward. Early in 1939, he was ordained as a Southern Baptist preacher by the authority of the St. John's River Association, and later that year, he held his first two-week evangelism meeting at the Baptist church in Welaka.

In 1940, Graham graduated from Bible college, and he continued his education at Wheaton College in Illinois, graduating with a degree in anthropology in 1943. In August of that year, he married fellow Wheaton College student Ruth Bell (to whom he would be married for the next sixty-four years). The newlyweds settled in Western Springs, twenty miles outside of Wheaton, where Graham pastored the First Baptist Church (later renamed to the Village Church, by Graham's suggestion, in order to appeal to non-Baptist believers in his area). As he gained experience on the platform, his confidence grew. He spoke of the Holy Spirit's role in communicating to believers and adhering to a lifestyle of upright behavior, and above all else, he preached that Christ came to die to save sinners from eternal damnation. From early on, many of Graham's sentences began with, "The Bible says…".

Within months of this transition to pastoring the Village Church, a man named Torrey Johnson approached Graham with an opportunity: Johnson's radio show, *Songs in the Night*, had fallen on hard times financially, and he was already so busy with ministerial demands at his church that he needed to let go of the broadcast. Graham, Johnson said, was the man he felt led to offer it to. Both men had heard of the other, and each was familiar with the other's ministry. It would cost a $150 per week to keep the program on the air, which meant that if Graham decided to keep the show running, he would need support from his local church. Graham responded that he needed some time to think about his decision, and he took the idea to his wife and the church board. After pulling a few strings and hiring a well-known radio announcer to help direct, Graham took over *Songs in the Night*. His church grew as a result, and people began attending the Village Church to see the fresh-faced radio personality as the recordings were happening during services. Mail poured in from throughout the Midwest, and offerings were sent to help support the show.

Although he would only run this program for about one year, it was enough time for Graham to get a feel for broadcasting, as well as to introduce him to the limitless possibilities that awaited him should he continue to bring his preaching outside of the church and into the media. It was a brand-new idea, but fascinated as he had been since a child with the radio, it felt natural for him to open his mind to such an outlet. There was no way he could have known during that year what he would become as a result of such a short stint on the air. And while Graham was sharpening his skills to embrace the man he would later become, people from all over the territory were inviting him to speak at special events.

Feeling the need to help support the troops during WWII, Graham enlisted in the Army and was appointed as a second lieutenant. His intention was to serve as a chaplain, but before he was able to complete the seminary chaplaincy course, he was struck with the mumps and was discharged after being bedridden for six weeks straight. (The war was almost over by this time.) When he had recovered, he heard once again from his friend, Torrey Johnson. As a result of that conversation, he resigned his pastoral post at the Village Church and became a full-time evangelist for Youth for Christ (YFC). Immediately, with Graham's organizational assistance, his congregations through YFC grew into multitudes, and the program soon became active in three hundred cities.[193] In 1946, YFC expanded into Europe, where Graham preached in front of huge crowds at least three times per day. The war was ending, and people responded dramatically to Graham's good-news gospel of Christ.

Before long, Dr. W. B. Riley, president of Northwestern Bible College in Minneapolis, sent an invitation for Graham to speak at his school in 1947. Graham agreed, but when he got there, Riley pulled him aside and informed him that he wanted Graham to be the succeeding president over the entire college. Graham was floored, and he didn't feel that collegiate administration was his calling, since he believed the Lord wanted him to be an evangelist for YFC. Riley explained that he was getting old, and wanted someone much younger to take his place. Graham humbly protested, but Riley persisted and eventually wore Graham down. Graham agreed to serve as president—but only on a temporary basis until another permanent head could be stationed. When Riley died eight weeks later, Graham, age thirty, assumed his chair, becoming the country's youngest college president in United States history. Graham served in this position for four years, intermittently holding evangelistic meetings whenever he could.

While away at one campaign, Graham met with fellow leaders to discuss proper ministerial practice. Money was one of the central items on the docket. Graham and his associates didn't feel right about playing on the emotions of those present at the meetings, so they agreed that though they would allow a collection plate to be passed around at offering time, they would rely heavily on support from local committees as they traveled. (This is one of many ways in which Graham's ministry differed from other revival personalities at the time. Even as early as the late 1940s, because of the lack of accountability for funds given at a tent meeting or rally, ministers could manipulate crowds into giving huge offerings—and no church board would be present to report what was given. Through Graham's system of securing financial backing via local committees, as well as establishing colleagues to collectively report each offering, he had established an accountability pattern that set the precedent for the rest of his ministry.)

During this time, while Graham was preparing for a tent revival in Los Angeles, California, he faced a serious internal struggle about whether to view the Bible as the whole, infallible, and inspired written Word of God. Through the assistance of Henrietta Mears, who hailed from the First Presbyterian Church in Hollywood, Graham found peace in believing the authority of the Bible. (From that day forward, his ministry and preaching would be greatly strengthened as a result.) The messages that came from Graham in the days ahead were more inspired than they had ever been, and the timing couldn't have been better, because God was about to do some pretty big things.

At the tent, Graham was introduced to some renowned Hollywood actors, actresses, and radio hosts. One of these, the illustrious "singing cowboy" Stuart Hamblen—known for his honky-tonk musical career, many successful radio shows along the West Coast, and his acting roles as the villain in several Western films opposite Gene Autry, John Wayne, Roy Rogers, Wild Bill Elliott, and Bob Steele—listened to

Graham's message with particular concern. Hamblen had been on a path of destruction involving alcohol and gambling for some time before his wife encouraged him to get help. When she had heard that evangelist Billy Graham was going to hold a revival near their home, she appealed to Hamblen to attend. When the meeting ended, Hamblen approached Graham and asked him to come on his radio show. Graham agreed. On the air, Hamblen openly advertised Graham's campaign, announcing that Hamblen, himself, would be there. Prior to the next meeting, the phone rang in Graham's room. It was Hamblen, and he was choking back tears on his end of the line. Graham agreed to meet with him immediately, and that very morning, Hamblen gave his heart to the Lord. From the *Texas State Historical Association*, we read:

> Hamblen's wild, boozing lifestyle might have gone indefinitely had his wife not introduced him to the young evangelist Billy Graham. She persuaded him to attend Graham's path-breaking tent revival campaign.... The next day Hamblen gave his testimony over the radio and declared that he was "hitting the sawdust trail." That public testimony allegedly influenced William Randolph Hearst's decision to order his newspaper chain to "puff Graham." [Hearst was the chief publisher of America's largest and most influential newspaper chain, known for its overwhelming impact on American journalism.] True to his word, Hamblen swore off alcohol and tobacco, sold his racehorses, and dedicated his life to Christ.[194]

(Later, Hamblen went on to host *The Cowboy Church of the Air* until 1952. He subsequently wrote and released many enormously famous Christian country songs, including: "This Ole' House," "This Ship of Mine," "Until Then," "It Is No Secret What God Can Do," "His Hands," and "Open Up Your Heart [and Let the Sunshine In]." For twenty years after his conversion, Hamblen and his wife hosted a television program, traveled the country to visit prisoners, and supported the Billy Graham Evangelistic Association, even making appearances in Graham's future crusades.)

Graham and his crew decided to extend their time in Los Angeles, as it appeared that God was opening doors there. When Graham arrived back at the tent the day after leading Hamblen to Christ, the atmosphere was *buzzing* with attention… Everywhere he looked, cameras were snapping photos and reporters were gathering information for their upcoming articles. When Graham asked a reporter what was going on, the response was, "You've just been kissed by William Randolph Hearst."[195] This meeting became Graham's first one televised, and by the end of the week, both major Los Angeles newspapers ran a story on Graham's revival. Those articles were shortly followed by coverage in Hearst's other papers in major cities across the US. Soon, *TIME Magazine* followed suit.

The tent was packed to the brim for the rest of that crusade, and other famous names were added to the salvation toll (including mobster Mickey Cohen's wiretapper Jim Vaus, former Olympian and prisoner of war Louis Zamperini, and actor Harvey Fritts). Four hundred and fifty ministers sat on the platform behind Graham, ready to assist the flocks of new converts when the invitation to accept Christ was given. The numbers of listeners grew so large by the end of the meetings that hundreds of people who had traveled to hear Graham speak ended up leaving because they couldn't get close enough to hear, even though Graham's voice was amplified through a microphone. By the close of the final meeting, Graham had preached sixty-five sermons to a full tent, and additional hundreds of messages to smaller groups.

Because of this one crusade alone, which has come to be known as the Los Angeles Crusade of 1949, evangelicalism became a prominent force in US culture, and from that day on, Graham was a national figure.

Graham went on to direct more than four hundred crusades in almost two hundred countries by the year 2005. At each one, he invited everyone who wanted to receive Christ as their Savior to the altar for prayer, where he often proceeded to provide them with free Bible study materials. According to an article in *TIME Magazine*, one of Graham's meetings in Moscow drew a crowd of 155,000 people, one-fourth of whom came forward at the closing.[196] As reported by *Christianity Today*, his crusade in Korea in 1973 collectively gathered 3.2 million people, *one million of whom came on the final day*.[197] Michael G. Long, author of *The Legacy of Billy Graham: Critical Reflections on America's Greatest Evangelist*, reported that through both personal encounters as well as his televangelism, Graham has reached 210 million people.[198] (Note: One individual who came to know the Lord through a televised Billy Graham crusade was Nita Horn, the wife of Thomas Horn, one of the authors of this book, back in the mid-1970s.)

Nobody with any clout has ever accused Billy Graham of being a prosperity preacher. Once, NBC even offered him a million dollars to do a show with Arthur Godfrey, but he kindly rejected the offer, deciding instead to pursue his crusades.

He was also known for his activism in racial integration. In 1953, during a rally in Tennessee, he tore down the ropes that divided the groups into racial clusters, and later in 1957, he preached alongside Martin Luther King Jr. in front of more than two million people (collectively) at Madison Square Garden, Times Square, and Yankee Stadium.

Since its establishment in 1950, the Billy Graham Evangelistic Association (BGEA) has risen to increasing distinction. At the time of this writing, Graham is still alive (he is ninety-seven years of age and suffers from Parkinson's disease); although he has retired from full-time ministry, the BGEA still organizes crusades in style similar to those he initiated. Numerous important ministries have come out of the BGEA, including the radio show *Hour of Decision*, the magazine *Decision*, a film production company called *World Wide Pictures*, and a youth training program called "Dare to Be a Daniel." In 2007, the Billy Graham Library became the headquarters for the BGEA, and the opening ceremony featured attendance by former US presidents Bill Clinton, Jimmy Carter, and George H. W. Bush. Over the years, Graham has written more than thirty books, most of which were best sellers, and some of which sold above one million copies within a few months of their release.

Unlike that of Oral Roberts, Billy Graham's reputation has remained nearly spotless throughout the years, and his motives as a whole have remained unquestioned. Although his beginning followed the tent revival trends set by ministers like Roberts, when he began televising after the Los Angeles Crusade of 1949, his popularity soared beyond that of any other televangelist, breaking viewing records and setting the standards high. Today he stands as one of the most pronounced modern evangelical Christian trendsetters in the history of the world, and though statistical reports have tried to assign numbers, only the kingdom of heaven can possibly know the number of souls that have ascended upwards after death as a result of his dedication.

Pentecostal Healer Kathryn Kuhlman

No study on the Age of Fire would be considered complete without covering the infamous healer Kathryn Kuhlman. Throughout the years, her ministry has been considered one of the most widely controversial. This bias is affected by several factors: 1) in an era when women were expected to sit quietly in church, dress humbly, and leave all theological interpretations to the men, Kuhlman spoke confidently on the platform, dressed in flowing gowns and high heels, and interpreted Scripture by her own theology; 2) during a time when Pentecostalism was becoming prevalent but was still hotly debated by more spiritually conservative Christian doctrines, Kuhlman, without shame or remorse, stood strong in her professions regarding the Holy Spirit, speaking in tongues, and healing (which may have come across less brazen from a man as well); 3) some of the healings attributed to her ministry were later investigated by a medical doctor who reported that the healings were not only false in the cases he followed up on, but one death was even a result of one women who *thought* she had been healed but wasn't (note, however, that the reliability of this investigation has been disputed; more on this later);

and 4) Kuhlman's name was brought into scandal when her personal administrator, Paul Bartholomew, sued her for breach of contract and alerted the world to the millions of dollars' worth of art and jewelry in her possession.

But before we chalk up Kuhlman's existence to the value given by a dirty laundry list, one must understand that there is another side to *this* story...

Born in the spring of 1907 to Emma and Joseph Kuhlman, Kathryn Kuhlman had a very close relationship with her father, whom she simply called "Papa." With her mother Emma, a Bible teacher, according to Kuhlman, no such relationship existed. Through Kuhlman's sermons, we glean that Emma disciplined Kuhlman so harshly that she had to take her daughter to the basement so the neighbors wouldn't hear the child scream. "Never once" did Kuhlman's mother show her any warmth or build her up, but when her papa arrived on the scene, she would run to him and jump into his arms, and "he would take away all the pain."[199] (Later, Emma would hug her daughter for the first time after one of Kuhlman's healing meetings.[200]) Joseph and Emma attended separate churches (though it is reported that Joseph's attendance was infrequent), and eventually, after finding a mounting number of excuses to be away from the home, Joseph prepared a room in his boarding stable where he would sleep overnight.

To find solace after being shaped by instability, from her earliest days Kuhlman studied the Word of God, believing wholeheartedly in the Holy Spirit and His ability to communicate on a personal level with believers. At fourteen, Kuhlman accepted Christ, and at sixteen, she moved away from home to live with her sister, Myrtle, who led an evangelistic tent ministry together with her husband, Everett. Everett and Myrtle were dedicated to their mission, but within the privacy of their own home, their marriage was under constant strain. As a result, by 1928, Everett took his tent and left for South Dakota, leaving Myrtle and Kuhlman behind. The two girls decided to carry on their own meetings, and Kuhlman began teaching at the Women's Club in Boise, Idaho, where she preached her first sermon to a congregation of ladies. Only weeks later, when funds for the meetings grew thin, Myrtle rejoined her husband, and Kuhlman went on to teach women for a short time in a modest mission hall before moving on to Twin Falls, Idaho. Around this time, she was ordained as a Baptist minister by the Evangelical Church Alliance.

The drive to preach to anyone who would hear her became so intense that, after breaking her leg in a winter tumble, she went against doctors' orders by standing to tell others of Christ and the Holy Spirit. On another occasion, she stayed outside in a turkey barn when there was no other available housing, just so she could remain on track with her ministry. In sermons years later, she told of many other freezing nights she spent in unheated guest lodging, determined that no force on earth would deter her from carrying out her calling.

Kuhlman's life in the following years held many remarkable moments when she professed unshakable faith in seemingly insurmountable obstacles: She was a *woman* minister, and that was all but unthinkable at the time; she had no formal theological training (her last year of public education had been the tenth grade); and times were desolate, as the Great Depression was at its peak. In her favor, however, was the spiritual hunger of countless numbers of Americans who fell to their knees in desperation before God, willing during their starvation to attend any church meetings they could find to receive hope. Some were even willing to overlook the fact that the message they were hearing came from not only a female, but a *young* female.

From 1933–1935, when Kuhlman was still in her twenties, she hired a business manager and moved her ministry to Pueblo, Colorado. After securing an old Montgomery Ward warehouse, she proceeded to hold meetings there, and these were later broadcast on a small radio station. Shortly after moving several more times, her ministry managed to gain a paper company warehouse in the larger city of Denver. Her gatherings grew rapidly, requiring yet another move to an old truck garage building, and then the numbers of attendees soared into the thousands during any given meeting. What had started as a string of sermons became a fully established church, with Kuhlman as the pastoral figure (she was never officially stationed as a "pastor" in any office, but was almost always fulfilling the duties of the position). Nothing interrupted her determination to preach, except for the death of the beloved Papa in a car accident just after Christmas Day in 1934. When she traveled home to say goodbye to him at his funeral, she felt devastated and angry...until she laid her hand on his shoulder as he lay in the casket. Upon contact with his clothing, she realized what she was touching wasn't her dad, but merely a fleshly image of him. The man on the inside was gone. She described later that this was the moment when the true power of Christ came upon her. She was able to let her father go, release her anger, and realize that Papa was more alive at that moment than ever before. He was just in another place.

Dealing with the death of her father was difficult. Kuhlman continued to minister, but her Papa was ever at the forefront of her mind. It is unclear when Kuhlman met the bad-news evangelist Burroughs A. Waltrip, as some alleged witnesses say they spotted the pair hugging as early as 1935, but in 1937, Waltrip convinced Kuhlman that his wife had left him, giving Kuhlman what she believed to be biblical grounds to marry him when he proposed. It wasn't until later that she discovered he had left his wife and two sons (likely to shed his burdens and woo Kuhlman as a single man). They married in 1938, against the sound advice of their peers, and, together, the two carried on a ministry that Waltrip had launched called the Radio Chapel. Immediately, Kuhlman regretted her decision to marry, confiding in her friends that it had been a huge mistake. However, she stood by her choice, and in the coming months—between the difficulties of keeping up with her own church and trying to apply herself to her new husband's ministry (were geographically far apart), and because of those who no longer took her seriously because of her marriage to a divorced man—her church fizzled, and she lost her congregation. Waltrip's Radio Church fell under financial disaster because of the scandalous relationship, and it, too, ended abruptly.

The ministry Kuhlman had worked so hard to get off the ground was over.

The following years of Kuhlman's marriage are described by vividly different biographical accounts—most all of which were based on hearsay. What we *do* know is that Waltrip and Kuhlman began traveling as an evangelist couple, but when it was discovered that Waltrip had left his wife and sons for another woman, and that the woman had agreed to an "immoral" matrimony with him, the couple was cordially *uninvited* to speak at most places along the Midwest. In 1944, after Kuhlman had spoken for a while under her maiden name, she left her husband and traveled the East Coast as an evangelist on her own. Whether her leaving him was an intentional marital separation or she had planned to come back to him, nobody knows for sure. One divorce had already done so much damage in her life (the divorce between Waltrip and his wife), and the act was seen as such a sin, that it stands to reason she *had* intended to leave him, but wanted to stay married to avoid controversy. (As history will tell, she never returned, and the couple divorced in 1947. She never saw him again.)

In 1946, Kuhlman landed in Franklin, Pennsylvania, where she was welcomed by a moderate crowd of people at a church she had been invited to. Her arrival there was a fresh start, and her reputation as the woman who married the wife-and-son-abandoner didn't seem to be much of an issue. Quickly, her messages were featured on radio programs all across Oil City, and her ministry appeared to be undergoing the earliest phases of repair. She traveled around the area speaking wherever she was welcomed, and when she was invited to hold meetings at evangelist Billy Sunday's old church—the Gospel Tabernacle in Franklin, seating fifteen hundred people—she readily agreed. This was the turning point of her healing ministry.

In the meantime, the world was hearing about a great traveling evangelist by the name of Oral Roberts. He was producing so many miracles that the country had begun to believe in these revival meetings as a natural go-to for anyone with afflictions…and then there was *Kuhlman,* not only believing in faith healing as well, but speaking in such a gentle, soothing voice over the air that she captivated her listeners in a way the more dominating male evangelists could not. The loud and command-ing male evangelists were intimidating and convicting, which had a time and place, for certain. But with the Great Depression and the country involved in the war, "gentle" and "soothing" was what many were drawn to. (Note that there were certainly moments of flamboyancy in Kuhl-man's services, but those do not define her typical personality.)

And it wasn't just her tone. Kuhlman detested the idea that people be told they were not healed "because their faith wasn't strong enough," and all around her, in the world of revival, those words were being bestowed inappropriately. To her, that phrase placed the power of healing in one's own ability to analyze the depths of his or her closeness with God to the point that any miracle observed was a matter of one's own manifestation. Over time, this one simple stipulation of faith was separating the believ-ers of God into groups: the elitists on one end, touched by God because *their* commitment was stronger—and the simpleminded, fickle on the other end, rejected by God until they got their hearts in the right place. It limited God to assume that He was unable to reach them because of their own spiritual immaturity. This took away from the glory that should have been God's through the very graceful nature of His heal-ing will. Sure, faith was most definitely a part of it. But when Kuhlman attended another evangelist's tent meeting and saw with her own eyes the number of people who sought healing and left still broken, her heart was broken right alongside them. When her approach to faith as a mat-ter of importance, but not as a dictator of God's power, was brought to the air and to her crowds, the blind, deaf, mute, crippled, and diseased were given a second wind of hope. Healing was available to *all*.[201]

In 1947, Kuhlman's Gospel Tabernacle meetings quickly became centered on the Holy Spirit and all He was capable of, including the healing of the human body. She did not reach out her hands and touch anyone at first. In fact, the first reported healing came from a small woman who, the night before, had been listening to Kuhlman's sermon from her seat. At the moment, Kuhlman was speaking not of healing, but of resurrection power, and the woman "felt the power of God flow through [her] body."[202] She knew at that moment she had been healed of her tumor, and when she visited her doctor the following day, he confirmed it.

Without the laying on of hands…

From that day forward, Kuhlman believed that all the ritualistic performances in healing tents were manmade. She rarely touched anyone, unless she was specifically asked. The second miracle came shortly after the lady with the tumor when, a week later, a WWI veteran recovered his sight. Another came soon after that, and then another. Before long, throngs of people crowded Kuhlman's meetings, and miraculous healings were reported all over the region—all without a healing line or personal touching, and most without other physical manifestations of the Holy Spirit that were occurring elsewhere at the time. It has been said that sometimes in a moment of pure silence (when there was no singing, preaching, praying, etc.), a metallic shuffling sound would break out all across the building, and when people began to look about to see the source of the noise, they would discover to their amazement that men and women everywhere were standing from their wheelchairs. For the next couple of years, this would be a regularity, and Kuhlman's ministry, although similar to those conducted by men, held its own flavor for those who sought love and acceptance instead of scolding.

When the board of trustees at the Gospel Tabernacle got into an argument with Kuhlman over receiving a percentage of the proceeds of her ministries (including funds that came from sources outside the tabernacle), Kuhlman was locked out of the building. Although her meetings there continued for a time after her zealous followers broke the padlocks off the doors, she knew the situation was unsustainable. She took her ministry to a larger location, and the healing carried on. After establishing Faith Chapel in Sugar Creek, Kuhlman's friends, associates, and devotees of her ministry pressed her to move to Pittsburgh. Feeling so dedicated to those in Sugar Creek who had embraced her when the rest of the world still held on to issues regarding her marriage to Waltrip, she made the comment: "The roof on Faith Temple in Sugar Creek will have to fall in before I'll move to Pittsburgh."[203] She had no way of knowing this statement would provoke the intervention of divine authority. On Thanksgiving Day in 1950, the roof on Faith Temple in Sugar Creek fell beneath the weight of a dense snowfall.

Weeks later, Kuhlman moved her preaching to an ideal location in Pittsburgh: Carnegie Hall. By this time, her radio broadcasts had drawn hundreds of thousands of listeners, and Carnegie Hall rendered immediate gatherings that were packed from wall to wall and down the aisles. For twenty-one years, Kuhlman remained in Carnegie Hall. She never took to the idea of televangelism, and very few of her services were filmed (although many pictures were taken). However, she did go on to appear on countless television shows outside her regular teachings (including her own, called "I Believe in Miracles"), and her radio audience continued to grow. She traveled to choice locations over the years, and was met with massive crowds and performed numerous healings. The Kathryn Kuhlman Foundation in later years made incredible donations, including building chapels around the world and paying for hundreds of wheelchairs to be sent to veterans of the Vietnam War. Between meetings, she wrote volumes of books on the subject of miracles and closeness with the Holy Spirit. Far more unbiased toward doctrinal division than other ministers of her time, eventually people from other faiths were drawn to her Pentecostalism as well, including Baptists and Catholics, and her broad smile paved the way for interdenominational harmony. In her later years, after she developed a heart condition, her body tired of the constant ministerial obligations, but she plodded onward without ceasing until her death in 1976. (Throughout her entire ministry, Kulhman publicly denounced the title of "faith healer," a label that haunted her in the press. She never once failed to attribute any miracles that occurred during her appearances to the power of Christ and the Holy Spirit.)

On November 8, 1975, the *Pittsburgh Gazette* ran a story regarding the investigation of one medical doctor, William Nolen, who claimed

Kuhlman was a fake. He believed that Kuhlman's intentions were worthy, but that her knowledge of the human body and nervous system was insufficient to accomplish the healings associated with her services. (Dr. Nolen's concerns were understandable, considering his profession.) To substantiate his suspicions, he gathered a short list of names of those who had claimed to have been healed during one of her meetings. He then followed to discover unflattering subsequent testimonies. For example, one woman who had cancer in her spine had thrown "off her brace and followed Kathryn's joyful command to run across the stage" during the meeting. But, the next day, "her vertebrae collapsed. Four months later, she was dead."[204] (Others from that meeting also shared that although they believed they had been healed while in Kuhlman's presence, their medical reports showed they had not been.) The media jumped on the story of the woman who had passed away as a result of believing in divine healing, Kuhlman was inundated with calls from journalists and television news reporters seeking a response, and the event triggered an explosion of doubt that surrounded Kuhlman's ministry. Yet, the press had much less interest in perpetuating the legitimacy of Nolen's investigation than in reporting the dirt on Kuhlman. The following short list summarizes why, in modern reflection, Nolen's report was biased and sketchy at best:

- Nolen only used a list of attendees from *one* of Kuhlman's meetings, and he *only* reported about those who had unflattering things to say. He did not relay the testimonies of those whose healings had been confirmed. (By the time his findings were released, nearly three million people across the nation had claimed to be healed, including through Kuhlman's television and radio programs—so, reflecting on less than thirty people from one single meeting hardly seems fair.)
- Following Nolen's report, many medical colleagues launched their own investigations that proved many of the healings had been confirmed. In one televised debate on *The Mike Douglas Show* in

1975, heart specialist H. Richard Casdorph, MD, PhD, brought a young girl to meet with Nolen in person. She had been healed of her bone cancer through Kuhlman's meeting at the Shrine Auditorium, and she and her mother "had x-rays and medical records to verify it."[205] (Casdorph later wrote a book called *The Miracles*, in which he showed numerous other Kuhlman-related healings to be real based on medical proof.)

- After his findings were challenged, Nolen, himself, determined that there may be some truth to the healing. From *Daughter of Destiny: The Only Authorized Biography [of] Kathryn Kuhlman* : "Even Dr. Nolen admitted when he attended that one miracle service in Minneapolis, he was almost persuaded (as King Agrippa was before the apostle Paul) to believe."[206]

Nolen is also at the center of a tragic misinterpretation of supernatural occurrences. Instead of saying that attendees of Kuhlman's meetings had been "slain in the Spirit" (which was not a priority for Kuhlman, but it happened nevertheless), he likened the experiences to hypnotism. The media again curled their fingers around such statements and blared rumors across the nation that Kuhlman fancied herself a clairvoyant hypnotist.

The number of those who would use Nolen's words to bring damage to Kuhlman far outweighed the number of those who were interested in unbiased truth and objectivity. And because one woman wasn't healed as she thought she had been, dying later as a result, the response on everyone's lips for years was, "No, Kathryn Kuhlman's a fraud! Didn't you hear about that lady who died because she ran across the stage at Kuhlman's meeting? That lady might still be alive if it weren't for that faith healer." Whereas statements like that might have been true in the spinal cancer case, that single woman's individual relationship with God and faith in her own healing would have had, as Kuhlman always said, more to do with her own miracle than Kuhlman did—and it's anyone's guess as to where that woman was with God the night she threw her brace aside.

Just after this scandalous uproar came another. Kuhlman's personal administrator, Paul Bartholomew, sued Kuhlman for breach of contract. The matter was settled out of court and later resolved. Because Bartholomew was disgruntled, he openly talked about Kuhlman's millions of dollars' worth of art and jewelry as a means of suggesting that her financial dealings were dishonest. This gave skeptics a second wave of gossip to dish out about her, and, sadly, those claims still ring as loudly today as they did in the '70s. What Bartholomew *did not* disclose, however, was from *where* Kuhlman had accumulated such treasures…

Kuhlman was something the world had never experienced. During her day, a female preacher wasn't necessarily unheard of, but, typically female preachers only spoke to fellow women—never to large groups. When Kuhlman's ministry resulted in miracles and crowds comparable to those of men like Oral Roberts, it propelled a category of mass admirers no *man* would have ever had. Not only were males all over the country in love with Kuhlman, showering her with gifts, wealthy *women* who had been healed through her ministry passed on their precious jewels and art pieces to Kuhlman as a moral obligation, expressing such sentiments as: "I would have paid it all out in doctor and hospital bills, so, since I was healed in Kathryn's meetings, why shouldn't I give these things to her?"[207] One woman stipulated in her will that *her entire estate, much of which was costly jewelry*, was to be left to Kuhlman.[208] Some of the most precious and sentimental of these gifts, Kuhlman kept for herself. In fact, she wasn't bashful about *wearing* the jewelry, which fed the buzz that she had been preying on the poor during her meetings and using their offerings to fund her lavish lifestyle. Other gifts "were usually put on a table in the office and picked over by members of her staff. Sometimes Kathryn would distribute them to friends in the ministry. For even a Kathryn Kuhlman had no use for one hundred jewelry boxes, or seventy-five dove pins, or thirty rhinestone bracelets."[209]

Contrary to the whispered rumors, Kuhlman "abhorred the method often used by some organizations of having people stand to their feet and pledge so much money," saying, "It just feeds the ego."[210] Considering some of the rich estates Kuhlman inherited, it's actually shocking how frugally she lived. Gorgeous and elaborate mansions were given to her freely, but she remained in her own home. She sold the insane number of valuables she was given, many of which were estimated at hundreds of thousands of dollars, to invest the proceeds back into the beneficiary functions of her foundation. When those in her own circle claimed that she was using offering money to purchase her treasures, she said, "As God is my judge, that isn't true!... You're perfectly free to visit and inspect my home."[211] Additionally, she and her lawyers repeatedly denied assertions that she was drawing in millions of dollars per year as a salary; no reliable sources ever validated those claims.

Nonetheless, as a result of how many people latched on to the rumors, many unreliable speculations about Kuhlman have surfaced as truth throughout the years, and today, her ministry is shrouded in unfortunate controversy.

To the millions of lives who were forever affected positively by her messages and ministry, Kuhlman was a saint. As a Pentecostal, and as a healer, she joined ranks with the most notorious names of her era, and greatly inspired the ministry of Benny Hinn. As a *woman*, she was an evangelical Christian pioneer, and it was her graceful yet persistent response to the attacks against her teaching in church that paved the way for some of today's paramount female ministers.

Conclusion

A vast number of other names significantly contributed to the growing Age of Fire. In this chapter, we have covered the three most-often referenced forerunners, but the following also played powerful roles in the spread of revival, and therefore need to be mentioned, if only briefly. Note that we are listing these names because of their association to revival—*not* as holy men who had solid, honest, upstanding lives, as *some* of their legacies have been extremely spotted by controversy:

- Jack Coe (1918–1956), Pentecostal tent revival minister. Ordained through the Assemblies of God in 1944. Simultaneously preached while serving in WWII. Attended a tent revival by Oral Roberts, measured the tent, and ordered a larger one (the largest in the world at that time). Began *Herald of Healing Magazine* circa 1951, reaching 250,000 subscribers by 1956. Stripped of his ordination by the Assemblies of God in 1953, due to his stance against earthly medical practice. Arrested in 1956 for practicing medicine without a license after he told the parents of a young boy with polio that his legs were healed (when they were not); the case was dropped in court because of Florida state exemptions regarding divine healing. Died—ironically from polio—just before Christmas of the same year.
- William Marrion Branham (1909–1965), extremely controversial tent revivalist; later credited as a cult leader. Claimed to be the eschatological "Prophet Elijah" of the Laodicean Church age. Played a key role in launching the healing revival, and set standards of business that would be adopted by other ministers of his time. Founded the popular *Voice of Healing Magazine* in 1948. Later shared the pulpit with cult leader and mass murderer Jim Jones of the Peoples Temple. Charged with tax evasion by the IRS in 1956. Died after a car accident in 1965; followers believed he would arise from death, so they delayed his burial almost four months. Teachings by Branham (largely considered absurdly heretical by modern conservative evangelical theologians) led to the development of Branhamism, the followers of which believed the year 1977 would be the beginning of the millennial reign of Christ; when that year came and went, date-setting Branhamists reconfigured their predictions to 1988; when that year came and went, remaining dedicated Branhamists continued to follow the teachings, claiming that Branham's statements about the millennium were merely a prediction, and not a prophecy. At the time considered a key leader in the healing revival; today generally forgotten.

- Asa Alonso Allen (most often A. A. Allen; 1911–1970), Pentecostal evangelist and tent revival minister. Born into a lifestyle of alcoholism. Ordained through the Assemblies of God in 1936. Attended a tent revival by Oral Roberts in 1949, leaving with newfound inspiration to heal others. Purchased his first tent for $8,500 in 1955, and became a key traveling evangelist of that era. After his arrest for drunk driving, he resigned from the Assemblies of God and was reordained by his "Miracle Revival Fellowship." Purchased Jack Coe's tent in 1958, increasing his seating capacity to twenty-two thousand. Appeared on over one hundred prominent radio and television networks at the crest of his career. Before his death in 1970, his ministries were producing more than sixty million publications per year on average; his *Miracle Magazine* was reaching 450,000 per month; and he was largely known for his interracial and interdenominational integration during services. Founded "Miracle Valley" circa 1959 (the land included A. A. Allen Revivals Inc. ministry headquarters, Miracle Valley Bible College, a church, office buildings, the residential "Ministry Valley Estates," and a publishing company with its own printing press). Divorced in 1967. Passed away in 1970 from liver damage caused by alcoholism; later buried in Miracle Valley.
- Marion Gordon Robertson (most frequently "Pat" Robertson; 1930–present), currently a successful media mogul in the world of Christian broadcasting. Joined the Marine Corps in 1948; promoted to first lieutenant in 1952. Obtained a law degree from Yale in 1955; later, became a Christian convert, set aside his potential law career, and obtained a master of divinity degree from New York Theological Seminary in 1959. Established the Christian Broadcasting Network (CBN) in 1961 in Virginia Beach, Virginia. Ordained as minister of the Southern Baptist Convention in 1961. Produced the pilot episode of *The 700 Club* television program in 1966 (still airing today as one of the longest-running programs in television history, viewed in 180 countries, broad-

cast in more than seventy languages, and of which Robertson is still a host). Founded CBN University (later Regent University) in 1977. Surrendered ministerial credentials to run for the republican US president in 1986–1988. Stands today as a best-selling author and record-setting harbinger of Christian television.

7

The Fourth Great Awakening

DUE TO THE TOLERATION and later embrace of Pentecostalism through the Age of Fire—as a result of tent revivals, healings, prophesying, the slaying in the Spirit, speaking in tongues, and the interpretation of tongues—mainstream Protestant Christianity no longer shunned Spirit-driven ideologies within the Church. By the mid-fifties, the Church at large underwent a complete reversal from offering a self-righteous smirk of disapproval anytime someone suggested the early practices of Acts 2 had a place in the service to almost universal acceptance.

This religious U-turn is often referred to as the "Charismatic Movement," within which ministers such as Oral Roberts, Billy Graham, and Kathryn Kuhlman played a major role. Some believe the Charismatic Movement took its firmest root in the year 1960, when American Episcopal priest Dennis Bennett received the baptism of the Holy Spirit, began speaking in tongues, and took his testimony to St. Mark's Episcopal Church in front of an audience of thousands in Van Nuys, California. He was asked to resign his leadership post, and to spare his church from mass media onslaught, he mercifully did so (but he personally went on to communicate directly with the media in the months following).

The Charismatic Movement was a predecessor for the next movement: the "'Jesus Freaks' Movement" (sometimes simply "Jesus Movement" or "Jesus People Movement"), that rose out of the counterculture of the 1960s.

Counterculture

The 1960s was an era packed with drastic social and political activism. From some angles, a person can trace the unfolding antiestablishment counterculture of the '60s to grass roots/freedom movements earlier on. There are those who suggest that the counterculture was merely an extension of growing, Age-of-Fire Pentecostalism, encouraging religious people to abandon every oppressive list of rules they had ever been taught about the restrained worship service in trade for Holy-Spirit-led excitement. In other words: If the Church was throwing its inhibitions to the wayside and challenging established hierarchal authority, and the Church was such an influence to societal behavior (which it has always been), then it should be expected that even secular groups would eventually join the fray and express themselves against secular hierarchy (the government). But this theory does not fully explain the nearly irrational (and sometimes *entirely* irrational) activism by secular groups of the era. Perhaps the most plausible explanation behind the counterculturism of the 1960s is that, with WWII just behind us and the Vietnam War at its peak, people everywhere were exhausted from daily bloody headlines and were ready to cast stones at anything that didn't immediately promise relief from the global schism.

However, despite these and other elucidations, a deeper look into the unbelievable *gravity* of antiestablishment cultural shifts within this decade leaves many scratching their heads: It wasn't just a movement led by a few grass-roots hippies hanging out behind a barn eating granola and swearing off the use of commercial skin cleansers. It wasn't just a bunch of teenagers suddenly revolting against their parents' tyrannical expectations of a high moral code and adopting voices of their own in order to demonstrate their own maturity in rebellion of church oppression—nor was it just that the Church got "caught up" in the enthusiasm of revival and started finding other social areas to target this new zeal when the gospel became old news. And although the war-exhaustion theory holds clout, it still doesn't completely warrant the vast radicalism behind the shift. The *entire country* was observing a colossal, all-and-sundry counterculture adherence that simply defies easy explanation. Moreover, the United Kingdom and all of the Western world were quickly a part of it as well, ruling out the notion that it would have merely been an American social development. Throughout history, the word "phenomenon" has been heard too many times in reference to this decade to assign one specific, pat cause.

Perhaps, then, the best way to proceed in this overview is to let the affairs of the decade speak for themselves. The following is a short list (although it may appear long, it's merely the tip of the iceberg) of significant national events that occurred during the 1960s:

1960

- U-2 Incident (May 1): An American spy plane was sent to scout Soviet airspace in search of nuclear threat during the Cold War. The plane was shot down by a Russian missile, and US President Dwight D. Eisenhower involved NASA in a cover-up, claiming the plane was lost. The lie was exposed when surviving CIA pilot Francis Gary Powers was captured alive by Russian authorities and exploited in the foreign press. The deception cast a huge shadow over Americans' trust in government honesty.
- "The Pill" (May 9): The FDA approved the first consistently dependable birth-control contraceptive pill, which played a key role in launching the Sexual Revolution, once pregnancy was no longer a central repercussion.

- Black Friday (May 13): Police forces drove an angry student crowd out of an official HUAC (House of Un-American Activities) meeting in City Hall, San Francisco, California, using crude firehoses. Others were dragged down the steps of the building and injured. This event attributed to the rise of student protests across the US.
- John F. Kennedy elected thirty-fifth US president (November 8): Victory for Kennedy occurred with barely more than a hundred and twelve thousand votes out of the near seventy million over that of Vice President Richard M. Nixon. The race was closer than it had been since 1916, and America was watching to see what promises both parties were making during the debates regarding tension with the Soviet Union. (One of Kennedy's intentions was to establish the Peace Corps.)

1961

- Kennedy's inaugural address (January 20): The famous words, "Ask not what your country can do for you; ask what *you* can do for your country," from the lips of the new US president ignited a sense of personal action within patriots of all ages. To some, these words were clearly a call to support the US military. For others who saw peace as the greatest national benefit, these words were a call to become active in the demands for worldwide ceasefire (which helps explain the incoming heaps of protests).
- Peace Corps (March 1): The establishment of a volunteer-run organization was born with the mission "to promote world peace and friendship through a Peace Corps, which shall make available to interested countries and areas men and women of the United States qualified for service abroad and willing to serve, under conditions of hardship if necessary, to help the peoples of such countries and areas in meeting their needs for trained manpower, particularly in meeting the basic needs of those living in the poorest areas of such countries, and to help promote a better understanding of the American

people on the part of the peoples served and a better understanding of other peoples on the part of the American people."[212]

- The first Freedom Ride (May 4): Civil Rights activists journeyed to and from major cities across Southern states to protest racial segregation. Riots and Ku Klux Klansmen attacks occurred upon the activists' arrival and departure, but the Freedom Riders stood firm, which brought further serious attention to the American Civil Rights cause.

- Women's Peace Strike (November 1): Approximately fifty thousand women in sixty US cities marched in this demonstration against nuclear weapon manufacturing (the largest peace protest put on by women in the twentieth century).

1962

- Operation Chopper (January 12): American military engaged in major combat in the Vietnam War for the first time.

- Operation Ranch Hand (January 18): Approximately twenty million gallons of herbicides and defoliants were sprayed by US aircraft over rural Vietnam soil for crop destruction, food deprivation, and the demolishing of vegetation coverage. This endeavor lasted until 1971.

- Marilyn Monroe's death from a drug overdose (August 5): This event assisted in catapulting prescription drug addiction to new highs, which led to thousands of accidental overdose deaths in subsequent years.

- Publication of *Silent Spring* (September 27): This book written by Rachel Carlson called for a whole new awareness of environmental disturbance as a result of synthetic pesticides. People everywhere reacted by insisting upon healthier environmental conscientiousness, and the US Environmental Protection Agency was formed as a result.

- Cuban Missile Crisis (October 16–28): The Soviets attempted to deploy nuclear missiles in Cuba. This confrontation was seen as an enormous threat to the US, and nearly launched the Cold War into a full-blown nuclear war.

1963

- Publication of *The Feminine Mystique* (February 19): This book by Betty Friedan took an in-depth look at the unhappiness of the "housewives role" in society. The modern feminist movement was born.
- Birmingham Campaign (April–May): Police fought back Civil Rights activists in the racially divided city of Birmingham, Alabama.
- English and Australian protest of the Vietnam War (May).
- "A Strategy of Peace" speech by John F. Kennedy (June 10): Kennedy had not only the attention of the nation, but of powerful world leaders, during this speech that called for a halt on all atmospheric nuclear weapons testing across the world. At the height of the Cold War, Kennedy's claim that America would "never *start* a war" was remarkably peaceful.
- Public school-sponsored Bible reading pronounced unconstitutional by the US Supreme Court (June 17).
- "I Have a Dream" (August 28): Martin Luther King Jr. delivered this speech to more than 250,000 Civil Rights activists on the steps of the Lincoln Memorial in Washington, DC.
- The Limited Test Ban Treaty (September 24): Political leaders from the US, the Soviet Union, and the United Kingdom signed a treaty that banned testing of nuclear weapons except underground. This also tapered nuclear radiation poisoning upon relative environments.
- Chicago student protest: Around 225,000 students protested enduring class racial segregation (October 27).
- Assassination of US President John F. Kennedy (November 22): America, as well as the world, was shocked. This event triggered a breakdown of social differences as the country banded together to mourn the loss of its leader. The people's concerns that had only

the previous day seemed crucially important suddenly did not need immediate attention or resolution, and the concept of the vulnerability of human lives—even for those with the highest public security—took on a life of its own. If the president wasn't safe, then nobody was. Such a dark reality hurled America into thoughts of national and international peace like never before, and affected every social and political sphere.

1964

- Chicago and Boston student protests (February 25–26): Tens of thousands of students protested enduring class racial segregation by skipping school.
- New York student protests (March 16): Around 25 percent of the state's students went on a strike to protest racial segregation.
- Cleveland student protests (April 20): About 85 percent of the black student population boycotted classes to protest racial segregation.
- Debut of the "Freep" (May 23): The *Los Angeles Free Press*, or "the Freep," was an underground newspaper edited and published by Art Kunkin, delivering a modern kind of radicalistic political view (primarily anti-war) that standard public papers would not print. The Freep cost more than twice the price of a standard public newspaper, but people were more than willing to pay. As the writers and columnists knew their readers had tired of the sanitized papers available to the public, they didn't shy away from extremist lingo, and the paper traveled between the hands of those who were most likely to riot, strike, picket, march, sit in the middle of the roads with signs, or sing on the sidewalks about the injustice of the international feuds, and the control it held over the American people's daily lives. At the peak of its publication, the paper had national distribution, printing around a hundred thousand copies per issue, but it is safe to assume that the numbers of readers greatly trumps the number of issues printed because, as it was an underground paper, it was hard to get

hold of, so many would share copies among friends. This paper helped subculture groups identify with others who held to the same convictions, and before long, what had been unorganized and futile anti-war rallies became suddenly organized and influential (eventually playing a significant role in the end of the Vietnam War).

- The first communal draft-card burning (May 12): This occurred in New York City.

- Sexually explicit films (June): When a theater was fined (and the owner of the theater criminally convicted) for showing a film that conflicted with Ohio's obscenity laws, the case was appealed in court, and subsequently dropped. Although obscenity disputes still occur at the time of this writing, depending on local laws, this case quickly paved the way for commercially available pornographic films throughout the US, and thus further fueling the Sexual Revolution.

- The Civil Rights Act (July 2): President Johnson signed this act wherein racial segregation, as well as inequality of employment opportunity, were banned under federal law.

- The Free Speech Movement (October 1): University of California, Berkeley, students protested on-campus political pursuits and demanded freedom of speech. One of the student leaders, Jack Weinberg, refused to cooperate with local law enforcement and was arrested, but fellow students surrounded the police car Weinberg was escorted to. For more than thirty hours, the police car was used as a stage for the student speakers, and eventually Weinberg's charges were dropped. Other uprisings occurred in the following months, and by December, the Free Speech Movement was in full swing in that locality, gaining much momentum across the states thereafter.

- Nobel Peace Prize (October 14): The prestigious award was presented to to Martin Luther King Jr.

1965

- The US initiation of aerial bombing in North Vietnam (February 8).

- Alice Herz protest (March 16): Eighty-two-year-old Herz, formerly a concentration camp prisoner under Francisco Franco's regime in Spain during WWII, set herself on fire in the streets to protest the Vietnam War, dying days later.
- Anti-Vietnam War protests (April 17): These escalated when the first major rally was conducted in Washington, DC, and an estimated twenty-five thousand attended.
- LSD (May): American chemist Owsley Stanley manufactured his first of many mass batches of "Owsley Acid" (LSD), becoming a primary psychedelic drug supplier to leaders of the counterculture movement.
- University of California, Berkeley, students and protesters' draft-card burning (May): This led to the establishment of the Vietnam Day Committee, a large organization of anti-war factions including pacifist religious citizens, students, labor unions, and many left-wing political groups.
- The Voting Act (August 6): This act was constituted under US law, allowing colored people the right to vote.
- Los Angeles riots (August 11–17): Riots broke out, claiming the lives of thirty-five citizens, and resulting in the destruction of around one thousand buildings.
- The burning of draft cards banned by US law (August 31).
- The first black star (September 15): Although colored people had been on television and in movies in minor roles for decades, Bill Cosby landed the first starring role in a television series (*I Spy*), quickly rising to international celebrity status.
- Musician Barry McGuire's "Eve of Destruction," a war-protest song: This recording reached #1 on the US Billboard Top 100 chart (September 25).
- Increasing number of war protests (October 15–16): Totals across the US grew to numbers above one hundred thousand.
- Baltimore protest (March 16): Thirty-one-year-old Norman Morrison, a Baltimore, Maryland, Quaker, set himself on fire while

holding his infant daughter (who survived) at the Pentagon to protest the Vietnam War, dying in minutes.

- Catholic protest (November 9): Twenty-two-year-old Roger Allan
  LaPorte, a leader of the Catholic Worker Movement, sets himself on
  fire to protest the Vietnam War, dying the next day.
- The *Fifth Estate* (November 19): This anti-authoritarian periodical
  had a similar effect on the counterculture of this decade as the aforementioned "Freep."
- More protests (November 27): An estimated thirty-five thousand
  protestors march outside the White House.
- Cultural expression (November–December): As freedom-of-speech
  movements escalate, national music sensations release bold tracks
  with anti-war, anti-establishment, and pro-drug lyrics, influencing
  the earliest hippie communes.

1966

- "Trips Festival" (January 21–23): This gathering of more than ten
  thousand listened to legendary recording artists and simultaneously
  partook in psychedelic drugs.
- Anti-Vietnam War rallies and demonstrations (March 25–27): An
  explosion in the number of rallies and demonstrations occurred
  across the US, as well as in nations around the globe.
- University of Chicago student protest (May 12): Students spoke out
  against the draft, taking over the administration offices.
- White House protest (May 15): An estimated ten thousand protestors and picketers march outside the White House.
- University of Wisconsin protest (May 18): An estimated ten thousand students protested the draft.
- A petition to end the Vietnam War signed (June 4): Almost sixty-
  five hundred respected clergymen and scholars signed the petition,
  and it was subsequently published in *The New York Times*.

- The "Miranda Rights" (June 13): The "You have the right to remain silent…" directives to those arrested of crimes was instituted.
- NOW (June 30): The feminist National Organization for Women was founded in Washington, DC.
- John Lennon (July): The Beatles singer/songwriter's "we're more popular than Jesus" comment spawned a reaction all across the world, resulting in mass burnings of their albums.
- Riots (July–September): Huge riots broke out in major cities all across the states; many deaths occurred, as did irreparable damage to countless city buildings.
- *The San Francisco Oracle* published in Haight-Ashbury (September 20): This underground newspaper had a similar effect on the counterculture of this decade as the aforementioned "Freep" and *Fifth Estate*.
- United States law ban on LSD (October 6): This did not stop the covert distribution, and only fanned the flames of the growing anti-establishment mindset. Many ban-protests ensued throughout the following months.

1967

- "Human Be-In" (January 14): San Francisco's Golden Gate Park hosted the event (whose name was a play on the words "human being"), a gathering of twenty thousand counterculture individuals to protest the ban on LSD, the draft, political control, environmental awareness, and self-empowerment.
- *The Responsibility of Intellectuals* (February 23): Noam Chomsky's anti-Vietnam essay challenging the intellectual US culture's reliance upon governmental authority was published in the *New York Review of Books*.
- Another "Be-In" (March 26): New York's Central Park hosted the next "Be-In" gathering of ten thousand.

- "Beyond Vietnam: A Time to Break Silence" (April 4): Martin Luther King Jr. delivered this anti-war speech in New York City.
- The National Mobilization Committee to End the War in Vietnam's rally of hundreds of thousands in anti-war protests (April 15): An estimated four hundred thousand protestors marched, sang, and picketed from New York's Central Park to the UN headquarters in New York City, led by Martin Luther King Jr., among others. A simultaneous march in San Francisco was led by Coretta Scott King (King Jr.'s wife) involving seventy-five thousand.
- Muhammed Ali's refusal of induction into the US military (April 28): He did this in opposition to the Vietnam War, setting an example for many to follow.
- London peace rave (April 29): Seven thousand attended the Pink Floyd-promoted televised psychedelic rave to endorse peace in London.
- *Seed* (May): *Seed* was a radical left-wing underground newspaper published in Chicago, having similar effect on the counterculture of this decade as the aforementioned "Freep," *Fifth Estate*, and *The San Francisco Oracle*.
- Student protestor deaths (May 14): James Earl Green and one other student were killed under law enforcement gunfire at a protest in Jackson State College, Mississippi.
- More protests (May 15–17): Student protestors opposed local law enforcement at Texas Southern University, stemming the death of one police officer and more than four hundred arrests.
- The National Mobilization Committee to End the War in Vietnam (May 20–21): This assembly of seven hundred leading anti-war activists gathered to organize future peace demonstrations in Washington, DC.
- More rioting (June–September): *Again*, huge riots broke out in major cities all across the states; *again*, many deaths occurred, as well as irreparable damage to countless city buildings.

- "Summer of Love" phenomenon (June–September): The counter-culture movement escalated to what is now known as the "Summer of Love" phenomenon in the Haight-Ashbury district of San Francisco. Teens and young mothers ran away from home to join the free-love society; television reporters crowded the streets to interview hippies; bystanders purchased bus tour tickets to observe the spectacle; the convergence of approximately one hundred thousand communally dwelling "flower children" were discussing politics, peace, drug use, psychedelic music, and the welcomed lack of sexual inhibition; and Charles Manson inaugurated himself as a guru of life to any and all who would hear. Articles, photos, and televised news reports blasted the states with updates from respected sources. Although there had certainly been hippie communities scattered across the US up to this point, the Summer of Love was a major assistor in the establishment of the hippie culture and communal living. Before long, other heavily populated cities followed suit, and the phenomenon became a national one.
- Detroit Riots (July 23–27): The deadliest riot outbreak in the history of the United States occurred after local law enforcement raided an unlicensed bar. As turmoil grew, as well as the crowds, Governor George W. Romney directed the Michigan Army National Guard to the city, and US President Lyndon B. Johnson (Kennedy's successor after the assassination) sent in air assault infantry as an attempt to terminate the disorder. In the end, forty-three were killed, almost five hundred were injured, more than seven thousand were arrested, and over two thousand buildings were burned.
- "Stop the Draft Week" (October): Protestors surrounded the US Army Induction Center in Oakland, California. More than one thousand registrants across the country returned their draft cards.
- *Hair* (October 17): The (then-off-Broadway) musical smash premiered in New York City. The production encapsulated hippie culture, featuring drug use and "tripping," self-empowerment, radical

reaction to political powers, sexual freedom, peace, and love. (As the reader has probably guessed, the title of the show was named after the longer hair that had been adopted by men within the hippie movement.)

- Brooklyn College strike (October 19): When military recruiters appeared at the Brooklyn College in New York, it launched a conflict involving thousands of students, who led a strike the next day.
- "March on the Pentagon" (October 20–21): The National Mobilization Committee to End the War in Vietnam rallied approximately one hundred thousand together in this anti-war protest in Washington, DC.
- San Jose State College protest (November 20): A student demonstration against military recruiters at the San Jose State College resulted in the use of tear gas by local police.
- Anti-war activists arrested (December 4–8): Almost six hundred anti-war activists were arrested while attempting to interfere with the operations of draft board centers.

1968

- Orangeburg Massacre (February 8): Police opened gunfire on one hundred and fifty racial segregation protestors at the South Carolina State University, killing three African-American males and injuring twenty-eight.
- Walter Cronkite's prediction (February 27): The *CBS News* anchor and incredibly influential American voice admitted on live television that he did not predict victory for the Vietnam War.
- National Advisory Commission on Civil Disorders (February 29): US President Johnson appointed Illinois Governor Otto Kerner to assist in the investigation of civil riots across the country, bringing about this report, in which recommendations were made for future societal unrest. The report indicated that, ironically, the social integration of black and white races was causing such strife that the

two peoples were more separated than ever before. (Whether or not that would be true in the coming years, the rioting occurring at the time this report was written shows that through the establishing of equality, pride intensified, the nation was split—the blacks on one side, the whites on the other—and the purpose toward peace was paradoxically disastrous before it got off the ground. It would take *decades* before most of the racial segregation was implemented socially, despite the law.)

- My Lai Massacre (March 16): US soldiers gang-raped Vietnamese women, then killed them along with the men, children, and infants in a small, nonhostile village in Southern Vietnam, and attempted to conceal their carnage. The news of this insane bloodshed did not reach the states until November of 1969, and when it did, it invoked colossal, worldwide outrage.
- March on US Embassy in London (March 17): Two hundred of the ten thousand protestors were arrested while marching on the US Embassy in London.
- Robert F. Kennedy's announcement (March 18): The brother of John F. Kennedy and US senator of New York announced his intention to run for president, openly condemning the Vietnam War.
- President Johnson's declaration (March 31): Johnson declared on television that he did not intend to seek a second term in the White House, and that he planned to focus all his attention on the war.
- Martin Luther King Jr. assassination (April 4): Extreme violence, rioting, and mass disorder broke out across the US when King wasassassinated at the Lorraine Motel in Memphis, TN.
- More anti-war protests (April 27): Tens of thousands marched in protest of the war in major cities all over the country.
- The Louisville Riots (May 24–27): These riots brought assistance from thousands of policemen and men in the National Guard; two young African-American males were killed.
- Robert F. Kennedy assassination (June 5): JFK's brother was shot and killed while at the front of the presidential election race.

- University of California, Berkeley, shutdown (July 28–30): The university was forced to shut down all operations because of protests.
- Democratic National Convention in Chicago (August 25–29): The meeting was largely derailed by protestors, eventually resulting in near failure as attention was diverted to disaster control; police were brutal in their attempts to drive back the angry crowds, and reporters were everywhere, bringing the calamity to international airwaves. Although a democratic presidential nominee was selected (the purpose of the national convention since Johnson had announced he was not running for another term and Robert Kennedy had been assassinated), the chaos fueled the antagonism to a breaking point: police beat young people; crowds fought back; tear gas permeated the city; mace was sprayed everywhere; chunks of concrete and sharp rocks were thrown far and wide… Unlike the previous riots, wherein law enforcement usually had only acted to temper the turmoil (not to instigate it further), during this convention, the police were actively involved in the violence, and news reporters caught much of it on film. Thus, this occasion in Chicago was considered the first "police riot." Activists *thought* that through this display, previously neutral or peaceful Americans would rally to their cause (which was different on a case-by-case basis depending on the group: anti-war, social/ racial integration, political, etc.), but their efforts backfired. Americans had felt the weight of bedlam and anarchy for too long, and now observing that the nations demoralization had reached even those who had been sworn to "protect and serve" struck a chord. The country was growing weary of radicalism. It was a turning point for our national psyche, certainly. However, the momentum of pandemonium was too strong to stop at this time, as our country had been long trained to respond to perceived injustice through loud and proud demonstrations.
- Freedom Trash Cans (September 7): Feminist groups united against the images portrayed of the perfect woman in what has become known as the "Miss America Protest." Although the protest occurred

outside the Miss America Pageant on the Atlantic City Boardwalk, the women's liberation movement was only partly to do with the pageant, and more to do with women's rights. Metal barrels and waste baskets were collected and painted with the words "FREEDOM TRASH CAN." Feminists who had traveled from all over the US lined up to these burning bins carrying "instruments of female torture": eyelash curlers, high heels, makeup, corsets and girdles, nylons, bras, beauty products of all kinds, objectifying literature and magazines, and various items from the kitchen. The aftermath of this demonstration launched the Women's Liberation Movement into the minds of every American. News companies were relieved to take a brief sabbatical from the war headlines and discuss beauty standards and other feminist agendas.

- President Johnson's order (October 31): The president ordered a stop to the aerial bombs in North Vietnam.
- The longest strike in US history (November 1968–March 1969): This strike began as members of the Black Student Union demanded an implementation of ethnic study programs, as well as the end of the Vietnam War.
- The *White Album* (November 22): The release of this recording by the Beatles later unintentionally inspired the Tate and LaBianca murders by the Manson Family.
- Earthrise (December 24): Environmental awareness took on an international rush after astronaut William Anders captured a photograph (called "Earthrise") of Earth from his orbit around the moon during the Apollo 8 mission.

1969

- Another protest (January 8–18): Students at Brandeis University in Waltham, Massachusetts, led a protest demanding the implementation of an African-American administrative department, which was granted.

- Richard M. Nixon's presidency (January 20): The thirty-seventh US president was sworn into office, ending eight years of democratic power in the White House.
- More protests (February 16): Students at Duke University in Durham, North Carolina, led a protest, demanding the implementation of a Black Studies program, which was granted.
- *Tinker v. Des Moines* (February 24): The US Supreme Court ruled in favor of public school attendees' rights to protest the war after this case.
- Nixon's statement (March 22): The newly elected President Nixon publicly condemned the dispiriting craze of campus violence and student takeovers of university administration.
- US military peak (April): The number of American soldiers in Vietnam reached almost five hundred and fifty thousand, its peak.
- Cornell University protest (April 19) Armed black students at Cornell University in Ithaca, New York, seized the student union building (Willard Straight Hall), demanding the implementation of an African-American studies program, which was granted.
- Colgate University protest (April 25–28): Students of this campus in Hamilton, New York, led a protest, demanding the implementation of an African-American studies program, which was eventually granted.
- Bloody Thursday (May 15): Student protestors opened gunfire on law enforcement in People's Park, Berkeley, California. One student died and hundreds were injured.
- 1969 Greenboro Uprising (May 21–25): Student protestors combatted law enforcement at the North Carolina Agricultural and Technical State University, requiring intercession from the National Guard; one student died, many were injured, and tear gas was dropped by helicopter.
- *Everything You Always Wanted to Know about Sex* (June): Sexual liberation climbed as a result of the publication of this book, which was an immediate bestseller and played a key role in the Sexual Revolution.

- Hippie culture (June–August): Newspapers, magazines, and television broadcasts across the nation reported on the increase of peace-loving hippie communes, how they lived, how they raised their children, and what their opinions were on politics, war, and the environment. This publicity assisted in the increase in the number of hippie communes.

- Stonewall Riots of Manhattan (June 28): The first major homosexual uprisings took place in Manhattan, New York. Within just a few short years of this uprising, gay and lesbian activist organizations were established all across the US and, by extension, the rest of the world shortly thereafter. By 1970, the first Gay Pride marches took place in Los Angeles, New York, Chicago, and San Francisco. To this day, most worldwide LGBT events are held toward the end of June in commemoration of the Stonewall Riots, as they are commonly considered to have launched the modern Homosexual Liberation movement.

- Apollo 11 (June 20): Humans first landed on the moon during the Apollo 11 space mission.

- Vietnamization (July 25): This was the first huge leap for the US toward eventually pulling out of the Vietnam War. President Nixon wished to end America's involvement, so he and government officials met and conjured up the "Nixon Doctrine" (frequently "Vietnamization"), wherein US troops would assist Southern Vietnam soldiers in training and expansion, while simultaneously improving their equipment. From there, the US troops would slowly come back to the states, allowing for self-sufficiency of Vietnam through a six-step withdrawal plan. Although the plan didn't go exactly as our government had anticipated at every turn, the news of Nixon's intentions spread across the states, and national celebratory buzz ensued at the first sight of the end of violence. (The vast scope of national reaction to this headline is complicated, went on for years, is still debated to this day, and it would require more space than we have here to discuss it at length. Suffice it to say, whether the plan was good, bad, or ignorant, it was a step in the direction America was demanding to see.)

- Manson murders (August 9–10): Sharon Tate, the LaBiancas, and several others were brutally murdered in a bloodbath killing spree by the Manson Family, making international news and causing conservatives to blame the hippies of the counterculture as the cause for promotion of violence.
- Woodstock (August 15–17): Up to five hundred thousand gathered for three days of music, love, and peace at the festival in New York.
- *Penthouse* (September): The first issue of the sexually explicit magazine hit newsstands across the US, *again* contributing to the Sexual Revolution mindset.
- March in Washington DC (November 15): The largest anti-war demonstration in US history occurred as over five hundred thousand marched in the nation's capitol.

Peace through Depravity

The 1960s was a time of radical voices. Most of the rallies, marches, riots, protests, and demonstrations—many of which turned violent—initialized as a result of individuals wishing to see the end of the war and racial tension in trade for peace, but it soon became something completely different altogether. As the war in Vietnam escalated, so, too, did the African-American civil rights movement, the Women's Rights movement, and the Sexual Revolution (among others). Even before Martin Luther King Jr. gave his 1963 "I Have a Dream" speech, the "dream" of peaceful and equalized interaction between human factions (racial, political, international, genders, etc.) inspired groups from coast to coast to become active in their quests for utopia. The more the passion grew, the louder the voices became, and the mission of peace was intermittently derailed over and over again through forces that were naturally opposite the cause: violence, demands, strong-arming, suppression, anger, imposition, and constant conflict.

After several years of this paradox, the United States lost much hope in the idea of *true* peace and love—the brand of which overpowered skirmishes and debate, bringing an entire nation into reconciliation for the good of mankind. And, as Christian history has often showed, it is when all hope is perceived as lost that people fall on their knees and find the answer.

The answer—as witnessed by hippies, flower children, wives, mothers, husbands, fathers, grandparents, teens, children, politicians, and activists—could only be found in the gospel.

The Jesus People/Jesus Freaks

The term "Jesus Freak" was originally viewed as a derogatory expression comparative to "Bible thumper" or "holy-roller." It carried connotations of belittling criticism by nonbelievers, although the term was a commonplace also among Christians toward those they saw as extremists. Yet, later, when phrases such as "on fire for Christ" or "radically saved" became heavily used within believers' circles, "Jesus Freak" was adopted by many Christians as a positive self-identification. It was an abandonment of self, an uncompromising obedience and loyalty to Christ. To those who were completely sold out for the gospel, being called a Jesus Freak was a compliment.

In 1995, the Christian music group DC Talk released an album called *Jesus Freak*, and the immensely popular title track held the following lyrics:

> People say I'm strange; does it make me a stranger,
> That my Best Friend was born in a manger?…
> What will people think when they hear that I'm a Jesus Freak?
> What will people do when they find that it's true?
> I don't really care if they label me a Jesus Freak.
> There ain't no disguising the truth.[213]

Although this Grammy Award-winning song wasn't written until the mid-'90s, it reflects the attitude of the Jesus Freak Movement from the mid-'60s and forward: If people were truly serious about the cause of Christ, then there "ain't no disguising" their status as a freak, if it meant a higher standard of faithfulness. Before long, a Christian who claimed *not* to be an uncompromising freak was ironically considered lackluster in his or her commitment. Radicalism had so long been the norm throughout our country that applying that same standard to Christianity was basically a requirement in order to be taken seriously.

Unlike some of the previous studies in this book that attribute revivals to the works of specific, influential power preachers, the Jesus People/ Jesus Freak movement was an unprogrammed phenomenon that began all over the states through non-clergy civilians, becoming its own energy, feeding itself, nurturing its own roots, and seismically revolutionizing religion and evangelical Christianity.

By the mid-1960s—with the same tenacity of the counterculture's civil, liberal, and political demonstrations (minus the violence and riots)—came floods of Jesus Freaks throughout main cities, holding positive signs, preaching the Word, pooling resources to feed and house the hungry and homeless, singing hymns of praise outside shopping centers, and sharing everything they had in the interest of witnessing to others about this "Son of God." Through similar publication methods as that of the "Freep," Jesus-centered magazines, pamphlets, and periodicals were printed and distributed by hand across all demographics without bias. With the same communal lifestyle as the flower children came opened doors to any and all to gather for scriptural study for days on end during meetings with no structured start or ending times, and before long, "churches" formed in the unlikeliest of places: personal homes, bus stations, coffee shops, restaurants, abandoned buildings, barns, parking lots, random fields, etc. "Pastors" were un-ordained lay teachers whose theology didn't need to be polished or reach the standards of an official church organization. In fact, people had stewed in the "anti-*this*, anti-*that*" pot for so long that "anti-hierarchal" wasn't a controversy, but a national expectation. Who needed an organized church, when Christ, *Himself*, wandered around on foot, establishing a "church" through a collective body of believers?

While not all of the gatherings rendered the same saintly imagery of Christ as had been established throughout centuries prior (the famous *TIME Magazine* cover of June 1971 comes to mind, on which Christ is painted as a psychedelic mystic in kaleidoscopic colors as the ultimate loving hippie), there is no doubt that this fresh association to Christ was sincere. Sermons were delivered in *joy*, not with demands. Preachers and teachers raised their voices to be heard with *smiles*, not with angry fists. Congregations sang with lyrics of *praise* and *love*, not with condescension, arrogance, pride, or hatred toward opposing opinion. The signs these Christ-followers held along sidewalks and roadways spoke of *inclusion*, not of protest. Their meetings were characterized by *hugs*, not by riots. The atmosphere surrounding them was one of *buoyancy*, not of anxiety or agitation.

To this group of believers, Christ was not the next slogan or superficial sentiment, but the Man who came to free whole nations from the very turmoil America had been facing for decades. He was the supreme anti-war activist, the absolute liberator, the nonpareil friend to people of all colors of races and nationalities…the sovereign *answer* to everything the people thirsted for. And yet, despite considering Christ to be the answer to all temporal grievances, they still saw him as the supernatural Savior and God, the awesome beginning and the end, and the merciful benefactor of sinners.

Christianity, beginning in the Summer of Love in the Haight-Ashbury district of San Francisco and moving across state lines to the rest of America, had entangled itself in a hippie twist, and for many exhausted souls who saw the hippie culture as one that predominantly promoted peace, love, and freedom, that is *exactly* what religion needed. Although some of the more conservative Christian leaders scoffed at the lay-Christ imagery and saw the Jesus Freaks as unhygienic and blasphemous street urchins who needed a good shave, others, such as sympathizer Billy

Graham of the Age of Fire, celebrated that "the Jesus People movement heralds a new spiritual awakening for America."[214]

And, despite expected opposition to the developing "hippie church," its expansion provided a much-needed middle ground: The conservatives had their buildings and administrative services, and the free-spirited had their wheat fields and long-haired disciples blowing bubbles in the wind while simultaneously quoting Scripture.

Now, *everyone* had a church where he or she could be embraced, not limited to regulated services that just *might* be filled with like-minded people.

And the world was, once again, on fire.

Conclusion

Today's church is heavily influenced by the Jesus Freak movement. Driving through Springfield, Missouri (in Tom Horn's locality), church billboards still speak the whispers of yesteryear's fourth Great Awakening, posting such phrases as "Come just as you are!" and "Christ loved all people, and so do we." One billboard that gains a lot of attention shows a man wearing distressed jeans and a regular T-shirt, with the caption: "These are my church clothes," implying that anyone entering the doors of that church will be welcomed no matter how casually he or she is attired. There is absolutely no way of knowing the depth of which the Jesus Freaks movement profoundly restructured our modern Church, or how many have been saved as a result of feeling that they are worthy of Christ's love simply because they are *human*, and not because they look/ dress/act a certain way. What we do know is that our modern Church has the Jesus Freaks and Jesus People to thank for their radical, revolutionary revitalization of the simplicity that is Christ's abounding love for all, whether or not the theology and service practice always stayed within the confines of what is considered acceptable.

Because this movement grew largely through its own making, no one person has been focused on biographically, as in the previous studies. However, once the momentum was in progress, several leaders materialized, the following of which are worthy of mention:

- Charles ("Chuck") Ward Smith (1927–2013), pastor and founder of the Calvary Chapel Church Fellowship: Graduate of LIFE Bible College. Ordained in the International Church of the Foursquare Gospel. Became pastor of a nondenominational church called the Calvary Chapel with a congregation of less than thirty. Prior to Smith's arrival, members of the Calvary Chapel had received a prophecy that Smith would take the pastorate, and that the church would grow to international recognition. This happened in a short few years, as Smith not only drew crowds with his informal and contemporary teaching style, but also by training other ministers who then planted other churches within the fellowship. Went on to write many books on theology and the love of Christ for His people. Died at the age of eighty-six of a heart attack after struggling with lung cancer.
- Lonnie Frisbee (1946–1993), Pentecostal evangelist, dancer, and award-winning painter who was and famously regarded as the "hippie preacher," as he maintained that appearance throughout his ministry: Ran away from home as a child several times. Exposed to much instability in a broken home. Joined the drug culture on a spiritual quest (which was popular at the time), mingled with the gay community on Laguna Beach at fifteen, and subsequently moved to the Haight-Ashbury district of San Francisco during the Summer of Love in 1967. Began reading the Bible while "tripping." Estranged from his family and friends after telling of a vision wherein he would be speaking of Christ to a sea of people. Dabbled in the occult, mysticism, and the paranormal for a time. Converted to Christianity, entered an informal commune/church

called the Living Room (storefront coffeehouse), and married former girlfriend Connie. Met Calvary Chapel pastor Chuck Smith circa 1969, moved in with him, and began ministering to, and baptizing, hippies on the beach. Brought new converts to Smith's home who had nowhere else to go, and when Smith's home was filled to the brim, co-founded the rehab-commune House of Miracles alongside John Higgins Jr. (a later leader in the Jesus Freak/Jesus People movement). House of Miracles proved to be a great success, quickly growing into nineteen communal homes, and when those were also filled, the Shiloh Youth Revival Centers were the replacement, rapidly budding into 175 communal centers across the US. (Because all were welcomed into these centers without documentation or records [so long as they had accepted Christ as their personal Savior], nobody is sure of how many converts came to the Shiloh houses for restoration. However, the most often stated number is one hundred thousand attendees at any given time.) Went on to appear in Kathryn Kuhlman's *I Believe in Miracles* show as well as in numerous other interviews and photo opportunities throughout the media hype of the Jesus Revolution. Divorced Connie in 1973 when she had an affair with Frisbee's ministry associate. Began to invite the youth of his congregation to ask for the power of the Holy Spirit circa 1980, manifestations of the Holy Spirit (including the slaying of the Spirit and speaking in tongues) resulted, spawning an enormous Pentecostal growth, including ministries taken back to home neighborhoods by the youth who had been affected by Frisbee's preaching. Traveled the globe with fellow minister John Wimber during a period of "signs and wonders," when many were healed at their meetings. Died at the age of forty-four from AIDS, possibly from a homosexual encounter. (Frisbee struggled off and on with homosexuality throughout his life. Many have stated that this was a result of his childhood instability, and that he had been the victim of a momentously horrifying sexual crime at the age of eight. Whereas this may very well be true, and much evidence supports it, it's also worth noting that the sexual liberation and "free love" shouts within the counterculture of the time would have provided ample temptation to partake of this lifestyle. In addition, due to the lack of learned theology in the somewhat liberal Jesus Church of the '60s and '70s, there is reason to believe even a minister would have approached this subject more liberally in such communal environments as those he helped launch.)

- John Richard Wimber (1934–1997), evangelical pastor, teacher on church growth, and one of the leading founders of the Vineyard Church/Vineyard Movement: Converted to evangelical Christianity in 1963. Led hundreds of others to conversion by 1970. Led more than ten Bible study groups at a time circa 1970, numbering an estimated total of five hundred attendants, collectively. Was the founding director of the Church Growth Department of the Institute of Evangelism and Church Growth in 1974–1978, during which time he led a church out of his home, initially as a minister of the Calvary Chapel, and later of the Anaheim Vineyard Christian Fellowship located elsewhere when his home was outgrown. (The Vineyard Movement and the Calvary Chapel Movement were similar, but differentiated in the subject of Holy Spirit gifts, which piloted the split between the two; Calvary methods of teaching centered almost solely on Christ and love, and Vineyard methods involved more of the Charismatic Movement/Pentecostal/Holy Spirit trends of the Age of Fire.) Traveled the globe with Lonnie Frisbee during the period of "signs and wonders." Because of his church-planting methods, the Vineyard Church opened thousands of churches across the country both during and after Wimber's lifetime. Influenced millions of other ministers who followed in his theological footsteps. Became an internationally famed Vineyard leader before his death from a brain hemorrhage at the age of sixty-three.

- Keith Gordon Green (1953–1982), pianist, singer, songwriter, and significant leader of the "Jesus Music" (which is today's "contemporary Christian music"): Roots in Jewish heritage; raised in Christian Science. Showed incredible musical talent from his earliest years. Talent featured in the *Los Angeles Times* at the age of eight, and subsequently involved in musical theater. Had written over forty original musical numbers by the age of ten. Signed a contract with Decca Records in 1965, releasing the secular song "A Go-Go Getter," becoming the youngest musical artist (eleven years old) to sign with the ASCAP (American Society of Composers, Authors, and Publishers). Quickly started becoming a teen idol through his appearances in secular magazines and television shows. Featured in *TIME Magazine* at twelve as an aspiring rock-'n'-roll musician. Mysteriously (although many Christians believe this was an act of God), Donny Osmond suddenly came into view as the latest dreamboat, and Green was forgotten completely by the secular music world. Joined the drug culture. Adopted "free love" ideology. Dabbled in mysticism. While "tripping," he became supernaturally aware of other presences surrounding him (which his biography relates as an initial belief in aliens and a later belief in demonic presences), and thereafter swore off drugs. Began studying theology and philosophy. Married Melody in 1973. The couple converted to evangelical Christianity, wrote songs for CBS Records, became involved in the Vineyard Christian Fellowship of Southern California, and took new converts into their home. Developed a communal society when his home was filled, purchasing one other home and renting an additional five in his neighborhood. None were turned away, including recovering drug addicts, prostitutes, young pregnant women, tough bikers, and the homeless. When this housing was outgrown, the Greens moved to Texas and increased land ownership to 140 acres by 1979. This ministry had become the Last Days Ministries (in 1977), later producing a pamphlet called *Last Days Newsletter*, which grew into the well-known *Last Days Magazine*. Signed with Sparrow Records in 1976, and later refused to charge for his live concerts, believing that anyone—including the poor—should be blessed by his lyrics however possible. After breaking from Sparrow Records to perform without interest in profit, he released—and personally funded through the mortgaging of his home—three other records; an estimated two hundred thousand were shipped from the Green's residence, the price of which was up to the purchaser (approximately sixty-one thousand were shipped for free). Released many renowned records (his own and those under Sparrow Records' label) until his death in a personal plane accident in 1982. By the mid-1980s, *Last Days Magazine* had more than five hundred thousand subscribers worldwide, and is still in circulation today. Green's music is heralded as a trailblazer of modern Christian music, and testimonies of lives affected by Green are uncountable. Green was posthumously inducted into the Gospel Music Hall of Fame in 2001 and honored with the ASCAP Crescendo Award in 2006. At the time of this writing, a feature-length film about the life of Keith Green is under development. The legacy of Green's music is such that many tribute recordings of his songs have been released by numerous contemporary Christian artists. Some of his most celebrated songs include: "He'll Take Care of the Rest," "No One Believes in Me Anymore," "When I Hear the Praises Start," "So You Wanna Go Back to Egypt," "Grace by Which I Stand," "Your Love Broke Through," "You Put This Love in My Heart," "Asleep in the Light," "Oh Lord, You're Beautiful," "The Lord Is My Shepherd" (a musical adaptation of Psalm 23), and "There Is a Redeemer" (written by wife Melody).

8

Spiritual Hindrance to Revival

The Infernal Struggle against What the World Really Needs

The Lord is a man of war: the Lord is his name.
—EXODUS 15:3

THE WORLD IS in desperate need of revival. Revivals have taken place in the past and are taking place today; but there are some powerful forces in today's world who don't want revival. And, quite predictably, they are doing everything in their power to hinder, thwart, and stop revival. Sadly, however, many in the Body of Christ don't even believe that these powerful forces exist.

A general survey of the evil in the world by the discerning Christian easily leads to the conclusion that "there is more going on than meets the eye." Indeed there is. Much more than ignorance and human perversity are painting this sinister picture. Open hostility to biblical values, insane crimes that are reported on a daily basis, and growing popularity of atheism strongly suggests that there is a war going on. The protagonist is malevolent but supremely intelligent. He is a master strategist who knows human nature and even the Word of God.

The Hidden War

Scripture does not allow us to conclude that every expression of evil in our world is due solely to fallen human nature. When Scripture says "we wrestle not against flesh and blood," it doesn't mean that we are wrestling against our fallen nature and our sinful proclivities, but rather "against principalities, against powers, against the rulers of the darkness of this world, against spiritual wickedness in high places" (Ephesians 6:12).

In Daniel chapter 10, we read of a conflict so hidden in a parallel reality that we would not be aware of its existence except that it has been revealed by God. Daniel had been praying, fasting, and humbling himself before God. His request had been heard in heaven, yet there was a problem. A messenger came in answer to Daniel's prayer and explained, "But the prince of the kingdom of Persia withstood me one and twenty days: but, lo, Michael, one of the chief princes, came to help me; and I remained there with the kings of Persia" (v. 13).

Unger's observation is revealing. He writes about demonic forces that "are those spirits that operate in the realm of governments of the satanic world system through the human agencies of kings, princes, and other governmental officials."[215] Are there any kings, princes and government officials in today's world who are inviting the forces of darkness into our lives?

Could this be an explanation, at least in part, of what is happening in America? Are the present decisions of the Supreme Court (Roe, Obergefell), the funding of Planned Parenthood, and many other assaults of Christian values the result of a breach in "forbidden gates"—portals to the other side that have been opened by national rebellion and apostasy in the churches of America?

Before we reject such a suggestion as ridiculous and off-the wall, remember that the Bible describes there is much going on behind the scenes and out of sight. A fierce battle with many casualties, often described as "spiritual warfare," is ongoing. Indeed, this warfare is real.

McGuire writes: "If you don't like what you see in reality, then you must learn how to enter this invisible realm and access what some call 'the Keys of the Kingdom.' These keys are spiritual mechanisms for changing reality. They are also referred to as spiritual weapons. They are the fastest, most efficient and powerful way to release power in the earth that change reality."[216]

Whether we acknowledge it or not, Christians are often casualties in this battle. The admonition, "neither give place to the devil" (Ephesians 4:27) suggests that some Christians do give place to the devil. The word "place" (*topos*) can be used in a variety of ways. It can mean a place to live or inhabit, as in Luke 2:7, where we are told that Mary and Joseph laid Jesus in a manger because there was no place (*topos*) for them at the inn. It can also be used to refer to a place where people eat, as at a dinner table (Luke 14:9). Sometimes a geographical region or area is described with the word *topos* (Luke 4:37). But the usage of this word is not only earthly and physical; Jesus said He has gone to prepare a *topos* for us in heaven (John 14:2–3).

The Christian life is not a free ride on easy street. Rather it is one of conflict requiring prayer, discernment, and a continual attempt to stay close to God. Of course, God never moves, but, as casualties of this battle, sometimes Christians move—away from God.

The apostle Paul reminded his readers that the Christian life is like being in the military. He wrote about waging war in a cosmic conflict (Ephesians 6:12), "fighting the good fight" (1 Timothy 1:18; 6:23), "waging war" (2 Corinthians 10:3), and living as a good soldier (2 Timothy 2:4). First-century Christians faced the challenge of living out the Kingdom of God in a world under siege by dark forces.

> ...for they lived with a warfare worldview that expected bad things to happen to good people. If the world is as thoroughly saturated with evil forces as they envisaged, then nightmarish suffering would not come as a great surprise. They understood (because Jesus taught) that, if the Lord of all creation suffered at

the hands of these evil forces, they could hardly expect to fare better (1 J[oh]n 5:20–21; cf. 1 Cor[inthians] 2:8). The New Testament tells "good people" to expect bad things![217]

Acknowledging the reality of this hidden war is extremely important for survival. McGuire asks: "How did America, a nation once heavily influenced by the Christian church and founded to a large degree by Christians, become a spiritual wasteland and a welcome home for what can only be described as the 'spirit of Antichrist?'"

One reason he gives is that "the foundational, scientific truthfulness of the Bible was undermined beginning with Charles Darwin's theory of evolution." In addition, McGuire writes that "huge segments of the evangelical church began to openly reject the Bible as the inspired and inerrant Word of God…the basic idea was that the Bible was only true in 'spiritual' matters and it was to be taken as an allegory or mythology in the areas of science, sexuality, economics, history, and other areas of life."

For McGuire, the big reason for this drift away from our Christian roots, however, "is also tied into a rejection of the authority of God's Word. In Ephesians 6:12, the apostle Paul writes, 'For we wrestle not against flesh and blood, but against principalities, against powers, against the rulers of the darkness of this world, against spiritual wickedness in high places.' God's Word teaches that we are to take the reality of spiritual warfare with Satan and demonic beings very seriously."[218]

What does all of this have to do with spiritual warfare and revival? Much in every way. The world in which we share Christ has been infiltrated at every level, as we are told in Scripture, with dark forces that are hostile to revival.

If we take Bible prophecy literally, as we should, it teaches us that in the last days the world will be united in a one-world government, one-world economic system, and one-world religion under the False Prophet and the Antichrist. Since the time of the Tower of Babel and the ancient mystery religions of ancient Babylon, the world has been moving steadily towards this prophetic destination point. It is clear that

Satan and his demons interact with, communicate with, and guide men and women just as the Holy Spirit does God's people. There are very powerful international bankers and people in positions of power who have dedicated themselves to fulfilling Satan's plan for mankind out of spiritual deception or choice—only God knows their hearts.[219]

America is in deep spiritual trouble. There are threats of every imaginable nature, ranging from military and economic and social to domestic and local. In every presidential election, campaigns are filled with rhetoric, each espousing its own brand of "solution." Yet, there is that inner gnawing sense of despair in every heart that none of these ideas will work. Might we be missing something very obvious? A simple parable may help.

There were two brothers, Jimmy and Billy. They were both in elementary school. Jimmy was doing real well, but Billy just wasn't getting it. Jimmy's teachers sent notes home and telling his parents how good he was doing: he was on time, did his homework conscientiously, and never talked without first raising his hand. The letters always included a happy smiling face. However, Billy was just the opposite. He was failing badly. Notes his teachers sent home had frowning faces on them. Billy's dad tried to help Billy improve his grades by using everything from a variety of rewards to a variety of threats and punishments. One day, his dad got real angry and even gave Billy a good beating. He even threatened to take away Billy's bicycle until his work and behavior in school improved. But it never did.

One day Billy's teacher asked his parents, "Have you had Billy's eyes checked lately? I think he has trouble seeing the board and reading his assignments. He said his eyes hurt." Sure enough, that was the problem. Once Billy started wearing glasses, his grades and behavior improved.

Just as Billy's parents were missing the obvious source of the problem, the church may be doing the same thing.

Are the problems that America faces of a different order than what the candidates are offering? Have demons found "the land of the free and the home of the brave" a stronghold?

God Is Sovereign, But Is He Pleased with the Current State of Affairs?

Some Christians have developed a theology of resignation. Since God is controlling everything, and since He, as God, always gets His way, He must be pretty happy with the current state of affairs. But do we realize what that means? If God is always getting His perfect will done, then any effort we make to change the situation—for example, putting an end to sex trafficking, stopping the illegal drug trade, and praying for national revival—is doomed to fail because we are fighting against God. So, Christians retreat into resignation and very piously attribute everything to the sovereignty of God: "Whatever will be will be, so what's the use?"

Many American Christians are paralyzed by this theology of resignation and will appeal to Romans 13:1– to make their case for non-resistance. Many will even refrain from voting. If the president pushes some outrageously evil and ungodly program, these Christians will say, "Well, God put him into office. Let's not be too critical." The unspoken assumption is: "To speak against a leader whom God has put in office is to speak against God."

Divine sovereignty is often thought of in terms of divine control and divine causation, also known as "omnicontrol." Misfortune, difficulty, and setbacks are often attributed to some secret plan of God. "Maybe we are getting what we deserve. We've been bad." Did God actually cause Israel's multiple rebellions and times of apostasy because He had a secret plan and really delighted in what was happening? Scripture says, "When I spake, ye did not hear; but did evil before mine eyes, and did choose that wherein I delighted NOT" (Isaiah 65:12, emphasis added).

To be sure, God does discipline His people in a variety of ways, but the discipline is for sin and rebellion, not out of caprice or because of some hidden plan that has not been revealed. The discipline is necessary, but its results are not an expression of joy on God's part. "For he doth NOT afflict willingly nor grieve the children of men" (Lamentations 3:33, emphasis added).

In a most poignant way, Jesus wept over Jerusalem: "How often would I have gathered thy children together, even as a hen gathereth her chickens under her wings [His will], and ye would not [their will]!" (Matthew 23:37). Jesus made it clear that Jerusalem's rebellion had a part to play in all of this: "For I say unto you, Ye shall not see me henceforth, TILL YE SHALL SAY, Blessed is he that cometh in the name of the Lord" (v. 39, emphasis added).

We live in a broken world populated by sick and hungry children; lives cut short by senseless violence; broken homes and marriages; poverty; and war. If all of this is God's doing, why are we taught to pray, "Thy kingdom come. Thy will be done in earth, as it is in heaven"? (Matthew 6:10).

A Warfare Worldview

The Bible presents a warfare worldview. There are invisible, but very hostile, intelligent entities that are seeking to impede or destroy the redemptive plans of God. Many of the pagan religions also speak of spirits, demons, and malevolent spirit entities. There is a never-ending battle between good and bad and light and darkness that will never end, because none of the good deities can ultimately vanquish their enemies. However, this theological dualism is not the biblical view.

In the biblical worldview, evil is intelligent and volitional. We are warned about Satan's "devices" (2 Corinthians 2:11) and "the wiles ["schemings"] of the devil" (Ephesians 6:11). However, in the biblical worldview, Satan is never presented as God's equal. For example, the demons had to get Jesus' permission to enter the herd of swine: "And forthwith Jesus gave them leave" (Mark 5:12–13), even as Satan could do nothing to Job apart from what God expressly allowed (Job 1:6–12).

In the background of Jesus' ministry is the thought that a spiritual war is in progress. Satan has taken something that is not his. Satan is referred to as the "prince [*archon*] of this world" (John 12:31; 14:30; 16:11).

Archon refers to the highest authority in a given place. There is a remarkable testimony to this in account of the temptations of Jesus. In Matthew 4:8–9, we read: "Again, the devil taketh him up into an exceeding high mountain, and showeth him all the kingdoms of the world, and the glory of them; And saith unto him, All these things will I give thee, if thou wilt fall down and worship me." Jesus never denied that these abilities were in Satan's possession. Why? First John 5:19 explains that "the whole world lieth in wickedness."

Jesus perceived many of the afflicted as being under attack from some kind of an alien and evil force in God's good creation. He claimed that some, though not all, sickness had something to do with this alien and evil force. In Luke 13, we read of "a woman which had a spirit of infirmity eighteen years" (v. 11). The ruler of the synagogue in which the miracle had taken place was indignant that Jesus "worked" on the Sabbath. Jesus' response is enlightening: "And ought not this woman, being a daughter of Abraham, whom Satan hath bound, lo, these eighteen years, be loosed from this bond on the Sabbath day?" (v. 16).

If someone asked why God became man and died on the cross, most Christians would answer: "To save us from the consequences of our sins." That is certainly a valid answer. Hebrews 2:14, however, completes the biblical picture: "Forasmuch then as the children are partakers of flesh and blood, he also himself likewise took part of the same, that through death he might destroy him that had the power of death, that is, the devil" (cf. also 1 John 3:8b). When Jesus drove out demonic forces, the kingdom was indeed expanding. Jesus was binding "the strong man" (Matthew 12:22–29).

One Almighty Triune God; Many "Gods"

Though there is only one true and living God who is supreme over the entire universe, the Bible acknowledges that there are other "gods" who enjoy a measure of autonomy by divine permission. This is a key point, so I repeat: These other "gods" "enjoy a measure of autonomy by divine permission." There is freedom in the world of rational beings, but it is not a stolen freedom. It is freedom granted by God. God doesn't will evil, but its existence is not a surprise to God. It is in this realm of free rational beings that evil, and evil beings, exist and do their work. Christians often have a two-tiered view of reality: The uncreated and Eternal God, and the world of created beings. However, there is a third, or middle tier: invisible spiritual beings, many who are malevolent in nature and, in large measure, do their own bidding.

I certainly don't want to get too philosophical or theological and delve into the morass of sovereignty, predestination, and the free, uncoerced actions of God's creatures. However, those of us who are praying and fasting for revival believe that "the effectual fervent prayer of a righteous man availeth much" (James 5:16). What we do, or don't do, really matters. There is a view of the sovereignty of God that is so heavy on the God side that it forgets the reality of second causes.

The apostle Paul writes, "I am made all things to all men, that I might by all means save some" (1 Corinthians 9:22). Second causes—our prayers and witness—have weight in the sight of God. How could that be? Because God so willed it.

First Timothy 4:16 says: "Take heed unto thyself, and unto the doctrine; continue in them: for in doing this thou shalt both save thyself, and them that hear thee." Paul is saying, "Timothy, if you do this you will save yourself, and you will also save those who hear you preach." Revival can come usually at great price and labor. It is unwise to use a one-sided view of divine sovereignty against working and praying for what we desperately need.

A common objection to this middle tier is that the scriptural references to other "gods" is really hyperbolic language and only references idols. Appeal is often made to Jeremiah 5:7: "Thy children have forsaken me, and sworn by them that are not gods."

However, the prophets sometimes speak of the nations in the same way. Isaiah 40:17 is an example: "All nations before him are as nothing;

and they are counted to him less than nothing, and vanity." Clearly, the prophet is not denying the existence of nations, so why should we take similar language to indicate that there are no gods when, in fact, there are many? Note the following biblical references:

- Psalms 86:8: "Among the gods there is none like unto thee, O Lord; neither are there any works like unto thy works."
- Psalms 96:4: "For the Lord is great, and greatly to be praised: he is to be feared above all gods."
- Psalms 135:5: "For I know that the Lord is great, and that our Lord is above all gods."
- Psalms 97:7: "Confounded be all they that serve graven images, that boast themselves of idols: worship him, all ye gods."
- Deuteronomy 3:24: "O Lord God, thou hast begun to show thy servant thy greatness, and thy mighty hand: for what God is there in heaven or in earth, that can do according to thy works, and according to thy might?"

Some might call this dualism; but it is not a dualism that removes God from His rightful place on the throne. Rather, it is a modified dualism that recognizes the sovereignty of God as well as the limited authority of other "gods." Psalms 97:7, which calls on the "gods" to worship the true and living God, shows that these "gods" are not just inanimate objects, as is also true of Judges 11:23–24: "So now the Lord God of Israel hath dispossessed the Amorites from before his people Israel, and shouldest thou possess it? Wilt not thou possess that which Chemosh thy god giveth thee to possess?"

The commandment of Exodus 20:3–4 is likewise instructive on this point. It is not a denial of other deities, but affirms their existence by forbidding their worship: "Thou shalt not make unto thee any graven image, or any likeness of anything that is in heaven above, or that is in the earth beneath, or that is in the water under the earth." The text doesn't say, "Don't make any graven images," but it says, "Don't make any graven images or representations of anything that is in the heaven above, or that is in the earth beneath, or that is in the water under the earth." The image represents something that is real.

"For the Lord is a great God," we read in Psalms 95:3, "and a great king above all gods." There is no denial here of the existence of other "gods." What is denied is that these other "gods" are greater than the Lord.

Gods, Idols, and Demons

The ancient world of the New Testament era was very much like our present-day era. A tourist visiting Athens, Greece, would get an overwhelming feeling of awe in seeing the Parthenon and adjacent structures—the Temple of Athena Nike, the theater of Dionysus, and many other magnificent edifices. Yet, when the apostle Paul was in Athens, he was not impressed by the architecture. Rather, he was deeply distressed that the city was full of idols (Acts 17:16). In his book, *Powers of Darkness: Principalities and Powers in Paul's Letters*, Clinton E. Arnold writes that pagans believed their gods were alive.

> Pagans believed their gods were alive and could help them in practical ways for their earthly needs and, in many instances, bring them a blissful afterlife. The early Christians, including Paul, saw these gods as alive too, but in a different sense. They believed demons, the powers of Satan, inspired and perpetuated these pagan gods. These idols greatly distressed Paul because they represented a supernaturally inspired opposition to the gospel which Paul came to proclaim.[220]

We have scriptural proof that the apostle Paul saw more in idols than just grotesque images and statues made of wood and stone. They actually brought their devotees into fellowship with demons. "What say

I then? That the idol is anything, or that which is offered in sacrifice to idols is anything? But I say, that the things which the Gentiles sacrifice, they sacrifice to devils [demons], and not to God: and I would not that ye should have fellowship with devils" (1 Corinthians 10:20). The apostle denies that the idol is "anything"—it's just wood, stone, or clay. However, there is a definite connection between the idol and demonic forces. The connection is so significant that it could lead to "fellowship with devils." Psalms 106:36–37 is similar, for we read that "they served their idols: which were a snare unto them. Yea, they sacrificed their sons and their daughters unto devils."

Some of the demons were associated with given locations. In the Old Testament, each group of people in a given locality worshipped its own particular Baal, and often named him after the city or locality where he was worshipped. There are many examples, such as Baal-hermon, Baal-hazor, Baal-gad, and Baal-peor. All of these idols—whether associated with a country, territory, city or a body of water—are in reality rebel angels masquerading as deity. The people's idolatrous worship brought them into fellowship with these evil spirits. God's anger with His people over their idolatry was that they are making false deities their hope.

The Bible never raises any doubt that the eternal, triune God whom Christians worship is supreme over all the universe. Nevertheless, we are taught, from Scripture that there are spiritual beings populating the universe, some of whom are designated "gods."

> For though there be that are called gods, whether in heaven or in earth, (as there be gods many, and lords many,) But to us there is but one God, the father, of whom are all things, and we in him; and one Lord Jesus Christ, by whom are all things, and we by him. (1 Corinthians 8:5–6)

The Old Testament speaks of the army of the Lord. "The chariots of God are twenty thousand, even thousands of angels: the Lord is among them, as in Sinai, in the holy place" (Psalms 68:16). Both Elijah's and

Elisha's servants was allowed to see that the Lord possesses a vast army of spirit warriors who aid His servants (2 Kings 2:11–12; 6:8–18). This helps us understand why God is called "the Lord of hosts" or "the Lord of armies." "O Lord God of hosts, who is a strong Lord like unto thee? or to thy faithfulness round about thee?" (Psalms 89:8).

Just prior to the description of the fall of Jericho is a Scripture verse presenting the Lord as a commander of armies.

> And it came to pass, when Joshua was by Jericho, that he lifted up his eyes and looked, and, behold there stood a man over against him with his sword drawn in his hand: and Joshua went unto him, and said unto him, Art thou for us, or for our adversaries? And he said, Nay; but as captain of the host of the Lord am I now come. And Joshua fell on his face to the earth, and did worship, and said unto him, What saith my Lord unto his servant. And the captain of the Lord's host said unto Joshua, Loose thy shoe from off thy foot; for the place whereon thou standest is holy. And Joshua did so. (Joshua 5:13–15)[221]

In view of this onslaught from the realm of darkness, Christians must neither be passive nor ignorant. Passivity and ignorance will destroy a person, a family, a community, and a nation. In these last days, Satan knows that his time is short. He has great wrath against those who are calling on God to bring revival. Consequently, he is furiously at work. Christians need never to forget the words of Revelation 12:12: "Woe to the inhabiters of the earth and of the sea! For the devil is come down unto you, having great wrath, because he knoweth that he hath but a short time."

The Ministry of Jesus as the Kingdom Advances

In the Gospels the advancement of the Kingdom is presented as a rout of dark forces—a fleeing of demons because power from God has come to earth. In Mark 1:15, Jesus appears, preaching the gospel. He says, "The time is fulfilled, and the kingdom of God is at hand: repent ye, and believe the gospel." Following this, Jesus builds an inner circle, a team to work with Him. He says, "Come ye after me, and I will make you to become fishers of men" (v. 17).

Jesus then begins to teach in the synagogue at Capernaum, where He meets a man with an unclean spirit (*pneuma akatharton*). This designation is used twenty-one times in the New Testament in the context of intense demonic activity that invades the mind, body, and spirit of an individual. "Unclean," in its Old Testament setting, referred to ritual impurity, but in the New Testament, it speaks of moral and spiritual defilement and, as such, could properly characterize our present age. These are "dirty demons" causing filthy perversions and damnable activities to be destigmatized by courts and so-called learned councils.

In Revelation 16:13, John sees "three unclean spirits like frogs come out of the mouth of the dragon, and out of the mouth of the beast, and out of the mouth of the false prophet." Future Babylon's indictment is that it has become "the habitation of devils, and the hold of every foul spirit, and a cage of every unclean and hateful bird. For all nations have drunk of the wine of the wrath of her fornication" (Revelation 18:2–3).

As an added insight, we must note that preterists must understand the book of Revelation as having already been fulfilled in the past. It supports their view that demonic activity is past because all the demons are now bound. If they would dare to let the book speak for itself, they would see that the demons are alive and well, and will be released as a swarm that will darken the skies in the future (Revelation chapter 9).

At any rate, there is a man there with an unclean spirit who cries out:

Let us alone; what have we to do with thee, thou Jesus of Nazareth? art thou come to destroy us? I know the who thou art, the Holy One of God. And Jesus rebuked him, saying, Hold thy peace, and come out of him. And when the unclean spirit had torn him, and cried with a loud voice, he came out of him. And they were all amazed, insomuch that they questioned among themselves, saying, What thing is this? What new doctrine is this? For with authority commandeth he even the unclean spirits, and they do obey him? (Mark 1:23–27)

Notice that this had a powerful effect on the people: "They were all amazed." They started talking among themselves and asked, "What new doctrine [or teaching] is this?" Such would suggest that the people prior to this time were plagued by dark forces and were virtually helpless to resist, but now that Jesus had come, a new period of spiritual deliverance and even conquest had arrived.

As we proceed, we notice that when they left the synagogue, Jesus, James, and John entered the house of Simon and Andrew. Peter's mother-in-law was sick with a fever. Verses 31–34 again show us that Jesus' ministry of advancing the kingdom involved healing and casting out demons.

Jesus continued His ministry with the healing of a paralytic on the Sabbath (Mark 2:1–12). After a short interlude of an unspecified duration, Jesus kept healing, setting large groups of people free from "plagues" (3:10) and driving out "unclean spirits" (3:11–12). In Mark 3:20–30, Jesus is charged with being in league with Beelzebub. Jesus makes it clear that His demonstrations of power show that He has bound "the strong man." Indeed, the coming of the Kingdom involved routing out evil spirits.

Boyd comments on this and says the kingdom of God "was something the New Testament authors prayed for, not something they considered already accomplished (Matt[hew] 6:10; L[u]k[e] 11:2). The only way it would be brought about was by overthrowing the illegitimate kingdom that was in place."[222]

Christian Persecution

The persecution of Christians has been a reality since the beginning of the New Testament era. Jesus told His followers to expect it. Civil government will be especially vicious because of the Christians' refusal to recognize the emperor—king, president, human potentate—as supreme. Jesus told the church at Smyrna, "The devil will cast some of you into prison" (Revelation 2:10). It is doubtful that Jesus meant that the devil will show up with a pitchfork wearing a red jumpsuit. He will accomplish his evil purposes using deceived people.

Again, in Revelation 2, we see evidence of Satan's hatred for the Body of Christ. In the Lord's message to the church at Pergamos, we read of Antipas (Greek: *antipas*, "against all") as being labeled "my faithful martyr." He was "slain among you, where Satan dwelleth" (Revelation 2:13).

Is there persecution in America and the world today that has a satanic origin? It is impossible to deny that there is. Revelation chapters 12 and 13 speak of Satan's rage against Christians. The red dragon persecutes the woman (Revelation 12:13) and wages war against her seed (Revelation 12:17). Though these are Tribulation passages, Satan's hatred of Christ and His people is continuous.

Perhaps one of the greatest opponents of biblical Christianity today (though certainly not the only opponent), is radical Islam. We would do well to focus on the demonic source of the opposition and to have compassion on the people whom Satan is using. Joel Richardson writes of our duty to God in our treatment of Muslims:

> Believers must demonstrate the Father's amazing, unrelenting love to Muslims. The Islamic world is not a culture of the cross. As such, when the Church truly lives as the body of Messiah crucified, Muslims will be touched. And many will be changed forever.... The praying Church must seize upon the prophetic promise that the Father has placed with Ishmael's name and cry out, "Father, once more, hear the cry of Ishmael! Do for his offspring what you have done for us. Open their eyes. Remove their blindness and reveal Jesus to them as the Son of God. Save a multitude of Muslims, O Father!"[223]

False Teaching

First Timothy 4:1 explains the effects spirit forces can have on a church's ministry and teaching: "Now the Spirit speaketh expressly, that in the latter times some shall depart from the faith, giving heed to seducing spirits, and doctrines of devils." According to the apostle Paul, there are those who will become apostates because they have given heed to dangerous spirit entities.

Paul relays this information to Pastor Timothy because the Holy Spirit spoke clearly to Paul about this emerging problem. Consequently, he is warning Timothy. There will be churches that will be subject to demonic influence through false teachers who have imbibed the teachings of demons. Of special significance is the effect that the teaching of demons will have on those who heed them: "Having their conscience seared with a hot iron." They will be unable to discern right from wrong, good from bad. It would appear that this is one of the reasons that there is so much bad doctrine being taught in so many modern churches. And since these churches' consciences are seared, warning and admonition has little effect.

Because of this reality, the apostle gives Timothy special instruction regarding those who have been infected: "In meekness instructing those that oppose themselves; if God peradventure will give them repentance to the acknowledging of the truth: And that they may recover themselves out of the snare of the devil, who are taken captive by him at his will" (2 Timothy 2:25–26).

Timothy is to instruct "in meekness." There is no thought here of brashness or berating such individuals. These individuals who have been led astray by the spirits are to be objects of compassion, not objects of scorn, for they "oppose themselves." Just as the Gadarene demoniac lived a self-destructive lifestyle (Mark 5:1–20), so, too, these individuals are harming themselves. They believe and practice that which is against their best interests.

Should We JustTake It,
or Should We Fight Back?

In some Christian circles, the words "spiritual warfare" make people fidget and roll their eyes. Perhaps with good reason. A number of techniques have developed that have no support in Scripture. They are quite dramatic and sensational, and, with good reason, some view them with skepticism. Their effect on the forces of darkness is to make them laugh with amusement.

Some warfare strategies involve confronting Satan and his helpers. Yet, Michael the archangel didn't. Rather, he said, "The Lord rebuke thee" (Jude 9). Nor is there any scriptural support for the contention that we need to first find out the name of the demon before we can hope for victory.

It seems to this author (Larry) that Arnold expresses great wisdom when he writes: "The silence of Scripture on the issue of strategy is quite evident. When we consider that the New Testament records the spread of the gospel into pagan lands (Syria, Asia Minor, Greece, and Italy) where idols and occultism held sway, it is very surprising to find no mention of a strategy that stresses discerning, naming, and praying down territorial spirits."[224]

We need a better way—a more biblical way—of looking at spiritual warfare. It is essential that we see spiritual warfare as that which is necessary for victorious Christian living in the modern world. The moment we come to faith in Christ, we are flung onto the battlefield, whether we know it or not. You can't live the Christian life without being confronted, sometimes on a daily basis, with the forces of darkness. Just as the early Christians burned their books of magic with their "tricks of the trade" and began to incorporate basic biblical principles that led to revival described with the words, "so mightily grew the word of God and prevailed" (Acts 19:19–20), we too, need to "burn" the methods that are sometimes used by the so-called "spiritual warfare experts." In short, we shouldn't be focused on a method of spiritual warfare, but on a *life* of spiritual warfare. Here's what that life looks like:

A person of prayer—In your prayers, ask God for guidance in how to pray and what to pray for. As in all prayer, petitions must be focused and specific. The Holy Spirit is the Guide and Energizer for effective prayer (Ephesians 6:18; Romans 8:26). Intercession needs to be guided by the Word of God and the Spirit of God. As the old saying goes, "If you aim at nothing you will hit it every time." An important part of your prayer is to specifically ask God to hinder the dark forces that are at work: (1) around you; (2) in your home; (3) in your church; (4) in your community and world. Be sure to praise God and thank Him for what He has already done in your life, and for what He is doing right now.

A person who seeks to win the lost—The gospel is the "power of God unto salvation" (Romans 1:16). Pray for the progress and advancement of the gospel. The apostle Paul asked the Thessalonians to "pray for us, that the word of the Lord may have free course, and be glorified, even as it is with you: And that we may be delivered from unreasonable and wicked men" (2 Thessalonians 3:1–2).

A person who guards his or her heart (Proverbs 4:23)—This is the person who follows the exhortation of 2 Corinthians 7:1: "Let us cleanse ourselves from all filthiness of the flesh AND spirit, perfecting holiness in the fear of God" (emphasis added). Filthiness is not only in the flesh, but also in the spirit.

A person who remembers that dark powers exploit the prevailing culture—Many victories are lost because Satan can use the prevailing culture to desensitize individuals to evil. Exposure to evil can make one comfortable with evil. Culture is not neutral. American culture is, by and large, downright hostile to godliness. We must strive to have more than Christian beliefs (that's only a starting point). Seek to have a Christian worldview. Christians with only Christian beliefs are easily duped by the darkness; Christians with a sound worldview will stand strong and persevere in righteousness.

A person who strives for personal and corporate purity—We must be careful about what we allow into our lives and what we allow into areas where we have some measure of leadership—such as homes, workplaces, and the local churches. "All things are lawful unto me, but all things are not expedient: all things are lawful for me, but I will not be brought under the power of any" (1 Corinthians 6:12).

A person who seeks to honor Ephesians 4:3: "Endeavoring to keep the unity of the Spirit in the bond of peace."—Satan wins many victories over cranky Christians who are willing to split hairs and find heretics under every pew. Scripture makes it abundantly clear that we are to contend for the faith (Jude 3), but some become very contentious and seem to think God endorses their mindless dogmatism and debatable matters. When Christians divide over minute issues of personal preference, the demons move in. We must make a distinction between personal opinions and biblically grounded truths that constitute the core doctrines of the Christian faith. If you have ever been in a church business meeting where people are fussing with one another, the Holy Spirit is grieved. And you know it.

A person who strives to bring peace and satisfaction to his or her home life and family—Unfortunately for some, this is the most challenging aspect of spiritual warfare. "Likewise, ye husbands, dwell with them according to knowledge, giving honor unto the wife, as unto the weaker vessel, and as being heirs TOGETHER of the grace of life; that your PRAYERS be not hindered" (1 Peter 3:7, emphasis added). If you do these things you will be in the choir of those who sing "the overcomers' victory song."

Revival is desperately needed. Human carnality and spiritual shortsightedness are great hindrances to what the world desperately needs. In addition, however, is the activity of a vast number of invisible beings whose great desire is to hinder and thwart revival unless we use the appropriate means to bring about their defeat.

9

Final Fire

Days of Glory Draw Near

GOD IS NEVER caught by surprise. He knows "the end from the beginning, and from ancient times the things that are not yet done" (Isaiah 46:10). Moreover, the counsels of eternity have already heard the echoes of the plan of redemption. Jesus Christ, the Lamb "without blemish and without spot: Who verily was foreordained before the foundation of the world, but was manifest in these last times for you" (1 Peter 1:19–20).

What do we see in our world that reminds us that we are drawing close to the days of final fire?

Signs of a Softening— What Are We to Make of It?

While terrorist attacks associated with Islamic fanatics in various parts of the world are gaining all the media attention, another move in the Islamic world is far more important, though it is virtually ignored in the media. Multitudes of Muslims are asking the question: "Do I want to be associated with a religion that brutally murders innocent people?"

A related question is also being asked by many Muslims: "Is terrorism the true side of Islam? Can I be a good Muslim and not be a murderous jihadist?"

The question that we must address is this: "Aren't there any Muslims in the world who abhor Islamic terrorism and radicalism and who are willing to publicly oppose the jihadists?"

Such a question has to be asked in the shadow of 9/11 and the many other acts of terrorism connected to Islam. Is Islam monolithic? Are all Muslims terrorists? Joel Rosenberg writes, "the mainstream media has, frankly, done a terrible job examining the internal tensions and enormous diversity of beliefs and practices within the Muslim Community"[225]. The non-jihadist Muslims are a "welcome breath of fresh air in a region being suffocated by the Radicals, and they deserve not only to be acknowledged by the free people of the West but to be appreciated, encouraged, and supported, for in many ways they represent our front line of defense in stopping the worst-case scenarios being planned by the radicals."[226]

This is one of the principal reasons why I (Larry) believe that that conservatives in the West, and especially in America, need to be very careful not to alienate this "front line of defense." While some might claim I am "soft on Islam," such is not the case. However, we do have to be honest about the facts and credible, and not carelessly lump all Muslims together. There are some Muslim groups that are speaking out, publicly, against jihad.

Though this phenomenon of faulting radical Islam by many Muslims is a relatively new phenomenon, it has roots in the past. Sayyad Imam Al-Sharif has been described as a "major" figure in the global jihad movement. He was one of Ayman Al-Zawahiri's oldest associates. His book, *The Essentials of Making Ready (For Jihad)* was the jihad manual for Al-Qaeda training camps in Afghanistan. However, in a manifesto written from an Egyptian prison, he made an about-face and said that the 9/11 attacks were "a catastrophe for all Muslims....Whoever approves their actions shares their sin." Among other things, he writes that "it is forbidden to harm foreigners and tourists in Muslim countries…it is treachery to kill people in a non-Muslim country after entering that country with its government's permission [a legal visa]."[227]

So where does this leave us in present years? Based on Gallup surveys, an overwhelming number of Muslims—more than nine in ten—are moderate in their views and are not inclined to violence and/or extremism. Substantial majorities in early all nations surveyed—94 percent in Egypt, 93 percent in Iran, and 90 percent in Indonesia—said that if they had the opportunity to draft a new constitution for their country, "they would guarantee freedom of speech, defined as 'allowing all citizens to express their opinion on the political, social and economic issues of the day.'"[228]

In a January 2015 NewsMax report titled "Egypt's New President Blasts Islamic Extremists," Todd Beamon writes:

> The new President of Egypt has directly confronted Islamic leaders in his country and challenged them to stand against extremism in their religion.
>
> "We are in need of a religious revolution," President Abdel-Fattah el-Sisi told imams on New Year's Day at al-Azhar University in Cairo.
>
> "You, imams, are responsible before Allah," el-Sisi said. "The entire world…is waiting for your next move…because [the Islamic world] is being torn, it is being destroyed, it is being lost—and it is being lost by our own hands."
>
> Since coming to power, el-Sisi "has cracked down hard on Islamist extremists. Meanwhile he has signaled support to the country's beleaguered Coptic Christian community, attending Christmas services at Cairo's Abbasaiya Cathedral and declaring that Egyptians should not view each other as Christians or Muslims but as Egyptians."[229]

This theme has been picked up in Saudi Arabia. A female Saudi television news anchor, Nadine Al-Budair, interrupted her own broadcast to criticize Muslims who claim that radical Islamic extremism doesn't represent the religion of Islam, and urged Muslims to "feel shame" over the deadly terrorist attacks like the one in Brussels in March of 2016. Muslims who argue that radical extremists "do not represent Islam or the Muslims" are nothing more than "hypocrites" and "smart alecks," she said. According to a translation by the Middle East Media Research Institute (MEMRI), Al-Budair argued:

> "We witness people competing in an attempt to be the first to prove that everything that is happening has nothing to do with the Muslims, and that the terrorists are highway robbers and homeless alcoholics and drug addicts," Al-Budair explained. "We all know that the number of the homeless in Europe is very high. They sleep in the streets and beg for alms, and some of them are alcoholics and drug addicts, but we do not expect these addicts or criminals to even consider coming here and blowing up a mosque or a street in our city. It is we [Muslims] who blow ourselves up. It is we who blow up others."[230]

In a Christianitytoday.com article titled, "The World's Biggest Muslim Organization Wants to Protect Christians," Jayson Casper writes, "Another major gathering of Islamic leaders denounces extremism.[231]

In January of 2016, 200 Muslim religious leaders, heads of state, and scholars, gathered in Morocco. They released the Marrakesh Declaration, a 750-word document calling for majority Muslim countries to protect the freedom of religious minorities, including Christians.

King Muhammad VI of Morocco has been at the forefront of reform. In the spring of 2011 he announced a broad revision of the Constitution. The King gave a speech to the nation on radio and TV and said, "By launching today the work of constitutional reform, we embark on a major phase in the process

of consolidation of our model of democracy and development."
The King said women's rights and political participation would
be strengthened. The changes guarantee that men and women
would have equal access to elected positions.[232]

Morocco has taken steps to protect the country from terrorist attacks.
The Clarion Project reports that "Morocco thwarts Islamic state chemical wWeapons attack." Ten suspects were arrested the day before they
were to carry out a suicide attack. Six jars of Sulphur-containing chemical fertilizer were seized along with chemicals which can create the teta-
nus toxin, along with four machine guns, tear gas and ammunition.[233]

The battle, however, has certainly not been won in Morocco. In
August of 2016, it was reported that a pregnant teenage Moroccan
girl set herself on fire after her eight rapists were released from prison.
Despite the police arresting eight suspects, a prosecutor decided to grant
the suspects a provisional release. They then threatened the victim, saying they would "publish pictures of the rape which they had taken with
their mobile phones unless she dropped the complaint against them."[234]

Progress, however, is being made in the Muslim world. In May
of 2016, another three hundred Muslim religious leaders from about
thirty countries did much the same. Gathering in Jakarta, Indonesia,
the country with the largest Muslim population and historically known
for its religious stability, the leaders denounced Islamic extremism and
addressed its causes.

The Indonesian conference was hosted by Nahdlatul Ulama (NU),
the largest Muslim organization in the world, and was opened by the
vice president of the officially-secular country.

NU's membership estimates range from thirty million to fifty million; most are in Indonesia. About 87 percent of Indonesia's population
of 250 million follow Islam; roughly ten percent are Christian. Hinduism and Buddhism comprise the remainder.[235]

Modern Jordan is remarkable in this respect. Under King Abdullah
II's reign, and during the Arab Spring, Jordan has weathered sweeping

reforms and constitutional changes. "King of the Hashemite Kingdom of Jordan and Custodian of the Holy Sites of Jerusalem" boasts that there is not a single political prisoner in Jordan. Abdullah II launched the Amman Message which has been endorsed by five hundred leading Muslim scholars. He has also come out in favor of the 2007 A Common Word Initiative—a groundbreaking initiative in Christian-Muslim engagement. Jordan has made application to UNESCO that al-Maghdas (Arabic for "Baptism"), one of the traditional sites for the baptism of Jesus (see John 1:28), be considered a World Heritage site.[236]

Queen Rania Al Abdullah of Jordan shares the same progressive attitudes. She recently spoke at the Abu Dhabi media summit and spoke out against violent Islamic extremism. Regarding the horrific images of rape, torture and beheadings broadcast by ISIS, the Queen said: "These images don't represent me any more than they represent you.... For the sake of each one of us...for Islam and the Arab world...for the future of our young people, we must create a new narrative and broadcast it to the world. Because if we don't decide what our identity is and what our legacy will be, the extremists will do it for us."[237]

At least one Muslim leader in America, contrary to the opinion of some, is pro-American Constitution. The Founder of the American Islamic Forum For Democracy (AIFD), M. Zuhdi Jasser, served eleven years as a medical officer in the US Navy. His tours of duty include medical department head aboard the USS El Paso, which deployed to Somalia during Operation Restore Hope. He has been chief resident at Bethesda Naval Hospital and staff internist for the Office of the Attending Physicians to the US Congress. Jasser is a respected physician currently in private practice in Phoenix, Arizona, and is past president of the Arizona Medical Association. One of the mission principles of the AIFD is "to advocate for the preservation of the founding principles of the U.S. Constitution.... AIFD looks to build the future of Islam through the concepts of liberty and freedom."[238]

In a rather remarkable indication of profound changes sweeping the Muslim world, we read that Kuwaiti media personality Yousuf 'Abd Al-

Karim Al-Zinkawi called on all Arab Muslims states to recognize Israel, openly and without delay, and stop calling it "the Zionist entity" and stop talking about "the Israeli occupation," terms that undermine Israel's legitimacy.

Since the Arab Spring, and in the last few years, a growing number of Arab policy makers have publicly supported open and full relations with the Jewish State. In January of 2016, Israel's Ministry of Foreign Affairs director—General Dore Gold—revealed that Israel maintains covert ties with almost all Arab countries.

Gold said Israel maintains contacts with "almost every Arab state, as long as it then does not make it to the front page of the daily newspapers," and said there is "the willingness in the Arab world for ties with Israel under the table," terming it as a "dramatic change."

In February, Prime Minister Benjamin Netanyahu called for a change in the way countries that have ties with Israel display and express them publicly, adding that Israel is experiencing a dramatic and positive shift in its ties with many countries, and primarily with the Arab world in the Middle East.

"Major Arab countries are changing their view of Israel…they don't see Israel anymore as their enemy, but they see Israel as their ally, especially in the battle against militant Islam," he said.[239]

Some of the Muslim Majority countries have having second thoughts about their identification with Islam as their state religion.

The highest court in Bangladesh has begun to hear arguments that challenge Islam's status as the official state religion. This development comes after a series of attacks against people of other religions—Hindus, Christians, and Muslim minorities, such as Shi'ites.

When Bangladesh was formed in 1971 after the nation split from Pakistan, it was declared a secular state. However, in 1988, the country's constitution was amended with Islam declared as the state religion. This is being challenged in the latest court battle and is being supported by religious minority leaders. No one knows how this will turn out in the near future, but it is reflective of a mega-shift in thinking.[240]

Perhaps most remarkable is the landmark ruling in March of 2016 of a Malaysian court upholding the rights of a Christian to convert from Islam. This judgment establishes a precedent in a country where religious conversions, particularly from Islam to Christianity, have been steeped in controversy. The significance of this is that this decision reaffirms the supremacy of the Federal Constitution over traditional Islamic law. Article 11 of the Malaysian Constitution defends every Malaysian's citizen's right to freedom of religion.

The plaintiff, Rooney Rebit, was asking judicial authorities to declare that his belief in Jesus Christ was a fundamental human right. The judge, Yew Kin Jie, said, "He is free to exercise his right of freedom to religion and he chose Christianity." Rebit embraced the Christian faith in 1999 and was baptized.

Cases of conversion in Malaysia have been highly controversial. There have been official dissension and charges of apostasy by Muslim clerics challenging verdicts by secular courts in Sharia tribunals.

The most prominent case involved Lina Joy, who converted from Islam to Christianity in 1998 at the age of 26. Her application to have her conversion legally recognized by Malaysian courts was rejected in 2007 after a six-year legal battle.[241]

The Muslim majority nation of Pakistan has made history by issuing a commemorative postage stamp of the Rs. 10 denomination "in recognition of the services for Pakistan of Dewan Bahadur S.P. Singha," a Christian. "This is a great news and honor for the Pakistani Christians and also the Singha family," said Nasir Saeed director of CLAAS-UK. "It is the first time in Pakistani history that any Pakistani Christian's image has been published on a postage stamp."[242]

Young adults in the Muslim world—and especially women—are challenging Muslim standards of dress, behavior and subservience. Evan Drajj was a recent contest winner and wrote:

I'm calling you "My not dear father" because, to me, you are nothing more than the biological causation of my existence in this world. Your efforts to program me for many years, like an ideological machine that was programmed to do this work, was not out of love for me; you did it to satisfy personal pleasure, as your religion dictates....

Father, I am now living life as I please. I didn't get morally and sexually degraded, as you and the rest of society thought I would when I took off my hijab and wore short skirts, or when I stayed up late to drink alcohol at bars—which you think will send me to hell, and make us act like animals.

I am now living alone, despite being a woman. My house hasn't become a house of harlotry, of men that just want to sleep with me, as you and your friends think. I can go anywhere I want by myself, I can take a taxi by myself, I visit my friends (men and women) and we stay up late and have fun without needing to worry about getting home for bedtime. Don't worry—none of them have tried to sleep with me or harass me, even though I live without a guardian.[243]

There are many bitter young women in Muslim countries—along with men, but perhaps to a lesser degree—who are striking back at all religions, including Christianity. They believe that revealed religion has caused all their problems. In effect, they are throwing out the proverbial baby with the dishwater. The softening in Muslim nations does open some doors for evangelism, but it can also close some doors for those who want to adopt secularism as the best course to chart. In our prayers for Muslim nations, in our evangelism, books and articles, Christians need to be extremely sensitive and alert to the pushback against all religions. This is a time of great opportunity, but the opportunity is clothed with a robe of danger. Pushback against Islam could be a pushback against all religious expression.

The gospel of Christ is a gospel of grace, love, and acceptance.

Sometimes it is hard for Christians to show grace, love, and acceptance to a group that is associated with mayhem, murder, and death. Former Muslim Nabeel Qureshi argues that you have to separate Muslims from Islam in your thinking if you are going to end up loving Muslims.

> On the one side you have people who are completely ignoring the history of Islam and what it might have to do with violent jihadists. On the other side of the picture people are looking at the theology and ignoring the complexities of the religious traditions such that Islam can be manifested as a peaceful practice but only in circumstances where people move beyond the foundational practices.
>
> I think the best thing that we can do at this point in time is to distinguish between Muslims and Islam. We haven't made that distinction in public media yet. And that's why you can't criticize Islam because people see that as criticism of Muslims. The conversation get shut down because of the accusations of islamophobia.[244]

Embrace The Cross

How then can we successfully bridge the gap with Muslims? First and foremost, we need to embrace the cross. When Christians exemplify the crucified life, we have made a big step in softening, or perhaps even neutralizing, the hostility many Muslims feel toward American Christians.

Jesus Christ is the "crucified God," to use a phrase that summarizes the session of the God-man on the cross. First Corinthians 2:8 says that angry people "crucified the Lord of glory." "Crucified" and "Lord" seem not to fit well in the same verse. The thief on the cross, however, seems to have made the connection: "Lord, remember me when thou comest into thy kingdom" (Luke 23:42).

Jesus is the "crucified God" and He is also "the image of the invisible God" (Colossians 1:15). Now we see it better. We can say "this is God and God is this."

We hear many names and titles applied to Jesus by pastors and Christian writers. In prayer He is often addressed as "Master," "Lord," "Dear Lord," and "Precious Jesus"; though seldom is He addressed as "Martyr," though that is exactly what He was. This is the name given to Him in Revelation 3:13: "the faithful and true witness." The Greek for this is *martus*, the word from which we get "martyr." Jesus witnesses to the love and faithfulness of God through death.

The connection of being a *martus* unto death is found in Revelation 1:5: "And from Jesus Christ, who is the faithful witness, and the first begotten of the dead." Jesus himself speaks of "Antipas, [who] was my faithful martyr, who was slain among you, where Satan dwelleth" (Revelation 2:13). In Revelation 17:6, John writes: "And I saw the woman drunken with the blood of the saints, and with the blood of the martyrs of Jesus."

Mitch pulls it all together when he observes that at the center of martyrdom is "Jesus Christ, the archetypal martyr, whose image and likeness shines through the heroism of every martyr in history. Taking this fact as an invitation, the challenge before us is to learn the secrets of martyrdom by walking upstream to its source—Christ Himself."[245]

This mysterious and hard-to-grasp truth is at the center of a theology of the cross. Most of the world looks to an invincible and almighty deity, but the God of the Bible identifies with sinful humanity. He experiences death—one of the penalties of sin—and daringly becomes GODFORSAKEN, underscored by Jesus' own words of dereliction, "My God, my God, why hast thou forsaken me?" (Matthew 27:46).

Paul's own life and ministry conformed to this "cruciform" pattern. It was marked by shame, suffering and degradation—even as Jesus' life and ministry were marked by shame, suffering, and degradation.

For I think that God hath set forth us the apostles last, as it were appointed to death: for we are made a spectacle unto the world,

and to angels, and to men.... Even unto the present hour we
both hunger, and thirst, and are naked, and are buffeted, and
have no certain dwelling place.... Being defamed, we intreat:
we are made the filth of the world, and are the offscouring of all
things unto this day. (1 Corinthians 4:9, 11, 13)

Paul's letter to the Corinthians, known today as "1 Corinthians,"
is a letter to a divided church, one in which there were theological and
personal issues that were not pleasing to God. A careful study of the
opening of the letter, and the way the apostle seeks to bring the church
into conformity with the will of God, will show that a theology of the
cross is pivotal. It is an example for us, too, in a day when division and
confusion characterize many local assemblies.

To this divided church the apostle writes: "For the preaching of the
cross is to them that perish foolishness; but unto us which are saved it
is the power of God" (1 Corinthians 1:18). If we want to know God's
wisdom, we have to look at the cross, and study it, and consider what
was accomplished through the cross, and how it was accomplished.

Paul effectively argues that the Corinthians' unity, which is so
fragile, is to be found in the fact that what Christ did for them on
the cross is for them individually and corporately. Some were followers of Paul, others of Cephas. So, Paul asks, "Is Christ divided? Was
Paul crucified for you?" (1:13). Paul refused to preach with the wisdom of words, "lest the cross of Christ should be made of none effect"
(1:17). "Furthermore," writes Graham Tomlin, "the cross answers not
just Corinthian quarrelling, but Corinthian arrogance as well. God's
wisdom is exemplified in His scandalous choice of a crucified Messiah as the means of salvation, a relatively low-status group of people
for the majority of His church in Corinth, and a weak, rhetorically
unskilled and spiritually exhausted apostle (1:26–2:5). Whereas these
Corinthian Christians disdained the poor and Paul, they demonstrate
God's wisdom. The cross thus deconstructs both competitiveness and
arrogance."[246]

As we push the frontiers of faith on the edge of "the end," the cross becomes our model. In his book *Trail of Fire*, Daniel K. Norris writes:

Jesus came to the world and said, "If anyone will come after Me, let him deny himself, and take up his cross daily, and follow me" (Luke 9:23). He then did something no worldly leader would ever do. He led the way. Worldly leaders ask for sacrifice from their followers first; Jesus showed that godly leaders first ask sacrifice from themselves! Jesus was the first to pick up the cross. He willingly laid down His life. Jesus came and walked opposite to the world. He fell out of line, and the religious and political antichrist spirits didn't like it.[247]

In the documentary, *The Global Jesus Revolution: Israel, Islam and the Gospel at the End of the Age*, the last section bears the title: "Reclaiming the Early Church's Theology of the Cross." Richardson says:

We hear the stories of Muslims coming to faith in Jesus. As wonderful as this is these things rarely come easily.… For most of the Western Church the cross provides us with the ability to live a most blessed and happy life. But if the church is to fulfill its last days mandate it must reclaim the theology of the cross as it was proclaimed by Jesus, the early apostles and the early church.[248]

This is a hard pill to swallow for many, yet Christians evangelizing on the cutting edge in dangerous areas have embraced this theology of the cross. In the above-cited documentary, Ali (not his real name; his face is concealed for security purposes), an evangelist ministering in Iran, states:

It's not like in the West where Jesus is like a local supermarket— "Come to Jesus and He'll give you this, …and you'll be happy… and you'll get all your needs given to you…" No! The Jesus I know says, "Come with me and suffer, because when you suffer with me, then you see my glory."

This is the way it was with Jesus. The beginning of the glory road for Him began with an agonizing death on the cross. The crown came after the cross. "Wherefore God also hath highly exalted him, and given him a name which is above every name" (Philippians 2:9).

But do suffering and martyrdom really have any saving value? Are they just things that happen because a lot of angry people out there strongly resent the spread of Christianity? No! Martyrdom is, supremely, an expression of who God is.

Richardson states:

In martyrdom we find the highest form of the testimony and witness of God. Both Jesus and Stephen asked the heavenly Father to forgive their attackers. They were both being martyred. Their patient forbearance in martyrdom was a testimony to the restraint and mercy of God. The day is coming when God will destroy His enemies. Martyrdom, however, is an expression of the nature and character of God in this age.

To embrace the cross, and to apply a theology of the cross, means embracing suffering and death. The cross was an instrument of execution. Jesus said, "Take up your cross and follow me" (Matthew 16:24). Obeying that command requires a great deal of moral fortitude and commitment to Jesus Christ as Lord.

There is pain and suffering for the martyr. To be ready to lose one's life voluntarily, perhaps violently and definitely prematurely, is no easy choice to make. Every cell in our bodies, and every thought flashing through our minds wants escape. The reality of Christ's lordship and command must far exceed the natural tendency toward self-preservation. If someone claps his hands in front of our faces, we blink. It's a reflex action—nothing to be ashamed of, but a reminder of our natural tendencies. God made us that way.

There is pain and suffering for the martyr's family. When Pakistani Christian wife and mother of five, Asia Bibi, was jailed, her husband and children experienced a great amount of suffering. Some family members do recover from the ordeal of losing a loved one, but some, because of the heartache and intense suffering, never recover. Disillusionment, deep spiritual struggles, broken marriages, and emotional distress are very real. God, however, does step in and bring grace to those who are suffering.

For those martyrs who have time to contemplate what is happening and see their death coming, God seems to grant a special "grace" to endure the impending ordeal. In many cases, God grants a surreal, tranquil spirit, a serenity of heart and mind that transcends understanding. That spirit of peace leads to a genuine surrender that is derived from an overarching eternal perspective on life. An unshakable faith in something better in store for them helped many martyrs to calmly bear the trial.[249]

The Cross and Foregoing Our Rights

A challenging and somewhat provocative statement that I (Larry) raised in a Sunday night service was this: "We should always insist on our rights." I then asked the group: "How would you defend this statement? What arguments would you marshal?"

Various comments were made: "The Bill of Rights is fundamental to maintain our freedoms"; "Americans have the right to life, liberty, and the pursuit of happiness"; "If we do not defend our rights, the strong will always defraud the weak."

Then, I made the same statement: "We should always insist on our rights," and asked the group to argue against that statement.

Some said that "based on the example of Jesus our greatest right is to forego our rights"; someone made the comment that "rights are important, but sometimes if we insist on our rights we will not love unconditionally"; "if everyone insists on their rights no one will excel and 'go the extra mile.'"

My point in raising this discussion was to lead the group to a study of 1 Corinthians 9. The apostle Paul makes several comments showing that he has the right to eat and drink, and that he has the right to have a spouse (v. 4–5). He asks, "Who goeth a warfare any time at his own charges? Who planteth a vineyard, and eatethy not of the fruit thereof? Or who feedeth a flock, and eateth not of the milk of the block?" (v. 7). No one goes to war and has to buy his own bullets. No one plants a vineyard without eating some of the crop.

Even God's law teaches that we have certain rights, even as does the laboring ox:

> For it is written in the law of Moses, thou shalt not muzzle the mouth of the ox that treadeth out the corn. Doth God take care for oxen? Or saith he it altogether for our sakes? For our sakes, no doubt, this is written: that he that ploweth should plow in hope; and that he that thresheth in hope should be partaker of his hope. If we have sown unto you spiritual things, is it a great thing if we shall reap your carnal things? If others be partakers of this power over you, are not we rather. (v. 9–12a)

The apostle says it is reasonable, both from the practice of others and the law of God, that he receive some assistance from the churches. But in the middle of verse 12, he makes the statement that he has gone beyond his rights: "Nevertheless, we have not used this power; but suffer all things, lest we should hinder the gospel of Christ." The apostle does the same thing again:

> Do ye not know that they which minister about holy things live of the things of the temple? And they which wait at the altar are

partakers with the altar. Even so hath the Lord ordained that they which preach the gospel should live of the gospel. But I have used none of these things.... For though I be free from all men, yet have I made myself servant unto all, that I might gain the more. (v. 13–15a, 19)

In the 1960s I (Larry) was a social caseworker for the Department of Social Services in a very large eastern city. The caseworkers had a union. We were all members of the union. One of the things that the union stressed was that we should not volunteer to do things that were out of our job description. In fact, even if a supervisor asked us to do that, we should refuse.

In principle, this sounded pretty good, and did have certain advantages. It protected caseworkers from abusive authority. However, I remember one situation in which there was broken glass on the floor. I got a broom and dustpan and swept up the glass. As a caseworker, this was not in my job description—it was my right to not sweep up broken glass—but, sensing the hazardous nature of broken glass, I voluntarily stepped out of my job title.

The apostle Paul, however, did not refuse a gift, a token of love and devotion given not out of necessity but out of appreciation. "Now ye Philippians know also, that in the beginning of the gospel, when I departed from Macedonia, no church communicated with me as concerning giving and receiving, but ye only. For even in Thessalonica ye sent once and again unto my necessity" (Philippians 4:15–6; see v. 18).

In 1 Corinthians 9, Paul writes that he didn't want to do anything, including claiming his rights, if it would jeopardize his effectiveness in proclaiming Christ (v. 15, 18, 23). Christian work can be quite taxing. Pastors, missionaries, and Bible teachers work long, hard hours, sometimes with very little remuneration. We all have bills to pay, but Christ gave all for us and we are called to give all for Him.

Embracing the cross is a necessity. People will often evaluate our sincerity. Paul surrendered his rights because he did not want to leave the slightest question regarding his sincerity. Sincerity communicates. It gives a powerful message. Moreover, because embracing the cross is voluntary, it demonstrates that it is better to want to do right than to have to do right. Surrendering our rights for a higher end demonstrates Christ-likeness in a powerful way.

Christians show that they have attained a high measure of Christian maturity when they surrender their rights. Love goes beyond duty. Love receives its full expression where duty ends.

Jesus Told Us What It Would Be Like

Jesus was brutally honest when He presented the demands of discipleship. He was so honest that we would have to conclude that he needed to take a sales seminar or He would be a flop as a leader.

Suppose I were a real estate salesman. You come to me and indicate that you are looking for a nice piece of land out in the country. A smile crosses my face. "I have just the spot for you."

I take you out to the parcel of land in my four-wheel-drive vehicle. It's equipped with special tires for mud, "just in case the road is a little wet," I inform you.

You ask me if there is water nearby. "Oh yes," I reply. "There is a stream that borders the property. It often floods and becomes a raging torrent. When that happens, the snakes move to higher ground—right where the old house sits, on a hill. And when that happens in the spring, the mosquitoes are really bad that year."

By this time, you have started to wonder what this parcel of property is like. You are having second thoughts concerning this particular piece of land. Your deep thinking is interrupted by my shifting into four-wheel low. The road has become a quagmire. The wheels are throwing mud up on the hood and at the windshield.

Finally, we pull out of the mud and come to a gate with a sign: "No Trespassing. Violators Will Be Shot!"

I honk my horn. I explain to you that there is a property dispute, and the right-of-way is in question. About fifteen minutes later, after several loud blasts on my horn, a very tall, bearded man walks up to the vehicle. He has a double-barreled shotgun cradled in his arm. He spits a wad of tobacco in front of my truck…

We can stop this little parable. We've heard enough. Would you be inclined to buy this piece of property? Probably not. A flood plain? Snakes and mosquitoes? A right-of-way dispute?

In the same way, Jesus told the truth about following Him. He was brutally honest and made no attempt to gloss over some of the issues that might cause people to NOT follow Him. In Matthew 10, Jesus says, in effect, "this is what you will meet as my disciple":

- Extreme danger: "Behold, I send you forth as sheep in the midst of wolves" (v. 16).
- Opposition: "But beware of men: for they will deliver you up to the councils, and they will scourge you in their synagogues (v. 17).
- Division in Families: "And the brother shall deliver up the brother to death, and the father the child" (v. 21).

Jesus, the martyr, was a witness to the truth. Motivated by love, He nevertheless made His enemies very angry. The trials of Jesus following His arrest are instructive. It must have been very high pressure, and then came the big question: "Art thou the Christ, the Son of the Blessed?" (Mark 14:61).

Jesus could have softened His answer by cleverly veiling the truth. He could have said, "Well, er, we are all children of God," or some other such thing. But acting out of the integrity of the divine nature, and in keeping with His full deity, He answered: "I am" (Mark 14:62).

When Jesus is brought before Pilate, once again He tells the truth about His identity. Pilate does not feel threatened by Jesus, but Pilate s somewhat distressed by the fact that the emperor would be unhappy to hear about the civil unrest in Jerusalem. Pilate questions Jesus: "Am I a Jew? Thine own nation and the chief priests have delivered thee unto me: what hast thou done?" (John. 18:35) Jesus, however, is dead serious about speaking the truth and acknowledges that He has a kingdom: "My kingdom is not of this world: if my kingdom were of this world, then would my servants fight, that I should not be delivered to the Jews: but now is my kingdom not from hence...thou sayest that I am a king. To this end was I born, and for this cause came I into the world" (v. 37).

The Christian martyr is like his Master. He follows truth no matter where it may lead—even to the point of execution.

When we see the Savior's hands and feet spiked to the wood of the cross, we can only learn one lesson for ourselves should we, some day—perhaps soon—face martyrdom: the martyr gives his life as an offering, both to God, and to mankind.

Christ was no surprised and hapless victim, caught up in a crowd of harsh and angry men. Bleeding and dying on the cross, the Son of God was making a willful love offering, as He said earlier: "Greater love hath no man that this, that a man lay down his life for his friends" (John 15:13).

A theology of the cross will help us to understand, in some small measure, the suffering that God's people experience—some of it even as part of the plan of God. "For unto you it is given in the behalf of Christ, not only to believe on him, but also to suffer for his sake" (Philippians 1:29). "It is given," certainly not by Satan. He doesn't grant faith in Christ. This is speaking about God's plan, His grand design, which obviously embraces suffering for His children. It may even include death, crucifixion, scourging and persecution. God uses good men and women to be agents of His judgment: "Wherefore, behold I send unto you prophets, and wise men, and scribes: and some of them ye shall kill and crucify: and some of them shall ye scourge in your synagogues, and persecute them from city to city: that upon you may come all the righteous blood shed upon the earth" (Matthew 23:34–35).

The Mystery of the Twenty-first Hostage

A rather sad, though compelling, account that shows what this means in the twenty-first century occurred in February 2015. ISIS released a shocking video of twenty-one men wearing orange jumpsuits being executed on a beach in Libya. In his book, *Apocalypse Rising*, Timothy Dailey explains a "mystery" associated with the executions.

> The victims were described as 21 Coptic Christian laborers. The scrolling caption announced their crime as being "people of the cross, followers of the hostile Egyptian Church." The men had traveled to Libya in search of work before they were kidnapped, marched onto the beach and executed by knife-wielding Islamists. To a man they refused to renounce their faith, each dying with the invocation "Lord Jesus Christ" on his lips....
>
> News reports of the killings on the beach in Libya mentioned "21 Copts." The Egyptian government, however, could confirm only twenty victims, leading to the mystery of the 21st hostage. It was later revealed that he was a citizen of the African country of Chad who had befriended the Copts and was captured along with them. The young man witnessed the incredible bravery of his friends in the face of imminent death.
>
> Finally, his turn came and the young man's interrogators demanded that he embrace Islam. Though not a Christian, he was so moved by the faith of his companions that when asked "Do you reject Christ?," he replied: "Their God is my God." He was summarily beheaded along with his newfound brothers.[250]

A Theology of Glory—A Counterfeit

It is natural to try to avoid suffering. However, some cleverly bypass the cross through a well-reasoned, but erroneous theology of glory.

"Theologies of glory" are approaches to Christianity (and to life) that try in various ways to minimize difficult and painful things, or to move past them rather than looking them square in the face and accepting them. Theologies of glory acknowledge the cross, but view it primarily as a means to an end—an unpleasant but necessary step on the way to personal improvement, the transformation of human potential. As Luther puts it, the theologian of glory "does not know God hidden in suffering. Therefore he prefers works to suffering, glory to the cross, strength to weakness, wisdom to folly, and, in general, good to evil." The theology of glory is the natural default setting for human beings addicted to control and measurement. This perspective puts us squarely in the driver's seat, after all.[251]

Though Luther did have a rather bombastic side to his character, he showed great depth of insight and understanding of the cross and its implications for the Christian life. In an in-depth paper, "Luther's Theology of the Cross, Carl R. Trueman writes:

The implications of this position are revolutionary. For a start, Luther is demanding that the entire theological vocabulary be revised in light of the cross. Take for example the word "power." When theologians of glory read about divine power in the Bible, or use the term in their own theology, they assume that it is analogous to human power. They supposed that they can arrive at an understanding of divine power by magnifying to an infinite degree the most powerful thing of which they can think. In light of the cross, however, this understanding of divine power is the very opposite of what divine power is all about. Divine power is revealed in the weakness of the cross, for it is in his apparent defeat at the hands of evil powers and corrupt earthly authorities that Jesus shows his divine power in the conquest of death and of all the powers of evil. So, when a Christian talks about divine power, or even about church or Christian power, it is to be conceived of in terms of the cross—power hidden in the form of weakness.[252]

When revival does come, and when multitudes of Christians of varying backgrounds will need to work together, Satan will most assuredly attack and create division. Many a great revival has been shortened and interrupted because of the flesh. Humility is paramount. Whether or not he consistently lived it, Luther believed that we are "little Christs to our neighbors, for in so doing we find out true identity as children of God." Trueman follows the implications of this and human relationships.

> The argument is explosive, giving a whole new understanding of Christian authority. Elders, for example, are not to be those renowned for throwing their weight around, for badgering others, and for using their position or wealth or credentials to enforce their own opinions. No, the truly Christian elder is the one who devotes his whole life to the painful, inconvenient, and humiliating service of others, for in so doing he demonstrates Christ-like authority, the kind of authority that Christ himself demonstrated throughout his incarnate life and supremely on the cross at Calvary.

A biblically rooted theology of the cross is to be the root dynamic for Christians. Jesus said: "I am among you as he that serveth" (Luke 22:27).

Sometimes there have been leadership abuses in churches and Christian ministries. We must not, and cannot, deny that. This has given fuel to our critics who charge that all the claims of Christian theism have no theological or philosophical value, but are merely a godless reaching for power. Allegedly, Christianity dominated the Western world not because of the truthfulness of its claims and the reality of the living Christ, but because men who claimed to be Christians had more power and money than anyone else. It is also claimed that the Church has used its theology to validate its claim to dominion.

Sad to say, there have been some who have used Christianity as a means of fulfilling their fleshly desires. In every group and organization, there are a few who do not represent what the organization really stands for. Most medical doctors do an important work and give themselves wholeheartedly to healing; yet a few don't. We shouldn't use the behavior of the few to mar the image of the majority.

How can Christians claim to be following the example of Jesus when some unprincipled individuals use their clerical authority to dominate the people under their watchcare? Their claim is false. A biblically grounded theology of the cross proves their words lie.

A Brief History of Outreach to Muslims

We've all heard much about Islam lately. We will probably hear a lot more about it in the next few years. *Dar al-Islam* is Arabic for "The House of Islam." It is the name of an invisible religious empire that stretches from West Africa to the Indonesian Archipelago, encompassing forty-nine nations and 1.6 billion adherents. Muslim evangelism for some thirteen centuries has been very disappointing. Yet, in the words of missiologist David Garrison, "Muslim movements to Jesus Christ are taking place in numbers we've never before seen."

What is a Muslim movement? Garrison defines it as at least "100 new church starts or 1,000 baptisms that occur over a two-decade period. Today, in more than 70 separate locations in 29 nations, new movements of Muslim-background followers of Christ are taking place.... In some countries the numbers within these new movements have grown to tens of thousands."[253]

For several centuries after the death of Muhammad in AD 630, there were no significant Muslim conversions to Christ. In the 970s, the Byzantine Emperor John Tzimisces invaded territory in Syria and Palestine. It is reported that some twelve thousand Muslim men, along with their wives and children, sought baptism from Byzantine Orthodox priests. They claimed the burden of taxation put upon them by their Muslim rulers was unbearable. Because of this, however, some have suggested, therefore, that their conversions are suspect. It was simply for the purpose of tax relief.[254]

A few centuries later, Francis of Assisi (1181–1226) walked across battle lines separating Crusader and Muslim armies near Damietta, Egypt, and sought to evangelize Muslims rather than conquer them. He had little success, but did manage to stay alive. His compassion was passed on to the order that followed him. His contemporary, Dominic de Guzman, had a similar burden for Muslims, but like Francis he had little success.

Though the Crusades (1096–1272) are often seen as Christian Europe's justifiable response to centuries of Islamic forays and attacks against Christians, this response was counterproductive and did nothing to advance the gospel. There was actually an increase in Muslim conversions as Muslim patriotic loyalties were strengthened in the face of European armies invading under the banner of the cross.[255]

While Muslim evangelism in the West saw very few, if any, converts, "Eurasian and Indonesian lay evangelists were making progress as they employed a more indigenous gospel witness," meaning evangelists were seeking to reach their own people.

A Javanese evangelist, Sadrach Surapranata (1835–1924), who came to be known as "The Apostle of Java," used a newly published Javanese Bible translation and aggressive apologetics to engage Muslim leaders. Rather than funneling converts into local Dutch Christian churches, Surapranata established indigenous communities of Javanese Christians. At the time of his death, between ten and twenty thousand Javanese Christians could be traced to his ministry. Garrison writes, "Though they represented only a fraction of the world's most populous Islamic country, these Kristen Jawa [Javanese Christians] marked a historic breakthrough, as the first uncoerced Muslim movement to Christ in nearly 13 centuries of Christian witness to the Muslim world."[256]

There were two other movements of Muslims to Christ in the nineteenth century. One was in Algeria under Charles Martial Lavigerie

(1825–1892), and the other was in Ethiopia under Shaikh Zakaryas (1845–1920). He began having troubling dreams that prompted him to obtain a Bible from Swedish missionaries in Asmara, modern Eritrea. Garrison puts it all in perspective when he writes:

> Though missions historians hailed the 19th century as "The Great Century" of Christian expansion around the world, the century closed with only two Muslim movements to Christ, comprising at least 1,000 baptized converts, and these only occurred nearly 13 centuries after the death of the Prophet Muhammad. It was 65 years into the 20th century before the next Muslim movement to Christ appeared, and this one took place under great duress.[257]

By 1965, Indonesia had one of the largest Communist parties in the world, but it was in during year that a coup took place that led to the death of a half million Indonesians. Anyone who had Communist Party or atheist leanings was either imprisoned or massacred. The new government demanded that every Indonesian declare to be a follower of one of the nation's historic religions: Islam, Protestantism, Catholicism, Hinduism, or Buddhism. A new day had dawned as some two million Indonesians entered Indonesia's Protestant and Catholic Churches. Harrison writes:

> Further Muslim movements to Christ in various corners of the Muslim world did not appear until the 1980s. Young Christians in the West, invigorated by the 1970s Jesus Movement, embraced the 1980's call to frontier missions to the world's remaining unreached people groups. Near the top of every list were the world's one billion unreached Muslims.
>
> The next movement emerged in the most unlikely of places. After the shock of the Iranian Revolution in 1979 many Iranians discovered that an Islamic state was not the panacea they had imagined. By the mid-1980s, Armenian Pentecostals in

Iran were seeing growing numbers of Shi'ite Muslims turning to them to hear the gospel. By the end of the 1980s, in the face of severe government persecution, thousands of Muslims were entering into the Christian faith.[258]

Some of the conversions are quite dramatic. Even terrorists have a change of heart and mind. In the foreword to the book, *Once an Arafat Man: A True Story of How a PLO Sniper Found a New Life*, author Joel Rosenberg tells of the conversion of Tass Saada.

Let me be brutally honest.

Tass Saada was a killer. That's why the first section of this book was incredibly difficult for me to read. This is not Anne of Green Gables. This is not The Sound of Music. If you are looking for a light, romantic story about growing up in the gorgeous splendor of Prince Edward Island, Canada, or about climbing very mountain in Austria—singing as you go—then move on, dear reader. This book is not for you.

Tass and his closest friends murdered Jews in Israel. They murdered civilians and soldiers alike. They attacked Christians in Jordan. Sometimes they tossed hand grenades at their homes. Sometimes they strafed God-fearing homes with machine-gun fire. They once tried to assassinate the crown prince of an Arab country. They nearly succeeded. And they did all this willingly. They did so eagerly. Tass certainly did. His nickname was once Jazzar—"butcher." It was a moniker he relished.[259]

Jesus: Showing Up in Some Strange and Dramatic Ways

In his first book documenting the amazing work of God among Muslims, Tom Doyle asks: "Who would you guess is the toughest sort of Muslim to reach? A terrorist, perhaps? Anyone willing to blow himself up to kill 'infidels' seems as committed to Islam as they come, right?"[260]

Doyle, who has spent many years working in Muslim countries and documenting the stories of converted Muslims, affirms that, yes, terrorists are hard to reach.

> That would be a reasonable speculation, of course, but I know of former terrorists walking with Jesus now in every Middle Eastern country. We work with many of them to reach other Muslims with the gospel. This new breed of disciples has been changed radically for Christ. The presence of the Holy Spirit is so strong in their lives, you would never suspect their shady pasts when you first meet them. These former terrorists are "Exhibit A" when it comes to the transforming power of Christ.
>
> Suicide bombers are tough, but as I see it, the hardest Muslims to reach are the imams. An imam is the leader of the local mosque. His job is to keep the Muslim flock in line with the Qur'an. These spiritual leaders are steeped in Islamic teaching and propaganda. As the guardians of Islam, imams live to defend their religion at all costs—usually the cost of the life of anyone who dares to convert to Christianity.[261]

Does God convert imams?

Doyle tells the story of Hassan, a Christian convert from Islam in Cairo, Egypt. Hassan had studied Islam for years, all for the purpose of knowing the beliefs of those whom he wanted to see saved. Late one night, Hassan was awakened by feeling a rough hand clamped firmly over his mouth. The intruder held the cold muzzle of a gun to his right temple. The man said, "Don't say a word. Get up and come with me."

They traveled down dark streets with the man roughly shoving Hassan ahead, and giving him directions, always keeping the gun in Hassan's side. They had jumped from one building to another. Even though it was a greater distance than Hassan would normally have even attempted, they both landed on the roof of an abandoned warehouse.

The assailant seized Hassan's right army again and forced him toward a hatchway in the abandoned warehouse. Hassan was sure he would never again see the night sky. He whispered, "Jesus, into Your hands I commit my spirit."

The man flinched almost imperceptibly at Hassan's prayer. Hassan noticed the fleeting cut of the man's eyes toward him. The grip on Hassan's arm tightened.

"Open the hatch door, and climb in quickly." The gun pointed the way.

Hassan saw himself struggle through the opening as if he were an actor in a movie thriller. He hoped the scene wouldn't end too quickly, and once inside the gloomy structure, the plot took a startling twist. He recounts what happened over the next several incredible minutes.

"I stepped into a foreboding room, lit with a single candle, fully expecting my immediate execution. Ten obviously Muslim men stood in a circle and stared at me as I entered. They ordered me to ˙ sit down. When I complied, the menacing atmosphere changed instantly. The mysterious group smiled at me."

The man who had kidnapped Hassan spoke first. "We are all imams, and we all studied at Al-Azhar University. During our time there, each of us had a dream about Jesus, and each of us has privately become a follower of Christ. For a time, we didn't dare tell anyone about this. It would, of course, have been our own death sentences. But finally, we could hide it no longer.

"We each prayed to Jesus for His help to learn what it means to be His follower. Over time, He brought us together, and you can imagine our amazement when the Holy Spirit revealed that there are other imams who have found Jesus as well. Now we meet here three times a week at night to pray for our families and for the people in our mosques to find Jesus too. We know you follow Christ. He led us to you."

Hassan recalls, "I was speechless. Then I was so relieved, I laughed for several minutes while the group watched."[262]

Isadreams.org says:

It is time for the Western Church to wake up to a great move of God.

Millions of Muslims are becoming Christians after Jesus appears to them in dreams and visions. The occurrences are so similar that many websites call Him "the man in white"—a glowing figure who often identifies Himself as Isa (Arabic for Jesus). These "Isa Dreams" have been happening for over 30 years while the West has slept, but no more! It is time to rouse ourselves, get informed, inform others, remove any barriers to belief and act together to support this growing harvest of Christ followers!

Muslims are Aware

Islam, a religion said to be delivered by an angel in Mohammed's dreams, is being profoundly shaken. The prophet Joel foretold a time when God's "Spirit would be poured out on all flesh...[they] will dream dreams." Only "angels" aren't appearing in these dreams—it is the Messiah! This wave of the Holy Spirit doesn't recognize nationalities, boundaries or laws. Campus Crusade workers in India frequently report people excitedly pointing to Jesus in the Jesus Movie exclaiming that they have seen that man in a dream![263]

It's always glorifying to God to realize how some individuals are brought to Christ. A Voice of the Martyrs field representative reported on a man who came to Christ while on a hajj in Saudi Arabia.

John—not his real name—was 23, had a wife and baby son, and

taught Islamic theology in his hometown in Afghanistan. His father, an influential Taliban leader, decided that John needed to make his pilgrimage to Mecca. He traveled to Saudi Arabia in November of 2011 with ten Taliban bodyguards. One night, as John slept, he dreamed of a man with a shining face and shining white clothes. The man said to John, "My son, I see that you are seeking after me, but the real faith is not here [in Mecca], and also I am not here."

John performed the duties of a faithful Muslim on a hajj, but he was struck with the hypocrisy he saw all around him. Muslims in Mecca weren't supposed to make money off of hajj pilgrims, but plenty of money was being made.

John walked with other hajj pilgrims to the city of Mina. That night he had another dream. John asked the Man in the dream, "Who are you?" The Man said:

> If I tell you who I am, you will lose seven things. You will lose the Quran and Muhammad. You will lose your parents. You will lose your child that you love. You will lose your relatives and every one will hate you. You will lose your wealth. You will be homeless and they will drive you from your country. If you don't accept the loss of these seven things, you won't be able to find me anymore. Before you were born, I had plans for you. What is your choice?

John said, "If you tell me your name I will believe in you." The Man answered, "I am your God. I am Jesus Christ."

John immediately left the hajj and returned to Afghanistan. He told his father that he had become a Christian. His father flew into a rage and began to beat him, and promised to cut out his tongue and burn his wife and young son.

John was brutally beaten and then thrown into a basement bunker on the property and was held there and tortured for eighteen months. His captors put snakes in the bunker and released a vicious guard dog.

In March of 2013, John was released and walked into his home. He was unshaven and disheveled. That night, after he cleaned himself up, he went to speak to his wife, eager to tell her about Jesus. She stopped him and said, "I have something to tell you first." Mary told John that throughout the time he was imprisoned in the bunker, she had been having dreams of Jesus. He comforted and encouraged her and promised that her husband would come home.

John and Mary fled from Afghanistan to another Central Asian country, going as far as they could before their money fan out. They did not fare very well because they identified themselves as Christian converts.

Mary was in great pain because of the beatings she had received form her father and father-in-law. When they went to the doctor, the doctor said that the unborn child that Mary was carrying had died, and that Mary would die a horrible death if the child were not removed. The doctor told them the procedure would cost five thousand dollars. They did not have the money.

John cried all night, and believed the Lord wanted him to anoint Mary while she slept. John anointed her and prayed that Jesus would heal his unborn son. Eventually John fell asleep.

The next morning, Mary was standing, and offered John a cup of tea. He did not know what to think, other than that Jesus had healed his wife. But what about his son? He and Mary went to the doctor, who had some good news: the baby was alive.[264]

A dream narrative posted by a Bosnian Muslim teenager, Emina Emlonic, focuses on Jesus.

I was in the desert alone, lost. As far as the horizon, there was nothing in sight but sand. I felt the sand on my bare feet. Then I saw something extraordinary. In the midst of that barrenness, an immense wooden cross emerged form the earth, rising up with sand spilling from it back to earth.

I felt then a spectator in my own dream, and the sight of the cross gave me neither fear nor joy. But I was curious and began moving, almost floating, towards it, the most magnificent… thing I'd ever seen or imagined, and as I came closer to the cross, I suddenly saw a man walking toward me: a broad-shouldered, long-striding man, with a dark complexion, long hair, and wearing a white robe.

And just as suddenly I ceased to be a witness to my dream. I was in it, walking toward the man walking toward me. I knew him immediately. He was Jesus. Without knowing why, I fell to my knees. He stood over me and touched my face with his right hand.

Pastor Frank Costenbader, founder of Manifold Hope Ministries, is the publisher of the Isa Dreams website. "The number of Isa dreams has seemed to grow tremendously since 2000, and in 2005 it seems to have kicked into another gear," Costenbader said. "There has been an explosion of testimonies on the Web in the past two years about people encountering Jesus in dreams and subsequently becoming followers of Jesus."[265]

In the Richardson documentary, *The Global Jesus Revolution*, Ali (not his real name), an evangelist on the field in Iran, says: "Out of ten people in Iran that I spoke to, eight would immediately come to Christ—the other two would come in two or three months…I felt I was living in Acts, because God would come, He would heal people."

Ali tells of a man with a most dramatic testimony. Ali asked him how he came to Christ. The man related the story of his vision.

A man came to his door and knocks. He is wearing white and has long hair. There are no churches nearby, no Christian witness. The Man in the vision tells him, "Write what I tell you." The man in the vision begins, and this man that Ali is talking to says he began to write what he was told: "In the beginning was the Word, and the Word was with God, and the Word was God…" He wrote the whole Gospel of John as it was dictated to him by the visitor.[266]

The Question Before Us

Will Christians in the West rise to meet the challenge? In the past, as well as in the present, Islam has destroyed whole cities populated by Christians. Fifty percent of the world is under some form of attack from Muslims. According to Dalton Thomas, a missionary with Frontier Alliance International, and others interviewed by Joel Richardson, there are 1.6 billion Muslims in the world. Only 6 percent of the missionaries are ministering specifically to Muslims. This means there are three missionaries for every one million Muslims.[267]

How do we respond in places like Iraq, Iran, and Libya? Some have suggested military intervention. Others have suggested total pacifism. Others suggest open dialogue—"Let's just talk." All these solutions will fail. As the video, *The Global Jesus Revolution,* affirms, "We must give a faithful witness in PROCLAMATION and DEMONSTRATION. We need an army of church planters, evangelists, and missionaries."

Because of the threat of Islam we must not be a "House of War," but rather "A House of Prayer. Islam is a culture of prayer. There are two houses of prayer. One is under the leadership of the Holy Spirit. The other is under the leadership of Islam. In the movie, *The Global Jesus Revolution,* Missy Huff, who ministers in an Islamic country, says, "It will take a prayer movement to contend with a prayer movement."

Perhaps the greatest threat to Muslim evangelism is not violence, but acorruption of the gospel. According to the Richardson movie cited above, the "Insider Movement" has produced Chrislam, an Islamicized gospel. Umar Milinde, a former Muslim sheikh, but now a Christian pastor in Uganda, had acid thrown in his face and is severely disfigured.

In public and in the movie he wears a pullover mask. Milinde cites 1 John 2:22 to show that what Muslims believe is a direct contradiction to the Bible: "Who is a liar but he that denieth that Jesus is the Christ? He is antichrist, that denieth the Father and the Son."

Yet the gospel of Jesus Christ is reaching Muslims. In the above-cited movie, Hormoz Shariat, "the Billy Graham of Iran," tells what he believes is the difference between Iran and the other Muslim-majority nations: "Iran knows that Islam is the problem. The other nations think it will produce utopia."

Questions Raised by the Demise of the Seven Churches

In 2009 Erwin Lutzer, pastor of Moody Memorial Church in Chicago, and his wife, made a visit to Turkey on a tour of the seven churches of Revelation chapters 2 and 3. The trip was an eye-opener. Lutzer said he was surprised at how a once-thriving Christian community was now completely overshadowed by the presence of Islam. Several questions came to Lutzer's mind that are worth pondering.

- Why did the Lord Jesus Christ allow Islam to triumph over Christianity in such an evident way?
- When a church dies, is it always the fault of the church, or are there other factors that contribute to its demise?
- Is persecution good for a church, or does persecution sometimes overwhelm a church?
- Does Islam's widespread victories over Christianity prove Islam is superior?
- Might God use Islam to bring judgment against the Western church?
- What might American churches look like in the next twenty-five to fifty years?[268]

Imagine how you, the reader, would have felt if you lived in one of the cities of the seven churches when the Turks came like a flood and conquered the area. What would you have felt if you were a part of the Body of Christ at Ephesus, or Pergamum or Sardis? You hear that the Turks are moving fast, with their swords drawn and the thunder of their horses' hooves shaking the ground. You will be given the option of converting to Islam to escape persecution, or you could choose to remain true to your Christian faith and live a life of servitude under Muslim rule. You might even be put to death.

Given those circumstances, Christianity did not have much chance of survival. Indeed, soon the demise of Christianity would be a finished fact. History tells us that in 1050, the region had 373 bishoprics and virtually all the citizens were members of the Orthodox Church, yet four hundred years later, there were only three bishops. With the coming of Islam in the Middle Ages, church buildings and monasteries were destroyed, priests and monks were killed, enslaved, or expelled. Cathedrals fell silent, or were burned to the ground.

Not all Christians were executed. Many were forced into servitude and agreed to an arrangement of servitude. They were known as *dhimmis*. They were to remain perpetual servants under oppressive taxation, had to follow strict codes of conduct, and were assured of continuous public humiliation under the Muslim overlords. In exchange for permission to stay alive, dhimmis had to agree to the following rules:

- They could not build new places of worship, and those that had been ruined in conquest could not be repaired or rebuilt.
- They had to house and feed Muslim soldiers.
- They had to offer hospitality to all Muslim travelers for three days.
- They could not seek to convert anyone to Christianity.
- If any of their kin wanted to convert to Islam, they could not prevent them from doing so.
- They could not raise a hand against or strike any Muslim.

- They could not wear garments that in any way resembled those worn by Muslims.
- They could carry no weapons.
- They could not display crosses or print or sell books pertaining to their religion.
- They could not bury their dead near dead Muslims.
- They could not build their homes on higher ground than Muslim homes.
- They had to give their seats to Muslims who wanted them.

In light of these repressive measures, the "wind that is blowing through the house of Islam" at the present time is truly remarkable.[269]

Perception Is Reality

A 20-year old Iraqi Christian woman tells how she is perceived by the Muslim culture, and how their erroneous views come from Christianity's association with the West:

> As a Christian I am a religious minority in Iraq, and society's view of us is highly incorrect because of the way Western Christians are portrayed in the media. Muslims see us in the same way they see foreigners—in terms of clothes, sex, and male-female friendships.... This misrepresentation is the reason I am not respected by the scholars and teachers at my university. I wish I could show them my religion, the good things, and teach them about it.[270]

This is a stark reminder that we need to develop a Kingdom culture, not an American identity. This may sound unpatriotic, but it's really not.

The Challenge to America

America, and indeed, the planet earth, is at a crossroads. The time is short and the Lord is at hand. There should be an urgency in our preaching and witness. Churches need not to be centers of entertainment, but houses of worship and praise. Because true worship can only occur when there is a true knowledge of God as He is revealed in the Word of God, churches must also be study centers where the Word of God is taught and applied.

The Great Apostasy— Will Satan Have the Last Word?

Many Christians will affirm that we are in the worst of times. Postmodernism seems to be advancing with alarming rapidity. Traditional values, which even nonbelievers once accepted without question, are now being swept away in a flood of new measures. The moral foundations of our culture are sinking into oblivion.

"Don't be surprised," we are told by the "experts." "This is what the Bible predicts: 'Let no man deceive you by any means: for that day shall not come, except there come a falling away first, and that man of sin be revealed, the son of perdition'" (2 Thessalonians 2:3).

When this and other Scriptures are cited, and the sad course of current events is described, it seems clear to many Christians that to talk of future revivals is madness at best, a kind of lunacy taught by fanatics and empty-headed dreamers.

But is this a correct assessment of Scripture, and is it taking into consideration all current events—especially those significant happenings that are not reported by mainstream media? Is the best we can hope for the triumph of evil worldwide?

Yes, the Bible does speak of apostasy; but the idea of apostasy is the falling away from something. It is apostasy in the Church. There is plenty of that today. Many churches no longer believe the Bible. The return of Jesus Christ and the Virgin Birth—many giggle at those teachings.

Even in the first century, the Lord Jesus Christ revealed His displeasure with the apostasy in some of the churches of Asia Minor. Regarding the church at Ephesus, He said, "But I have somewhat against thee, because thou hast left thy first love" (Revelation 2:4).

To the church at Pergamos, the Lord Jesus said, "I have a few things against thee, because thou has there them that hold the doctrine of Balaam.... Repent, or else I will come unto thee quickly and will fight against them with the sword of my mouth" (Revelation 2:14, 16).

Yes, there was apostasy in the churches of the past, and there is apostasy in the churches of the present. Mainline denominations are now caving in and ordaining gay and lesbian pastors. The thought that Jesus is "the only" way—something clearly taught in the Bible— is being viewed as a hangover from the narrow-minded bigotry of the past. Many Lutheran churches no longer follow the teachings of Luther. Many Presbyterian churches no longer follow the historic creeds and the venerable Westminster Confession of Faith." And yes, the Wesleys would be shocked at the radical transformation that has come upon modern Methodism. And yes, as we are told in 1 Peter 4:17: "For the time is come that judgment must begin at the house of God."

But that's in the house of God. Those are churches falling away from the historic faith once delivered to the saints. But what about in places like Egypt, Syria, and Iraq. What about in places that have been overrun by Islam for over 1,400 years, like Jordan and Morocco, or other places like China and Russia that have been overrun with secular materialism? You can't talk about apostasy—a falling away from the faith—in those places. They have not been centers of Christianity, or if they were in the past, that past was in the distant past.

In Acts 2:17, we read: "And it shall come to past in the last days, saith God, I will pour out of my Spirit upon all flesh: and your sons and your daughters shall prophesy, and your young men shall see visions, and your old men shall dream dreams."

Note the worlds "all flesh," "sons and daughters," "young men... and your old men." None of these groups were affected on Pentecost. The prophecy in Joel 2 is far broader than what occurred two thousand years ago. These are promises that have yet to be fulfilled.

Acts 2:20 tells us when all of this will be fulfilled. It will be "before that great and notable day of the Lord come."

For more than three-quarters of a century, Southwest Radio Ministries has opened its broadcasts with the words: "God is still on the throne, and prayer changes things." Those words are still true. The situation is depressing in America, but let's not forget something very important: God is raising up His servants to stand up and push back.

Roe v. Wade is a tragedy. The Supreme Court goofed, but that hasn't stopped thousands of pro-life crisis pregnancy centers from opening all over America. And who would deny that atheism is on the march? But God has raised up a mighty army of Christian apologists. They have answered every charge. They've made the atheists look foolish.

And what about Darwin and Dawkins and their spiritual clones? God has answered them, too. He has raised up ministries such as Answers in Genesis and the Institute of Creation Research. It can't be denied: We are fighting back.

We are standing tall!

Don't let the secular media fool you into thinking that God is dead. "God is not dead. He is surely alive. He is roaring like a lion."

I (Larry) am not a postmillennialist and do not believe we will present a converted world to the Lord Jesus Christ when He returns. But I am not a gloomy, "stop-the-world-I-want-to- get-off" premillennialist either. "But," someone will ask, "what about the alarming increase in evil?" Of course, we shouldn't be surprised. The Bible warns us that "evil men will wax worse and worse" (2 Timothy 3:13). But note, the text is speaking about "evil men." It doesn't mean that everybody is "waxing worse and worse."

In 2 Timothy, the apostle Paul wrote about those who are "ever learning, and never able to come to the knowledge of truth." Then he writes, "Now as Jannes and Jambres withstood Moses, so do these also resist the truth: men of corrupt minds, reprobate concerning the faith. But they shall proceed no further: for their folly shall be manifest unto all men, as theirs also was" (2 Timothy 3:7–9).

The Bible never even remotely suggests that the gospel witness will be snuffed out by evil people. They would like to—but God won't let it happen. The message is too wonderful and the lost souls are too precious.

Honesty mandates that we have to acknowledge that there is a lot that militates against the expansion of Christianity. The "New Atheism," as it is called, is the old atheism on steroids—much more aggressive and "in your face." The West is seeing a massive influx of Muslim refugees, many bringing their religion to Europe and America. However, the very common assertion that Islam is outpacing Christianity needs reevaluation. Dr. Rodney Stark, a researcher into religious trends and movements based in Baylor University, writes:

> As recently as April 2015, the Pew Research Center declared that Muslims will soon overtake Christians by way of superior fertility. They won't…Islam generates very little growth through conversions, while Christianity enjoys a substantial conversion rate, especially in nations located in what my colleague Philip Jenkins describes as the "global south"—Asia, Sub-Saharan Africa, and Latin America. And these conversions do not include the millions of converts being gained in China. Thus, current growth trends project an increasingly Christian world.[271]

Others are coming up with pretty much the same conclusion. Pastor Chris Mathis writes that "we are living in the greatest times the world has ever seen. God, by His Divine plan, chose for us to be alive right now in this time—not in the days of the Welsh Revival, or in the days of Azusa or any other time in Church history." Mathis explains:

I was recently reading some statistics about church growth in other parts of the world, and I was astonished at how different they are compared to the church in the U.S. in the past. The article stated that, in China, there is a person born again every three seconds, which comes to 28,000 people every 24 hours! I minister in Brazil often, and that country is seeing a revival sweep across it that is bringing societal transformation. At a service I recently ministered at in Brazil, the service didn't start until 10 P.M. My thoughts were, "Who is going to show up to a service that starts that late?" To my surprise, when I arrived, the pace was packed with 2,000 young adults who were 18 years of age and under. They were there to seek God and worship. I was blown away. Try calling a service at 10 P.M. in most places in America and see how many show.

What is the key to this type of move in these other places? As I have sought the Lord over this question, He keeps taking me back to this one key—hunger. Those who are hungry for God will be filled. It's kingdom economics; where there is a demand there will be a supply. God will always pour Himself out on those that are desperate for Him.[272]

Will Satan have the last word? It all depends. The Holy Spirit is bringing revival and transforming individuals, churches, and even communities. Some churches are growing at a phenomenal rate. Of course, not all large churches are large because God has made them that way; yet, we can't ignore the fact that some are.

In 1995, God began to impress a young Christian leader named Satish Kumar in Hyderabad, India, that he would one day have a very large church. In 2005, Pastor Kumar planted Calvary Temple with twenty-five members. In 2015—just ten years later—Calvary Temple now numbers 130,000 members. Sixty thousand have been added in a recent three-year period. A few years ago, Dr. Michael L. Brown, social commentator, Christian apologist, Hebrew scholar, and fervent prayer warrior asking God for revival, visited Calvary Temple. There are certain things that Dr. Brown noticed about the church:

1. Prayer and fasting. When it came time to constructing their main building that seats 18,000, Pastor Satish called for forty days of prayer and fasting. Night after night crowds gathered on vacant property. Despite the heat and the heavy rains, thousands gathered, sitting with their umbrellas, while Pastor Satish led the huge congregation. He called for a protracted time of prayer and fasting, adding up to 120 days. They were able to build the facility in fifty-two days.

2. Uncompromising preaching. Despite conducting five services of two hours each on Sundays, Satish preaches a full message at each, lasting sixty to seventy minutes. The first service starts at 6:00 a.m.; the last ends around 8:00 p.m.. In addition, the pastor gives a thirty-minute teaching to 1,200 key church workers late Sunday afternoon. The messages hit sin hard, call for repentance and faith, and focus on the cross.

3. Caring for the flock. Every member of the church gets a swipe card and registers his or her attendance by swiping the card on a kiosk at one of the doors. Individuals who miss a service receive phone call from one of the staff members to see if they are having a special need. Western Christians might find this somewhat meddlesome and legalistic, but it is not viewed that way in India. It is a sign to the people that the pastor and staff care and want to help in case of need. The church also provides ten thousand meals every Sunday for poorer members. The church provides medication for these members at a 50 percent discount.

4. Mountain-moving faith. Pastor Satish believes that victory comes through faith, and he preaches in such a way that lifts up Jesus Christ in His glory and encourages confidence in God.

5. Support for Israel. Pastor Satish has two flags on his desk. One is the flag of India, the other is an Israeli flag. When members swipe

their cards at the kiosk, they are greeted with the Hebrew word *Shalom*.

6. A willingness to work. Brown observes that Indian pastors are hard workers, as are many Indians. Pastor Satish regularly puts in sixteen-hour days. "Yet," writes Brown, "what struck me while we were together was that he did not seem burned out in the least, even seeming relaxed as we talked. And his family members I met seemed excited and blessed as well."

7. Wise use of media. Pastor Satish became very popular in India. There were several sponsors who wanted him on TV, and as more sponsors came forward, his broadcasts began to increase. At present, his messages air on about three hundred different programs each month, in several Indian languages. As a result, there are more than five thousand new visitors each week, many of whom become committed church members.[273]

We hear reports like this and marvel. Some are angry, however, because it sounds like man is twisting God's arm. "Can God be forced to do something, like build a large church with thousands of people?" Certainly not. God is greater than man. However, God has sovereignly willed that under certain circumstances He will respond and work. There are those who wait on God, but God is waiting on us.

Maintaining Biblical Standards— And Loving Those Who Don't

God gave mankind His Word because of love. Ethical imperatives and behavioral standards revealed in the Bible are for our own good.

In Ephesians 6, verse 1 and following, we read: "Children, obey your parents in the Lord: for this is right. Honor thy father and mother; which is the first commandment with promise; that it may be well with thee, and thou mayest live long on the earth." God's standards were given not to harm us but to bless us: "that it may be well with thee, and thou mayest live long on the earth."

First Peter 3:10 is similar: "For he that will love life and see good days, let him refrain his tongue from evil, and his lips that they speak no guile: Let him eschew evil, and do good; let him seek peace and ensue it."

Repeatedly we are reminded that God gave us His Word for our good. Hence, we must maintain, defend, and affirm the moral standards given in God's Word. Those who come up with alternate lifestyles that conflict with biblical norms are hurting no one but themselves and all those who listen to their false teachings. The Bible is the revelation of God. How dare we tamper with it.

Because this is true, it is a natural, knee-jerk reaction to hate those who are harming our society, our culture, and our families. When people depart from wholesome and helpful biblical stands and teach others to do so, it is natural to regard them as enemies—and to hate them.

If you feel that immigrants, gays, liberals, conservatives, gun owners and constitutionalists are harming society, the natural reaction is to hate them. This is one of the reasons there is so much violence in our world. It's because there is so much hatred, and there is so much hatred because there are so many groups with their different beliefs and values, all pushing those beliefs and values.

Christian must break this chain of hatred and violence.

How do we do that? By resisting two popular myths. First, if you do not approve of a person's lifestyle, you must necessarily fear, or hate, that person. Ssecond, in order to love someone, you must be in full agreement with everything he or she does and accept hs or her views as normative. Jesus did not approve of sinful lifestyles, but He didn't hate people. He didn't approve of adultery, hypocrisy, and murder, yet He loved adulterers, hypocrites, and murderers.

There were some pastors in America who rejoiced that Omar Mateen killed some fifty gays in Orlando, Florida. The only thing that made these pastors unhappy was that Mateen did not kill another fifty more. That's not the way Christians are supposed to think.

Many Christians have a very restricted and narrow view of worldliness. It can be summarized in this way: "I don't smoke, or chew, or run around with women who do."

Someone could refrain from smoking and chewing, and running around with women who do—and still be worldly. Do you know how? By hating. When we hate someone we are being worldly.

There are a lot of militant advocacy groups who are promoting and pushing some really radical lifestyles. We need to stand against those lifestyles—without hating those who are promoting them. Christians must not remain silent in the face of evil. But neither can we become hateful. So, when you do oppose evil—as you must—watch your attitude. We have to follow the scriptural mandate to overcome evil with good. That's the Lord's instructions for His people:

> If it be possible, as much as lieth in you, live peaceably with all men. Dearly beloved, avenge not yourselves, but rather give place unto wrath: for it is written, Vengeance is mine; I will repay, saith the Lord. Therefore if thine enemy hunger, feed him; if he thirst, give him drink: for in so doing thou shalt heap coals of fire on his head. Be not overcome of evil, but overcome evil with good. (Romans 12:18–21)

There are many examples of people being overcome by smoke. One day a man saw a house that was on fire. A young woman was outside. She was screaming because her baby was trapped in the house. A Good Samaritan ran into the house to rescue the baby. The newspapers reported that he was a hero, but he was overcome by the smoke. He and the baby died. This man was overcome—conquered and defeated—by the noxious fumes in the smoke. We must not be conquered and defeated by evil.

The Bible says, "Be not overcome of evil." In Romans 12:9 we read: "Abhor that which is evil." The Bible does not say "Abhor he who is evil." There are many evil people around, but the Bible never says to hate them. We are to hate the moral evil that drives them.

"Evil" here is not natural evil—evil from earthquakes, typhoons and tornados. The Bible is speaking about moral evil. Moral evil is the result of an intentional action, or inaction, of a rational human being— murder is an example. In natural evil, there is no rational intent on the part of a human being.

How do we overcome evil with good? Romans 12:20 tells us: "Therefore if thine enemy hunger, feed him; if he thirst, give him drink." We overcome evil with good by showing kindness to our enemy.

Do we all have enemies? Hopefully, we don't all have enemies who want to murder us, but everyone has enemies. It's impossible to live as an obedient Christian without having enemies, just as it is impossible to live as an obedient Christian without facing conflict. Dealing with enemies, and conflict resolution are skills we all need to develop.

Remembering that Revivals Are Not Perfect

Another aspect of the challenge to America is to remember that in a true revival there is a synergy between God and man. God does not need man for revival; yet God has often brought revival through human instrumentality. Sometimes revival comes through prayer, at other times revival comes through preaching. The principle is "draw nigh to God, and he will draw nigh to you. Cleanse your hands, ye sinners; and purify your hearts, ye double minded" (James 4:8). There's a condition, and we are part of the condition: "If my people which are called by my name…" (2 Chronicles 7:14).

The Pensacola/ Brownsville Revival, so named after the Brownsville Assemblies of God Church, has garnered both praise and condemnation. Some claim that it was marked by fanaticism, but others claim it transformed many lives. Question: Can both be true? If you answer "no," my next question is: "Why? By what rule of divinity can there not be good and bad in a move of God that involves sinful human beings? Charismatic leader, social commentator, and biblical scholar, Michael L. Brown, PhD, describes his experiences at Brownsville in this way:

> A time of extraordinary spiritual intensity, everything happening with such urgency…80 or 90 hours of ministry a week… all night prayer meetings…people getting saved in the parking lot waiting on line to get in…the highs spiritually speaking were like nothing I've known and the lows were like nothing I've known…like a ship in a storm; the wind is blowing, the waves are rolling in; it's incessant…and then there are some criticizing you.[274]

J. Lee Grady, another charismatic leader, former editor of *Charisma* for eleven years, also comments on Brownsville. He has no doubt that the revival at Brownsville was genuine. He took his first trip to Brownsville in 1995 and was moved by the powerful preaching of evangelist Steve Hill who challenged the audience and demanded repentance from spiritual compromise. Grady writes, "Wailing was commonly heard during those meetings. Some people shook under the weight of conviction.… My life was changed there.… One night, in the midst of the pandemonium near the stage, I ran over to where Hill was praying. He grabbed my head and screamed, 'Fire! Fire! More, Lord!' I was one of the thousands who fell backward on that floor. I was not pretending."

Grady also notes that the church that hosted hundreds of thousands of visitors has shrunk to a few hundred members. It is deep in debt, according to Grady, and now owes millions of dollars on a building that is far larger than the attendance. "I don't question whether the Holy Spirit was in that place. But today, more than ten years after the Pensacola Outpouring occurred, I am asking other questions."[275]

Sometimes we miss the work of God because we have different ideas of what a revival really does. What about the "Jesus People Movement" or the "Jesus Revolution"? Do Christians today remember more vividly the nudity, drugs, and free love of Woodstock than they do the "Jesus Revolution"? Michael Brown writes:

> Yes, the Jesus People Movement was a bona fide work of the Spirit, bringing tens of thousands of hippies and rebels into the kingdom. From 1970 until 1975, in particular, radically lost young people became radically saved. (I was one of the them!). Rock musicians high on drugs had genuine visions of Jesus and quit getting high. Student activists came under divine conviction and, in tears, surrendered their lives to the Lord. Long-haired, guru-following, bead-wearing spiritual seekers came into traditional churches in droves.[276]

The Azusa Street Revival is, perhaps, one of the most striking examples of the mixed nature of revivals. It marked the origin of the Modern Pentecostal Movement, and was led by William J. Seymour, an African American preacher. It began on April 9, 1906, and continued until 1915.

Azusa Street was characterized by ecstatic experiences and dramatic worship services, speaking in tongues, and various miracles of healing. It was highly controversial and was criticized both by secular observers and orthodox Christian believers. Yet, most would admit that it did change many lives for the better, though some of the charges from Christian orthodoxy had merit. The position of this author (Larry) is that it was prompted by the Holy Spirit at a time when the Spirit's working was going to become increasingly necessary in a century of war, world conflict, and increasing demonic activity. The problems came not from the revival itself, but with those who were in charge of administering its work.

The Azusa Revival could have continued, but even those who are friends of the Pentecostal Movement and who can be considered "charismatic" in the full sense of the word have found some issues that caused the revival to end. J. D. King, drector of the World Revival Network and associate pastor of World Revival Church, gives several reasons.

One of the big reasons was the sudden loss of the mailing list in 1909 for the Apostolic Faith Mission. Florence Crawford, described by J. D. King as "the strong-willed secretary of the Apostolic Faith Mission," abruptly left town with the extensive roster of subscribers. Without the mailing list the group's paper and support, appeals could no longer be circulated. The paper was used to report on the work of the Holy Spirit and to disseminate testimonies of people whose lives had been transformed through the revival.

Another issue involved the theological differences that were causing division. King writes: "Early Pentecostal and Holiness people were very cantankerous and independent. It is often hard for them to agree with others for any length of time. Many would break rank over the smallest differences of opinion."

An intense theological struggle was brewing. It centered over the appropriation and experience of sanctification. Seymour believed that sanctification was an instantaneous work, which was the standard view of holiness preachers at the time. Another key figure in the movement, William Durham, believed it was more gradual. He was in conflict with the standard Pentecostal-Holiness view.

Some even debated whether or not neck ties should be worn since they were viewed as nothing more than a "frivolous adornment." Others were convinced that building a storm shelter was wrong because it showed a "lack of faith." Thrown into this cauldron of bubbling opinions was the upset caused when Seymour married Jane Evans Moore in 1908, which may have precipitated some degree of friction with Florence Crawford.

King makes a perceptive statement when he says, "I think there is one important lesson that the revival at Azusa Street provides for us. It helps us to understand that revivals seldom end because of trouble without. No, revivals end because of the trouble within."[277]

Unusual Manifestations

One of the most consistently challenged aspects of some revivals has been the unusual manifestations. In this category are included miraculous healings, shouting, shakes, falling on the floor, and other attention-getting responses of those present in the meetings. Charges that "such craziness never happened in the Bible," "this is obviously demonic," "this is not God-honoring," and other such comments are often made.

Paul King, cited earlier, in his online article "Supernatural Physical Manifestations in the Evangelical and Holiness Revival Movements," has done an extensive study of the comments of the leaders of revivals in the past on such manifestations. King writes about the unusual phenomena associated with the "Toronto Blessing" and the Pensacola/Brownsville revival, such as "holy laughter," shaking, and other controversial occurrences that have often led to strong criticisms regarding whether these revivals were genuine or "just a lot of emotional hype." In his article, King is convinced that leaders of past revival movements neither accepted such phenomena as proof that God was present in power, nor were such phenomena rejected outright.

The phenomenon of falling under the power of the Spirit occurred in the revivals of Jonathan Edwards. His assessment was that a person may "fail of bodily strength" due to fear of hell and the conviction of the Holy Spirit or due to a foretaste of heaven. John Wesley recognized falling to the ground as a manifestation from God, and records many such instances in his ministry. In fact, George Whitefield criticized Wesley for permitting the phenomena until it began happening at his own meetings. The Kentucky revivals of 1800–1801, which involved Baptists, Methodists and Presbyterians, was replete with similar demonstrations. In the early 1800s, the revivals led by Methodist circuit riding preacher Peter Cartwright (who was converted in the Kentucky revivals) were often accompanied by people falling under God's power, including some Baptists. Finney's ministry also frequently manifested fainting or swooning, what he called "falling under the power of God." The Welsh revival of 1859 was accompanied by swooning as "waves of power often overwhelmed" people. In the 1860s, Andrew Murray's church started to speak out against people who began to shout and cry and swoon in a revival in his church, until a visitor from America told him about similar manifestations in American revivals.[278]

Cane Ridge, Kentucky (1801)

Barton Stone, Pastor of the Presbyterian congregation in Cane Ridge, Kentucky, described the Cane Ridge Revival in 1801:

> The effects of this meeting through the country were like fire in a dry stubble driven by a strong wind. All felt its influence more or less…the whole country appeared to be in motion to the place [of the meetings], and multitudes of all denominations attended. All seemed heartily to unite in the work and in Christian love. Party spirit shrunk away. To give a true description of this meeting cannot be done; it would border on the marvelous. It continued five days and nights without ceasing. Many, very many will through eternity remember it with thanksgiving and praise.[279]

At the time of the Cane Ridge Revival, the United States was barely a quarter of a century old. Jonathan Edwards, and many others, had been used mightily by God to bring about the First Great Awakening, but the effects of that great work of God were beginning to wane. The nation was expanding. There were new challenges and new growth, bringing prosperity—and a falling away in fervor for the Lord. People moved farther and farther from churches and were at the edge of the frontier, where whiskey and guns controlled life.

Having church meetings was a challenge. There were no interstates, and people lived far from established congregations. It was impossible to expect really large crowds. This need birthed the Camp Meeting movement. People often came from hundreds of miles away. Some were invited by families near churches and meeting places. Others pitched tents so they could have a "home" near the meeting. Camp meetings were a necessity, but they provided a sense of community and Christian fellowship, a perfect environment in which the Holy Spirit could work.

Word had gotten out that large crowds had gathered at various camp meetings, and that God was working in ways that had not been seen before. The camp meeting at Cane Ridge would have an opening service on Friday evening, which would be followed by a day of fasting, prayer, and preaching on Saturday. Then on Sunday, communion would be celebrated. Pastor Stone anticipated a large crowd and invited seventeen ministers from different denominations to minister to the large crowd he anticipated.

That particular Friday evening, at the beginning of the move of God, it rained hard, and most stayed in their tents. On Saturday morning the sky cleared. Thousands gathered with a hunger and anticipation that could only have been planted in hearts by God. The church building could not accommodate all the people. Raised platforms were constructed outside the church where preachers could stand and preach. Some stood on stumps and gave their messages. The crowds grew. By afternoon, there were far more people than anyone had anticipated. Daniel Norris summarizes what happened that Saturday afternoon:

> In the crowd that afternoon was a mother standing with her two
> teenage daughters at her side. They were listening to a minister
> who stood before them on a stump. He preached with pow-
> erful words about the deadly consequences of sin. As they lis-
> tened, the two daughters were suddenly seized with conviction.
> They cried out from the depths of their souls and then fell to the
> ground like two dead women.

This was a new sight for everyone in the crowd. The mother, a devout woman who loved the Lord, became quite distressed. She began to frantically fan their faces in an attempt to wake them up, but to no avail. It was an hour later when one of her daughters stirred just long enough to cry out with a piercing scream, "Mercy, Lord! Mercy!" She then fell back into her trancelike state. Both girls lay there motionless for hours upon the ground with the most awful look of terrors upon their faces. From time to time they would wake up enough to cry out for mercy once more before returning to their agonizing slumber.[280]

There was great excitement rippling through the camp. One of the daughters who had been in a trance woke up. She opened her mouth and began to preach the gospel and warn sinners, and a new crowd began to gather.

Similar things were happening around the camp, and others began to preach. At first, it was the ministers who were preaching, but as the day wore on, many others stood up to speak and to share. "It was not uncommon to see a man or woman struck down to the ground just as the two young ladies had been and then rise up with an intense urge to preach. These untrained ministers suddenly declared the wonders of God." Those who gathered around the speakers would often fall to the ground, sometimes as many as a hundred at a time.[281]

This must have been a strange sight to Reverend Stone and his flock. The fact that there were twenty-five to thirty thousand men, women, and children on the grounds was a sight in and of itself, but then something else began to happen.

Falling was just one of the peculiar manifestations that took place that day. As the evening approached, many found themselves unable to control their bodies. Someone called these strange actions "the jerks," and the name seemed appropriate. Sometimes it would affect just a head or an arm or a leg, and the body part would twitch or jerk in the most unusual fashion. A few of these movements took over their entire bodies. One man was seen bending so far forward that his head nearly touched the ground; then he would bend just as far backward. Strange as it may seem, not a single person complained that these jerks caused them any discomfort.[282]

South Africa (1860)

A transforming work of God came to the Cape Colony, South Africa (the Western Cape on South Africa's Atlantic coast), in 1860. The Dutch overlords refused to let any language other than Dutch be spoken within the churches, even though few people understood it. However, reports of the Second Great Awakening in America had been received in South Africa, and had created a hunger for a similar work of God. A prayer conference was organized in Worcester, some seventy-five miles from Cape Town, to discuss and pray for an awakening in the Cape. Hundreds of ministers, elders, and deacons attended. Among them was a young minister named Andrew Murray, the well-known devotional writer.

Murray, at that time, had been appointed pastor of a Dutch Reformed Church in Worcester. At the meeting was a gentleman from the United States who told of the Great Awakening that had been taking place in America. The report of such a revival in America provoked Murray and others to pray fervently for a similar work of God in South Africa. Murray began a series of messages on the necessity of a new Pentecost.

Murray's messages calling for revival particularly struck the heart of a young Dutch woman by the name of Miss Van Blerk. She had spent a great deal of time on a farm owned by her uncle and was saddened by the vulgarity and coarseness of many of the Africans who worked in the fields.

Van Blerk longed to see the Africans meet Jesus. She began to pray with two of her friends who shared the same passion. The three prayed regularly for months. The more they prayed, the more the burden increased. But when it came, the breakthrough was heavenly.

The first outpouring took place one evening in early September in the old school house that sat in the center of her uncle's farm. Several farmhands and Africans gathered that night for a chapel service Van Blerk hosted. What follows was absolute pandemonium. The Spirit of God descended upon the meeting and great conviction struck the room. Africans were a deeply emotional people, and in the meeting that emotion poured out in a steady, torrential flood. They cried aloud for mercy and pleaded with the lord with a deep anguish of the soul. The scene took Miss Van Blerk by surprise. It came so suddenly that she ran from the room to find help in leading people to Jesus.[283]

When Reverend Murray arrived, however, he was deeply troubled and warned the congregation that this display of emotion must stop. He warned the people and told them to control themselves and tried to bring the meeting to order. He insisted that he was their pastor and had been sent from God, and what they were doing was not honoring to God.

One of the spiritual leaders of the congregation approached Murray and told him it was impossible to stop what was happening.

Murray was offended and left the meeting at once. He contended that God could not be the orchestrator of such disorder. It wasn't long before the fire that fell on the farmhouse found its way to Murray's church. It too came suddenly on a Sunday evening in a meeting with the young people of the church.[284]

Reports tell of an unusual sound outside. J. C. deVries, one of the church's leaders, looked out the window as the sound outside grew louder. It was distant and faint at first, but it grew louder like the roll of thunder.

It came like a violent wind and filled the very room in which they gathered. It was deafening. The effect on the meeting was instantaneous. Every young man and woman began to fall upon their faces before the Lord. They cried out with groaning, weeping and wailing. It was very much like what had taken place on the farm.[285]

While Murray couldn't deny that people's lives were being changed and that there was an unknown, but much welcomed, hunger for spiritual things, he could not approve of what he considered excessive emotionalism. "People, I am your minister sent from God. Silence!" But there was no silence.

"God is a God of order," he told himself over and over again. Yet he couldn't get past the stirring within his spirit that it truly was God who was at work in what seemed to him to be utter confusion. Was this the answer to his prayers? Could it truly be God? These questions were in his mind as he took the pulpit in the main hall of the church.[286]

The mysterious roar that had been heard a week before again started. The sound filled the church. Though Murray tried to restore order in the church, it was to no avail. The harder he tried to stop what was happening, the more intense it became.

He turned to see a man standing at his side whom he did not recognize. For the pastor it might well have been an angel sent from the Lord, as his appearance had a similar effect. The man looked straight into Murray's eyes and with a stern compassion offered the minister some encouraging words that would set this move of God into place: "I think you are the minister of this congregation: be careful what you do, for it is the Spirit of God that is at work here. I have just come from America, and this is precisely what I witnessed there."[287]

We can also cite the account of Rifqa Bary, the 16-year-old Muslim girl who, in 2009, ran away from her new home in Ohio, claiming that her father, a devout Muslim, had abused and threatened to kill her because of her Christian faith. The media reported on the legal battles between the critics of Islam and its defenders, sparking a national debate about the treatment of women and converts within Islam and how they should be protected.

Bary recounts that one day, as a little girl in Sri Lanka, she was playing and running in circles when she felt compelled to stop. "From that moment I felt something strange and new. A Presence, quiet and comforting, hovering, nearly tangible. It pressed closer and closer.... I knew Someone was there, a strong Man who seemed to stir the breeze as he moved."[288]

A few years later, Rifqa met Aiden by name. He was a Christian. Rifqa wanted to know how a Christian prays. He said, "I pray like I am talking to you right now—in English. I just talk to God from my heart." Rifqa mused to herself, "There's something about the way Christians talk to their God." Rifqa later asked herself, "This God that Aiden prayed to—could He be the same Presence I encountered in my garden in Sri Lanka as a small child?"[289]

Many years later, after her ordeal was nearly over, and she had gotten a lot of legal help, Rifqa was diagnosed with a strange kind of cancer. That was strange for her, because that type of cancer only afflicts very young children, or very old women, and Rifqa was neither. After a thorough exam, an Indian doctor consulted with her. "Rifqa, I need to tell you the truth, okay? You generously have one year to live even with the best treatment we can offer."

Rifqa began her cancer treatments, with expected results: loss of hair, sickness, and deep depression. She decided to stop all treatments, to her oncologist's dismay.

> I knew it sounded crazy. Was crazy. It didn't make sense to me either. But I knew in my spirit that God was calling me to do this, and I decided I would rather die in obedience to Him than live in disobedience and possibly survive the treatment. The same whisper that lifted me up from my hiding place that Sunday morning behind a tree at my parents' apartment was the same voice that asked me to do something everybody in my life protested. I was saying the same thing as before.… I wasn't going through with the hysterectomy, and I wasn't going through with any more chemo treatments.

Rifqa's cancer disappeared. She is alive and well. At the time of my (Larry's) interview with her in 2015, she was in college studying philosophy and preparing for a legal career.[290]

Christian conservatives, fundamentalists, discernment ministries, and others of like mind have generally been suspicious of miracles and unusual phenomena, and with good reason. Some of it is a lot of hype—but not all of it. Even the revivals of the past have produced some unusual manifestations, and miracles.

Heidi Baker, co-founder and director of Iris Global, has served tirelessly in Mozambique, Africa. Iris Global includes free health clinics that service the poor and sick; feeding programs; primary and secondary schools; and more than five thousand churches in Mozambique and more than ten thousand churches in over twenty nations. Growing up as a pretty blonde kid in Southern California did not deter her from surrendering it all and ministering, with her husband Rolland, in some of the poorest and most dangerous areas of Africa.

In the book, *Love Like Fire: The Story of Heidi Baker, Mother to Nations*, Cassandra Soars, who spent some ten years in Africa with the Bakers, writes of the miraculous healings and other works of God seen in the Bakers' ministry. Not every prayer was answered the way the prayer was intended, but many of them were answered specifically, dramatically, and miraculously. Heidi did not challenge people to not resort to medical doctors, and she actually enlisted one to come to Africa to perform surgery on a blind man whom she could not heal.

> Heidi couldn't have been more delighted to see the body of Christ function as it was meant to. She was realizing that perhaps healing looked different in different scenarios. Maybe sometimes God chose to heal supernaturally and sometimes through doctors or medicine. Was it any less a miracle that medical doctors had been able to develop cures for diseases that we could purchase at the pharmacy?[291]

Both Heidi and Rolland suffered some debilitating issues despite their prayers, yet the evidence of miracles cannot be denied. The book relates the story of Akhil, a little boy who was crippled with "jelly legs," and who could not heal himself, but who prayed for crippled children who were healed.

> In one of the villages there was a four- or five-year-old girl who was unable to walk. Heidi described the little girl's legs as "jelly legs." As soon as Akhil saw the girl, he marched up to her. When Akhil reached the little girl, he put his hands on her shoulders and said confidently, "In the name of Jesus."
>
> Instantly the little girl's legs straightened and were able to support the weight of her body. They watched as the girl's mother held her hands above her head as she took her very first steps.
>
> In that moment, Heidi couldn't have been prouder of Akhil. Many in the village who were of a different faith background, came to believe in Jesus, who healed the little girl through a little boy not much older than her.

Sometimes it just didn't make sense. Akhil could pray for a little girl with jelly legs and see her healed while he continued to hobble around.[292]

A few years ago, Dr. Candy Brown from Indiana University traveled to Pemba, Mozambique, to conduct a detailed scientific research study. Dr. Brown wanted to measure the results of Heidi Baker and her team's prayers on Mozambicans who were deaf and/or blind. "The results of the study were astounding, proving that the miracles and healings were not fabricated or merely the power of suggestion."

Dr. Brown's "Study of the Therapeutic Effects of Proximal Intercessory Prayer (STEPP) on Auditory and Visual Impairments in Rural Mozambique" was published in the September 2010 issue of the *Southern Medical Journal*. The study used an audiometer to test individual's hearing levels. For those who had vision problems, the clinical researchers used vision charts. Dr. Brown stated that the results produced by the healings were far greater than studies have shown about the slight improvements that come from hypnosis and suggestion.[293]

Love That Is Fearless

What motivates people to acts of courage in the face of great danger? In his book, *Killing Christians: Living the Faith Where It's Not Safe to Believe*, Tom Doyle recounts the stories of Christians who have been converted to Christ from Islam. Apostasy is punishable by death in many Muslim areas. Yet the love that Christ implants in the heart is fearless. Men and women who have had a saving encounter with the resurrected Christ are supernaturally energized and have dramatically believed the words of Jesus in Matthew 10:28: "And fear not them which kill the body, but are not able to kill the soul." The names of the individuals in the stories that Doyle tells are changed, but the stories are substantially as relayed to Doyle.

Somalia—How can evangelists get Bibles into a hostile nation? By personally bringing Bibles into the country in a coffin. Doyle tells the story of Azzam Aziz Mubarak hiding under a three-day old corpse. The stench is stifling. On some occasions when the coffins reached their destinations, there were two corpses inside!

No Muslim would dare open a casket, let alone look beneath the remains. "Under dead people, Bibles could get to believers and saints in Somalia, and endangered believers and saints (as if they weren't all endangered!) could get out to Kenya."[294]

Mosul, Iraq—A mosque in Mosul (ancient Nineveh) is not where you would advertise: "Get your Bible at the Mosul Mosque." But this is virtually what Shukri Hananiyah did. He had been having dreams and visions of a man in white, but didn't know who it was until he had been given a New Testament. On at least one occasion, he and his wife Khadija had the same dream.

Shukri believed that the best place to engage Muslims with the gospel of Christ was at a mosque. Khadija agreed, but added, "It's probably the most dangerous, too." Shukri had made up his mind. He was under orders from the Lord Jesus Christ. Shukri went to the Great Mosque in Mosul. He was excited that he was walking in the footsteps of Jonah and Nahum. He had three boxes of Arabic Bibles that he gave out. Everyone seemed very cordial. God had opened the door for Shukri. The following week, however, he was grabbed. Six men in *dishdashas*—an ankle-length garment—formed a circle around him. Under three of the *disdashas*, Shukri spied the bulge of AK-47s. "I believe I saw you last week at the mosque but didn't have a chance to introduce myself. I am a messenger from the Lord Jesus Christ."[295] The man who had grabbed Shukri pulled a large knife from under his garment and smiled back: "We are from ISIS."

Khadija explains that Shukri was tortured and then killed. He was slashed with knives several times before they shot him ten times. Khadija said she was completely numb for an hour. How would she raise little Sarah and Walid? Khadija, a very brave and committed servant of Jesus Christ, wrote:

How could I fight against the will of God? He sent Shukri and me to Mosul to bring the fragrance of Christ to this dark and evil city. As we had prayed, we reasoned that we would be martyred for our glorious Lord someday, and it would be an honor. But now that Shukri was really gone, it did not feel so honorable.

I share these words several months after I lost my beloved Shukri. I am not sure I would have been able to compose myself and voice my feelings before now. I ache for him. It's hard to put into words how much I miss my husband. He loved me with the love of Christ. And little Sarah and Walid were lost without their loving abu! But the Lord's grace is rebuilding their shattered hearts.[296]

Khadija reports that the two couples who came to their home after Shukri's first Friday at the mosque have become followers of Jesus. After they were saved they were taught how to share their faith. At the writing of Doyle's book, there are twenty-three Christians who now worship in Mosul. Khadija continues to write:

Yet, you must know this. We are not leaving. God put us in Iraq, and here is where we will stay. Perhaps you, too, have been called to persist at something God has called you to. I am convinced it is our duty as servants of the Most High to stay, go, or continue doing whatever He says until He tells us otherwise.[297]

Fallujah, Iraq—Always in the crosshairs, Fallujah was the battlefield for Saddam Hussein against the Shiites, against the Americans, and against other "coalition" soldiers. After Saddam's capture, it was the scene of daily shootouts between Al-Qaeda and ISIS. This was the only life that Tasyir Awad knew until Jesus paid him a visit.

While in high school Tassie, as he was known, met an American soldier on a house-sweeping mission through the teenager's neighborhood. Tassie doesn't remember his name, but he remembers the soldier as "Joe

America." The soldier gave Tassie a pocket-sized Arabic Bible. He said to Tassie: "Your family was gracious to us, and they are good people. I pray that the Lord of heaven watches out for you and them."

Tassie intended to throw the little Bible into the first garbage can he saw. He was almost afraid to touch the little testament. He had been taught that the Bible of the Christians and Jews was a corruption of Allah's pure word. Touching the little Bible was like touching a snake. Nevertheless, Tassie was bored. Reading the Bible might be good for a few laughs. Tassie opened the Bible and read the words: "I am the light of the world."

That night, Tassie had a dream. A man approached Tassie in a darkened room. The visitor called the boy by name and immediately light flooded the room: "Tassie, I am the light of the world. I will show you the way. Will you follow me?"

Tassie did decide to follow Jesus. He committed his life to Christ. Three years later, he was almost murdered for his faith. But Tassie had a mission. Love for Jesus and love for those in Iraq helped him bravely stay the course.

Syria and Jordan—Because of love, Christians are different. Grace transforms. It is transformed people who draw others to the light. Tom Doyle relates the story of a Syrian family fleeing Damascus and walking some sixty-five miles to safety in Amman, Jordan. Dori, the mother, was walking with her two teenagers, Hania and Saeeb. They were out of food and water, and Dori was begging—just a few bottles of water would keep them alive. Doyle writes: "At the highway she flagged down a truck. The driver pulled off the road and opened the door. Yes, he would help. He had food, but he wanted a sample of what was hidden beneath her clothing first…"

Another truck came and slowed down. The driver opened the door and tried to force her into the truck, but she broke free and fell to the ground, face down in the sand. Another truck was coming. What would Dori do? She still needed food and water. She was not very religious. She wondered if it would be legitimate if she gave herself to the next driver to save the lives of her family from starvation.

She peered over her shoulder as a semi braked to a halt at the spot the other truck had just left. The door swung open, and a man jumped to the ground. He raised his arms toward Dori.

"I saw what happened! I won't hurt you! I want to help."

Dori sized up the new stranger and believed him. "I need food."

"I have bread. Do you need water, too?"

"Yes. For me and for my children."

The man nodded and turned to the truck. He extracted several bags from a compartment under the cab.

"Here. This is yours." He approached Dori and handed her bags containing several bottles of water and four uncut loaves of bread. As she took the provisions, her helper looked at her kindly. "Begging along the highway could get you killed—or at the very least kidnapped and sold on the black market. Whatever is wrong, I hope you'll be careful."

Dori stiffened. "My children are hungry, and my husband is missing. It was the only thing left to do."

"I understand." The man paused and then bowed slightly in Dori's direction. "My name is Osama. It's an honor to help you. I pray this tides you over until you are safe in Jordan. I assume that's where you're going."

The man had read the situation well. "I'm Dori, and yes, I'm going to Jordan." Dori looked at the ground and shook her head. "I can never thank you enough."

The stranger's next words startled the grateful woman: "The Lord Jesus bless you, Dori. Look to Him. He will be your shelter."[298]

Transformation: Revivals That Impact the Community—and Beyond

As we read about revivals in Scripture, we notice that when healing and renewal come to a people and a place, it indeed affects the entire community and impacts the culture and even the productivity of the land. Second Chronicles 7:14 states: "If my people, which are called by my name, shall humble themselves, and pray, and seek my face, and turn from their wicked ways; then will I hear from heaven, and will forgive their sin, and will heal their land."

Another passage of note is Psalm 67:1–2, 5-6: "God be merciful unto us, and bless us; and cause his face to shine upon us.... That thy way may be known upon earth, thy saving health among all nations.... Let the people praise thee, O God; let all the people praise thee. Then shall the earth yield her increase; and God, even our own God, shall bless us."

George Otis Jr. is president of the Sentinel Group, a Seattle-area ministry that assists Christians who are eager to prepare their communities for a revival that brings transformation. He has also produced a series of nine award-winning "transformations documentaries," reporting on transforming revivals in different parts of the world.

During almost two decades, Otis' quest to understand and document revivals has led him into more than thirty-one nations on six continents. Since Otis and his colleagues began doing documentaries on transformed communities in the mid-1990s, they have encountered nearly eight hundred examples. Sadly, as of late 2011, only two of these could be found within the borders of the United States.

I (Larry) did some in-studio programs with Otis and was impressed with the man and his work. Not everyone, however, has reached the same conclusion. He has been charged with being a "dominionist," "on the fringe," and "associated with fringe groups." We could go on, but such would serve no meaningful end. Now, maybe I, too, have moved to "the fringe" in the judgment of some.

In a recent edition of Charismamag.com, Otis lays out his views in an article titled "Why Revival Tarries...in America":

There is much talk in Christian circles these days about redeeming the various "mountains" of society. Advocates float terms like "kingdom reformation" and "cultural mandate" while a steady stream of books and conferences promote strategies for transforming everything from Hollywood to Washington, D.C. I am sympathetic to calls for social healing and godly change agents, but I'm afraid these sympathies are not accompanied by much optimism that we can win the so-called culture war—assuming this is even our mission in the first place.

My initial concern is the fact that social activism does not require God to come down in power (interventionist revival). What if our problems are so deeply entrenched that we can't make a difference? Faithful witnessing, for example, will not bring an end to years of war or drought. Nor will well-run Christian businesses bring about pervasive conviction of sin. Apart from the aid of divine hydraulics, some loads are simply too heavy to lift.

...Society doesn't care about our arguments. In fact, it resents them. In the absence of God's presence people are not asking, "Who is He?" They are asking, "Where is He?"

The one thing that sets us apart is missing—all because of a fatal calculus that our projects (or comforts) are so important that we can't let more important things interfere with them!

...Transforming revival is not the morning newspaper or a prerecorded sports event. It is not a product that can be ordered from a catalog or an experience for which one schedules an appointment. It is not something we can just "fit in." If we want to see it, we'll need to cultivate an appetite for it.[299]

In his video documentary, *Appalachian Dawn*, Otis reports on the sad state of Clay County Kentucky and its county seat, the city of Manchester, a small city of 1,200 nestled in the hills of southeast Kentucky. The city was in a continual decline, as drugs, crime, and government corruption took their deadly toll. Significantly, the website for the city of Manchester reports how a prayer meeting and the commitment of area churches impactedthe city for good. The city now calls itself, by decision of the city council, the "City of Hope." The city website reads:

Manchester is being constantly referred to as the "City of Hope." People throughout the country have seen and heard about Manchester and Clay County. It hasn't always been good either. About four years ago it all started with a small prayer group made up of different are churches whop rayed for an end to illegal drug sales, illegal drug use, and for real transformation to come to the city and county. Since this humble beginning Manchester has been featured on the CBN 700 Club twice as well as other national media outlets. Certain local Christian leaders involved have been contacted from 43 states and several foreign countries stating how they have been inspired by the story of Manchester. Stating that the story of Manchester has restored hope for them in their cities. This recurring theme of hope has been stated over and over and so much so that a resolution was entered and passed by a unanimous vote before the city council that Manchester be tagged as the "City of hope. This tag will be in the form of a small placard attached under the city limits sign at each entrance into the city. The prayer group still meets and prays each Saturday morning for our city.[300]

Otis has been charged with a lot of theological blunders, one of them being an overcharged postmillennialism that is looking for a "Christianized world" to meet Jesus Christ when He returns. However, his comments make it clear that this is not his view.

There is nothing in Scripture to suggest the Second Coming of Christ will be welcome by a six-billion-voice choir. Darkness will increase before it is vanquished forever. But as it spreads and intensifies, it will also accentuate any light that is shining. And herein lies our hope…and opportunity. By prevailing with

God in prayer and preparing his way through obedient action, we become "bearers" and "welcomers" of light in this darkening hour. As the Kingdom of God is put on exhibit in neighborhoods, towns, cities, and nations, a weary and demoralized world is made aware of a shimmering way of escape. The role is ours if we are willing to allow the pain and urgency of this present darkness to transform our passive dissatisfaction into active desperation. May God give us the courage.[301]

It is my (Larry's) conviction that God wants to bring revival, is bringing revival in certain parts of the world, and wants to bring revival to many more regions prior to the Rapture of the Church. Too many Christians say they believe in the supernatural and will decry the "social gospel" and other movements within Christianity that leave out a supernatural new birth, belief in the resurrection of Christ, and the resurrection of the saints. These are Christians who believe in the fundamentals of the faith. However, is it possible to be a good fundamentalist and not really believe in the supernatural?

A reading of the New Testament, especially the book of Acts, will show that the New Testament Church did not limit the supernatural to the fundamentals of the faith. They had a vision of what God was going to do and lived supernaturally every day. They saw signs and wonders and miracles as regular features of the Christian life.

The two greatest hindrances to revival are: (1) failing to meet the requirements for revival as summarized in 2 Chronicles 7:14; (2) limiting God with ideas that come from preconceived notions, theories, and neatly packaged theological formulations.

Theology is very important and seeks to make sense of the themes of the Bible. However, when a particular theology becomes so rigid and is highly esteemed in the sight of the men who created it, it limits God and truly becomes a hindrance to revival. It becomes like the idols of old—the works of men's hands—that men worship out of reverence for themselves.

Notes

1. http://www.nytimes.com/2013/02/13/world/europe/pope-benedict-xvi-resignation.html?_r=0.
2. Eric Schmitt, "In Battle to Defang ISIS, U.S. Targets Its Psychology," *New York Times*, December 28, 2014, last accessed February 18, 2016, http://www.nytimes.com/2014/12/29/us/politics/in-battle-to-defang-isis-us-targets-its-psychology-.html?_r=0.
3. Ibid.
4. David Commins, *The Wahhabi Mission and Saudi Arabia* (IB Tauris, London, New York: 2006), vi.
5. Front page of the As-Sunnah Foundation of America website, ASFA, last accessed February 17, 2016, http://sunnah.org/wp/.
6. Zubair Qamar, "Wahhabism: Understanding the Roots and Role Models of Islamic Extremism," under the "Introduction" header, last accessed February 17, 2016, http://www.sunnah.org/articles/Wahhabiarticleedit.htm.
7. Ibid.
8. "ISIS Spokesman Declares Caliphate, Rebrands Group as 'Islamic State,'" Jihadist News, last updated June 29, 2014, last accessed February 17, 2016, https://news.siteintelgroup.com/Jihadist-News/isis-spokesman-declares-caliphate-rebrands-group-as-islamic-state.html.
9. Eric Schmitt, "In Battle to Defang ISIS," http://www.nytimes.com/2014/12/29/us/politics/in-battle-to-defang-isis-us-targets-its-psychology-.html?_r=0.

10. George Weigel, "ISIS, Genocide," https://www.firstthings.com/web-exclusives/2016/02/isis-genocide-and-us; emphasis added.

11. Anugrah Kumar, "Over 100 NGOs, Leaders to Obama: ISIS Atrocities Against Christians, Other Minorities, Are Genocide," *Christian Post*, February 18, 2016, http://www.christianpost.com/news/obama-isis-atrocities-christians-minorities-genocide-international-religious-freedom-roundtable-158043/.

12. Ibid.

13. "Leading Sunni Sheikh Yousef Al-Qaradhawi and Other Sheikhs Herald the Coming Conquest in Rome," *MEMRI: The Middle East Media Research Institute*, posted December 6, 2002, last accessed February 18, 2016, http://www.memri.org/report/en/0/0/0/0/0/0/774.htm.

14. "Leading Sunni Sheikh," http://www.memri.org/report/en/0/0/0/0/0/0/774.htm.

15. "In New Message Following Being Declared a 'Caliph,'..." *MEMRI: The Middle East Media Research Institute*, posted July 1, 2014, last accessed February 18, 2016, http://www.memrijttm.org/content/view_print/blog/7607; emphasis added.

16. "Pertaining to the Conquest of Constantinople and the Appearance of Dajjal and Descent of Jesus Son of Mary (Jesus Christ)," *The Only Quran*, last accessed February 18, 2016, http://www.theonlyquran.com/hadith/Sahih-Muslim/?volume=41&chapter=9.

17. Sophie Jane Evans, "ISIS's Chilling Death March to the End of the World: Jihadists Release Video Depicting Their Apocalyptic Vision of a Future Battle Culminating in Rome," *DailyMail*, December 11, 2015, last accessed February 18, 2016, http://www.dailymail.co.uk/news/article-3356503/ISIS-s-chilling-death-march-end-world-Jihadists-release-video-depicting-vision-future-battle-culminating-Colosseum.html.

18. Sam Prince, "WATCH: New ISIS Video Shows Armageddon Battle with the West," *Heavy News*, December 11, 2015, last accessed February 18, 2016, http://heavy.com/news/2015/12/new-isis-islamic-state-news-video-see-you-in-dabiq-rome-muslim-extremists-rome-crusaders-colosseum-malahim-meeting-at-dabiq-italy-west-war-uncensored-full-youtube/.

19. Video can be seen at the following article: Anthony Bond, Kara O'Neill, Kelly-Ann Mills, "ISIS Release Chilling New 'End of the World' Video Showing Final Battle with Crusaders," *Mirror News*, December 11,

2015, last accessed February 18, 2016, http://www.mirror.co.uk/news/world-news/isis-release-sickening-new-video-6995563.

20. Tyler Durden, "ISIS Releases New Apocalyptic Video Depicting 'Final' Battle with 'Crusaders' in Syria," December 12, 2015, *Zero Hedge*, last accessed February 18, 2016, http://www.zerohedge.com/news/2015-12-12/isis-releases-new-apocalyptic-video-depicting-final-battle-crusaders-syria.

21. http://time.com/3745462/vatican-ISIS-syria-iraq-middle-east/.

22. http://www1.cbn.com/cbnnews/world/2014/August/Pope-Francis-US-Action-against-ISIS-a-Just-War.

23. https://en.wikipedia.org/wiki/Just_war_theory.

24. http://www.cruxnow.com/church/2015/03/13/vatican-backs-military-force-to-stop-ISIS-genocide/.

25. http://www.breitbart.com/big-government/2015/11/15/paris-pope-francis-tells-christians-ready-end-world/.

26. http://www.dailymail.co.uk/news/article-3356503/ISIS-s-chilling-death-march-end-world-Jihadists-release-video-depicting-vision-future-battle-culminating-Colosseum.html.

27. http://www.nbcnews.com/storyline/pope-francis-visits-america/ISIS-magazine-dabiq-singles-out-pope-francis-ahead-u-s-n431681.

28. http://nypost.com/2015/03/10/pope-francis-if-im-assassinated-at-least-make-it-painless/.

29. http://www.ncregister.com/daily-news/pope-francis-consecrating-the-world-to-mary-culminates-fatima-celebration/.

30 Thomas Horn, Cris Putnam, *Petrus Romanus* (Crane, MO: Defender Publishing, 2012), 454.

31 Thomas Horn, *Zenith 2016* (Crane, MO: Defender Publishing, 2013), 371.

32. http://catholictruthblog.com/2013/12/30/was-pope-francis-canonically-elected/.

33. Rev. Herman Bernard Kramer, *The Book of Destiny* (Belleville, IL: Buechler Publishing Company, 1955), 277.

34. http://nation.foxnews.com/2016/01/10/report-obama-wants-become-un-secretary-general-netanyahu-doing-everything-he-can-stop-him.

35. http://www.discoveringislam.org/end_of_time.htm.

36. Numbers reported in this section are taken from: "America's Changing Religious Landscape: Christians Decline Sharply as Share of Population; Unaffiliated and Other Faiths Continue to Grow," *Pew Research Center*,

May 12, 2015, last accessed January 1, 2016, http://www.pewforum. org/2015/05/12/americas-changing-religious-landscape/.

37. Ibid.

38. Traditionally, Wycliffe is given the birth date of 1324. However, nobody is certain about the exact day on which he was born. Records indicate that it was between 1320 and 1331.

39. "John Wyclif," *New Advent Catholic Encyclopedia*, last accessed January 5, 2016, http://www.newadvent.org/cathen/15722a.htm.

40. Thomas Murray, F.A.S., *The Life of John Wycliffe* (John Boyd, 37 George Street, Edinburgh: 1828), 21.

41. Ibid., 19.

42. Ibid., 22.

43. Carol M. Miller, "The St. Scholastica Day Riot: Oxford after the Black Death," *Annual Proceedings of the Florida Conference of Historians, Volume 1* (Orange Park, Florida: 1993, with contributions made by Jacksonville University and Lake City Community College), 29–43.

44. Reverend Robert Vaughan, D. D., "Introductory Memoir," *Tracts and Treatises of John de Wycliffe* (The Wycliffe Society, London, Blackburn and Pardon: 1845), x.

45. "John Wyclif," *Stanford Encyclopedia of Philosophy*, September 18, 2001, last accessed January 7, 2016, http://plato.stanford.edu/archives/win2011/entries/wyclif/.

46. "Jan Hus," *New Advent Catholic Encyclopedia*, last accessed January 7, 2016, http://www.newadvent.org/cathen/07584b.htm.

47. The students and leaders who left Charles University of Prague have been reported between five thousand and twenty thousand, and it is difficult to know the exact number of those who left, as a result of historical discrepancy between the governing sections. However, all records agree that this division was a costly one, which delivered the university to far less international importance. The numbers "5,000 to 20,000" are the most common report. See: "Jan Hus," *New Advent*, http://www.newadvent.org/cathen/07584b.htm.

48. Edward N. Peters, J. C., J. C. D., *A Modern Guide to Indulgences: Rediscovering This Often Misinterpreted Teaching* (Hillenbrand Books, Chicago, IL: 2008), 13.

49. "John Huss: Pre-Reformation Reformer," *Christian History*, August 8, 2008, last accessed January 7, 2016: http://www.christianitytoday.com/ch/131christians/martyrs/huss.html?start=2.

50. Ibid.
51. Ibid.
52. "Council of Constance," *New Advent Catholic Encyclopedia*, last accessed January 7, 2016, http://www.newadvent.org/cathen/04288a.htm.
53. "John Huss," *Christian History*, http://www.christianitytoday.com/ch/131christians/martyrs/huss.html?start=2.
54. "Council of Constance," *New Advent*, http://www.newadvent.org/cathen/04288a.htm.
55. "John Huss," *Christian History*, http://www.christianitytoday.com/ch/131christians/martyrs/huss.html?start=2.
56. "Council of Constance," *New Advent*, http://www.newadvent.org/cathen/04288a.htm.
57. Ibid.
58. "The Astro-Hungarian Monarchy," under the heading "The Middle Ages," *New Advent Catholic Encyclopedia*, last accessed January 7, 2016, http://www.newadvent.org/cathen/02121b.htm.
59. "Hussites," *New Advent Catholic Encyclopedia*, last accessed January 7, 2016, http://www.newadvent.org/cathen/07585a.htm.
60. Ibid.
61. "Conciliarism," *The Catholic Dictionary*, accessed January 11, 2016, https://www.catholicculture.org/culture/library/dictionary/index.cfm?id=32689.
62. Martin E. Marty, *Martin Luther: A Life* (Penguin Publishing Group, London: 2004; Kindle Edition, 2008), Kindle Locations 158–159.
63. Ibid., Kindle Locations 184–188.
64. Ibid., Kindle Locations 206–210.
65. To bring clarity to why Luther cried out to St. Anna that he would be a monk, and then dedicated himself instead as a friar, for those less familiar with classic Catholic terminology: The terms "friar" and "monk" are to a degree interchangeable in communal lifestyle and dedication, the main difference being that friars have more connection to the outside world, such as public ministry, to which Luther felt desperately called.
66. Martin E. Marty, *Martin Luther*, Kindle Locations 302–303.
67. James M. Kittelson, *Luther the Reformer: The Story of the Man and His Career* (Fortress Press, Minneapolis: 2003), 78.
68. Martin E. Marty, *Martin Luther*, Kindle Locations 274–281.
69. Ibid., Kindle Locations 307–308.
70. Ibid., Kindle Locations 317–318.

71. Ibid., Kindle Locations 423–424.
72. "Martin Luther," *New Advent Catholic Encyclopedia*, last accessed January 13, 2016, http://www.newadvent.org/cathen/09438b.htm.
73. Martin Luther, "The Ninety-Five Theses."
74. Martin E. Marty, *Martin Luther*, Kindle Locations 611–632.
75. Ibid., Kindle Locations 697–700.
76. "Martin Luther," *New Advent*, http://www.newadvent.org/cathen/09438b.htm.
77. Ulrich von Hutten, Franz von Sickingen, and Silvester von Schaumberg were named as Lutheran supporters here: "Martin Luther," *New Advent*, http://www.newadvent.org/cathen/09438b.htm.
78. Martin E. Marty, *Martin Luther*, Kindle Locations 716–717.
79. "Martin Luther," *New Advent*, http://www.newadvent.org/cathen/09438b.htm.
80. Martin E. Marty, *Martin Luther*, Kindle Locations 941–943.
81. "Martin Luther," *New Advent*, http://www.newadvent.org/cathen/09438b.htm. Also note that Luther's exact response has been challenged by Protestant researchers. Many variations of his precise words appear in both biographical and encyclopedia accounts. However, each variation essentially delivers the same integrity and meaning of what has been quoted here.
82. Ibid.
83. Martin E. Marty, *Martin Luther*, Kindle Locations 1097–1101.
84. "Martin Luther," *New Advent*, http://www.newadvent.org/cathen/09438b.htm.
85. Ibid.
86. Ibid.
87. Ibid.
88. Ibid.
89. Thomas Murray, *The Life of John Wycliffe*, 21.
90. Michael Hughes, *Early Modern Germany: 1477–1806* (Macmillian Press, London: 1992), 45.
91. Martin E. Marty, *Martin Luther*, Kindle Locations 1297–1316.
92. Ibid., Kindle Locations 1331–1335.
93. George M. Marsden, *Jonathan Edwards: A Life* (Yale University Press, New Haven and London: 2003; Kindle Edition), Kindle Locations 300–301.
94. Ibid., Kindle Locations 304–306.

95. Ibid., Kindle Locations 433–436.

96. Timothy Edwards, sermon on Acts 16:29–30, pp. 11–12, 1695 (Washington University Library). As quoted by: Kenneth Minkema, *The Edwardses: A Ministerial Family in Eighteenth-Century New England* (University of Connecticut: 1988), 82.

97. George M. Marsden, *Jonathan Edwards*, Kindle Locations 422–433.

98. Ibid., Kindle Locations 532–536.

99. Ibid., Kindle Locations 576–577.

100. The "unconditional election" is a term referring to the belief that God has pre-appointed salvation by grace to some, but not all, believers. The opposite of this is "reprobation," referring to those who will receive eternal damnation for sin, including the original sin by the Fall of Man. Although not all modern Calvinists agree that it is this simple, and that human choice does play a role in determining one's afterlife, many still adhere to the doctrine of predestination, suggesting that the fates of every human is foreordained, and the elect will be called in due time. As mentioned earlier in the "Protestant Reformation" chapter, Calvinism is highly debated.

101. Original source: Clarence H. Faust and Thomas H. Johnson, *Jonathan Edwards: Representative Selections* (New York, American Book Company: 1935). Page number to this original source is unknown as these authors have quoted from a secondary and digital source online. See: "Personal Narrative: An Electronic Edition; Jonathan Edwards 1703–1758," *Early Americas Digital Archive*, last accessed January 26, 2016, http://mith.umd.edu/eada/html/display.php?docs=edwards_personalnarrative.xml.

102. George M. Marsden, *Jonathan Edwards*, Kindle Locations 653–654.

103. "Personal Narrative," *Early Americas Digital Archive*, http://mith.umd.edu/eada/html/display.php?docs=edwards_personalnarrative.xml.

104. Ibid. Italics original; bold added.

105. George M. Marsden, *Jonathan Edwards*, Kindle Locations 1725–1728.

106. Ibid., Kindle Locations 1756–1757.

107. Ibid., Kindle Locations 1927–1936.

108. Ibid., Kindle Locations 1828–1831.

109. Ibid., Kindle Locations 1913–1917.

110. Ibid., Kindle Locations 2224–2225.

111. Jonathan Edwards, *A Divine and Supernatural Light, Immediately Imparted to the Soul by the Spirit of God, Shown to Be Both a Scriptural, and Rational Doctrine* (S. Kneeland & T. Green, Boston: 1734), 4–5. Accessed

electronically January 28, 2016 through the Digital Commons of the University of Nebraska: http://digitalcommons.unl.edu/cgi/viewcontent.cgi?article=1056&context=etas.

112. "The Holy Club," *Christianity Today*, last accessed January 28, 2016, http://www.ctlibrary.com/ch/1983/issue2/216.html.

113. Ibid.

114. John Charles Ryle, *A Sketch of the Life and Labors of George Whitefield* (Anson D. F. Randolf, New York: 1854), 21.

115. Ibid., 22.

116. Ibid., 25–27; emphasis added.

117. Ibid., 34.

118. Ibid., 29.

119. Ibid., 47.

120. Harry S. Stout, *The Divine Dramatist: George Whitefield and the Rise of Modern Evangelicalism* (Eerdmans, Grand Rapids, Michigan: 1991), 117; emphasis added.

121. George M. Marsden, *Jonathan Edwards*, Kindle Locations 2899–2903.

122. At one point, Whitefield and Edwards found an issue to disagree upon, but it had little bearing on the effect of the revival. The two men remained fixed allies for the cause. As a result of their disagreement, however, Whitefield did not intimately bond with Edwards at any time in their lives like he had with Benjamin Franklin.

123. "George Whitefield, 1714–1770, English Evangelist," *Believer's Web*, last accessed January 29, 2016, http://www.believersweb.org/view.cfm?ID=94.

124. Ibid.

125. Richard McNemar, *The Kentucky Revival* (Trumpet Press, Lawton, OK: 1808; Kindle Edition, Great Plains Press: 2011), Kindle Locations 214–226.

126. As quoted by: John B. Boles, *The Great Revival: Beginnings of the Bible Belt* (University Press of Kentucky: 1972; 1996; Kindle Edition), Kindle Locations 215–217.

127. Ibid.

128. John Boles, *The Great Revival*, Kindle Locations 226–229.

129. Ibid., Kindle Locations 396–400.

130. Ibid., Kindle Locations 400–401.

131. Ibid., Kindle Locations 420–421.

132. Ibid., Kindle Locations 473–474.

133. Reverend Barton Stone, as quoted by: John Mark Hicks, "Assurance, Stone-Campbell History, and Calvinism," *John Mark Hicks Ministries*, last accessed February 25, 2016, http://johnmarkhicks.com/2008/05/10/assurance-stone-campbell-history-and-calvinism/.

134. John Boles, *The Great Revival*, Kindle Locations 720–722.

135. As quoted by: Mark Galli, "Revival at Cane Ridge: What Exactly Happened at the Most Important Camp Meeting in American History?" *Christianity Today*, last accessed March 1, 2016, http://www.christianitytoday.com/history/issues/issue-45/revival-at-cane-ridge.html.

136. Mark Galli, "Revival at Cane Ridge," http://www.christianitytoday.com/history/issues/issue-45/revival-at-cane-ridge.html.

137. Richard McNemar, *The Kentucky Revival*, Kindle Locations 440–447.

138. Ibid., Kindle Locations 399–423; emphasis added.

139. Ibid., Kindle Locations 424–428; emphasis added.

140. Ibid., Kindle Locations 467–477; emphasis added.

141. Kevin Belmonte, *D.L. Moody—A Life: Innovator, Evangelist, World Changer* (Moody Publishers: 2014; Kindle Edition), 20.

142. Ibid., 21.

143. Paul Dwight Moody, *The Shorter Life of D. L. Moody* (Bible Institute Colportage Association: 1900), 21.

144. Kevin Belmonte, *D.L. Moody*, 44.

145. Ibid.

146. Ibid., 48.

147. Ibid., 53.

148. Ibid., 62.

149. D. L. Moody, *Twelve Select Sermons* (F. H. Revell, Chicago: 1884), 60–61.

150. Kevin Belmonte, *D.L. Moody*, 64.

151. Ibid., 67.

152. Ibid., 83.

153. As quoted by: Lyle W. Dorsett, *A Passion for Souls: The Life of D. L. Moody* (Moody Publishers: 2003), 156.

154. Ibid.

155. Kevin Belmonte, *D.L. Moody*, 106.

156. Ibid., 116.

157. Edwin Hodder, *The Life and Work of the 7th Earl of Shaftesbury* (Cassell & Co., London: 1887), 688–689.

158. Kevin Belmonte, *D.L. Moody*, 119–122.

159. Ibid., 267.
160. Yehuda Bauer, *Rethinking the Holocaust* (Yale University Press, New Haven and London: 2001), 48.
161. Robert John van Pelt, *The Case for Auschwitz: Evidence from the Irving Trial* (Indiana University Press, Bloomington and Indianapolis: 2002), 4.
162. Marilyn J. Harran and John Roth, *The Holocaust Chronicle: A History In Words and Pictures* (Publications International, Ltd: 200), 384. Accessed electronically February 3, 2016, http://www.holocaustchronicle.org/StaticPages/384.html.
163. Ibid.
164. Andreas Hillgruber, "War in the East and Extermination of the Jews," *The Nazi Holocaust Part 3, The "Final Solution": The Implementation of Mass Murder Volume 1* (Meckler, Westpoint, CT: 1989), 103.
165. Dr. Anwar El-Shahawny, *Allah and Space* (Xlibris: 2010), 141–142.
166. See: "Nazi Propaganda Film about Theresienstadt/Terezin," *United States Holocaust Memorial Museum*, last accessed February 4, 2016, http://www.ushmm.org/online/film/display/detail.php?file_num=565.
167. Ibid.
168. Eric Hanin, "War on Our Minds: The American Mass Media in World War II" (PhD dissertation, University of Rochester, 1976), chapter 4, note 6.
169. "The United States and the Holocaust," *United States Holocaust Memorial Museum*, last accessed February 4, 2016, http://www.ushmm.org/wlc/en/article.php?ModuleId=10005182; emphasis added.
170. Theodor Herzl, *A Jewish State: An Attempt at a Modern Solution of the Jewish Question* (Maccabean Publishing Co., New York: 1904), 102.
171. Declaration of the Fist Zionist Conference (1897), as quoted by: David Gerald Fincham, April 17, 2015, *Mondoweiss*, last accessed February 6, 2016, http://mondoweiss.net/2015/04/understanding-jewish-national/.
172. Tomer Kleinman, "Israel and the Holocaust," *UCSB History Archives*, last accessed February 5, 2016, http://www.history.ucsb.edu/projects/holocaust/Research/Proseminar/tomerkleinman.htm; bold text original.
173. Benny Morris, *1948: A History of the First Arab-Israeli War* (Yale University Press, New Haven and London: 2008), 179.
174. Rabbi Yechiel Eckstein, "Ancient Jewish History: The Bible on Jewish Links to the Holy Land," *Jewish Virtual Library*, last accessed February 8, 2016, https://www.jewishvirtuallibrary.org/jsource/Judaism/biblejew.html.
175. Frank Newport, "In U.S., Four in 10 Report Attending Church in Last

Week," December 24, 2013, last accessed February 8, 2016, http://www.gallup.com/poll/166613/four-report-attending-church-last-week.aspx.

176. Ted Olsen, "Why the Oral Roberts Obituaries Are Wrong," *Christianity Today*, December 16, 2009, last accessed February 9, 2016, http://www.christianitytoday.com/ct/2009/decemberweb-only/151-34.0.html.

177. Oral Roberts, *Oral Roberts' Life Story: As Told by Himself* (Faithful Editions: 2015; Kindle Edition), Kindle Locations 272.

178. Ibid., Kindle Locations 196–204.

179. Ibid., Kindle Locations 204–205.

180. Ibid., Kindle Locations 415–416.

181. Ibid., Kindle Locations 551–555.

182. Ibid., Kindle Locations 615–619.

183. Ibid., Kindle Locations 657–659.

184. Justin Juozapavicius, "Evangelist Oral Roberts Dies in Calif. at Age 91," *CTPost*, December 15, 2009, last accessed February 9, 2016, http://www.ctpost.com/news/article/Evangelist-Oral-Roberts-dies-in-Calif-at-age-91-288912.php.

185. Oral Roberts, *Oral Roberts' Life Story*, Kindle Locations 1724–1725. Note, however, that the death tolls reported herein was drawn from another source reporting the fire, not from Roberts' book.

186. Ted Olsen, "Why the Oral Roberts Obituaries Are Wrong," http://www.christianitytoday.com/ct/2009/decemberweb-only/151-34.0.html.

187. Ted Olsen, "Why the Oral Roberts Obituaries Are Wrong," http://www.christianitytoday.com/ct/2009/decemberweb-only/151-34.0.html.

188. Justin Juozapavicius, "Evangelist Oral Roberts," http://www.ctpost.com/news/article/Evangelist-Oral-Roberts-dies-in-Calif-at-age-91-288912.php; emphasis added.

189. W. Terry Whalin, *Billy Graham: A Biography of America's Greatest Evangelist* (Morgan James Publishing, New York: 2015; Kindle Edition) 5.

190. Ibid.

191. Ibid., 16.

192. Ibid., 24.

193. Ibid., 48.

194. "Hamblen, Carl Stuart," *Texas State Historical Association*, last accessed February 9, 2016, https://tshaonline.org/handbook/online/articles/fhafq.

195. W. Terry Whalin, *Billy Graham*, 63.

196. Nancy Gibbs and Richard N. Ostling, "God's Billy Pulpit," *TIME*

Magazine, November 15, 1993, last accessed February 9, 2016, http://content.time.com/time/magazine/article/0,9171,979573,00.html.

197. Rob Moll, "Prophecy and Politics," March 1, 20016, *Christianity Today*, last accessed February 9, 2016, http://www.christianitytoday.com/ct/2006/march/17.32.html.

198. Michael G. Long, *The Legacy of Billy Graham: Critical Reflections on America's Greatest Evangelist* (John Knox Press, Westminster: 2008), 3.

199. Roberts Liardon, *Kathryn Kuhlman: A Spiritual Biography of God's Miracle Worker* (Whitaker House : 2005; Kindle Edition), Kindle Locations 277–300.

200. Ibid., Kindle Location 435.

201. Ibid., Kindle Locations 795–821.

202. Ibid., Kindle Locations 833–834.

203. Ibid., Kindle Locations 874–875.

204. Reverend Lester Kinsolving, "Kuhlman Tested by MD's Probe," *The Pittsburg Gazette*, November 8, 1975. Archived here: https://news.google.com/newspapers?id=cOQNAAAAIBAJ&sjid=iG0DAAAAIBAJ&pg=5291,834959&dq=kathryn+kuhlman+william+nolen&hl=en.

205. Jamie Buckingham, *Daughter of Destiny: The Only Authorized Biography [of] Kathryn Kuhlman* (Bridge Logos Foundation, Alachua, Florida: 1999; Kindle Edition), 224.

206. Ibid., 226.

207. Ibid., 122.

208. Ibid.

209. Ibid., 162.

210. Ibid., 161.

211. Reverend Lester Kinsolving, "Kuhlman Tested," https://news.google.com/newspapers?id=cOQNAAAAIBAJ&sjid=iG0DAAAAIBAJ&pg=5291,834959&dq=kathryn+kuhlman+william+nolen&hl=en.

212. Peace Corps, "RPCV Members of Congress Help Celebrate 52 Years of the Peace Corps Act," *Peace Corps Passport*, September 23, 2013, last accessed February 14, 2016, http://passport.peacecorps.gov/2013/09/23/rpcv-members-of-congress-help-celebrate-52-years-of-the-peace-corps-act/.

213. Lyrics to "Jesus Freak" on the album *Jesus Freak* by DC Talk. Written by Mark Heimermann and Toby McKeehan, produced by John Mark Painter, Mark Heimermann and Toby McKeehan, released by ForeFront/Virgin Records on November 21, 1995.

214. Chris Armstrong, "Tell Billy Graham: 'The Jesus People Love Him,'"

Christianity Today, August 2008, last accessed February 16, 2016, http://www.christianitytoday.com/history/2008/august/tell-billy-graham-jesus-people-love-him.html.

215. Merrill F. Unger, *Unger's Commentary on The Old Testament* (Chattanooga: AMG Publishers, 2002), 1674.
216. Paul McGuire, *Standing Down Goliath* (Los Angeles: M House Publishers, 2014), 163.
217. Gregory A. Boyd, *God at War: The Bible and Spiritual Conflict* (Downers Grove: IVP Academic, 1997), 283.
218. Paul McGuire, "The Evangelical Church, Apostasy, and Change Agents: The Destiny of America in the Last Days," in *Blood On The Altar: The Coming War Between Christian vs. Christian*, Thomas Horn, General Editor (Crane, MO: Defender, 2014), 171–172.
219. Ibid., 173.
220. Clinton E. Arnold, *Powers of Darkness: Principalities & Powers in Paul's Letters* (Downers Grove: IVP Academic, 1992), 35–36.
221. See p. 114–142 of Boyd, op cit, for a more complete treatment.
222. Ibid., 185.
223. Joel Richardson, *Mideast Beast: The Scriptural Case for an Islamic Antichrist* (Washington, DC: WND Books, 2012), 256–257.
224. Clinton E. Arnold, *3 Crucial Questions About Spiritual Warfare* (Grand Rapids: Baker, 1997), 161.
225. Joel C. Rosenberg, *Inside the Revolution: How the Followers of Jihad, Jefferson and Jesus Are Battling to Dominate the Middle East and Transform the World* (Carol Stream: Tyndale House Publishers, Inc., 2009), 215.
226. Ibid., 216.
227. Ibid., 236–237.
228. Ibid., 219.
229. www.newsmax,com/Newsfront/egypt-President-egypt-sisi/2015/01/11/id/617848.
230. www.christianpost.com/news/female-arab-journalist-muslims-who-say-extremists-do-not-represent-islam-are-hypocrites-161398.
231. www.christianitytoday.com/gleanings/2016/may/more-than-300-islamic-leaders-denounce-extremism.html.
232. https://www.theguardian.com/world/2011/mar/09/morocco-constitutional-reform-king.
233. https://www.clarionproject.org/news/morocco-thwarts-islamic-state-chemical-weapons-attack.

234. https/www.clarionproject.org/news/
     Moroccan-teen-self-immodates-after-rapists-released.
235. www.christianitytoday.com/gleanings/2016/may/more-than-300-
     islamic-leaders-denounce-extremism.htm.
236. www.the muslim 500.com/profile/king-abdullah-ii-jordan.
237. www.patheos.com/blogs/progressivesecularhumanist/2014/11/
     queen-rania-of-jordan-moderate-muslim.
238. aifdemocracy.org.
239. unitedwithisrael.org/
     Israel-has-ties-with-most-arab-countries-foreign-ministry-offcial-says.
240. www.dailymail.co.uk/news/article-3473136/
     bangladesh-considering-abandoning-islam-official-religion.
241. https.//worldwatchworldmonitor.org/2016/03/4374627/.
242. www.asiatribune.com/node/88916.
243. www.clarionproject.org/news/honor-diaries-film-about-womens-rights.
244. www.christianpost.com/news/nabeel-qureshi-christian-can-love-
     muslims-even-if-they-are-trying-to-kill-you.
245. cuf.org/2002/07/learning-from-jesus-the-martyr.
246. www.theologynetwork.org/christian-beliefs/the-cross/
     theology-of-the-cross-subversive-theology-for-a-postmodern-world.
247. Daniel K. Norris, *Trial of Fire: True Stories from the Most Powerful Moves of
     God* (Lake Mary: Charisma House, 2016), p. 138–139.
248. *The Global Jesus Revolution: Israel, Islam and the Gospel at the End of the Age.*
     WND Films. Written and directed by Joel Richardson, 2016.
249. Marvin J. Newell, *A Martyr's Grace: Stories of Those Who Gave All for Christ
     & His Cause* (Chicago: Moody Publishers, 2006), 201.
250. Timothy Dailey, *Apocalypse Rising: Chaos in the Middle East, the Fall of
     the West, and Other Signs of the End Times* (Chosen: Minneapolis, 2016),
     182–183.
251. www.christianpost.com/news/
     theology-of-glory-vs-theology-of-the-cross-78119/.
252. www.opc.org/new_horizons/NH05/10b.html.
253. David Garrison, *A Wind in the House of Islam: How God Is Drawing
     Muslims around the World to Faith in Jesus Christ* (Monument: WIGTake
     Resources, 2014), 5.
254. Ibid., 6–7.
255. Ibid., 7
256. Ibid., 13–14.

257. Ibid., 15.

258. Ibid., 16.

259. Joel Rosenberg, Foreword, *Once An Arafat Man: The True Story of How A PLO Sniper Found a New Life,* by Tass Saada with Dean Merrill (Carol Stream: Tyndale Publishers, Inc., 2002), ix.

260. Tom Doyle, with Greg Webster, *Dreams and Visions: Is Jesus Awakening the Muslim World?* (Nashville: Thomas Nelson, 2012), 17.

261. Ibid., 18.

262. Ibid., 20–21.

263. 39www.isadreams.org/wake-up-to-dreams/.

264. *The Voice of the Martyrs* (January 2015), 4–8.

265. 41www.wnd.com/2014/11/ rising-number-of- muslims-reporting-dreams-about- jesus.

266. *Revolution,* Joel Richardson.

267. Ibid.

268. Erwin Lutzer, with Steve Miller, *The Cross in The Shadow of the Crescent* (Eugene: Harvest House, 2013), 25, 36.

269. Ibid., 63–64.

270. www.clarionproject.org.

271. Rodney Stark, *Triumph of Faith: Why the World Is More Religious Than Ever* (Intercollegiate Studies Institute, 2015), 19.

272. www.charismanews.com/opinions/57029-revival-has-hit-america.

273. www.charismamag.com/spirit/church-ministry/25114-7-lessons-from-the-world-s-fastest-growing-church.

274. www.youtube.com/watch?v=z3v5jvbJnV.

275. 51www.1cbn.com/spirituallife/what-happened-to-brownsville's-fire

276. Michael F. Brown, *Revolution in the Church: Challenging the Religious System with a Call for Radical Change* (Grand Rapids: Chosen Books, 2002), 31.

277. www.charismamag/life/women/26097-why-the-azusa-street-revival-ended.

278. http://pneumareview.com/supernatural-physical-manifestations-in-the-evangelical-and-holiness-revival-movements-pking/.

279. Norris, 34.

280. Ibid., 39.

281. Ibid., 40.

282. Ibid., 40–41.

283. Ibid., 74.

284. Ibid., 75.

285. Ibid., 76.

286. Ibid., 78.

287. Ibid., 80–81.

288. Rifqa Bary, *Why I Risked Everything to Leave Islam and Follow Jesus* (Colorado Springs: WaterBrook Press, 2015), 3.

289. Ibid., 24.

290. Ibid., 200–209.

291. Heidi Baker, *Love Like Fire: The Story of Heidi Baker: Mother to Nations* (Lake Mary: Charisma House, 2016), 151.

292. Ibid., 229.

293. Ibid., 227–228.

294. Tom Doyle, *Killing Christians: Living the Faith Where It's Not Safe to Believe* (Nashville: Thomas Nelson, 2015), 3.

295. Ibid., 99.

296. Ibid., 10.

297. Ibid.

298. Ibid., 56–57.

299. www.charismamage.com/spirit/revival/14934/-why-revival-tarries-in-america.

300. www.cityofmanchesterky.org.

301. www.crosswalk.com/faith/prayer/how-to-pray-for-gods-transforming-power-in-your-city.